STAN~~~~~ ~~~~~~~

John Baxter is a f~~~~~~~ ~~~~~~~~~~~ d broad-
caster, whose book~~~~~~~~~~~~~~~~~~~~~~ ollywood
*Exiles, The Cinem~~~~~~~~~~~~~~~~~~~~~ nema of
John Ford*, and bi~~~~~~~~~~~~~~~~~~~ *Appalling
Talent*), Fellini, Buñ~~~~~~~~~~~~~~ ~pielberg.

John Baxter was born and brought up in Australia, has
worked in London and taught in the United States, and now
lives in Paris with his wife Marie-Dominique Montel. His
biography of Woody Allen is published by HarperCollins in
the autumn of 1998.

Further reviews for *Stanley Kubrick*:

'John Baxter's superb biography sets out with enormous
relish to unravel this mystery [of Kubrick's reclusiveness]. His
earlier biographies, of Buñuel, Fellini, Ken Russell and Spielberg, are among the best in their field, and his account of
Kubrick's somewhat tortured soul is written in the same vivid
prose. Needless to say he wasn't granted an audience with the
brooding Kubrick; but he is eager to track down the ambiguities of character and motive that he sees so thinly disguised in
the films.'   J.G.BALLARD, *New Statesman*

'The ingenious John Baxter has had to compile this blow-by-
blow account of a bumpy career without catching sight of the
rare bird... This history of an extraordinary career is barbed
with the anecdotes of those who fell for Stanley's charm; and
those who simply fell, under Kubrick's slave-driving techniques... *Stanley Kubrick* is the sharpest book on cinema
since Jake Eberts and Terry Ilott's *My Indecision Is Final*, the
history of Goldcrest Films.'

BRIAN ALDISS, *Daily Telegraph*

'Judicious and well-researched.'

PHILLIP FRENCH, *Observer*

'...tells us as much about Kubrick as we can probably hope to
know.'   JONATHAN ROMNEY, *Guardian*

By the same author

BUÑUEL
FELLINI
THE HOLLYWOOD EXILES
STUNT: THE GREAT MOVIE STUNTMEN
THE CINEMA OF JOSEF VON STERNBERG
THE GANGSTER FILM
SCIENCE FICTION IN THE CINEMA
HOLLYWOOD IN THE THIRTIES
HOLLYWOOD IN THE SIXTIES
SIXTY YEARS OF HOLLYWOOD
KEN RUSSELL: AN APPALLING TALENT
STEVEN SPIELBERG: THE UNAUTHORISED BIOGRAPHY

JOHN BAXTER

STANLEY KUBRICK

A BIOGRAPHY

HarperCollins*Publishers*

HarperCollins*Publishers*
77–85 Fulham Palace Road,
Hammersmith, London W6 8JB

This paperback edition 1998

1 3 5 7 9 8 6 4 2

First published in Great Britain by
HarperCollins*Publishers* 1997

ISBN 0 00 638445 5

Set in Sabon

Printed and bound in Great Britain by
Caledonian International Book Manufacturing Ltd, Glasgow

For Marie-Dominique and Louise

–there is an importance of beauty
Which can't be accounted for by there and then–

BERNARD SPENCER, 'Part of Plenty'

Contents

Illustrations

Kubrick in 1951, on location for his first feature, *Fear and Desire*. (*Museum of Modern Art*)

Kubrick and his first wife Toba on location for *Fear and Desire*. (*Museum of Modern Art*)

Virginia Leith, the film's female lead, in a provocative publicity still taken by Kubrick. (*Museum of Modern Art*)

Joseph Burstyn's strident publicity for the re-release of the film with Buñuel's *El Bruto*. (*Museum of Modern Art*)

The *Fear and Desire* unit. (*Museum of Modern Art*)

Jamie Smith and Frank Silvera battle amid the shop-window dummies in the action climax of *Killer's Kiss*. (*Museum of Modern Art*)

Timothy Carey as the marksman Nikki Arano in *The Killing*. (*Author's collection*)

A masked Sterling Hayden leads the racetrack robbery in *The Killing*. (*Author's collection*)

Kubrick and his partner James B. Harris with Kirk Douglas during the shooting of *Paths of Glory*. (*British Film Institute*)

Kubrick on the set of *Paths of Glory* with Kirk Douglas and actress Suzanne Christian, later his second wife. (*Museum of Modern Art*)

Kubrick receiving Adolphe Menjou's complaints about his role as General Broulard.

Laurence Olivier and Tony Curtis in the sequence deleted from *Spartacus*. (*Author's collection*)

Kirk Douglas tries to talk Kubrick round to his vision of *Spartacus*. (*Museum of Modern Art*)

Dolores Haze, aka Lolita, as first glimpsed by Humbert Humbert in Kubrick's adaptation of Vladimir Nabokov's novel. (*British Film Institute*)

Kubrick with fourteen-year-old Sue Lyon, his choice to star in *Lolita*. (*Author's collection*)

Humbert Humbert (James Mason), grappling with Charlotte Haze (Shelley Winters), gazes longingly at the photograph of his stepdaughter. (*British Film Institute*)

Kubrick and director of photography Gilbert Taylor line up a shot in Ken Adam's War Room set for *Dr Strangelove*. (*British Film Institute*)

Russian Amabassador DeSadesky (Peter Bull) and President Merkin
Muffley (Peter Sellers) in the deleted pie-fight sequence. (*Estate of Arthur
Fellig; Weegee the Famous/International Center for Photography, New
York*)

Kubrick directs Sellers as the sinister Dr Strangelove. (*British Film Institute*)

Frank Poole (Gary Lockwood) and Dave Bowman (Keir Dullea) in *2001: A
Space Odyssey*. (*Author's collection*)

Poole jogs round the living quarters of the *Discovery*.

Kubrick shooting the sequence. (*Author's collection*)

The exterior of the $750,000 Vickers-Armstrong centrifuge. (*Andrew
Birkin*)

Heywood Floyd and his party descend into the excavation in Tycho where
the monolith was unearthed. (*Author's collection*)

Marlon Brando with Karl Malden in *One-Eyed Jacks*, which Kubrick
prepared but Brando directed. (*Author's collection*)

Kubrick lining up the shot in which Alex (Malcolm McDowell) attacks the
Cat Lady in *A Clockwork Orange*. (*British Film Institute*)

Mrs Alexander (Adrienne Corri) about to be raped by Alex and his *droogs*
while Kubrick operates the camera. (*British Film Institute*)

Kubrick on the prison set with Michael Bryant and Malcolm McDowell.
(*British Film Institute*)

Kubrick on the prison chapel set. (*British Film Institute*)

One of Kubrick's cost-cutting technical innovations: a wheelchair adapted
into a camera platform. (*British Film Institute*)

Kubrick directs *Barry Lyndon*. (*Author's collection*)

Marisa Berenson as Lady Lyndon. (*British Film Institute*)

Lady Lyndon and her chaplain, the Reverend Runt (Murray Melvin), in one
of the gaming-room scenes which Kubrick insisted be shot by candlelight. (*British Film Institute*)

Kubrick on the set of *The Shining*. (*British Film Institute*)

Kubrick with director of photography John Alcott. (*British Film Institute*)

Lee Ermey as Sergeant Hartman rages at the recruits in *Full Metal Jacket*.
(*British Film Institute*)

The death of Cowboy (Arliss Howard), from *Full Metal Jacket*. (*British
Film Institute*)

Acknowledgements

Jean-Pierre Thierry suggested this book. He thought Stanley Kubrick was an obvious subject, given the way I never stopped talking about *The Shining* and *Full Metal Jacket*. Once he brought it up, Kubrick did seem an obvious subject for a biography, but an impossible one. Surely Kubrick's passion for privacy, frequently and powerfully expressed, would be respected by his friends and colleagues. A chance conversation with his brother-in-law and business manager Jan Harlan at a party seemed to confirm this view. Nobody was going to talk to me about Stanley.

Thus is the bright hue of resolution sicklied o'er with the pale cast of thought. Because researching this book was less a question of seeking out material than of restraining the flow. Ten-minute interviews turned into three- and four-hour monologues during which people wept and laughed – well, mostly wept, really – as they recounted what it had been like to work with Kubrick. Halfway down the steps, they would turn back to say, 'Listen, did I tell you about the time...?'

Everyone, it seems, has a Kubrick story, but my particular gratitude goes to the following who offered theirs, and made my work so illuminating and pleasurable.

Ken Adam, Brian Aldiss, Richard Anderson, Professor Bob Anderson, Jean-Claude Barsacq, Louis Begley, Andrew Birkin, Michel Ciment, Bernard Cohn, Adrienne Corri, Roger de Vito, Jules Feiffer, Jerry Goldsmith, Curtis Harrington, James B. Harris, Michael Herr, Tana Hoban, William Hootkins, Neil Hornick, Diane Johnson, Allen Jones, Alan Kaufman, Gavin Lambert, Scott Martin at Shepperton Studios, the late James Mason, John G. Morris, Jerry and Janice Pam, David Perry, Sir David Puttnam, Frederic Raphael, Shane Rimmer, the late Bob Shaw, Kerry Shale, Alexander Singer, David Slavitt, Gordon Stainforth, Fred Stettner, Erika Stoll, Bertrand Tavernier, Walter Trueman, Lisa Tuttle, David Vaughan and Paul Vaughan, John Ward, Derek Ware, John Whitwell and William Read Woodfield.

Denise Bethel directed me to the International Center for Photography in New York, the curator of which, Miles Barth, made available Weegee's 'lost' stills from *Dr Strangelove*. Charles Silver, Ron Magliozzi and Mary Corliss of the Museum of Modern Art, New York, were their customary courteous and helpful selves. Michael Neal made available his limitless knowledge of erotica by elucidating the more obscure *couloirs* of *Lolita* and the Olympia Press. The National Film Theatre, London, kindly supplied a tape of Paul Mazursky's lecture there. Paolo Cherchi Usai and his staff at George Eastman House in Rochester NY made available both their rare copy of *Fear and Desire* and their documentation on the film's distribution. Without the help of the American Chess Federation and Chess Foundation, I would never have found Alan Kaufman and learned of Kubrick's early life in New York.

Arvad Kompanetz drove me around the Bronx in a blizzard on the track of Kubrick's childhood haunts. June Cullen of Griffith University in Queensland directed me to Kevin Rockett in Dublin and Commandant Peter Young of Ireland's National Military Archive, both of whom illuminated the politics surrounding the production of *Barry Lyndon*. Bill Warren lent books, arranged interviews and otherwise helped with research. Professor Matthew Bernstein drew my attention to a number of articles on Dalton Trumbo and his contribution to *Spartacus*. The BBC's Mark Burman suggested additional sources from his own programme research. Adrian Turner supplied unpublished interviews, letters and clippings, and with his wife Andrea took me on a tour of Childwick Bury and Kubrick country. Adrian also read the manuscript and made a number of insightful suggestions for improving it, as did David Stratton, Bill Warren, Michael Ciment and David Thompson.

David Thompson also provided much valuable documentation, including copies of the complete versions of *The Shining*, *Making The Shining* and *Killer's Kiss*, and of Kubrick's early documentaries, and John Brosnan gave access to a number of rare interviews as well as to material recorded for his books *Future Tense*, *Movie Magic* and *The Primal Screen*. Lee Hill made available sections of his forthcoming biography of Terry Southern, and was unstinting in clarifying the thorny relationship between Southern and Kubrick. Patrick McGilligan also kindly allowed me to quote from Lee's interview with Southern in a forthcoming edition of his *Backstory* series. Weidenfeld & Nicolson gave me permission to quote passages from Vladimir Nabokov's *Lolita*.

In Paris, Kristi Jaas helped with document research and interviews, and Tuki Jancquel with translations. Jackie and Patrick Morreau never complained when their home was turned into a combined office, answering service and hospitality suite. Brian Troath tracked down the rarest books, and without Mary Troath's indefatigable research, this book would have been greatly diminished. Richard Johnson proved once again the most supportive and diplomatic of editors. To all of these people and to the others who helped, not least my wife Marie-Dominique, my profound gratitude.

John Baxter
Paris, 1997

I renounce nothing of that which is the Mind. I want only
to transport my mind elsewhere with its laws and its organs.
I do not surrender myself to the sexual mechanism of the
mind, but on the contrary within this mechanism I seek to
isolate those discoveries which lucid reason does not provide.
I surrender to the fever of dreams, but only in order to
derive from them new laws. I seek multiplication, subtlety,
the intellectual eye in delirium, not rash vaticination.

There is a knife which I do not forget.

ANTONIN ARTAUD, *Correspondance de la momie*
(translated by Helen Weaver)

Prologue:

The Skull King

'Stanley Kubrick is a talented shit.'

Kirk Douglas

It's high summer in America. Dwight D. Eisenhower, by the grace of God of these United States President, has just added another to the number; Alaska makes forty-nine. Fidel Castro has seized control of Cuba, the Dalai Lama fled from Tibet. Nikita Khrushchev is the Premier of the Soviet Union and is about to visit the United States – but not Disneyland: it's too dangerous, decree his hosts. An unmanned space probe, Luna 2, has made man's first contact with the moon by crashing into it. The big movies are William Wyler's *Ben-Hur*, Alfred Hitchcock's *North by Northwest* and Billy Wilder's *Some Like it Hot*. Elvis Presley is serving his army hitch in Germany, so the record of the year is Bobby Darin's sugary finger-snappin' take on Kurt Weill and Bertolt Brecht's ballad of Mackie Messer – 'Mac the Knife' to teenagers everywhere.

It's 1959 in God's own country – everywhere but on a hot hillside in Southern California's San Fernando Valley, just over the hill from Greater Los Angeles. There, despite the occasional distant roar of rockets from the test beds of Rocketdyne Corporation and the mutter of traffic on Barham Boulevard, it is 71 B.C., and the common people are getting restless.

'If he doesn't get this shot done soon,' mutters a grip, 'we're going to have a slave revolt right here.'

Three hundred extras dressed in scratchy brown homespun are scattered over a grassy slope in the hot sun. Each holds a large card with a number on it. None looks happy. From a gantry of planks and scaffolding twelve metres in the air, a young man in crumpled cotton trousers, an open-necked white shirt and slip-ons, with black hair and thick eyebrows, a Camel smoking between his fingers, looks down on the scene. In a Bronx monotone he murmurs something to his assistant, who picks up a microphone.

'Number 23. Move to the left,' his voice booms. 'Number 104 – writhe!' The figure doesn't respond.

'George,' says the minion, 'Stanley wants 104 to writhe.'

The assistant director picks his way through the crowd, then threads his way back.

'It's a dummy,' he yells up to the gantry.

The face of the director remains expressionless. He says something inaudible to the assistant.

'Stanley says, put some wires on it and *make* it writhe.'

At thirty-two, Stanley Kubrick is the youngest person ever to direct a Hollywood epic. Kirk Douglas, the film's star and executive producer, gave it to him after firing the older, less malleable Anthony Mann at the end of the first week. On a weekend's notice, Kubrick, known for little more than a low-budget crime film, *The Killing*, and a First World War drama, *Paths of Glory*, suddenly found himself in charge of a $12 million enterprise with twenty-seven tons of robes, tunics and aluminium armour made to measure in Rome, and a no-less-heavyweight cast that included Sir Laurence Olivier, Charles Laughton and Peter Ustinov, playing senators, slaves and dictators.

But if the experience is weighing him down, Kubrick shows no sign of it. He has already fired the leading lady and infuriated Kirk Douglas by taking the film at his own deliberate pace. The star has an uneasy feeling he's hired the wrong man. Hoping for a kid he can push around, he's found himself saddled instead with a film-maker of steely resolve who sometimes seems almost to rival him in ego and stubbornness. Tony Curtis, one of the co-stars, recalls:

Kubrick had his own approach to film-making. He wanted to see the actors' faces. He didn't want cameras always in a wide shot twenty-five feet away, he wanted close-ups, he wanted to keep the camera moving. That was his style.

The production manager, even Kirk Douglas, were all hustling Stanley. 'Let's go faster, Stanley . . . No, you don't need a shot like that!' . . . and Stanley saying, 'That's the way I want it.'

What inflated the film and the budget to a different number was Kubrick's concept and ideas of interesting camera set-ups. He wanted to do only two camera set-ups a day, the studio wanted to do about thirty-two, so he had to compromise – about eight a day. He wanted to do long panning shots, getting lots of people in, and following the key actor. If you watch the film carefully, you'll see he does that.

Screenwriter Dalton Trumbo, blacklisted for his Communist sympathies and barred from screen credit, estimates he wrote a quarter of a million words on the film. One of Kubrick's first acts is to cut some of them – specifically all but two lines from the first half-hour of Douglas's role.

After one script conference, the question of whose name is to appear on the screen as writer comes up. Douglas and Universal Pictures are both leery about crediting Trumbo and arousing the wrath of the political right.

'Use *my* name,' Kubrick suggests suddenly.

'Stanley,' Douglas says, after a significant look at producer Eddie Lewis, 'wouldn't you feel embarrassed to put your name on a script that someone else wrote?'

'No,' Kubrick says – nor would he have been the least defensive if Douglas had followed his suggestion. There is a core of self-assurance and obstinacy to Kubrick that would do credit to a general, a president, an emperor, even a messiah. He is incapable of embarrassment. If he had any tendency to such a failing, he has long since trained himself out of it.

Watching Kubrick meticulously at work setting up his post-battle scene, Douglas fumes at the delays. He is almost ready to replace his director yet again, except that Kubrick is getting good material. And there is more than money invested in the production. Douglas's reputation is on the line.

He'd intended to shoot the film in Rome, where locations, extras and resources are cheap, but Edward Muhl, president of Universal Pictures, prevailed on him to make it in Hollywood. This, Muhl believes, will be the film that stems the flood of 'runaway' producers heading for Europe. Universal is the most factory-like of all Hollywood studios, with a rigid hierarchy of technicians and a tradition of using second-rate directors to churn out films that stay under budget and put black ink on the books. Douglas's production will give work to the hundreds of high-priced technicians on the payroll. Up on the hill above the studio, Muhl decrees that neon letters five metres high spell out the film's name:

SPARTACUS

There is something imperial about the gesture, redolent of the SPQR ('Senatus Populusque Romanus' – 'For the Senate and People of Rome') which appeared on the standards of Rome's legions, or the 'In hoc Signo, Vinces' ('In this Sign, Conquer') that marked the Christian cross as the symbol of the Holy Roman Empire – and, though nobody cares to say it in so many words, of the injunction of Roman matrons as they handed battle-bound sons their weapons: 'Return with this shield – or on it.'

The director of photography assigned to the film is Russell Metty, at fifty-three a twenty-year veteran of Hollywood. He's shot *The Stranger* and *Touch of Evil* for Orson Welles, *Bringing up Baby* for Howard Hawks, but also everything else assigned to him: *Kiss the Blood Off My Hands*, *Magnificent Obsession* and, just before *Spartacus*, *Midnight Lace* with Doris Day. Face flushed under a grey crewcut, he runs his unit with an autocratic hand that usually grips a coffee cup of Jack Daniel's. Metty is accustomed to having directors explain their requirements for a scene, after which he will growl, 'OK. Go sit down,' and put his crew to work setting the lights. He resents the young director's seizure of his authority, and his detailed directions about lenses and light. Kubrick's years as a photo-journalist for *Look* magazine aren't wasted.

After Metty lights a scene with Herbert Lom, playing the slippery agent of some Cilician pirates with whom Spartacus is negotiating to get out of Italy with his slave army, Kubrick looks through the camera and tells him, 'I can't see the actors' faces.'

Furious, Metty kicks a small spotlight beside his chair. It rolls into the shot.

'*Now* is there enough light?' he snarls.

'Now there's too *much* light,' Kubrick says, unperturbed.

The duel of wills comes to a climax when Kubrick tries to shoot the aftermath of the final battle, where the sun rises over a hillside

littered with corpses. His first attempt, using the system of numbering the extras, a method which worked on *Paths of Glory*, doesn't
satisfy him. He sends everyone home and, to the horror of Douglas
and Eddie Lewis, tells them he'll shoot it at the studio, where he
can control the light.

Two weeks later, he asks stills photographer Billy Woodfield to
bring his Polaroid to Universal's biggest sound stage. The space is
jammed with extras lounging across the best hillside the studio's
design department under Alexander Golitzen can build. Woodfield
will never forget it:

> Stanley showed me what he was going to do. The shot began
> on a bloody hand, then tracked back across a stream red with
> blood, more dead people, dead horses, then a cyclorama that
> went on and on. It was all in forced perspective, so they had
> midget people at the back to make the distances look greater,
> and dummies, and everything you can imagine. Stanley had con-
> ceived it so that at a certain point the camera passes a rock, at
> which point he would cut, restage the action, and pick it up on
> the other side in one continuous movement.
>
> Stanley called out, 'Light 'em.' And there were arcs every-
> where! They had gotten every arc in Hollywood to create this
> sunset.

Only a mighty studio can create sunsets like this one. It's a sunset
for Scarlett and Rhett, for Shiloh, for the Resurrection. The elec-
tricians have used enough vermilion and crimson gels to cover a
football field. Woodfield continued:

> And he says, 'What do you think?'
>   'About what?'
>   'Does it look like a sunset to you?'
>   'It looks like a *Russ Metty* sunset.'
>   'Exactly. Take a picture of it.'
>   We didn't have colour Polaroids in those days, but I took a
> black and white picture. He looked at it and said, 'It really
> stinks.'
>   So he cancels the shoot.

Metty apparently went to Ed Muhl and said, 'I quit.' Muhl said, 'You can't quit. You're under contract.'

'Then let me do my job.'

And Stanley said, 'You can do your job by sitting in your chair and shutting up. I'll be the director of photography.'

I wasn't at the meeting, but that was the gist of it. After that, Metty didn't do anything. Stanley would tell his crew what to do, they'd look at Metty, and Metty would nod. Stanley lit the film – and Metty got an Academy Award!

The truth is, Kubrick, even as he scorns the material, his star and the demands of the studio front office, relishes the chance to control such a massive project. It is, he senses, what he has been heading towards all his life. Leaving school at sixteen to become a professional photographer, hustling chess games in Greenwich Village to save money for his first feature, then winning his way to Hollywood and fighting the system to make *Paths of Glory* – it all leads inexorably to this moment.

Sitting on a camera crane during a pause in the scene where the gladiators break out of Peter Ustinov's school, he tells Woodfield, 'This is going to be my best film.'

The photographer demurs. 'It's just a piece of Technicolor plastic, Stanley. *Paths of Glory* is your best film.'

But Kubrick shakes his head. Woodfield doesn't understand. Nobody does. Years later, actress Adrienne Corri, irritated by Kubrick's manner on *A Clockwork Orange*, would bring a copy of Ingres' picture of Jupiter onto the set and prop it in his chair.

'That's who you think you are,' she would say. The accusation would amuse Kubrick. But he'd never deny that he believed her to be right.

'Film is a battleground,' says the director Sam Fuller, in one of the most famous of all statements about cinema. 'Love, hate, action, death. In a word, emotion.' Stanley Kubrick would agree. A connoisseur of war who, on one of his rare holidays, takes his family on a tour of the Normandy landing beaches, he sees the set as a battlefield, and himself as its general. Establishing control of a production and the people on it is integral to his method. 'If Kubrick hadn't been a film director,' says his star in *A Clockwork Orange*,

Malcolm McDowell, 'he'd have been a General Chief of Staff of the US Forces. No matter what it is – even if it's a question of buying a shampoo – it goes through him. He just likes total control.' Why? Partly it's innate. Kubrick is shy, and shyness magnified by natural intellectual superiority into a posture of heartless disdain isn't uncommon in artists. Calder Willingham, who co-scripted *Paths of Glory*, accuses Kubrick of 'a near psychopathic indifference to and coldness toward the human beings in the story – a failing, I might add, which has sadly limited the work of Kubrick throughout his career; he doesn't like people much: they interest him mainly when they do unspeakably hideous things or when their idiocy is so malignant as to be horrifyingly amusing'. Barbara Greene has written of her cousin, the novelist Graham Greene, in similar terms. 'Apart from three or four people he was really fond of,' she says, 'I felt that the rest of humanity was to him like a heap of insects that he liked to examine, as a scientist might examine his specimens, coldly and clearly.' For some people, it comes with the creative territory.

Kubrick is a loving husband, a devoted father to his two daughters and stepdaughter, and not without sentiment, affection or compassion. But public statements of feeling are rare in his life, and exhibitions of it rarer still. Only one person has ever seen him cry in public, and that was a long time ago.

Most of Kubrick's mental and physical isolation is an act of rational will. He admires machines: his third wife Christiane says, 'Stanley would be happy with eight tape recorders and one pair of pants.' Surrounded since adolescence by cameras, television sets and short-wave radios, he has aspired, not always successfully, to their precision. But at the same time, he knows that mechanisms malfunction. This realisation is the key to his life and work. It explains both why he won't fly or drive fast, and why he has made *2001: A Space Odyssey* and *Dr Strangelove*, both films about technologies that fail.

Jack Nicholson, his star in *The Shining* and the actor he had intended to cast in his long-time pet project, *Napoleon*, penetrates Kubrick's character quicker than most. 'Just because you're a perfectionist,' he says, 'doesn't mean you're perfect.' But to aspire to perfection is surely no shame. Nicholson, no diplomat himself, is Kubrick's wary but warm admirer. 'Stanley's good on sound,' he offers as an example. 'So are a lot of directors, but Stanley's good on designing a new harness [for the microphone]. Stanley's good on the colour of the mike. Stanley's good about the merchant he bought the mike from. Stanley's good about the merchant's daughter who needs some dental work. Stanley's *good*.'

Chapter Two

Kubrick in Class

'Life is a burden to me. Nothing gives me any pleasure.
I find only sadness in everything around me. It is very
difficult because the ways of those with whom I live,
and probably always shall live, are as different from
mine as moonlight is from sunlight.'

Napoleon Bonaparte at seventeen

Stanley Kubrick would always display an affinity for what he imagined to be his Austrian roots, but while it's true that his great-grandparents did come from Galicia, then part of Austria, the region, now shared between south-east Poland and west Ukraine, was far from Vienna.

Hersh Kubrik arrived at Ellis Island, via Liverpool, on the ill-fated *Lusitania* on 27 December 1899. At the age of forty-seven he'd left behind his wife and two grown-up children: a son, Elias, aged twenty-two, and a daughter, Bela, of twenty. With him was his second wife, Leie Fuchs, and their baby daughter Annie. It was the classic case of the middle-aged man making a new start with a younger woman. Two more children, both sons, would be born in America: Joseph in 1902 and Michael in 1904. Hersh found work in his trade of tailoring, and wrote to the children of his first marriage about the opportunities in America. In 1902 his son Elias, also a tailor, arrived in New York with his young wife Rosa, *née* Spiegelblatt, a nineteen-year-old Romanian girl who was pregnant with their first child.

Jacob Cubrick, as his birth certificate spelled his name, was born in New York on 21 May 1902. At the time, the family lived at 125

Rivington Street in lower Manhattan, in the heart of New York's noisy and congested garment district. Elias and Rosa soon produced two more children: Hester Merel in 1904, and Lily in 1906. Elias prospered, and by the 1920s he was in business with Jacob Maslen, formerly Mazlen, as Kubrick & Maslen, manufacturers of ladies' coats. Hester, then known as Ester, and Lily, renamed Lillian, worked in the rag trade too, one as a book-keeper, the other as a pants-presser.

As the eldest, and the only son, Jacob had more than his fair share of the family's attention. It helped that he was handsome and intelligent, with a challenging gaze and, in adulthood, a suave moustache. He didn't look especially Jewish, and as his sisters had done, he quickly discarded his Jewish name for the more cosmopolitan Jacques, or Jack. Like most elder sons, he was marked down early for a profession. He studied medicine, graduating from the New York Homeopathic Medical College and Flower Hospital in 1927. Free to choose the spelling of his name, the new graduate signed himself Jacques E. Kubrick.

In 1927 Jacques married Gertrude Perveler, christened Sadie, like him the child of Austrian immigrants. Gert, as she was always known, was also the eldest of three children, her younger brothers being Joseph David and Martin. Martin went into the pharmacy business, and was to have a crucial effect on the career of Gert and Jacques's first child, Stanley, who was born on 26 June 1928. By then Jacques had put the garment district behind him, and moved to the Bronx.

Even today, the Bronx is a windy, rocky place, with a sense of sky everywhere. In winter the wind bites, borrowing its chill from the Hudson River basalt that underlies this part of the east coast United States. There is nothing soft here. The few parks are rugged outcrops of stone to which the grass clings nervously, like a climber. Except in the more sheltered streets there are few trees. Apartment blocks tend to be low, and to huddle together. The few large buildings, mostly schools or turn-of-the-century National Guard armouries that double as assembly halls and sports stadia, are massive and overbearing. It's clean and bright and bracing here, but you would not call it welcoming.

Mostly given over to farms and fields as late as 1900, the Bronx developed speedily as Manhattan's swelling population spilled onto the rocky heights across the East River. In 1909, the six-lane Grand Concourse was built across the roughly square promontory. Lined with banks, department stores, huge cinemas and apartment buildings on the European pattern, boasting uniformed doormen, concierges and gardens with fountains, the Concourse hoped to replicate the spaciousness and opulence of Vienna's Ringstrasse and Berlin's Unter den Linden.

Along the spine of the Grand Concourse, the Bronx evolved and expanded. 'Developers responded to increasing demand by building apartment houses on the side streets and avenues,' says one history of the area, 'creating a dense urban fabric, a canyon-like community along narrow, winding hillside streets, punctuated by broad avenues and a grand central boulevard. The extension of subway services to the Concourse in the twenties and thirties accelerated growth.' Though the social standing and ethnic mix of the district would change as black families migrated from uptown Manhattan and Harlem into the South Bronx, creating a dangerous slum, the Bronx remained throughout the years before World War II largely middle class and white.

Stanley Kubrick was born in Manhattan, in the Lying-In Hospital at 307 2nd Avenue, where Jacques had done his obstetrics training. But it was to the Bronx that his parents took him home. The six-storey brick apartment block at 2160 Clinton Avenue, between East 181st and East 182nd Street, was typical of the new buildings in the Bronx that housed the upwardly mobile immigrant community of which the Kubricks were a part. Jacques set up a surgery on the corner of East 158th Street and Courtlandt Avenue, and took a residency at Morrisania City Hospital, specialising in otolaryngology. On 21 May 1934 Jacques and Gert's second child, Barbara Mary, was born.

Soon after Barbara's birth, Stanley was enrolled in Public School 3 in the Bronx. In June 1938 he moved to Public School 90. In neither school did he do well. During his first term at PS 3 he missed exactly as many days as he attended – fifty-six. The following year he had an equally poor record, and academic insufficiency would continue to dog him. His report cards from PS 90 also show a damning 'U' – for unsatisfactory – in the areas of Personality, Works and Plays Well with Others, Completes Work, Is Generally Careful,

Respects Rights of Others and Speaks Clearly. Only his Cleanliness and Personal Habits were found acceptable. In intelligence tests, however, he rated above average. Young Stanley was a closed personality waiting to be unlocked.

Within a year of his birth, a congress of international psychiatrists meeting in Manhattan decided that it was couples with two dissimilar and opposing personalities, rather than two brilliant parents, who are most likely to produce a genius. 'The tension,' they concluded, 'exerts a driving force and produces the instability of temperament, emotional pressure and restive impulsiveness which are the earmarks of genius.' Stanley Kubrick bears out the theory. As an adult he seldom spoke about his mother or his sister, but it's evident that his father was the source of most major elements in his character. Jack Kubrick gave him his first camera, and taught him chess. From his shelves, Kubrick first started reading Greek and Roman myths and the Grimm brothers' fables that instilled a lifelong affinity with Europe. But to Kubrick's few friends, Jack Kubrick remained shadowy. 'I had very minimal contact with his father,' says Stanley Kubrick's high-school buddy and later collaborator, Alexander Singer. 'I knew him as a grey eminence, a presence somewhere in Stanley's life. He represented a fairly conventional relationship to a teenager's notion of inhibition; the father figure was always there to limit his adventure.'

Stanley Kubrick was born into an America that would disappear before he could experience it. That America was wealthy, though within a year the Crash would render one third of it, in Roosevelt's phrase, ill-housed, ill-clothed and ill-nourished. It prohibited alcohol, but the law would be repealed before Kubrick ever touched a drink. Many films were still silent, but he would grow up with sound cinema, just as he would see many of the European artists who had been Hollywood's cultural heroes for the last decade supplanted by home-grown performers who stamped world cinema with the imprint of Hollywood.

For the student of war that Kubrick was to become, 1928 offered few hints of the carnage that would dominate the next decade. Safe behind the isolationism of the Monroe Doctrine, and content to let the limping League of Nations handle other people's wars, few Americans knew or cared what happened overseas. In 1929, President Calvin Coolidge had repudiated the promise of Emma Lazarus's

poem on the plinth of the Statue of Liberty to accept Europe's
'huddled masses yearning to breathe free', and cut European immi-
gration to a trickle; a nation in economic depression had no room
for newcomers. From then until the first of Hitler's pogroms, more
people left America to live abroad than arrived as immigrants.
Europe was the place for a cut-price holiday, or to loaf through a
career as novelist or painter on dollars from home that could be
exchanged at absurdly inflated rates in London, Paris or Rome.

Under its first Labour Prime Minister, Ramsay Macdonald,
Britain was calm and prosperous. Treaties of friendship rather than
declarations of war papered the corridors of power. A succession
of protectionist presidents had built a United States four-squarely
in favour of affluence at home and freedom from foreign entanglements. Those who knew of Hitler or Mussolini saw them as up-and-
coming European politicians with some interesting ideas that might
be tried out in the United States with profit.

There was much talk of technocracy – government by scientists.
'What seems to be inevitable in the future,' H.G. Wells had said in
1899, 'is rule by an aristocracy of organisers, men who manage
railroads and similar vast enterprises.' Wells would not have cared
for the reality, of government controlled by soundbites and headed
by actors and TV executives, and nor did Kubrick, whose conviction
that life can, and should, be run on rational, even mechanical lines
took root early. If that meant he would have to live alone in his
tower, like John Masterman, the administrator king of Fritz Lang's
Metropolis, it was a price he was ready to pay.

As the family of a doctor, the Kubricks were prosperous by Bronx
standards. 'He lived in a *house*,' said Alexander Singer. 'I didn't
know anybody who lived in a house. We all lived in apartments.
He lived in the West Bronx, north rather than south, in the middle
of a semi-residential area. A pleasant enough street in its time. Trees
and so on. It was one of the first houses I ever visited.'

Kubrick spent many summer Saturdays at the Bronx's major
leisure attraction, Yankee Stadium, and fantasised about playing
for the New York Yankees baseball team. As a photographer for
Look, he was to shoot a photo-essay documenting the shifts in
emotion on the faces of two boys watching a game there – rapt
expressions that recall his own excitement.

People in the Bronx, however, like those all over America, relied for much of their entertainment on the movies. Cinemas like the RKO Fordham and Loew's gigantic Paradise on the Grand Concourse showed the latest studio productions as soon as they opened. From the time he was six or seven until well into his teens, Kubrick caught most of their twice-weekly double bills, though once he became committed to a film career and enamoured of the European cinema, he retrospectively deleted any youthful enthusiasms. If he ever saw – or, if he saw them, enjoyed – *The Wizard of Oz*, *Gone with the Wind* or *Meet me in St Louis*, we will probably never know.

Kubrick's educational standard remained poor. In June 1940, as he approached his twelfth birthday, his parents sent him to California to stay with his uncle Martin Perveler. Perveler was flourishing in the pharmacy business which would eventually make him a millionaire. Kubrick spent the next two semesters at school in Pasadena, the satellite town of Los Angeles, cementing a relationship with his uncle, his aunt Marion and their daughter Patricia Ann that was to prove valuable when he began making movies.

In September 1941 Kubrick returned to the Bronx and re-enrolled in PC 90 for his last year of grammar school. California did not appear to have galvanised him as his father had hoped, and Jack's disappointment in his son was confirmed. Hoping to find something to stimulate his imagination, he taught him chess, for which Stanley showed an unexpected passion that would continue for the rest of his life.

For his thirteenth birthday Kubrick received from his father a gift that was also to have a far-reaching influence, a Graflex camera. The American-made Graflex belonged to the last generation of semi-portable cameras, soon to be supplanted by the lightweight metal-framed German Leica, which photographers like Henri Cartier-Bresson were pioneering in Europe. At 20cm x 18cm x 4cm, and weighing 3.8 kilos, the Graflex, with a pebbled black surface like lizardskin, was as big as a child's shoebox. It mainly used cut film the size of a small postcard, loaded in ten-exposure magazines, but a removable back made it possible to fit a 35mm adapter, which became Kubrick's favourite option. The photographer framed his picture from above, on a ground glass the size of a notepad and shaded by a collapsible fabric hood, the pterodactyl-like folds of which added to the Graflex's impression of antediluvian clumsiness, an effect further emphasised by the enormous 165mm, 17cm-wide lens, which looked like a staring eye.

Kubrick's affinity for photography was as instant as that he felt for chess. Photography is the art of the solitary, the voyeur, and it was this characteristic that was to predominate in his adult character. Production designer Ken Adam noticed it when they were viewing transparencies of stately homes as possible locations for *Barry Lyndon*. 'He would stare at the interior of a bedroom, say, and discover details that would never have occurred to me, but on which he then put important connotations. I would be interested in the architecture, the furnishings, purely as they related to possible filming. Stanley wasn't. He was fascinated by the details of who might have lived here; what they did; what they thought.'

Other local boys were also interested in photography, and Kubrick found one in the nearby apartment of Marvin Traub, who was four months older than Stanley, and had been given a twin-lens reflex camera as a bar-mitzvah gift. Better still, Marvin had turned a corner of his bedroom into a darkroom, complete with enlarger.

Kubrick became a regular visitor to the Traub apartment, to the extent that the family began to resent it. 'Oh, Kubrick the *nudnik* is here again,' said Marvin's mother. 'Doesn't this kid have his own apartment? Why is he down here?' Stanley and Marvin also went on photographic excursions around the Bronx. He carried the Graflex in a paper shopping bag, partly because it was too large and heavy for a light shoulderstrap like the one on which Marvin carried his, but also because the sight of so large a camera might alert his subjects. But with the camera hidden in a bag, the top open so that he could sight down it and the lens peering out through a hole torn in the paper, Kubrick could take pictures virtually unnoticed.

The weight of the Graflex and the awkward shooting position it dictated, seldom higher than the navel and often almost on the floor, influenced Kubrick's development as a director. In his early films he often shot from lower angles than other cameramen, and sometimes from ground level, laying the camera on its back and lying on his stomach to get shots looking straight up between the knees of his subjects. In later years, his preference for seeing his pictures full-size on the ground glass before he shot them translated into a preoccupation with composition and framing. No director is so insistent that his films must be screened sharp from corner to corner, and with the correct aperture plates in the projectors to recreate precisely the framing he saw through the camera's view-finder.

Kubrick admired Arthur Fellig, a diminutive freelance news pho-tographer with an improbably squeaky voice who roamed New York with a heavy Speed Graphic drop-fronted bellows camera only marginally more awkward than the Graflex. The secret of Fellig's success was a radio kept tuned permanently to the police band. His apparent prescience, which often brought him to the scene of a crime before the police, let alone rival cameramen, earned him the nickname 'Weegee', after the Ouija Board with which competitors assumed he must locate his juiciest subjects: his prints were stamped on the back with the peremptory direction 'Credit Weegee the Famous.' Once he became a director, Kubrick was to be just as obsessive an eavesdropper on international short-wave traffic as Fellig had been on the police band, and he would hire Fellig to act as special stills photographer on Dr Strangelove.

Weegee had a profound but largely unacknowledged influence on the low-budget, low-light, low-life crime movies of so-called film noir. One of his books, The Naked City, inspired the 1949 film of the same name, much of which director Jules Dassin shot on actual locations in the seedier corners of New York, often with hidden cameras.

Frequently Fellig photographed the dead: slumped suicides, car crash victims, corpses leaking blood onto the sidewalk, casualties of tenement fires limp in the arms of firefighters. Kubrick's work as both photographer and director was equally detached. Introducing a collection of his photo-journalism published in 1994, Italian critic Enrico Ghezzi pointed out that Kubrick's human subjects are 'plucked from a sort of auteur version of Candid Camera, [and] sport an ambiguous, almost animal expressiveness. Snapshot enigmas. As if they were dead. The life of Kubrick, a recluse film-maker withdrawn in his manor, is the life of someone dead to the world. Someone who leaves only "dead" time embalmed in his films. [Someone] to be interpreted, like a classical author, [his work] already completed, of centuries ago; almost like someone that can only be imagined.'

William Howard Taft High School in the Bronx, at 240 East 172nd Street, where Kubrick enrolled in 1942 for the 1943 intake, had only been completed in 1941. It would be the only school Kubrick attended for any length of time in his brief education. A block-long eight-storey building, it stands bleak as a brick on a hill overlooking a district of forties apartment blocks, most of them with some pretensions to elegance in their neo-classical decoration. Wide steps at its main entrance at one narrow end lead into a foyer decorated in dark red marble and terrazzo, echoing the quasi-Graeco-Roman reliefs on the apartment buildings. Beyond is a theatre and assembly hall as large as a thirties movie house. At the other end of the building, the hill has been sheered away to create a playing field, an asphalted space above which the building's blank face hovers, invigilating even when the students aren't actually in class. This façade and the buttresses that run along one margin, supporting the wall that holds back the uphill soil, create a sense of institutional confinement, closer to prison than school, that must have had a numbing effect on the pupils incarcerated there.

Kubrick's three years at Taft, from 1943 to 1945, were the unhappiest of his life. IQ tests rated him above average, but formal learning bored him. Alex Singer recalls, 'Stanley and I had boundless curiosity, but not about the things they were teaching.' Kubrick agrees. 'I think the big mistake in schools is trying to teach children anything. Interest can produce learning on a scale compared to fear as a nuclear explosion to a firecracker. I never learned anything at school and I didn't read a book for pleasure until I was nineteen years old.'

His school days were dominated less by a search for learning than by fear: 'Fear of getting failing grades,' he wrote later, 'fear of not staying with your class.' He got Fs by betraying his lack of interest in set books like George Eliot's *Silas Marner*, and failed English totally one year, forcing him to make up the lost grade during the summer. When he graduated, it was with a mediocre 70.1 average, his only high marks those in Physics.

Grades, however, don't tell the whole story. Kubrick could and would work if his interest was engaged: this was the man who, despite his disdain for George Eliot, created in *Barry Lyndon* the cinema's best adaptation of Thackeray. Once he left school and was no longer required to do so, he read voraciously. 'A great story is a kind of miracle,' he has said. 'I've never written a story myself, which is probably why I have so much respect for it. I started out, before I became a film-maker, always thinking, you know, if I couldn't play for the Yankees I'd like to be a novelist. The people I first admired were not film directors, but novelists, like Conrad.'

What sort of novelist would Kubrick have made? Pretty dismal, in all probability. He has never written anything but film-scripts, and in those cases he almost always worked in collaboration, and from an existing work. What Kubrick admired in Conrad was the same thing respected in him by two other great visualists of the cinema, Orson Welles and David Lean: his flair for investing an image with narrative power.

Taft interested Kubrick as a photo subject far more than it ever did as a seat of learning. He became a contributor to its student paper and photographer for the yearbook. Walter Trueman, who wrote a sports column for the paper, remembers him as a social outcast whose only skill was the ability to take his camera apart and reassemble it. In his films, Kubrick was often to show characters demonstrating their intelligence with some similarly intricate mechanical skill: Dave Bowman disconnecting HAL in *2001*; Patrick Magee palming a card in *Barry Lyndon* and Ryan O'Neal collecting debts with his skill at swordplay; Matthew Modine assembling a rifle in *Full Metal Jacket*.

Kubrick at school was anything but likeable. In Trueman's yearbook he wrote sarcastically, 'I'm sure we'll be reading your stories in the *Daily Worker*' – the organ of the Communist Party. Another contemporary characterised Kubrick as 'close to being the class creep. He never got to classes on time, was irregular in attendance, and made terrible marks. In his defence it must be admitted that, for some reason, he drew the worst teachers. They would immediately take an active dislike to him and really pound on him.' An exception to Kubrick's blanket dismissal of Taft's teaching staff was Aaron Traister, who caught his imagination by teaching Shakespeare not as poetry but as living theatre, acting out roles for the class rather than simply droning the text. A few years later, Kubrick made one of his first professional sales with a photo-essay on Traister.

Through the school magazine, Kubrick met other like-minded and alienated boys. One was Bernard Cooperman, with whom he shared the photographic chores. He had a particular friendship, though, with Alexander Singer, rated 'the school intellectual' by his classmates, and despised accordingly. 'We met when we were both about sixteen,' says Singer. 'He had first made contact with me because of some things I'd written for the school literary art magazine. I'd written stories and illustrated them.' Kubrick made an immediate and indelible impression on Singer, both through his personality and his social circumstances. 'There was a sense of organised activity directed at a goal that is, to put it mildly, uncommon with teenagers,' recalls Singer. 'Stanley didn't disport himself as a "rich kid", but in the blue-collar environment in which I was mostly enmeshed, he represented a middle class I had no experience of.' As soon as he was eligible for a licence, Kubrick also drove the family car. 'I knew nobody who owned a car, let alone could drive it,' Singer remembers. 'That kind of mobility was simply outside my experience.'

Almost as impressive was another friend of Kubrick's and a fellow contributor to the Taft magazine, Howard Sackler, later to be a highly successful playwright. Even then handsome and assured, Sackler was already making a reputation. Singer says, 'I also knew him as one of the smart kids. There was an odd smugness, a kind of arrogance he radiated. I would have said a kind of perversity of nature; he was the kind of youngster who's capable of emotional cruelty. There was a slightly feverish quality about him. The rumour was that he was a Lothario, or more specifically a gigolo: older women used him, or he used older women. It was an almost inconceivably remote notion to a bunch of teenage boys who can barely get off the notion that they must somehow do something with their erections. He was someone who was doing something almost unimaginable. He was a figure both of envy, and of things outside what you imagined the world contained.'

Against the odds, Kubrick too had a sex life, which made him relatively comfortable in Sackler's company. While still at Taft, he started dating a pretty fellow student, Toba Metz, who lived in the new apartment block to which the Kubricks had moved at 1414

Shakespeare Avenue. 'She was quite striking,' says Alex Singer. 'Italian-looking, perhaps. But without any sense of Kubrick's potential. It was a mismatch. She seemed relatively ordinary as people go, and he was not.' Kubrick tried to 'fix up' Singer, but Alex had none of Kubrick's or Sackler's casual cool that allowed them to remain detached and unemotional with women. 'I couldn't date girls. I only wanted to sleep with them or marry them.'

At Taft Kubrick discovered another enthusiasm, for jazz. Popular music at the time was dominated by the big swing bands, each with its drummer who, elevated on his dais, crashed out a flashy solo in every arrangement. Gene Krupa, first with Benny Goodman's band, then as the head of his own, was typical of this group. Chewing gum and flailing furiously in his double-breasted white sharkskin suit, he embodied a driving sense of the period's search for self-gratification in the face of worldwide conflict. Krupa and his colleagues exercised as powerful a fascination for teenagers as did rock guitarists like Jimi Hendrix in the seventies, and Kubrick decided to become a drummer.

An ulterior motive behind Kubrick's sudden interest in jazz is suggested by Fred Stettner, who was in the class ahead of him. 'He was trying to get in with the jocks, who were all the stars of the school, and also people in the band, who were the second stars in the school – yours truly being the trombone player – and wanted to hang round with the cheerleaders, because we all hung round with the cheerleaders . . . and he was somewhat of a nerd, in today's standard . . . And he was a pain in the ass with his camera, he was always annoying people and taking pictures. And lots of these people didn't want their pictures taken, as I recall . . . He wasn't socially adept.'

Kubrick did make the school orchestra and, more important to him, became the drummer of the nine-man Swing Band, whose singer Edith Gorme would later, as Eydie Gorme, become a notable jazz vocalist. He also got to hang out with the cheerleaders, shooting them for the yearbook and the school magazine.

In April 1945, President Franklin Roosevelt died. Kubrick, on his way to school, noticed a news vendor framed by posters announcing the death, and photographed him. Kubrick told everyone it was a lucky shot, the snatching of what a critic, writing about Cartier-

Bresson's work, called 'the decisive moment'. To Walter Trueman, however, he confessed he'd sweated blood persuading the old man to look appropriately dejected – an early example of his taxing method with actors.

Skipping school, he hurried home to process the picture, and took it to the Manhattan office of *Look*. Launched in 1937, *Look* was widely regarded as the most innovative of the many picture magazines pushed onto the market to compete with the Luce empire's *Life*, which had started publishing in 1936. All of these magazines exploited the new technology of wire-photos and high-quality reproduction and printing, but, as a weekly, *Life* inevitably snatched the scoops, while its black-and-white presses, the best in the world, made it the aim of every serious news photographer and photojournalist. As a fortnightly which printed ten days ahead, *Look* couldn't hope to fight *Life* on its home ground; in a famous lapse, its December 1941 issue had no mention of Pearl Harbor, which *Life* splashed across most of its pages. Instead it pioneered colour covers and advertising, and published more thoughtful and occasionally playful features leavened with some serious photojournalism. (Having outlasted all but its toughest competitor, *Life*, *Look* survived until 1971, folding, with notable irony, in National Magazine Week.)

The picture editor who finally saw Kubrick, Helen O'Brian, had a rule about never turning away a picture without at least looking at it. She liked the news-stand shot enough to offer him $25, and was taken aback when he asked her to wait while he showed it to the *New York Daily News*. 'They only offered ten,' he told her when he returned, 'so you can have it.' Intrigued by a high-school boy with this much *chutzpah*, O'Brian asked to see any other pictures that reached *Look*'s standard. On his way out of her office, Kubrick passed the 'bull pen' where freelance photographers hung out, waiting for an assignment. To any other ambitious teenage photographer, this gang of surly pros grown old and grizzled in pursuit of a good picture might have been daunting. To Kubrick, however, they represented a challenge.

Look used the picture in its issue of 26 June 1945, to illustrate a feature on the careers of FDR and his successor, Harry Truman. After that, Kubrick sold pictures regularly to *Look*, starting with a shot of motorists queuing for rationed gasoline, which made him

$100. He followed with his first photo-essay, a series of pictures of Aaron Traister's shenanigans before his Shakespeare class. Staff journalists wrote the text for these stories: Kubrick's role, like that of most photographers at the time, was to deliver the pictures and let others caption them. As photographers won the trust of the editors, they would sometimes be sent out with a concept, and given orders to illustrate it. Kubrick learned early the habit of looking to others for his narratives, and devoting his energies to illuminating them.

Before long, he was a regular in *Look*'s bull pen, a startling sight in red-and-blue checked shirt and orange corduroy trousers, both of them too short for his gangling limbs. 'He was constantly at war with the older staff, who preferred the larger formats,' a *Look* editor remembered. 'They couldn't stand the graininess of 35mm or the gall of Stanley for using it.' He frowned. 'We still bought his pictures, though.'

The Traister project was one of Kubrick's last at Taft before graduation. His grades were so dismal he had no chance of getting into any respectable university, and the labour market was swamped by returning servicemen better qualified than himself, and with a stronger call on the nation's generosity. He began auditing classes at City College in the hope of eventually being allowed to enrol. He confided his frustration to Helen O'Brian and, in a weak moment, she offered him a job as apprentice photographer. He joined *Look* in April 1945. He wasn't yet seventeen.

Chapter Three

Kubrick in the City

*'The only people for me are the mad ones, the ones who
are mad to live, mad to talk, mad to be saved, desirous
of everything at the same time, the ones who never
yawn or say a commonplace thing, but burn, burn, burn
like fabulous yellow roman candles exploding like
spiders across the stars . . .'*

Jack Kerouac, *On the Road*

Kubrick left Taft with a momentum envied by his contemporaries,
none of whom could hope to equal it. 'Most of us were still worried
about whether our flies were open or closed,' Alex Singer says.
'Stanley may have been worried about that too, but he was on
Look's staff, and *Look* at that time was in the class of *Life*, and
its reproduction was even better. Stanley had very carefully made
that possible. He'd gone through a very deliberate set of plans
to get there. Whether it was thought out entirely is beside the
point.'

Look's assignments ranged from the banal to the eccentric. In
October 1945 Kubrick shot, again from hiding, a series of photos
showing two boys watching a baseball game. In April 1946 the
magazine published *A Short Short in a Movie Balcony*, evidently
shot before he joined the staff, since the copy speaks of 'a freelance
photographer' who, with a friend, 'recently visited a Bronx movie.
They selected a total stranger, and the photographer's friend sat
down beside her. She was completely unaware that a photographer
was recording the scene a few seats away on infra-red film.' The
four photographs show a handsome Jewish boy sitting next to the

girl, lighting a cigarette, turning towards her – and being slapped in the face because of some (unseen) sexual advance. The posed look of the couple, especially in the shot of the slap, and the high contrast of the pictures, inconsistent with infra-red, make it clear they were staged, and taken with flash. The boy was Bernard Cooperman, Kubrick's fellow photographer from Taft, and the girl a classmate. In proposing the feature, Kubrick was almost certainly inspired by a series of flash pictures Arthur Fellig took of New York cinema audiences at about the same time. Kubrick only explained part of his plan to Cooperman, who was told simply to begin pawing the girl. *She* had been instructed to hit him as hard as she could. Cooperman said the slap almost loosened his teeth.

Two more series for *Look*, one of covert shots of people at a zoo staring at monkeys (20 August 1946), the other of patients in a dentist's waiting room (1 October 1946), are more typical of Kubrick. They show his growing technical competence, as well as the ability to crystallise character in an expression or pose. He even won the cover on 5 August 1947, though only with an anodyne picture of a little boy surprised by a squirt from a tap. This picture, and two other photo-series, to illustrate features on the *Boston Blackie* radio show (8 January 1946) and imaginary illnesses (17 September 1946), suggest that Kubrick's interest in photojournalism was flagging. *Look*, however, pressed more ambitious assignments on him. In 1948 the magazine would send him to Portugal to shoot pictures for a travel piece. He covered a circus during its winter layoff in Sarasota, Florida, followed Senator Robert Taft as he stumped Ohio in search of re-election, and shot stills for a feature about the young Montgomery Clift.

William Read Woodfield, stills photographer on *Spartacus* and later a successful TV producer, can imagine the effect of this job on young Kubrick. 'When you're a seventeen-year-old photographer on the staff of *Look* magazine and you go out and do a story, you are in total control of that story. What you frame, what you take, the mood you take it in, the pictures you mark for printing, what you turn in – you are in complete control. And it is a wonderful feeling.' Still, Kubrick found his work for *Look* 'pretty meaningless. What kind of photography can you do on a college costume party,' he complained, 'or on stories like "Is an Athlete Stronger than a Baby?"' He used some of his new wealth to take flying lessons, and in August 1947 he was issued with a pilot's certificate for single-engined aircraft.

Kubrick married his high-school girlfriend Toba Metz on 28 May 1948 in Mount Vernon, NY. He was eighteen, she a year younger. They moved into a tiny apartment at 37 West 16th Street, off 6th Avenue. There was even room to keep a dog, so Kubrick bought a Doberman Pinscher, which deterred visitors almost as much as it did burglars. His family had owned a large dog, and all his life Kubrick was to remain attached to dogs – inordinately, some people think. Freud asserts that the relationship between a dog and his owner replicates that of parent and child, with one difference: 'there is no ambivalence, no element of hostility.'

Greenwich Village in 1948 was filled with men who'd returned from the war but had no intention of picking up their old lives. Many were taking advantage of the GI Bill to get a college education and had gravitated to the Village, drawn by a Bohemian reputation that went back to the First World War. As some became bored with education and joined the drop-outs, cranks, political radicals and mostly unpublished writers and poets milling around downtown Manhattan, a community began to form which John Clellon Holmes would christen in a 1952 *New York Times* piece 'the beat generation'.

Kubrick was on the fringe of this surge in American popular culture, but not really part of it. Literature still didn't interest him. He and Toba, known to most of his friends as 'Toby', spent their spare time in the Village's bars and cafés listening to jazz, and in the downtown art cinemas that showed *avant garde* and foreign films. He was already looking beyond still photography, to cinema. As he saw it, he had mastered photography, and his years of watching films had taught him everything he thought he would ever need to know about film story-telling. Acting, design and music, as far as they related to underlining the film image, interested him hardly at all. Now all he need do was study the masters and discover a means of taking the first step towards emulating and, in time, surpassing them.

Once Kubrick discovered the Museum of Modern Art's theatre on West 53rd Street, he saw, he claimed, each daily change of programme. The Museum's film library reflected the taste of its curator Iris Barry, a defiantly left-wing Briton with an appetite for radical politics and gin. During the war she'd taken on Luis Buñuel as head of MoMa's documentary programme, which produced Spanish-language versions of propaganda films for circulation in South America. Another employee, the Soviet film historian Jay Leyda, was also, like Buñuel, a communist. The Museum's collection reflected their radicalism, favouring Soviet cinema and the European *avant garde* over Hollywood, and stressing the maverick tradition of American cinema as exemplified by directors like Erich von Stroheim, for whom Kubrick never lost his enthusiasm. When a young assistant on *2001: A Space Odyssey*, Andrew Birkin, showed him a script treatment he'd written for a little-known Frank Norris novel called *McTeague*, Kubrick explained that von Stroheim had already adapted it, and borrowed a print of *Greed* for Birkin to study.

Chess remained an absorbing interest for Kubrick, and the Village offered plentiful opportunities to play it. Almost as soon as he moved away from home, Kubrick scraped up $50 to join the Marshall Chess Club at 23 West 10th Street. Ex-US chess champion Frank Marshall ran his club from a one-family brownstone that a group of friends had bought as his retirement home. In its ballroom-like dining room, filled with orderly rows of chess tables, a generation of American grand masters was nurtured. When times were better, Kubrick also joined the more select Manhattan Chess Club, then situated uptown, on 100 Central Park South, opposite the St Moritz Hotel.

Alan Kaufman, now executive director of the US Chess Federation, was a young member of the Marshall Club in the early fifties, and a friend of Kubrick. Both relished its elitism. 'I consider chess to be a sort of religion,' says Kaufman, 'and this was a temple of the religion, and people who came there were co-religionists. It's in the nature of chess clubs to reorganise the people who come. You line up the people according to their rating. Young or old makes no difference; rich or poor, educated or uneducated; bathed or unwashed, you take your place in the hierarchy by how well you play chess.'

Kubrick warmed to this supercharged meritocracy. Most evenings, he played at the Manhattan or the Marshall. In the mornings and early afternoons, when the clubs were closed, he prowled the cafés and bars where old men hunched over games at a few tables in the rear. Sometimes he watched the games of speed chess, or 'skittles', played for side bets of 25 cents in Washington Square, or in establishments like the New York Academy of Chess and Checkers on 42nd Street, better known as 'The Flea House'.

Chess has remained important to Kubrick, though he rejects the superficial correlation between his sense of spatial relationships as a director and the dynamics of the board. The latest research confirms this. 'Chess ability,' says one report of the nineties, 'is quite specific and not a function of general memory or cognitive expertise.' The 'chess mind' is one that can retain thousands of games, and consider and reject hundreds of alternatives before choosing the best move for a particular situation. But its strategies are instinctive rather than rational – a quality not always applicable in the real world. Many successful generals, businessmen and film-makers play mediocre chess.

'If chess has any relationship to film-making,' Kubrick told Alexander Walker, 'it would be in the way it helps you develop patience and discipline in choosing between alternatives at a time when an impulsive decision seems very attractive. Otherwise it is necessary [in chess] to have perfect intuition – and this is something very dangerous for an artist to rely on.' What Kubrick most remembered from chess, he acknowledged later, was the sense of combat: the rush of pleasure and excitement, the pounding of the heart as one saw the right, the *only* move – and the need to hide your knowledge until the trap could be sprung. Better than winning was *knowing*.

The New York chess scene encouraged those aspects of Kubrick's character which psychologists call 'passive/aggressive'. He had developed, like many men who shared this personality defect – T.E. Lawrence, Howard Hughes – the tendency, which David Garnett noted in Lawrence, of 'backing into the limelight'. There was a narcissism in Kubrick's shyness, a tendency to choose the act of self-effacement which would most stridently draw attention to itself. Whether reading a newspaper by the light of a movie screen, hunched over a chess board under a street lamp in Washington Square or, later in his life, lurking in a private enclave in the English countryside, he was as much on show as if he'd been doing *Hamlet* on Broadway.

*

Ambitious, like Kubrick, to make movies, but more conventional
and systematic in the way he went about it, Alex Singer found a
job as office boy at 'The March of Time', the documentary news
film series sponsored by the publishers of *Life* and *Time* magazines.
Since 1935 the company had released a monthly documentary short,
usually twenty minutes long, that combined newsreel footage with
re-enacted incidents in an attempt, initially highly successful, to
give documentary the audience appeal of features. Although Orson
Welles parodied its hectoring commentaries and self-important
theme music in *Citizen Kane* as 'News on the March', 'The March
of Time' had been a high-flying and high-spending series in its day,
and exerted a marked influence on public opinion, especially with
its exposé of Louisiana Governor and Presidential hopeful Huey
Long, and a number of films which turned confiscated Nazi propaganda footage against Hitler by using it to attack his regime.

In his spare time Singer wrote scripts, including an ambitious
version of Homer's *Iliad*, which he storyboarded in nine hundred
continuity sketches. He showed these to Kubrick, who took the
project to Helen O'Brian on his behalf. She had enough clout to get
it to Dore Schary, MGM's recently appointed head of production. A
studio reader pointed out, diplomatically, that since the studio was
filming the Roman epic *Quo Vadis?*, no resources existed for a
Greek extravaganza that, moreover, he estimated would cost around
$6 million. 'I was crushed,' said Singer.

Kubrick suggested he write a simpler story, one on which they
might collaborate. After a number of tries, Singer succeeded:

It was for a twenty-minute 16mm black-and-white film, a very
teenage-y thing. The lonely young man at the beach almost makes
contact with the pretty girl. It was written with some artfulness
and some device.

My next step, which seemed to be inevitable, was to do a
series of continuity sketches which, in effect, set the camera
positions for every single one of the shots. At that time I didn't
reckon there was any other way to make film except to do it
totally. But I had unwittingly reduced Stanley's function to something rather mechanical. He looked at this work and told me
how much he liked it, and felt it was a fine piece of work, and
I should by all means go ahead and do it, but that he would

have no part of it. Because I had in fact taken the total creative life of the thing and shaped it. That was the last time I aspired to equality in the relationship. It was a singular moment that I remembered very well. It was on a double decker bus going down 5th Avenue, and I had a presentiment at that point of how our fates were to separate and go. From that point on, Stanley's projects were Stanley's projects. For one thing, he'd paid for them. And that's what happened to *Day of the Fight*.

Unaware of the shakiness of 'The March of Time's' financial status, and the fact that cinemas were increasingly refusing to pay anything at all for shorts, Singer believed that the series, which in palmier days had paid as much as $40,000 for short films, represented a lucrative market. He persuaded Kubrick that a documentary could both establish them in the business and show a solid profit.

Late in 1948, *Look* assigned Kubrick to cover one day in the life of a young middleweight boxer, twenty-four-year-old Walter Cartier. *Prizefighter* appeared in the issue for 18 January 1949. In his most ambitious piece of photo-journalism, Kubrick followed Cartier through the day of a big fight: waking up in his apartment with his twin brother, who was also his manager; weighing in; consulting his trainer; the afternoon spent on a boat around Staten Island with his girlfriend; a visit to his young nephew, for whom he assembled a toy boat; and finally the fight in Jersey City, which he won on a knockout.

Boxing made a powerful impact on Kubrick. In 1948, the sport still retained the overtones of machismo and blood lust accumulated over a century. Friday-night fights remained as much a fixture of the entertainment week for many working-class and immigrant men as was the Saturday-night visit to the movies. 'When I was young, growing up in the tenements of New York in the years after World War II,' wrote sporting journalist Pete Hamill, 'prizefighting was the great dark prince of sports ... Boxing exuded the dangerous glamour of the urban night. We travelled on Friday evenings by subway to the old Madison Square Garden. Before the fights, the lobby was jammed with neighbourhood tough guys and off-duty cops. There were a lot of pinkie rings. Some guys brought their women with them, great fleshy creatures with blinding hair and glistening scarlet lips. Everybody smoked. And the very air seemed charged with the coming blood rite. We were all there to see violence transformed into art.'

One of Kubrick's photographs in particular, the image chosen to open the piece, and accorded a respectful full page, exuded this sense. Waiting with his manager in the changing room, dressed for the ring, bare-chested, gloved hands in his lap, Cartier looks up and away, gathering his strength for the fight. The single ceiling light shadows his eyes and emphasises his high cheekbones and the broad, hairless expanse of his chest. Shooting from his favourite low angle, Kubrick turns him into an icon of masculinity – of, some would say, homo-eroticism. It's obvious from this single image that Kubrick would have more to say about boxing, so remote from the sunny world of Yankee Stadium which until then had been his main experience of professional sport.

Although Kubrick continued on the staff at *Look*, *Prizefighter*, with its nineteen photos taking up seven full pages, suggests the direction of his future career. It might have been meant as the blueprint of a film.

Convinced he was ready for movies, Kubrick sank his savings of 4½ years at *Look*, along with whatever he could borrow, into a twelve-minute documentary about Cartier. Burt Zucker, a young man who ran the Camera Equipment Company at 1600 Broadway, rented Kubrick a 35mm spring-wound silent Eyemo, the standard camera of World War II combat photographers, and spent a morning teaching him how to use it. Later he would instruct Kubrick in the use of the synchroniser, splicer and Moviola he also rented.

Day of the Fight reprised *Prizefighter* by following Cartier through the day of another bout, deleting his Staten Island idyll and his visit to his nephew. By dropping all reference to his girl and to his family, except his attentive brother, Kubrick implies that Cartier has no aim in life except to win. He is transformed into that favourite character of Kubrick's later films, the driven man.

Day of the Fight might be an illustration of Pete Hamill's essay, although it was filmed almost half a century before he wrote it. From the opening shot, of a poster for the fight nailed to a lamp-post, with a mist-shrouded city street in the background, Kubrick accumulates atmosphere. As in *Prizefighter*, he dwells on the nervous build-up to the fight and Cartier's near-symbiotic relationship with his brother Vincent, a lawyer from New Jersey who becomes his manager on the day of his bouts, moving into the Greenwich Village apartment Cartier normally shares with his aunt.

The men wake in the same double bed, attend mass and take communion together, and Vincent is at his corner that night when Walter convincingly decks his opponent. We learn about the Cartier boys through their surroundings. The crucifix above the bed and the *pietà* they pass on their way to mass imply a spirituality not evident in *Prizefighter*. Empty streets and the deserted church lift their story into stylisation, an effect underlined by the lack of the 'live' sound that was to contribute so much to the atmosphere of *cinéma vérité*. Instead, it has a solemn 'March of Time'-type commentary ('This is the story of a fight and of a fighter'), written by Robert Rein and delivered by Douglas Edwards in the solemn house style. Again following style, the film opens with a full panel assuring audiences 'All Events Depicted In This Film Are True'. Kubrick took credit as director, cameraman (though Alex Singer shot almost as much as he did) and twice as producer – once on the opening title ('A Stanley Kubrick Production') and again at the end ('Produced and directed by . . .'). 'I did everything myself,' Kubrick later claimed, 'from keeping an accounting book to dubbing the punches and footsteps.' Singer recognised instantly that he was watching a fine director in the making. 'He did that sports short as if he were doing *War and Peace*,' he says. 'He was meticulous with everything, from scripting to editing. Stanley was a full-blown film-maker instantly.'

Day of the Fight has dated far less than one would expect. Instead of following the formal style of Soviet and British documentary, with their looming compositions and heavily shadowed close-ups of faces carefully kept free of make-up, he exploited what he'd learned sneaking still shots around New York in available light with his Graflex. Years before the French documentary-makers invented *cinéma vérité* or the teams of Drew Leacock Pennebaker and the Maysles brothers introduced hand-held camerawork and live sound to American cinema via their 'Living Camera' documentaries, Kubrick anticipated their pale, undramatic shooting and slice-of-life effects. In the process he made Walter Cartier look so good that the young boxer had a successful acting career, appearing in films like Elia Kazan's *A Face in the Crowd* and the Phil Silvers TV series *Sergeant Bilko*.

Alex Singer gets an assistant director credit. He also introduced Kubrick to a friend, Gerald Fried, who became the film's composer. Typically focused on the photographic mechanics, Kubrick hadn't considered a score, but Fried convinced him that the film needed one to have any chance of commercial release. Fried's music, though sparse, cost more to record and mix than Kubrick expected. After having shot the film for less than $1000, he found himself spending over $3000 to record and lay the sound effects, music and commentary. But the music became an integral part of the film, and Fried would go on to score Kubrick's first four features.

Day of the Fight is an assured debut, and would have been a worthy inclusion on 'The March of Time'. Unfortunately, as Kubrick and Singer discovered when they submitted it, television had supplanted the current-affairs short feature, and *Time* was preparing to close down the series. The young film-makers took the film to one of the few distributors still handling shorts, RKO-Pathé. RKO, then a pariah among studios, was under the wayward management of Howard Hughes, who was supposed to have visited his possession only once, directed his staff, 'Paint it,' and left.

The company bought *Day of the Fight*, as it bought many documentaries. Of the fifteen films RKO released in 1950, it produced only three, the rest coming from independents. What little success it enjoyed at the Academy Awards during this period was for documentaries like *Kon-Tiki*, about Thor Heyerdahl's voyage across the Pacific on a raft, and the nature shorts like *Beaver Valley* it distributed for Disney.

RKO paid Kubrick a disappointingly small $4000 – a mere $100 profit. However, the company did have another project for him, about a New Mexico padre, Father Fred Stadtmueller, whose parish was so large that he commuted between his eleven congregations in a Piper Cub. Burton Benjamin, soon a major influence in network TV documentary but in those days manager of RKO's 'Screenliner' film series, offered Kubrick $1500 to make a film about the flying priest.

Like *Day of the Fight*, the nine-minute film covers a brief period – two days in this case – in the life of an ordinary man working in an extraordinary job. The archetypal old-fashioned patriarchal priest,

Stadtmueller says mass at a number of his outlying churches, offici-
ates at a funeral, exercises moral control over the bickering kids in
his home diocese, and flies an ailing child and its mother to hospital.
There's little of Kubrick in the film, except for two trademark shots,
one from the floor of the plane looking up at Stadtmueller, the other
a final long track back from him standing on a dusty airstrip by his
plane.

Kubrick called the film 'Sky Pilot', a pun on the slang term for
priest, but Benjamin preferred the more prosaic title *Flying Padre*.
It opened in March 1951. A week later, on 26 April, *Day of the
Fight* went out as part of the supporting programme to *My Forbidden Past*, starring Robert Mitchum. Watching his film on the
big screen at the Paramount in New York transformed Kubrick. He
decided to quit *Look* and become a full-time film-maker.

RKO had no more work after *Flying Padre*, and Kubrick, reluctant to return to photo-journalism, started drawing unemployment
insurance and educating himself in film. There were few books
on the cinema in the early fifties, but Alex Singer, with his usual
punctiliousness, read them all, and persuaded Kubrick to do the
same. The best were the texts written in the twenties and thirties
by Soviet film-makers determined to stake out ideological claims to
the high ground of film theory. Jay Leyda's translation of Sergei
Eisenstein's *Film Form* came out in 1949, to join Eisenstein's earlier
The Film Sense. In the same year *Film Technique*, by Vsevelod
Pudovkin, director of *Mother* and other works of symbolic 'realism',
was reissued in a new edition, combined with his book *Film
Acting*.

Kubrick devoured all of them, but, typically, not without questioning some of their premises. He was sceptical about the instinctive
and personal methods of film-making proposed by the flamboyant
and often self-important Eisenstein, though he admired *Alexander
Nevsky*, in particular its set-piece Battle on the Ice. A clash between
the invading Teutonic Knights and the forces of Russia united under
Nevsky, the battle took place on a frozen lake. Undeterred by the
fact that he was filming in high summer, Eisenstein edited the skirmish so skilfully to Prokofiev's music that the sequence became a
classic. Kubrick was as seduced as anyone by Eisenstein's rhythmic
editing and the skill with which he disguised the cheapness of his
costumes and the dearth of extras. Later, however, he dismissed

Eisenstein's work as 'the triumph of cinematic style over heavy-handed, often simple-minded content.' He preferred Pudovkin, much more a nuts-and-bolts man. Pudovkin was preoccupied with editing, about which he wrote with the practical directness of someone who had been doing it all his life. In *Film Acting* he was equally pragmatic, insisting that a performer need not express emotion overtly, as on stage, or even express it at all; a good editor could create a performance in the cutting room. 'The film is not shot,' said Pudovkin, 'but built up from separate strips of celluloid that are its raw material.'

To an introvert like Kubrick, preoccupied with control, Pudovkin's adulation of editing sounded sweet. Cutting assumed a near-mystical importance to him. It was, he decided, the only original and unique art form in film. As he explained to a journalist much later, 'Everything else [in film] comes from something else. Writing, of course, is writing, acting comes from the theatre, and cinematography comes from photography. Editing is unique to film. You can see something from different points of view almost simultaneously, and it creates a new experience.'

Kubrick's film career would coalesce around this insight. Instead of finding, as many directors did, the intellectual 'spine' of a film in the script before starting work, then shooting each scene to illuminate some part of that concept, Kubrick felt his way to the final version of a film by shooting each scene from many angles and demanding scores of takes on each line. Then, over months in the cutting room, he arranged and rearranged the tens of thousands of scraps of film to fit a vision that only really began to emerge during editing.

With more time on his hands, Kubrick began to make friends. Some were film-makers, like the animator Faith Hubley. Kubrick haunted her cutting room and those of the other editors and directors who rented space at 1600 Broadway, the informal centre of film-making in Manhattan. Others were fellow photographers, like Bert Stern and Diane Arbus, who often took Kubrick to Saturday-night charades parties in the Village. He also got to know obsessive chess players, like Arthur Feldman, Amos Kaminski and in particular Alan Kaufman. Since they shared his interest in jazz, Kubrick and Toba sometimes joined Kaufman at one of the city's many clubs.

Kubrick's tastes had widened, and Kaufman recalls hearing New Orleans clarinettist George Lewis with them at Childs, a midtown café.

Kaufman remembers the Kubrick of 1950–51 as 'skinny and dark. He looked introverted and quiet. He walked with his head down. Sometimes he'd wear an old suit and a shirt without a tie. Unimpressive, I would say.' That changed when he began talking about his future. 'He was a quiet, shy kind of guy, but when you got him going he'd tell you about the movies he was going to make. "I'm going to make this movie; I'm going to make that movie . . ." Generally speaking, people didn't believe him. It sounded like just another young man with boastful ideas.'

To eke out his unemployment insurance, Kubrick began hustling chess games, a popular practice among younger players. Kaufman and his friends would play at The Flea House until they had won enough to pay for a meal, then, after dinner, hustle enough for a movie. Kubrick preferred to play in the Washington Square area, near MacDougal and West 4th Streets. The fixed concrete boards were free – at The Flea House players paid by the hour – and the open air offered the maximum number of *kibitzers* – spectators – and *potzers* – patsies. By timing his games carefully, Kubrick occupied a shaded board by day but switched to one under a street light as night fell. He remembered a typical take for a twelve-hour day as around $3 – 'which goes a long way,' he told a friend years later, 'if all you are buying with it is food' – but he almost certainly made much more.

Playing chess for money developed other useful skills. 'When I think of Stanley and chess,' says the British critic and writer Gavin Lambert, who became his assistant and friend, 'it's in relationship to the element of gamesmanship.' Alan Kaufman agrees. 'There used to be a guy down there [in Washington Square] who called himself The Master. He wasn't a chess grand master, but he'd use that title to intimidate his opponents. "You'd play that move against The Master? Such arrogance! You can't get away with that move against The Master!" I remember the remarks he used to make to unsettle his opponents. In offhand chess and play for money, comments are not only accepted, but they become part of the entertainment of the game, so that people calling one another names, or needling one another in the form of insults, sometimes produces a result in the game by upsetting the opponent, but more often are just amusement for the bystanders.'

Kubrick saw through The Master, and pigeonholed him as a semi-*potzer* – defined by Kubrick's friend and chess opponent of the sixties, the physicist Jeremy Bernstein, as 'the possessor of a flashy but fundamentally unsound game that was full of pseudo-traps designed to enmesh even lesser *potzers* and to ensure the quickest possible win.' But Kubrick learned from The Master and others like him a battery of psychological games that he used throughout his film-making career to keep both opponents and friends off-balance. The urgent nocturnal summons, the lawyer's letter appearing out of the blue, the sudden phone call revealing his unexpected possession of information, the abrupt change of mood during filming or the demand for some enigmatic object or obscure alteration to script, set or performance: these became tools of Kubrick's trade.

Even chess played its part. 'I always got this feeling that Stanley was a mind-game guy,' says a technician on *Full Metal Jacket* who watched Kubrick play chess with Arliss Howard, one of the actors. 'He loved to wind people up; wind the spring and see how long it took to make them pop.' Simply challenging an actor or critic to a game of chess could place them at a disadvantage, and Kubrick's comments on the flow of play would wear down their resistance. George C. Scott brought his sense of Hollywood importance to *Dr Strangelove* – 'but Stanley beat him a few times at chess,' said his friend Lyn Tornabene, entertainment editor of *Cosmopolitan* magazine, 'and showed him who was boss.' Colleagues smiled behind their hands at Kubrick's apparently casual invitation to a recalcitrant collaborator, 'How about a little game?' On *The Shining*, Kubrick played with Shelley Duvall, further complicating what had become for the actress an exhausting experience. Years later, when she was again in London, Kubrick, to whom she hadn't talked since the film wrapped, rang her and asked if she'd like to play again. 'I thought about it,' Duvall recalled with a shudder. 'And then I thought, "No . . ."'

*

Kubrick's years in and around Greenwich Village, playing chess, reading, listening to jazz, provided the only real education, both intellectual and sentimental, of his life. Faith Hubley recalls him always carrying a crumpled paperback of extracts from great novels. He would stop people in the street and demand, 'Dostoevsky, what do you think?' – his affectation of intellectualism undercut by the fact that he often mispronounced the authors' names. He left the Village with his adult lifestyle already formed. By the time he reached Hollywood in 1955, he was already aloof, uncommunicative, preferring his own company and that of one woman, spending much of the night working, and the days asleep. It was the way of life that the heroes of his films would follow. Johnny the lonely criminal planner in *The Killing*, Dax the intellectual lawyer-turned-soldier in *Paths of Glory*, the astronauts in *2001: A Space Odyssey*, the gang members of *A Clockwork Orange*, the 'grunts' of *Full Metal Jacket*, Barry Lyndon and, most obviously, Jack Torrance in *The Shining*, all find most satisfaction in their own company.

Gavin Lambert sees affinities between Kubrick's character and way of life and those of Marcel Proust, who also worked all night and came to limit his personal contacts to a handful of servants and friends. 'I think he is shy, in the sense that social life doesn't come very easily to him, or that he enjoys it all that much. I think he's learned to protect himself from the world. I think he's a bit paranoid, and that's the paranoid person's self-defence, to be inaccessible. I think it's amazing that someone who's so withdrawn from the world can make these movies that are so full of observation. Like Proust.

'I think that Stanley, in his early days in New York, saw just enough of the world: as much as he needed to see what was going on and what it was all about, and that he didn't want to have any more to do with it. So ever since then he's lived this sort of fortress life.'

Once he was launched as a film-maker, Kubrick would increasingly avoid any intimacy, except as part of the casual and evanescent camaraderie of the film unit. Kevyn Major Howard, one of the young actors in *Full Metal Jacket*, says, 'I think he enjoys the male comradeship of making films. He's surrounded by women at home and he likes to talk guns and sports. We'd sit around making our own food like guys in a logging camp.' But logging, like film-making,

44 STANLEY KUBRICK

doesn't last forever, and Kubrick could be confident that, after the few months of shooting, he would be left alone again in productive isolation, during which he could concentrate on the only activity that really satisfied him – making movies. The British author Brian Aldiss, who worked with him for many years on an unproduced science fiction project, 'A.I.' (for 'artificial intelligence'), believes that Kubrick is 'schizoid, like René Descartes. Descartes said, "I think, therefore I am." For Kubrick, it's "I film, therefore I am."'

Chapter Four

Kubrick on the Threshold

> 'Human beings make a strange flora and fauna. From a
> distance they appear negligible; close up, they are apt to
> appear ugly and malicious. More than anything they
> need to be surrounded by sufficient space – space even
> more than time.'
>
> Henry Miller, *Tropic of Cancer*

Throughout the early fifties, Kubrick's film-going became even more
intensive. As well as every change of programme at the Museum of
Modern Art, he saw at least two new first-release films each weekend. He scoured the pages of *PM* magazine, which listed films all
over the five boroughs, and would travel as far as Staten Island for
an obscure revival.

In particular, he caught every new film at the Guild and World
Cinemas near Times Square, where distributor Joseph Burstyn pre-
sented all the important works of Italian neo-realism, including
Rossellini's *Rome: Open City* and *Paisà*, and de Sica's *Bicycle
Thieves*. The lesson of neo-realism – that one could make movies
with amateur performers on real locations – wasn't lost on Kubrick.
He also found inspiration in that flashiest and most outrageous of
French film-makers, Jean Cocteau. He often quoted the passage in
Cocteau's 1949 film *Orphée* where the students demand of Orpheus,
poet star of the Parisian cafés, 'How may we please you?' Their
idol responds casually, 'Astonish me.'

Kubrick resolved to astonish. In the summer of 1950, he persuaded his friend from Taft, Howard Sackler, now, as Howard O.
Sackler, installed in Greenwich Village as a poet, to write a feature

46 STANLEY KUBRICK

screenplay provisionally titled 'The Trap', and later 'Shape of Fear'. Its inspiration was the war in Korea which erupted on 25 June when the North Koreans invaded their southern neighbour. But while the script has plenty of resonances with World War II films like *A Walk in the Sun* and *The Story of GI Joe*, where small groups of American soldiers find themselves trapped behind enemy lines and unable to communicate with the local peasants, Kubrick never identifies the nationalities of his antagonists, nor the war in which they're fighting.

Sackler's script played on the way combat externalises internal fears and hatreds. Stranded in heavily wooded country when their plane crashes, Lieutenant Corby and three enlisted men, Fletcher, Sidney and their sergeant, Mac, try to build a raft and float to safety down the river. Scouting the area, they find an enemy base commanded by a general. Mac, the toughest and most experienced of the group, persuades Corby that killing the general will redeem their so-far sorry performance, and give meaning and dignity to their lives.

The first attack, on a small outpost, is successful, and two of the enemy are killed while eating a meal, but complications set in when the group surprises three girls trying to net fish in the river. One is captured and tied to a tree, and Sidney is left to guard her. But, apparently crazed from shellshock, he embarks on a rambling speech filled with references to *The Tempest*, then unties the ropes, with the evident intention of raping the girl. When she runs, he shoots her dead and flees into the forest.

Attacking the enemy camp, Corby and Fletcher are surprised to find that the general and his aide are their own identical twins – a fact interpreted by critic Gene Phillips, who has discussed the film with Kubrick, to mean that 'the basic brotherhood of mankind cannot be destroyed even by war, for the enemy is but a reflection of one's self.' Corby and Fletcher kill their opposite numbers anyway. Mortally wounded in the skirmish, Mac floats downriver on the raft, and is reunited first with a now-calmer Sidney, then, in death, with Colby and Fletcher.

With its anonymous but threatening location, its toying with multiple personality and the evocation of *The Tempest* – critic David Thomson would compare Kubrick to 'a Prospero who has kept people off the island' – the film anticipated Kubrick's later fascination with science fiction. Modern science fiction, preoccupied with gadgetry, held no interest for him, but he never forgot the myths and fantasies he read as a child. 'Shape of Fear' also evoked the Teutonic forest of Grimm, a setting to which Kubrick returned in *The Shining*. In a summary for his distributor, he described the film as an 'odyssey' – the myth that would also inspire his most famous film.

This was Kubrick's first, but by no means last, film about men at war. (He himself has never fought. Eligible for the draft at the time of Korea, he was, according to Alexander Singer, 'turned down by the army on some oddball thing'.) A few years later, a *New York Times* magazine interviewer asked him why he seemed so fixated on criminals and soldiers. Kubrick told her he found both groups fascinating because, in his Manichaean vision of life, they were 'doomed from the start':

The criminal is always interesting on the screen because he is a paradox of violent contrasts. The soldier is absorbing because all the circumstances surrounding him have a kind of charged intensity. For all its horror, war is pure drama, probably because it is one of the few remaining situations where men stand up for and speak up for what they believe to be their principles. The criminal and the soldier have the virtue of being *for* something or *against* something in a world where many people have learned to accept a grey nothingness, to strike an unreal series of poses in order to be considered 'normal' or 'average'. It's difficult to say who is engaged in the greater conspiracy – the criminal, the soldier, or us.

The hand of Eugene O'Neill lay heavily on Sackler's text for the film, which employed a series of fashionable theatrical devices, including actors playing both hero and villain, characters spouting unexpectedly intense philosophical statements, and stream of consciousness – interpreted literally in this case, with Mac having a long mental soliloquy as he floats down a river in darkness and mist.

By contrast, the peasant girl, a late addition to the script, is a cliché of Hollywood war films, where the isolated unit is conventionally polarised by the combined sexual challenge and potential for useful intelligence of an attractive but uncommunicative captive. Such helpless women, often physically bound, at the mercy of groups of men, would turn up frequently in Kubrick's films.

Needing forests and a river, Kubrick planned to shoot 'Shape of Fear' in upstate New York, but California promised better weather. Normally a feature film, especially on 35mm and filmed on location, would have been beyond his resources. However, a Mitchell camera with four lenses (but no sound recording capability) cost a mere $25 a day to hire, and New York's fringe theatre seethed with actors who would work for nothing to appear in a movie. By meticulously planning the film shot by shot, editing in the camera and using no synchronised dialogue, Kubrick calculated he could make it in a fraction of the time of a Hollywood unit, and with almost no waste of stock, much as Rossellini had done with *Rome: Open City*, which used scraps of 35mm film bought from street photographers.

With typical audacity, Kubrick approached the *New York Times* and persuaded it to write a feature about his project. The story, headlined 'Young Man with Ideas and a Camera', appeared on 14 January 1951 under the byline of Thomas M. Pryor, but the laudatory text could easily have been written by Kubrick himself:

> Stanley says he has figured out every camera angle and that after he finds the proper location 'in some wooded area of Southern California', shooting should run smoothly and be concluded in fifteen to twenty-one days. He will bring four professional 'but not known name actors' out to the coast from Broadway and, because Stanley himself is not a member of the movie cameramen's union, he will engage a professional cinematographer. The one requirement is that the cameraman must agree in advance to follow the blueprint laid out by Stanley, who will direct and produce the film.

The *Times* piece conferred credibility on Kubrick, and his father and other members of the family invested $10,000 in him. A few days later, with Sackler's bulky script under his arm, Kubrick walked into the office of producer Richard de Rochemont, brother of Louis de Rochemont, who supervised 'The March of Time', and asked him to produce it, raising the rest of the money he needed. De Rochemont explained that he didn't have time, as he was involved in producing a series about Abraham Lincoln for the new TV series *Omnibus*, but he admired Kubrick's drive, and marked him down as a young man to watch.

Undeterred, Kubrick flew to Los Angeles and asked his uncle Martin Perveler to back the film. Perveler, by now the owner of a string of drugstores, could well afford to do so, and he was enough of a businessman to recognise, as de Rochemont had done, that Kubrick was going places. He proposed a deal under which he would become an investor in his nephew's entire career, taking a percentage of his earnings for life. Kubrick refused, and was at the airport and ready to board a plane back to New York when his uncle caught up with him and agreed to finance just 'Shape of Fear'.

As he expected, Kubrick had no trouble finding actors. Two unknowns, Kenneth Harp and Steve Coit, played Corby and Fletcher. Howard Sackler spotted young Paul Mazursky in an off-Broadway production of Leonid Andreyev's *He Who Gets Slapped*, and suggested he try out for the hysterical Sidney. Still a student at Brooklyn College, Mazursky made the long journey to 14th Street and, with nervous glances at Kubrick's Doberman, gave an audition.

'That's fine,' Kubrick said. 'You've got the part. You realise you'll need to spend a month in California?'

'Well, if it's OK with the Dean,' Mazursky said worriedly.

With Toba and Sackler, Kubrick spent six weeks scouting locations in California, and chose the heavily wooded San Gabriel Mountains and a river near Bakersfield, as well as some woodland at Azuga, near Los Angeles. Also in California he hired Virginia Leith, a slim and sensual-looking photographer's model who'd done a little TV, for the peasant girl, and, to play the more demanding role of Mac, Frank Silvera. The swarthy Jamaican-born Silvera was a proponent of the Method school of acting with some movie experience, having played in Elia Kazan's *Viva Zapata!* with Marlon Brando.

In the summer of 1951 Kubrick returned to California to start shooting. On paper the actors were paid hundreds of dollars a week, but actually they drew a pittance, deferring the rest of their fees until the film went into profit. Four of Kubrick's friends served as crew. Bob Dierkes, a studio assistant from *Look*, was production manager, Chet Fabian did make-up, and Herbert Leibowitz built the minimal sets. Steve Hahn, credited as assistant director, was also a member of the cameramen's union. It's clear, however, from the lapidary care lavished on framing and lighting, that Kubrick controlled the photography. Four anonymous Mexicans hired in Los Angeles acted as grips.

As independent productions go, 'Shape of Fear' encountered fewer technical problems than most. The weather stayed fine, and Kubrick was able to achieve the visual excellence he demanded. Few first films are so beautifully lit and composed – sometimes absurdly so: a hand plunged into a tin plate of stew during the attack on the enemy looks like a study by the master of photographic chiaroscuro Edward Steichen, while each dying or dead soldier is given a close-up worthy of Ava Gardner.

Kubrick rose to the film's technical problems with the interest in technology that became typical of his career. Too strapped for cash to rent a fog machine for Mac's drift down the misty river, he discovered that Hollywood's devices burned a soluble oil called Nujol, and improvised one by loading an insecticide sprayer with mineral oil and water. The resulting miasma choked everyone, though the effect was impressively atmospheric.

Toba acted as script girl, but her sour expression in stills of the production shows that she found the experience tiresome. The marriage, never sound, didn't survive the strain of shooting. She and Kubrick separated immediately after returning to New York, and filed for divorce later that year.

In September 1951 Kubrick arrived back in the east at the end of thirty days' shooting with fifteen thousand metres of exposed film, only a tenth of what a professional unit would have shot. Photographically, the material was excellent, but as Kubrick began the painstaking process of editing it became clear that he'd severely underestimated the cost and complexity of creating a soundtrack. The score he commissioned from Gerald Fried required twenty-three musicians and much expensive studio time. He also had to coax all the actors into a recording studio to loop their dialogue. The cost of the film ballooned to $53,000, of which investors owned 39.5 per cent. The rest remained with Kubrick – as did the responsibility of paying to complete the film.

When the American Federation of Musicians began threatening to 'black' the film unless its members were paid, Kubrick turned to

Richard de Rochemont, who placated the union and paid $500 towards the bill out of his own pocket, securing an agreement that no action would be taken against the film.

Kubrick, meanwhile, had suspended work on dubbing 'Shape of Fear' and gone looking for work as a cameraman and director of sponsored documentaries. Embarrassed, he never in later years mentioned any short films other than *Day of the Fight* and *Flying Padre*. However, in a summary of his career sent to veteran New York film critic Theodore Huff in February 1953, he wrote that he had worked on 'Misc. television and state dept. trivia intersperced [sic].'

Only two short films directed by Kubrick have been identified, of which one is known still to exist. The first was a documentary, title unknown, length uncertain, made in 1952 about the World Assembly of Youth, an early attempt by the US State Department, which sponsored the film, to mobilise college-aged kids to carry out socially worthy projects, an initiative that was to have its pay-off in John Kennedy's Peace Corps.

The other, a thirty-minute documentary in colour, *The Seafarers*, resurfaced in the eighties. It was commissioned by the Atlantic and Gulf Coast District of the Seafarers' International Union, which hoped to encourage membership by showing a typical day in the life of seamen on shore, waiting for a ship, and the facilities offered by the union to help them. In addition to the hiring hall at which the men gather to look for work, these include a library, where they're shown, somewhat self-consciously, writing letters and wrangling over grievances with a union representative, and a Marine Hospital for ageing and injured sailors. There's little sign of the mature Kubrick, and his reluctance to acknowledge *The Seafarers* is understandable.

De Rochemont nudged director Norman Lloyd into hiring Kubrick to direct second unit for the *Omnibus* series *Mr Lincoln*. Underwritten by the Ford Foundation in the hope of raising American TV's intellectual level, the series, hosted by the urbane Alastair Cooke, struggled with varying success from 1952 to 1959 to wave the banner of intellect in the face of a flood of game shows and sitcoms.

Usually relegated to the cultural ghetto of Sunday afternoons, it roosted at all three networks at various times during its seven-year

life, often alarming both programmers and audiences with its catholic and challenging choice of material, which ranged from *King
Lear* with Orson Welles (making his TV debut) to Cyril Ritchard
in Gilbert and Sullivan's *HMS Pinafore*.

In its first season, *Omnibus*'s executive producer Robert Saudek
truculently nailed his colours to the mast by commissioning his
old college room-mate James Agee to write a five-part dramatised
biography of Abraham Lincoln. *Mr Lincoln* starred raw-boned and
rangy character actor Royal Dano, courageous casting for a series
which would have had trouble drawing audiences even with a Hollywood star in the role.

Agee, who deeply admired Lincoln, had established himself as
one of the finest writers on rural America with his book *Let us
now Praise Famous Men*, a documentary novel about sharecropper
families during the Depression, then gone on to become the most
lucid and acute of film critics, after which he graduated to writing
screenplays like *The Night of the Hunter* and *The African Queen*.
Despite being ruined in health by alcohol, chain-smoking and a
recent heart attack, Agee, who resembled the young Lincoln,
approached *Mr Lincoln* with relish, even including a cameo role
for himself as Jack Kelso, a hard-drinking fishing friend of the
President. *Mr Lincoln* gave Kubrick a chance to meet the man whose
criticism for the *Nation* and *Life* had been one of his inspirations.
Though Agee had given up film reviewing in 1948, he promised to
take a look at Kubrick's feature when it was finished. They probably
discussed two projects on which Agee was working, since both are
echoed in Kubrick's later work. One was Stephen Crane's short
story 'The Blue Hotel', about a card game in a snowbound Nebraska
hotel that ends in murder. Agee had adapted it into a feature script
for Huntington Hartford, the eccentric millionaire heir to the A&P
supermarket fortune, who had ambitions to produce films, but Agee
so over-elaborated the story with technical ideas gleaned from years
of criticism that it proved impossible to shoot. Instead he turned it
into an *Omnibus* episode which Kubrick undoubtedly saw. Years
later, he acknowledged *The Blue Hotel* as one inspiration of *The
Shining*.

Agee's second script, never produced or even published, was written for Charlie Chaplin under the working title 'Scientists and
Tramp'. Chaplin had warmed to Agee when he was the only critic

to praise his 1947 film *Monsieur Verdoux*, which took a flippant approach to the story of Landru, a French *bourgeois* who murdered a series of women for their money. Finding that Agee wanted to leave film journalism and become a screenwriter, Chaplin suggested that he write a script about their shared fear of nuclear war. Agee's sixty-three-page treatment began with a view from space of the nearly-ruined earth, now run by evil scientists – characters he based on the doctors who had made a misery of his many spells in hospital. To combine comedy with nuclear destruction was novel, and remained so until Kubrick made *Dr Strangelove* ten years later.

Apart from Agee, Kubrick didn't make any friends on *Mr Lincoln*. Shooting exteriors and crowd scenes in Hodgenville, Kentucky, he gave interviews to local papers which suggested that this was a Stanley Kubrick film. Norman Lloyd, directing Dierkes, Joanne Woodward, Jack Warden and Agee in locations in the east, was not amused. Once Kubrick had finished in Kentucky, he joined Lloyd in New Salem, Illinois, and offered to become his assistant. Incensed by the interviews, Lloyd told him he didn't need his services, and Kubrick was unemployed once more.

By June 1952, Kubrick had finished the editing and post-synching of 'Shape of Fear'. It ran sixty-six minutes, barely long enough to qualify as a feature. Hiring one of the many small preview theatres around New York which rented by the hour, he showed the film to Mark van Doren, the scholar who'd been the *Nation*'s film critic in the thirties, and whose classes at Columbia he'd attended as an observer. Van Doren wrote a hyperbolic recommendation, calling the film 'brilliant and unforgettable, using the simplest materials toward the most profound and surprising result – a fable that has the feeling of truth, a fairy tale that belongs to this world after all . . . The incident of the girl bound to a tree will make movie history once it is seen; it is at once beautiful, terrifying and weird; nothing like it has ever been seen in a film before, and it alone guarantees that the future of Stanley Kubrick is worth watching for those who want to discover high talent at the moment it appears.'

James Agee, as promised, also attended a preview. 'Pained and strained', in Kubrick's words, the writer was so ill that he had to pause every few steps for breath, and could barely climb the stairs to his own apartment. After the screening, Agee met Kubrick for a drink in a 6th Avenue bar in Greenwich Village. He retained enough Southern good manners to tell the young director, 'There are too many good things in the film to call it arty.' Kubrick took this as a compliment, and publicised it widely.

Not everyone was as diplomatic as Agee. Curtis Harrington, an experimental film-maker subsequently successful in Hollywood as director of *Games* and a number of horror films, was invited by a critic friend to one preview. 'The film was not well received,' Harrington remembers. 'In particular, Paul Mazursky's performance was laughed at. There were giggles in the wrong places, and it all seemed a bit overdone and overwrought. And afterwards, Stanley was in tears. I was very touched that this young film-maker had been so upset by the reaction to the film. Some of *my* films hadn't been well received, but it never brought tears to my eyes.'

Gavin Lambert was in New York collecting pieces for *Sight and Sound* magazine at the time, and a friend took him to a screening of 'Shape of Fear'. 'I think it's incredibly awful,' Lambert said as the lights went up, 'and I think he's incredibly talented' – a reaction probably closer to Agee's than the writer had been prepared to voice. Kubrick, who was sitting in front of them, turned and introduced himself. The two men became friends. Lambert supported Kubrick in his reviews, and Kubrick later briefly employed Lambert when he lived in Los Angeles.

In November 1952, armed with his notices from van Doren and Agee, Kubrick approached Joseph Burstyn, who had distributed most of the Italian neo-realist films in America. Normally he only handled foreign films, but Kubrick's vigorous pitch letter caught his attention, and Burstyn took on 'Shape of Fear' – which, nevertheless, he suggested renaming *Fear and Desire*. It went on his schedule for spring 1953 release. His terms weren't princely. The cost of prints and advertising came out of income, and Burstyn's accountants were accustomed to ensuring that films never quite reached the point at which the producer and director earned a profit. But Paolo Cherchi Usai, chairman of the Film Department at Eastman House in Rochester, New York, which acquired Burstyn's records after his death, along with the surviving prints of *Fear and Desire*, is probably right to say, 'At this point it was no longer a question of a fair return on his investment. Kubrick's goal was simply to see the film screened publicly and get a response from the critics.'

Now with a distributor who was enthusiastic about the film – 'He's a genius! He's a genius!' Burstyn was heard to utter – Kubrick persuaded Richard de Rochemont to take over its management. Martin Perveler was induced to invest some more money, and in January 1953 the three men signed a new contract. Perveler agreed to refund the $500 de Rochemont had put up to placate the musicians' union, and to waive his right to first call on the film's receipts. In recognition of his involvement, de Rochemont would receive 2 per cent of Kubrick's share of the film.

Fear and Desire previewed for New York's press on 26 March 1953, before opening at the Guild Theater on 31 March. Burstyn was no shrinking violet when it came to publicity. He'd promoted *Rome: Open City* with the slogan 'Sexier than Hollywood Ever Dared!' Now he persuaded Walter Winchell, New York's most influential gossip columnist and radio commentator, to plug *Fear and Desire* by remarking, 'The wolves are breathless about Virginia Leith,' a line used prominently in pushing the film. To back it up, Kubrick shot some stills of Leith in her dressing room, wearing a tight satin breast-band that emphasised her erect nipples. The image, which appears nowhere in the film, dominated the film's advertising.

Since most of the films running in art cinemas were Italian or French, the press, for patriotic reasons if no other, welcomed a young American director. *Time*, *Newsweek*, the *New Yorker* and the *New York Times* all reviewed *Fear and Desire*, as did *Variety*, *Motion Picture Herald*, *Theater Arts*, *Commonweal*, the *Herald Tribune* and *Saturday Review*. In general, they approved. *Variety* called it 'a literate, unhackneyed war drama, outstanding for its fresh camera treatment and poetic dialogue.' All downplayed Sackler's clumsy script and highlighted its superior photography and, above all, the ambition and promise of its young director. Against this, John McCarten in the *New Yorker* articulated something closer to the long-term estimate of the film when he dismissed it on every count. He made a sole exception for the attractiveness of Virginia Leith – 'But then it's spring.'

Despite the reviews, *Fear and Desire* made little impact at the box office. With art-house cinemas sparse outside New York and Los Angeles, the non-theatrical 16mm market minimal, and film festivals largely unknown, there was nowhere else for it to go.

However, it had served its purpose in introducing its cast and production team to the industry. Virginia Leith went on to play supporting parts in Hollywood dramas like Nunnally Johnson's *Black Widow* and Richard Fleischer's *Violent Saturday*. Paul Mazursky, though he gives the film's most mannered performance, went to Hollywood too, played a delinquent student in Richard Brooks's *The Blackboard Jungle*, and later made a career as a director. Howard Sackler won the Pulitzer Prize in 1969 with his play *The Great White Hope*, about the African-American boxer Jack Johnson, and became a successful screenwriter. Even Kubrick's backers got their money back eventually.

Kubrick too gained a new credibility from the film. Over the years, however, he distanced himself from *Fear and Desire*, dismissing it as an embarrassing apprentice work, 'a very inept and pretentious effort . . . little more than a 35mm version of what a class of film students would do in 16mm. Our ideas were good, but we just didn't know how to put them across dramatically.' He's widely believed to have overseen the destruction of the negative shortly after Burstyn died in 1953. Certainly he did everything to keep the film out of circulation, specifically excluding it from retrospectives of his work. In 1994, when prints began to reappear in archives, he asked Warner Brothers, the studio with which he worked through most of the eighties and nineties, to issue a letter in his name calling *Fear and Desire* 'a bumbling amateur film exercise' and 'a completely inept oddity, boring and pretentious'. Of the lessons he learned making it, he will only say, 'Pain is a good teacher.'

Chapter Five

Kubrick and Crime

> 'At the same time I feel more shaken, confused, and
> ignorant, through my own actions, than I can remember
> having felt before. Yet my sense of confusion, ignorance,
> guilt and disintegrity is not to be cured by reversing and
> betraying such few things as in all faith and vigilance
> and scepticism not only of authority but of myself, still
> seem to me to be so.'
>
> James Agee, letter to Father James Harold Flye,
> 28 June 1938

Before the Korean War petered out in a nervous armistice in July
1953, Kubrick's friend Alex Singer had been drafted, and posted
with a number of other young men with film experience to the US
Army's Signal Corps Photographic Center in Paramount's old
studios in Astoria, Long Island. 'We were all acting as cameramen
and assistant directors and script supervisors,' says Singer, 'and
working with civilian crews. We were all getting a film education.
I went home to my wife every night in Greenwich Village, where
Stanley also lived at the time. It was the best army service anyone
ever had.'

Among the other young men posted to Astoria was James B.
Harris, universally known as Jimmy. He and Singer struck up a
friendship, though the two could hardly have been more different.
Slight and soft-spoken, as a boy Jimmy Harris had wanted, like
Kubrick, to become a jazz drummer, but it took a year at Juilliard
to teach him he'd never reach professional standard. Since his father,
a wealthy New York insurance broker, had funded some film distribution deals, Jimmy joined a film export company as office boy and

shipping clerk, from where he moved to Realart, buying foreign films for US distribution.

'My sense,' recalls Singer, 'was that Jimmy, at twenty-two, was as shrewd and as hard a money dealer as he would ever be. They were the first really wealthy people I ever knew.' Singer persuaded Harris to produce a ten-minute film, citing Kubrick as having made an entire independent feature on a shoestring. Harris saw *Fear and Desire* and, while not really liking it, was impressed that Kubrick had managed to get it made and screened.

Singer and Harris made their film. Singer directed, and another member of the unit wrote the script. James Gaffney, also in the army, edited it, and through him Kubrick met his brother Bob, a long-time associate. They borrowed equipment from the army, and shot the film in the Manhattan apartment of Harris's parents.

Kubrick came to watch, and to shoot some stills. It was easy for him to be gracious in such a situation, and he carried off the moment with *savoir faire*. 'What I liked about him was, he was so encouraging,' enthused Harris. 'Here we were, fumbling along with this short subject, but he treated us as if we were all in the same boat, which I never forgot.' They didn't meet again for more than a year, but Harris held on to his sense of Kubrick as a man on the way up.

After its first release, Joseph Burstyn gave *Fear and Desire* a second lease of life by showing it as part of a double bill with Luis Buñuel's *El Bruto*, retitled *The Male Brute*. Made on a shoestring in Mexico City, Buñuel's melodrama starred Pedro Armendariz as a slow-witted slaughterman who acts as a strong-arm man for local slumlords until he's morally regenerated by the love of a good woman. Putting *Fear and Desire* on the same programme was a compliment of sorts, though Burstyn negated much of its effect with his usual lurid advertising. The marquee read, 'First Time Together – 2 Sexational Thrillers for Adults Only.' *Fear and Desire* was plugged with the line 'Trapped – A Desperate Man and a Strange Half-Animal Girl!!'

After three years during which he'd thought of little but *Fear and Desire*, a chastened Kubrick returned to unemployment. Following his divorce from Toba he was alone for the first time in Manhattan, but didn't remain so for long. Actresses, dancers and footloose girls in search of fulfilment, freedom and a place to sleep surged through the streets of Greenwich Village. Kubrick soon had a mistress, and was thinking of marriage – the aim, many friends believe, of all his emotional entanglements. 'I don't think he can talk to women,' says Adrienne Corri, who acted in *A Clockwork Orange*. 'I think you fall into various categories: you are a wife and mother; you have great tits . . . very few of them have brains.' James Harris is inclined to agree. 'I think his pursuit of women was mostly a distraction,' he says. 'His attitude was: "It's easier to be married, and get down to work."'

Ruth Sobotka danced with the New York City Ballet, but defied the stereotype of the stringy, angular *danseuse*. Dark and voluptuous, with excellent legs, she radiated vivacity and sensuality. Three years older than Kubrick, she'd come to New York as a child in the thirties from Vienna – another point of attraction for Kubrick – and settled in Pittsburgh, where her father, an architect, took a job teaching at Carnegie Tech. Ruth studied scenic design at Carnegie, but after graduation took up ballet.

'She was a very European-looking woman,' remembers Alex Singer. 'Quite striking face and body. She was closer to the sort of person who made some kind of sense with Stanley. She was part of the artist's world. Stanley never seemed to be concerned with material things. He wanted them, but they had very much a secondary priority to him. I was much quicker at saying, "I must have . . ." But he achieved them very much sooner. His eye was on the sparrow pretty continuously, and that paid off. Ruth seemed right at that time in his life because she understood the hard times of young artists.'

The British-born ballet scholar and biographer of Sir Frederick Ashton, David Vaughan, was Sobotka's close friend until her premature death in 1967. 'She was an extraordinarily generous person,' he says. 'She took in waifs and strays.' Vaughan was one of them. He'd arrived in New York from London in October 1950 on a scholarship to the School of American Ballet, and Ruth befriended him. In the summer of 1951 he helped her paint a new apartment at 22 East 10th Street, between 2nd and 1st Avenues, and later that year he moved in to share it. He was living there when Ruth, then waiting tables at the Limelight Café in the Village, met Kubrick in late 1952.

Young, struggling artists brought out Ruth's maternal instinct.

'She had intense and sometimes brief relationships with men who were not yet established in whatever artistic endeavour they were involved in,' says Vaughan. 'She had affairs with two scenic designers, one of whom, after they split up, became famous. Her relationship with Stanley came to an end when he became a prominent director.'

As long as Kubrick was a novice, however, the relationship flourished. He taught her chess, but she taught him much more about art, ballet and literature. Greenwich Village's bookshop and coffee house scene was flourishing, and with it a new libertarian and international culture. The rise of the paperback had opened the floodgates of European literature, and American shops were filled with the cheap, fat Dover editions of writers Kubrick had known until then only from movie credits.

He discovered the short stories and plays of Arthur Schnitzler, one of which Max Ophuls had adapted for *La Ronde*, and Stefan Zweig, whose *novelle* supplied the original for the same director's *Letter from an Unknown Woman*. Freud caught his interest, and he took to pressing *A General Introduction to Psychoanalysis* on friends. His imagination was ignited by the work of certain American radicals who'd taken their inspiration from Europe, particularly Henry Miller, whose observations, particularly the more Rabelaisian ones, he took to quoting.

With Ruth's encouragement, Kubrick let his hair grow, and abandoned his conservative clothes for something more untidy. 'He'd back into Klein's,' said Ruth, 'and grab anything black off the rack, whether it fitted or not.' People flinched when he arrived for business meetings in an open-necked shirt and brown cotton pants, or a loose suit and sneakers, but Jimmy Harris acknowledges that, a few years later, most of show business had adopted his style.

As their attachment became more passionate, Kubrick moved into Ruth's 10th Street apartment, and David Vaughan moved out. The three remained close, however. 'Ruth and Stanley and I would go to movies all the time, every night,' recalls Vaughan. 'We would go to some double bill on 42nd Street or wherever. Stanley just wanted to see every movie that was made. He was just studying them.'

*

Anxious to keep up the momentum of *Fear and Desire*, Kubrick began developing a new screenplay. The style of urban thriller the French christened *film noir* had seen its greatest days in the late forties, and its stories of suave gang bosses sending out their minions to chase the hero down dark, wet city streets were wearing thin. Replacing them was a new, more violent crime story with its roots in the pulp and true-crime magazines of the thirties.

Some of the new writers drew on existentialism for their characters, others on pornography and the gaudier tabloids. Though he probably read the more thoughtful writers, like David Goodis (*Dark Passage*, *Cassidy's Girl*) and Horace McCoy (*Kiss Tomorrow Goodbye*, *They Shoot Horses, Don't They?*), Kubrick preferred Jim Thompson, a hard-drinking Communist pulp and true-crime writer whose novels exuded the sweat and stink of flop-houses and drunk tanks.

Thompson and Kubrick were soon to have an intense and troublesome professional relationship, but that, and the films it produced, were still in the future. For the Kubrick of 1953, the most accessible, easiest-imitated and least challenging hard-boiled writer was Mickey Spillane, whose sado-masochistic tales of murder and retribution placed him at the spearhead of the genre. Spillane's most notorious novel, the 1947 *I, The Jury*, ends with his hero, Mike Hammer, unmoved by her stripping naked to seduce him, shooting his treacherous lover Charlotte in the stomach with a .45.

Her eyes had pain in them now, the pain preceding death. Pain and unbelief.

'How c-could you?' she gasped.

I had only a moment before talking to a corpse, but I got it in.

'It was easy,' I said.

'Spillane,' a respectful Kubrick would tell Irene Kane, his star in *Killer's Kiss*, 'knows all there is to know about reaching audiences.' More than thirty years later, Kubrick would have Drill Sergeant Hartman in *Full Metal Jacket* demand of a recruit who'd got a job as a reporter on the Marine newspaper, 'Who do you think you are – Mickey Spillane?'

Inspired by Spillane, Kubrick developed an original story set in the sleazier corners of downtown Manhattan. He told the critic Hollis Alpert that he simply jotted down all the action scenes he could imagine taking place a few minutes from his apartment. Pleasureland, the film's dance hall, is at 49th and Broadway, almost next door to Childs, where he and his chess friend Alan Kaufman had heard jazz clarinettist George Lewis play. A ballet scene for Ruth would be shot at the Theatre de Lys in the Village, just a few blocks from his home. Most of an impressive chase across the roofs against a foggy city skyline would be filmed ten minutes from 10th Street. It was an early example of the territorial preoccupation that would drive him, decades later, to demand that every location for *Barry Lyndon* and other films be found within driving distance of his home.

Having listed a boxing match, a dance-hall seduction, a rooftop chase, a near-rape in a rooming house and a climactic fight in a garment warehouse, he handed the list to Howard Sackler, who, in Kubrick's words, 'hacked out [a script called] "Kiss Me, Kill Me"' that included all of them. Despite this, Sackler's name appears nowhere on *Killer's Kiss*, as 'Kiss Me, Kill Me' was retitled; at the time he was anxious to establish himself as a poet and serious playwright, and may not have wished to have his name on something as raw as Kubrick's thriller. There's no screenplay credit at all. Kubrick takes a full panel credit for the story, and the production, editing and camera credits as well of what he called, in another reference to the myths of his childhood, 'A Minotaur Production'.

Whatever Sackler's contribution, the roots of the new film were really in *Day of the Fight*. The main characters are Davy Gordon, an unsuccessful boxer who lives in Greenwich Village, Gloria Price, a dime-a-dance girl with a room in the same building, and Vince Rapallo, a middle-aged dance-hall owner infatuated with her. When Gloria, after having sex once with Vince, rejects his next advances, mocking him as 'an old man who smells bad', he tries to kill her. Davy intervenes, and the loners fall in love. Rapallo, in revenge, sends two men to dispose of Davy, who's about to take Gloria away to his uncle's farm in Oregon, but by accident the thugs kill Davy's trainer instead. The story climaxes in Davy rescuing Gloria after a chase over the roofs of warehouses of the garment district, and a battle with Rapallo in a store-room full of shop-window dummies

– settings Kubrick had come to know well from the rag-trade connections of his grandparents.

A family friend, Maurice 'Moe' Bousel, who owned two Bronx drugstores, invested $40,000 in the film, in several instalments. Kubrick calculated this would be enough if everyone deferred salary; had they been paid, making the film would have cost almost twice as much. *Fear and Desire* had taught him that actors would sacrifice regular money for a good part. Unknown Jamie Smith played Davy. Frank Silvera agreed to play Vince Rapallo if he received top billing for what was really a supporting role. He signed a contract for $1000 a week, of which he pocketed only $100. Kubrick even tried to get *Mr Lincoln*'s director Norman Lloyd to appear, telling him the film was called 'The Nymph and the Maniac'. Lloyd declined. Ruth designed and decorated the minimal sets. David Vaughan choreographed the ballet scene, and played some small roles. Kubrick also extended to equipment hire his insight about the incipient generosity of people in the film business, persuading a Manhattan camera company to lend him a Mitchell for studio work and an Eclair for hand-held sequences, and to wait for payment.

Alex Singer shot stills for the film. 'The picture was made for an astonishingly small amount of money,' he says, 'and it was done with every bit of the fastidiousness and care of everything else he's ever done. This is a perfectionist, an absolute perfectionist. I tried to put the same rules into force in my own career, and it cost me a lot before I could shake it. Because unless you also have the freedom to exercise it, very few people survive that. It's an obsessive thing, and has nothing to do with commerce.'

But commerce was very much on Kubrick's mind. *Killer's Kiss* marked a new direction, both in his career and his production style. *Fear and Desire* had been made out of youthful enthusiasm; Kubrick's obvious commitment and refusal to compromise won over his cast and crew. To work on such a film was noble, self-sacrificing. With *Killer's Kiss*, however, he set his eye firmly on Hollywood.

'Stanley's a fascinating character,' wrote the film's star, Irene Kane. 'He thinks movies should move, with a minimum of dialogue, and he's all for sex and sadism. Talks about Mickey Spillane, and how the public eats it up. He's also totally sure of himself. Knows where he's going, how he's going to get there, and who's going to pick up the tab for the trip.'

To play Gloria, Kubrick tried a number of actresses before photographer Bert Stern introduced him to Kane, a model who also lived in the Village (but who would later, under the name Chris Chase, find her niche as a journalist and author). A thin, long-necked blonde with short hair, she wasn't everyone's idea of a dance-hall hostess. So daunted was she by the prospect of a starring role that she panicked when Kubrick suggested it, bolted to the corner of her tiny apartment and crouched behind the television set. 'Your friend's pretty,' Kubrick calmly remarked to Stern, 'but she's a little odd.'

Undeterred, he returned next day with a script, from which he read to her, explaining at length his conception of Gloria. Far from being a born member of Manhattan low-life, he explained, she had been brought up in comfort and security on Long Island. Racked, however, by an incestuous love of her father and by the suicide of her sister Iris, whom their father forced to give up ballet and marry for money, Gloria expiates her guilt by taking the most sordid job she can find, as a dime-a-dance girl, and becoming the mistress of its middle-aged gangster proprietor.

Kane was impressed, less by the complexity of the motivation Kubrick suggested than by his passion as he did so. An hour later, she had been coaxed into an impromptu audition. She apologised for her throaty voice. Kubrick said he liked it. 'You're going to be a great star,' he told her. Dazzled, she signed a contract for $650 a week. Only a hint of her elaborate motivation would appear in the finished film, her voice would be dubbed, and her $650 salary would dwindle to $65 a week, less tax – but such was Kubrick's ability to hypnotise that 'the day I reported for work,' she recalled, 'I nearly died of happiness.'

Killer's Kiss was shot through the autumn and winter of 1954. 'Places in *noir* reveal character,' critic Foster Hirsch emphasises in his study of *film noir*. 'The cramped tenements, the joyless middle-class apartments, the dingy furnished rooms that populate the genre carry the history of their inhabitants. Settings are chosen for thematic reinforcement. Cars and trains and boxing arenas figure prominently in *noir* stories because they provide visual metaphors of enclosure and entrapment.'

Kubrick had learned these lessons well. He unashamedly recycled *Day of the Fight* for the first reel of *Killer's Kiss*, even repeating the shot of a fight poster dangling from a lamp-post. The rest of the film is an anthology of *noir* moments, many of them rescued from cliché by Kubrick's skill in lighting and framing: the steep staircase leading to Pleasureland, with the minatory sign, 'Watch Your Step'; the murder of the trainer, Jerry, in an alley, the victim clawing at locked doors crudely lettered 'No Toilet' while the two killers, little more than shadows, stalk him remorselessly; the fight in the mannequin factory, cribbed from the Girl Hunt ballet of Vincente Minnelli's *The Band Wagon* and soon to become a Hollywood cliché, but no less impressive for that. The scene was so spectacular that Kubrick invited Moe Bousel and his family to watch it being shot. 'It was almost worth the money he eventually lost,' commented critic Hollis Alpert, but Kubrick insists that all the backers of his early films got their money back, however delayed.

Then, as later, visuals were never the problem with Kubrick's films. It was the story that creaked and groaned. 'We have shot a bunch of endings for this plate of hash,' Kane wrote to her sister, 'and by now I don't know if I'm a bad guy or a good guy. There's one version where I kill the villain, there's another version where I try to seduce him, and there's been more killing and resurrection than you'll find in the Bible.'

Iris's lengthy dance solo, with Gloria's doleful voice-over, served the double purpose of showing off Ruth, whom Kubrick married in 1954, and padding out an uncomfortably short film. Kubrick also inserted a couple of dream sequences. One was a series of point-of-view shots in negative from a car speeding down an alley, which foreshadows the conclusion of *2001*. The other showed Davy in boxing shorts and gloves crossing 5th Avenue at 42nd Street in the midday crowds. Accustomed to oddity in that area, nobody paid any attention, a fact which, for some reason, caused Kubrick to cut the scene, though one would have thought the passers-by's insouciance would contribute to the scene's dreamlike quality.

Other contrivances worked better, including a scene where David Vaughan and Alec Rubin as drunken Shriners come dancing along Broadway in their fezzes while Davy is waiting for Gloria outside

Pleasureland, and playfully steal his scarf. He gives chase, setting up the scene in which Rapallo's thugs kill his trainer by mistake.

Gloria's character lacks definition. Her two erotic scenes with Rapallo, one where she lets him make love to her in his office while watching Davy lose his fight on TV, the other in which, as his prisoner in a warehouse, she offers herself submissively in return for her life, make little sense unless one knows that, in Kubrick's subtext, Rapallo is a surrogate for the father she desires. Only a comment at the end of Iris's dancing scene, that Gloria took the Pleasureland job as a form of expiation – 'At least Iris never had to dance in a place like that, a human zoo' – ties Gloria to her bizarre backstory.

The scene of Gloria bound and menaced in the warehouse, so like the sequence of the girl prisoner in *Fear and Desire*, makes this psychological subtext seem even more nakedly contrived. It would appear from his films that Kubrick is excited by the image of helpless and sexually threatened women: Varinia, the slave wife of *Spartacus*, the girl captive at the end of *Paths of Glory* forced to sing to the soldiers, the women gang-raped in *A Clockwork Orange* and the helpless Viet Cong cadre at the end of *Full Metal Jacket* belong to the same brutalised sisterhood. Elsewhere, Kubrick's women – Charlotte Haze in *Lolita*, Lady Lyndon in *Barry Lyndon* – are complaisant and servile or, in *The Killing*, *Dr Strangelove* and *2001: A Space Odyssey*, either extraneous to the story or virtually non-existent.

Davy's determination to save Gloria and carry her off to Oregon also seems puzzling, since they are strangers until he saves her from Rapallo's attempted rape. Had the two made love after the rescue, their bonding might make more sense. Indeed, Kubrick had such a scene in mind, and tried to film it. 'The other day I was playing a love scene,' Kane told her sister, 'when, in the middle of a kiss, [Jamie] suddenly reached up and grabbed my left chest, very firmly, as the camera ground away. I leaped to my feet screaming and calling Jamie and Stanley bad names (they'd clearly set the whole thing up behind my back) and Stanley gave me the foreign markets lecture ... "Bully for Europe," I said, "but I'm narrow-minded, and I want you to burn that film."'

It's not certain that Kubrick did destroy the footage. Gavin Lambert implied that the print he saw for his review in *Sight and Sound* contained such a scene, but in the most complete version of *Killer's Kiss* (which runs for eighty minutes, rather than the sixty-seven minutes cited in most filmographies), Davy simply puts an exhausted Gloria to bed and, while she sleeps, fascinatedly fondles the stockings and underwear hung on a string to dry.

The atmosphere on the production deteriorated as shooting dragged on. 'I'm in the hands of a maniac,' Kane wrote to her sister, 'who looks fully seventeen years old, has black hair that grows down over his neck, quotes widely from Henry Miller – the dirty parts – and takes time out from shooting to discuss with his girl-friend the sex habits of some canaries who are living in her apartment.' Kubrick's style also upset the owner of a processing lab, not used to grubby young directors telling him how they wanted their negative treated. 'He came into my office dressed like a bum,' said the man, who threw him out. The boss of Titra Film, a subtitling company at 1600 Broadway, felt the same way, but agreed to let Kubrick edit on his Moviola as long as he shaved and took the occasional shower. Max Glenn, who worked at Titra, also became the film's camera operator.

Kubrick had hired Nat Boxer, later the sound designer for Francis Ford Coppola on *The Conversation* and *Apocalypse Now*, to record sound for the film, but the arrangement ended in disaster. Working in a Greenwich Village loft, Kubrick kept the sound crew waiting outside the locked door for hours while he lit the set. When they were finally admitted, Boxer tried to place his microphones. 'But when we went in and placed the microphone where we normally would, there must have been seventeen shadows in the picture. What do still photographers know about the problems of a movie? Well, he looked at the set and said, "Is that the way you do it? You mean you're going to put the microphone *there*? But that's impossible."' Boxer was fired, and Kubrick recorded the sound on a non-professional Webcor tape recorder.

Frank Silvera complained that he'd turned down an off-Broadway play to stick with the film. The grips and gaffers also rebelled at the cold, the long hours and the lack of money. Kubrick, according to Kane, 'listened to the whole thing, then very sweetly told every-body to take off, we were finished for the day. After we got in the car, I asked him how he could be so patient, and he grinned. "Baby, nobody's going to get anything out of this movie but me."'

There had been no money to record the film's dialogue or sound effects on location. All Kubrick and his actors had to work with in re-recording their lines was the inferior guide track recorded on the Webcor. 'All the dialogue was post-synched,' said Kubrick, 'which accounts for the slightly zombie-like quality to some of the acting. Money began to run out in the editing stage, and being unable to afford even an editing assistant, I had to spend four months just laying in the sound effects, footstep by footstep.' Kane refused to spend even more time on the film and fled to Florida. Radio actress Peggy Lobbin dubbed her entire role.

Kubrick also added a commentary for Davy, and another for Gloria during Ruth's dance. In part, like the film's other deviations from standard narrative, they help us accept some of the wilder improbabilities: Gloria's abrupt shifts of character, Davy's puzzling decision to leave the ring and join his uncle farming in Oregon, taking Gloria with him, and Gloria's even more unaccountable decision to go. Later, Kubrick specifically repudiated this gratuit-ously sunny ending. All logic demands that Gloria stand Davy up, leaving him alone with his suitcase and his despair among the indif-ferent crowds at the railway station, musing bitterly on his fate. But Kubrick was already thinking of the film as a calling card which might win him the entrée to Hollywood. And Hollywood liked happy endings.

The voice-over was to become one of Kubrick's favourite narrative devices, subtly modified to fit the tone of each film. *Fear and Desire* has a voice-of-God introduction and a rambling first-person solil-oquy for Mac. The voice in *Killer's Kiss* is also first-person subjec-tive, but that in *The Killing* is third-person objective again ('At 2.25 that afternoon, Johnny Clay was still in the city. He knew exactly how long it would take . . .'). *Lolita*'s voice-over marks a departure, since the voice is that of Humbert Humbert, as, in *A Clockwork Orange*, it is Alex who provides the commentary. In *Barry Lyndon*, however, we hear Thackeray's weary musings, faultlessly articulated by Michael Hordern. In *Full Metal Jacket*, Matthew Modine speaks an occasional line from Gustav Hasford's novel on which the film is based.

Spoken or written words provide Kubrick, and us, with a secure connection to reality. When they are absent, as in *Paths of Glory*,

Dr Strangelove, 2001: A Space Odyssey and *The Shining,* the films inhabit the most restless and remote of Kubrick's worlds, those of random violence and supernatural fantasy, where all bonds are snapped and we are adrift in a hostile universe.

Kubrick showed *Killer's Kiss* to any distributor who would look at it. Joseph Burstyn had died in November 1953 of a stroke during a flight to Paris, closing one possible outlet, and the rest proved unwelcoming. Many felt, as does the *film noir* historian Foster Hirsch, that the film lacked originality. 'Clearly derived from other movies rather than from life,' he says, *'Killer's Kiss* has a ready-made, hand-me-down quality ... so self-consciously steeped in *noir* conventions that [it looks] like an anthology of genre stylistics.'

Eventually United Artists bought it, but only for $75,000, almost exactly its production cost, including the salaries which cast and crew had deferred. They released it in September 1955, rightly expecting that it wouldn't run until Christmas. In contrast to *Fear and Desire, Killer's Kiss* was reviewed perfunctorily, befitting its place as a B-film destined to make up the bottom half of random double bills all over the country. The *New York Times* didn't even bother, and those journals that did were dismissive. The film embarrassed Kubrick. He later told Alex Walker, 'While *Fear and Desire* had been a serious effort, ineptly done, *Killer's Kiss* ... proved, I think, to be a frivolous effort done with conceivably more expertise though still down in the student level of film-making.' It joined the growing list of films he preferred not to talk about.

Chapter Six

Kubrick at the Track

'Crime is just a left-handed form of human endeavour.'

Louis Calhern in John Huston's *The Asphalt Jungle*, script
by Ben Maddow and Huston from W.R. Burnett's novel

After his demobilisation from the Signal Corps Photographic Unit in
1954, Jimmy Harris launched a TV distribution company, Flamingo
Films, with Sy Weintraub and a school friend, David L. Wolper.
He also produced a series of short films about baseball. His real
ambitions, however, were fixed on features.

By chance, in mid-1955 he bumped into Kubrick in front of
1600 Broadway. Kubrick invited him to a screening of *Killer's Kiss*.
Shortly after, they met in Flamingo's Madison Avenue office. Kubrick asked Harris to help him sell *Fear and Desire* to TV, but Joseph
Burstyn's business proved to be in such confusion following his
sudden death that nobody could draw up the necessary papers.

The talk turned to the future. Kubrick explained that United
Artists, impressed with the economy of *Killer's Kiss*, had shown
some interest in another film, ideally a cheap $100,000 quickie.
Harris thought Kubrick deserved better. 'I felt that both *Fear and
Desire* and *Killer's Kiss* were tremendous examples of incipient
genius,' he says. 'Stanley was on his way to becoming a terrific
film-maker.' Collaboration blossomed, and they decided to go into
business as Harris–Kubrick Films. 'I can buy you a property,' Harris
told a delighted Kubrick, 'and hire you actors.'

'We found one another at exactly the right time,' Harris says.
'We became very close friends, and we decided to become full
partners. We had to have corporate papers but we never had any

agreement in writing between us. Stanley said, "We're two articulate people. If we ever have a disagreement, we ought to be able to talk it out." '

As in most relationships between a creative person and a business-man, distinctions soon began to blur. Harris found that his partner, far from being a pure artist, was determined to succeed commer-cially. 'Stanley wanted to make successful movies,' says Harris. 'Movies that people went to see. Box-office hits. However, to achieve that, he would never ever take anything away from the way he wanted to do the picture. He wanted to have it all. He would never make concessions or violate his own integrity in terms of the artistic approach and thrust of the movie in order to please at the box office.'

Harris's role also changed over the course of the partnership. He emerged as a more creative collaborator than Kubrick expected or wanted, while Kubrick's interest in finance and distribution grew. Harris finally become a director, while Kubrick metamorphosed into his own producer.

A disconsolate Alex Singer watched his two friends gravitate towards one another. 'It was fairly obvious that Jimmy wasn't going to help *me* with money,' he says, 'because I hadn't done enough. Jimmy was a real find. He was obviously interested in making films, and had the resources to make a difference. And for someone like Stanley, it was a real leg-up.'

Singer did benefit from the production of *Killer's Kiss*, if indirectly. Sympathising with someone so obviously in Kubrick's thrall, Irene Kane sent him to *Modern Romances*, a magazine of the photo comic-strips the Italians call *fumetti*. 'I became their principal photographer,' says Singer. 'They had been using terrible models, and shooting on amateurish sets. I hired real actors and actresses, went on location, improvised scenes and shot the pictures. I also lit them in motion-picture lighting. I taught myself how to direct by improvising scenes with real actors.' Free at last of the perceived need to compete with Kubrick, Singer developed into an effective Hollywood director of films like *A Cold Wind in August*.

In 1955 Harris–Kubrick Films opened an office on West 57th Street. Soon after, an item in the *New York Post* column of Jimmy Cannon, 'Nobody Asked Me But . . .', caught Harris's eye. Lionel White's novel *Clean Break*, Cannon commented, contained some of the most authentic horse-racing descriptions he'd ever read. His interest piqued, Harris found the book in Scribner's bookshop on 5th Avenue and galloped through it. Everything about it felt right. It was new, so it was unlikely that anybody else would have thought about filming it. And the subject, a racetrack robbery, was both unusual and visual. Though *Clean Break* was his first novel, Lionel White had been around for years, writing and editing true-crime magazines like *Underworld Detective*, *Detective World* and *Homicide Detective*. He drew on that background when, at fifty, he crashed the fiction market. *Clean Break* employed interlocking flashbacks and a wealth of circumstantial detail of times, dates, weather, clothing, to recreate the detail of the robbery as experienced by the half-dozen people involved.

'This is what Stanley needs,' thought Harris. 'Something that's got a story all worked out.' Kubrick shared his enthusiasm, so Harris approached White's representatives, the Jaffe Agency in Los Angeles – to be told that Frank Sinatra was already negotiating for the book as a follow-up to *Suddenly*, his 1954 film about a gangster's attempt to assassinate the President. But while Sinatra dithered, Harris's $10,000 offer won the rights. He immediately called United Artists to tell them – only to discover that, having distributed *Suddenly*, UA knew White's book and had assumed they'd be handling Sinatra's production of it. Harris rang off with the sense that UA didn't want their version of *Clean Break*.

He wasn't far wrong. A fresh administration under Arthur Krim and Robert Benjamin had just dragged UA out of a long period in the red. Their policy was now to invest substantially in proven star vehicles by well-known independent producers, and take a slice of their profits, rather than waste time with the nickel-and-dime movies typified by *Killer's Kiss*, which clogged their books but which they were forced by contract to continue distributing to a market drastically eroded by television. Over the next five years UA would finance films from the cream of independents: Mike Todd, Stanley Kramer, the Mirisch brothers, as well as the top-star companies: Kirk Douglas's Bryna, John Wayne's Batjac, Burt Lancaster's Hecht–Hill–Lancaster. *Clean Break* with Sinatra interested them. *Clean Break* from Harris–Kubrick, with no star attached, was at best an unknown quantity, at worst a liability.

Kubrick and Harris persisted. Their most urgent need was for a screenwriter, and Kubrick thought of Jim Thompson, the hard-boiled author who combined the power of Spillane with a more literary flair for dialogue. Lou Ford, the deputy sheriff protagonist of his best book, *The Killer Inside Me*, is a psychopath and murderer, but Thompson elects to tell his story through Ford's eyes. Kubrick had toyed with the idea of filming the novel as their first production, but suspected – rightly – that no studio would fund so bleak a story; it wasn't filmed until 1976, by Burt Kennedy, and then not well.

To their delight, Harris and Kubrick found Thompson living in New York, in suburban Sunnyside. They asked him into the office for a chat. Thompson could hardly have been more of a contrast to the dapper Harris and the shaggy, untidy Kubrick. A tall, doleful Nebraskan, he'd been born over the jail where his father was sheriff, a job Thompson Snr lost amid charges of embezzlement. This gave his son a lifelong empathy with the moral problems of lawmen and criminals, whom he often showed as almost identical in personality. 'It became Thompson's dismaying gift,' writes his biographer Robert Polito, 'to recreate his monsters from the inside out, as it were, to roost deep within their snaky psyches, and to embody through imaginative art their terrifying yet beguiling voices on the page.'

By 1955, Thompson, a long-time active Communist, alcoholic and chronically unreliable employee, often in ill health and given to bouts of self-pity, had alienated much of the crime-writing community. Many companies refused to publish him, and he survived precariously by writing true-crime stories under assumed names and contracting for novels which he delivered late or not at all. Desperate for work, he'd joined the *New York Daily News*, not as a reporter but as a rewrite man, smartening up the copy of infinitely less able colleagues. When he lost even this job, a terminal descent into booze and misery seemed inevitable. Gavin Lambert remembers him as looking like 'someone in their last hangover'.

Thompson was an odd choice to script *Clean Break*, never having written a screenplay, but Kubrick coveted his hard-boiled dialogue. That left him free to control the film's look and pace – areas where he was on more certain ground. 'Stanley was responsible for outlining what the scenes in the picture were going to be,' says Harris, 'and Jim was then going to write the dialogue. I guess Stanley structured the thing – though we followed the structure of the book. People begged us to make a straight-line story. But we had enough sense to realise this structure was the most interesting thing about the story.'

The better to be near 'those boys', as he called his twenty-six-year-old employers, Thompson left his family in Sunnyside and moved into a midtown Manhattan hotel. He went home at weekends, and Kubrick occasionally drove out there to argue some script point. His arrival threw the sedate Thompsons into panic. 'He just drove us all insane,' Thompson's daughter Sharon told Robert Polito. 'He was a beatnik before beatniks were in. He had the long hair and the weird clothes. They'd go to a nice restaurant, and my dad would be thinking, "Oh God, they're not going to let Stanley in!" He would be really worried about this. My dad was very refined in many ways.'

In less refined moments, Thompson, broke and/or drunk, would call up Kubrick or Harris for a loan or advance. 'Those boys' were soon inextricably involved with the writer. In June, to get back $1000 they had paid him in advances, they commissioned from Thompson a novella, provisionally called 'Lunatic at Large', about 'an American soldier and a psychopathic female with homicidal tendencies'. The idea was to develop it as a film, but neither Harris nor Kubrick liked the seventy-six pages of typescript Thompson delivered, and it was filed away. When admirers of Thompson checked the folder in Harris–Kubrick files after his death, it contained only the last three pages. Asked about the story, Harris says, 'I don't really remember, but I can't believe it was any good. If it had been, we'd have put it into production, or at least had a script written.' 'Lunatic at Large' has become one of the most famous 'lost' detective stories.

The characters of *Clean Break* frankly derive from W.R. Burnett's novel *The Asphalt Jungle*, John Huston's 1950 film of which both Kubrick and Harris admired. Unlike the typical denizens of *film noir*, the criminals in both books are ordinary, even likeable. Unfailingly polite, they help one another out, refuse to accept money for services, are affectionate, friendly and kind. It's those outside the group who are vicious, greedy and cruel, and who thwart the robbery. As in most of Jim Thompson's books, we root for the criminals and are dismayed when they fail.

Johnny Clay is just out of Alcatraz, where he's spent five years planning the robbery of the racetrack, which he hopes will net $2 million. He's assembled a miscellaneous group to help him: George, an ineffectual cashier at the track; its barman Mike O'Reilly; Marvin Unger, an ageing book-keeper who embezzles to fund the caper; Randy Kennan, a cop with a gambling habit; Maurice Oboukhoff, a chess-playing wrestler; and Nikki Arano, the gun collector and dealer who creates the essential diversion by shooting the favourite in a race just as it's about to pass the post.

Also in contrast to the professional hoods and tuxedoed gang boss of *Killer's Kiss* and other *films noirs*, these people are amateurs with credible, even prosaic motives. George hopes to impress a sluttish wife, and O'Reilly to cure his ailing one. Kennan owes money to a bookmaker no less polite and soft-spoken than everyone else in the film. Unger, who has a lifelong contempt for gambling, helps Johnny because of an implicitly homosexual affection. In one of the film's most moving scenes, he tries to delay Johnny's impending marriage by suggesting that the two of them go away together for a while. Johnny gently disengages himself, but Unger's love saves him when, having disobeyed orders and gone to the track, he helps Johnny escape from a cop who's spotted him leaving the scene.

The robbery is a success, but the gang never get their money. George's wife Sherry wheedles the plan out of him, then alerts her lover Val. The worm turns, fortuitously, when Val tries to hijack the robbery just before the share-out, and George kills him and his confederate in a bloodbath that leaves only him alive. Staggering home, George shoots Sherry, then dies himself. Johnny gets away with the whole $2 million, only to lose it when his suitcase bursts open at La Guardia Airport and the notes are blown everywhere by a rush of air from a propeller.

Jimmy Harris suggested this ending, reminiscent of Huston's *The Treasure of the Sierra Madre*, one of many additions to the script made by the partners. The contributions of Thompson, the original author Lionel White and Harris–Kubrick aren't hard to separate. White created the fragmented structure and authentic racetrack atmosphere; Thompson clarified the book's motivations, making explicit the homo-eroticism of Unger's friendship with Johnny, and substituting an ill wife for O'Reilly's tramp daughter. Kubrick drew everything together in the documentary format pioneered in *Naked City*. He also delved into his Greenwich Village experiences to flesh out characters like Maurice, the wrestler who provides a diversion during the robbery. An old chess buddy, Kola Kwarian, played him, and Kubrick set the scene where Johnny meets him at the 'Academy of Chess and Checkers', based on the New York 'Flea House' where Kubrick used to play. Maurice's ruminations on the implacability of fate also recall *Fear and Desire*.

Harris–Kubrick had no Hollywood agent, so they mailed a number of copies of the script, now called 'Day of Violence', to Lionel White's representative, Robert Goldfarb of the Jaffe Agency, who recalled, 'I guess we were the nearest they had to a Hollywood connection at the time. I remember that [the scripts] arrived one day in a cardboard carton big enough to live in, the kind of box which might have contained rolls of toilet paper at the supermarket. The script itself was typed on legal-size pages running sideways and bound at the top. It was humongous – maybe three hundred pages long – not at all in a conventional form physically. The whole thing smacked of amateur night.'

Another agent at Jaffe's, Ronnie Lubin, represented Harris–Kubrick in their negotiations with United Artists, who remained dubious about the project. They felt it needed a big star, and suggested Harris wait eighteen months until Victor Mature was available. 'It didn't take us long to figure out they weren't offering us anything,' Harris says. 'If we had a name, we could take the film to any studio and get a deal.'

Sterling Hayden, who'd played opposite Sinatra in *Suddenly*, as well as taking a role similar to Johnny Clay in *The Asphalt Jungle*, topped Harris–Kubrick's list, but the actor, who made movies simply to finance voyages on his boat, was elusive, so Harris drove to Stratton, Connecticut, to see another prominent heavy, Jack Palance, who was appearing there in Shakespeare. 'I went there and left [the script] in his dressing room,' says Harris. 'I was so naïve. I thought people would read it the moment you gave it to them, and they'd naturally love it, as we did, and be breaking down our door. But he never got back to me, so a week later I called him. The telephone voice was so negative and so dead, I thought I was talking to a cold flounder. It puts you so on the defensive. You expect to hear, "I'm so glad you called. I loved your script. When can we do it?" But you felt he didn't know who you were or what you were talking about. It was the beginning of a great education in what this business is all about.'

Harris found Kubrick's lack of a track record a major drawback to producing *Clean Break*. 'I swore to Stanley that, on this or any other project, I would never ditch him as director just to keep the film alive. When you've got the money up and the backers don't think this director can handle the project, a lot of people will say, "You've got to let me off the hook with this." But we were kids, and we had a long way to go. And I believed in Stanley. He was a friend, and it's fun working with your friends.'

One agent rang to ask, 'Who have you got for the film?' Assuming he was talking about directors, Harris said, 'Kubrick.' 'Did you say you've got *Coop*?' said the man, thinking he meant Gary Cooper. Then, out of the blue, Bill Schifrin, the famously aggressive agent who represented Sterling Hayden, called. 'This is a pretty good script,' he said, 'and Sterling likes it, but who's the director? Is he Stanley Kramer?'

Hayden agreed to do the film for $40,000, and Harris informed United Artists with some enthusiasm that they had their star. To his disappointment, the company was anything but impressed. After *The Asphalt Jungle*, Hayden, under investigation by the anti-Communist House UnAmerican Activities Committee in 1951, 'named names', discrediting himself with most of his friends. Marginalised within Hollywood, he made a string of cheap Westerns, most of which ended up on UA's books, so unpopular that they were rented out not even for a percentage of the box office but for $100 a booking.

Grudgingly, UA offered to invest $200,000 in 'Day of Violence'. If it cost more than that, they warned, Harris–Kubrick would have to pay the excess; Harris became, in effect, the film's production guarantor. Also, in distributing profits, UA would have first call, so that Harris–Kubrick would begin making money only after UA recouped its investment – a point which, with 'creative accounting', receded like a mirage the closer one approached it. Head of Production Max Youngstein urged Harris to scale down the film, starting by giving Hayden the elbow. With some cheaper has-been in the main role, the whole thing could be shot on a studio backlot. 'Nobody will know the difference,' he told him, 'and you boys won't get hurt.'

Harris and Kubrick, however, wouldn't give in, though the pressures to do so mounted. Every east-coast racetrack neighed in dismay at the thought of allowing a robbery film onto their premises. West-coast tracks, more accustomed to the movies, were less nervous. It became increasingly clear that the film would have to be shot in California, so in the late summer of 1955 Kubrick and Harris set about relocating their homes and wives to Los Angeles.

Alex Singer had been offered an Associate Producer credit on the film, 'but I'm not sure how much associate producing I did. I was being paid off for an important move: I'd introduced him to Jimmy Harris.' His first task in this onerous position was to drive Harris's car to California. Kubrick also nominated Ruth to do the sets, a cost-cutting measure in which Harris acquiesced doubtfully, and about which he was to become increasingly unsure.

United Artists had no studio space of its own, so Harris rented offices in Charlie Chaplin's old headquarters, then called the Kling Studios, at the corner of Sunset and La Brea. Kubrick and Ruth found an apartment not far away, on Doheny near Sunset, in an eccentric thirties building that from the outside resembled an *art deco* pagoda. From the start, however, Kubrick showed no enthusiasm for California. People he'd met in New York, like experimental film-maker Curtis Harrington and Gavin Lambert, now working there as a novelist and screenwriter, loved Los Angeles. They introduced him to what they regarded as its secret delights, like the home of so-called 'male witch' Samson DeBrier on Barton Avenue in Hollywood, a mecca for every oddball in the city. Guests at DeBrier's *soirées* included Igor Stravinsky, James Dean and Kenneth Anger, who shot his *Inauguration of the Pleasure Dome* there. One visitor described the house as 'a gentle junkyard, a repository of rotting portières, chipped gilt frames, Regency ballgowns on wooden dress dummies, disintegrating first editions stacked on floors, tables and love-seats; of dusty whorehouse mirrors, of gold-plated peacocks with zircon wings, of photographs of Gide, who was Samson's closest companion, of death masks, including one of James Dean.' It sounds like, and could be, the model for Quilty's decaying mansion in *Lolita*.

Lambert in particular relished these *Sunset Boulevard* fossils of a Hollywood before the coming of sound, and wrote an influential set of stories about them, set in the 'slide area' of crumbling cliffs along the Pacific. 'But all of that meant nothing to Stanley,' laments Lambert. 'I don't think he ever liked it out here. I always think of Stanley as an indoors person. I see him always living in some place that's a little inaccessible, not very brightly lit – in long shots. As you come into the room, there is this figure, over in the corner, in the dark, deceptively low key.'

Kubrick and Lambert often went to movies, where Kubrick continued his habit of reading a newspaper when bored. Neither Kubrick nor Ruth were great cooks, so they were glad of Curtis Harrington, who was. They often visited his cramped apartment off Vine Street for meals and talk. Harrington, who shared Ruth's passion for ballet, felt her to be decidedly un-Hollywood, and unhappy there. Others too commented on the couple's – but especially Ruth's – palpable nostalgia for New York. Lambert thought Ruth 'likeable but unhappy'. Hollywood gossip and studio politics didn't interest her. 'She was not a devious person at all.'

Alex Singer also sensed a tension between the couple, especially at the point where they interacted creatively, in the production of the film. He feels Kubrick was already manoeuvring to exclude Ruth from his professional life. Harris was equally unsympathetic to her. 'She wanted to be right in there with us, a partner,' he says. 'And my attitude was: who needs her? She would have liked to sit in on all the script meetings and decisions. She even wanted her name on the door. But a ballet dancer from the Village, I didn't want around. I guess she thought she was Mrs Kubrick, and that gave her the right. She was a forerunner of a lot of the Women's Lib people. I think Stanley agreed with me, and maybe I put some pressure on him to keep the project between us.'

Harris hired a professional production manager, Clarence Eurist, to compile a budget and shooting schedule for the film, now retitled yet again, as 'Bed of Fear'. 'And it put us into shock,' recalls Harris, 'because the figure was $330,000. And that only gave us twenty-four days of shooting.' Nor did the budget include any payments for either Harris or Kubrick, each of whom was deferring all but $5000 of their salaries. UA was adamant in sticking to its $200,000 offer, so Harris kicked in his savings of $80,000 and borrowed $50,000 more from his father. 'We're buying a career,' he told him. 'If we make a cheap, lousy movie, we'll never get anywhere. But if we make the kind of movie Stanley and I can do, it could be the start of everything.' Harris Snr obliged. However, as Harris–Kubrick embarked on pre-production in the fall of 1955, it was in the knowledge that not a dollar could be wasted.

As cameraman, Harris hired Lucien Ballard. Twenty years Kubrick's senior, a veteran who'd begun with Josef von Sternberg in the mid-thirties and since then shot everything from Archie Mayo's *Orchestra Wives* with the Glenn Miller Band to comedy shorts with the Three Stooges, Ballard had still not achieved his best work, which was to be his lighting of the Westerns of Sam Peckinpah. In 1955 he'd just ended a four-year contract with 20th Century-Fox and was marking time on low-budget thrillers and Westerns for independents, picking up the threads of a career derailed by a marriage to the glamorous and promiscuous Merle Oberon that culminated in Ballard smashing through the window of a Rome hotel to surprise her in bed with her lover, Count Giorgio Cini. The resulting scandalous divorce prevented him from working at all between 1948 and 1951.

Still startlingly handsome, tall and broad-shouldered, with a chiselled face and copper skin that hinted at his part-Cherokee heritage, Ballard presented Kubrick with an unignorable challenge, both as film-maker and man. It came to a head when Kubrick sent him to shoot footage of a racetrack for use under the titles. According to Alex Singer, 'Ballard was a splendid cameraman, but he couldn't do documentary work to save his life. They went out with a whole crew and four cameras, and came back with trash. Stanley wanted to fire him, but Jimmy and I said, "Wait a minute. He can't do that sort of stuff. It's the sort of stuff you or I could do." Stanley said, "I have to work on the script. You go and do it."'

With the clockwork single-lens Eyemo, the only piece of film-making equipment Harris–Kubrick owned, and a bagful of film in thirty-metre loads, Singer covered a day in the life of the Golden Gate track at Bay Meadows, in San Francisco. Singer had a good eye, and the footage, all shot with available light, was excellent, with the slightly grainy texture one subconsciously associates with authenticity. 'Stanley was delighted with what I shot,' says Singer

– so delighted that, instead of simply using it under the titles, he spread it through the film, repeating shots of the horses being led out and urged into the starting gate at the start of each flashback in the intricate structure. All that remains of the work by Ballard's teams are some shots from the infield of racing horses. Seeing the completed film was Ballard's first intimation that Singer had been backstopping him – not the last time Kubrick would behave in this way towards a cameraman.

Kubrick, who had seen almost every major Hollywood movie of the previous decade, had no trouble casting what was now called *The Killing*. The film features an anthology of B-movie veterans: Jay C. Flippen as Unger; Elisha Cook Jr of *The Big Sleep* and *The Maltese Falcon* as George; Ted de Corsia from *The Naked City* as Randy; Jay Adler as his courteous and meticulously well-spoken bookie; Marie Windsor, sensual star of classic *films noirs* like *The Narrow Margin*, as Sherry. For Johnny's adoring girl Fay, Kubrick hired Coleen Grey from *Kiss of Death* – a diplomatic choice, since she was Max Youngstein's mistress. Joe Sawyer, henchman in scores of thirties crime films, was cast against type as the bartender. Val, Sherry's lover, was Vince Edwards, later TV's most famous doctor in the long-running *Ben Casey* series. Soft-spoken Joe Turkel, who was to appear in more Kubrick films than anyone, plays a gunman. For Nikki, Kubrick chose gangling, horse-faced Timothy Carey, whose crooked smile and whining voice put his eccentric signature on every film in which he appeared.

Kubrick finished shooting in twenty-four days, as scheduled. Sterling Hayden, who sat in on rushes, was astonished at his expertise. 'I haven't seen rushes like these since *The Asphalt Jungle*,' he said. But it wasn't a warm relationship. 'Stanley was cold and detached,' recalled Hayden. 'Very mechanical, always confident. I've worked with few directors who are that good.' An electrician told Alex Singer, 'I've been in this business thirty years, and I'm learning stuff from this kid.'

Unlike later films, on which Kubrick would earn a reputation for multiple takes and a tendency to follow any interesting technical sidetrack, no matter how unpromising, *The Killing* was shot with such precision that it needed little work in the cutting room. 'He's like the Russian documentarists who could put the same footage together five different ways,' said Hayden, 'so it really didn't matter

what the actor did – Kubrick would know what to do with it.'
Jimmy Harris agrees. 'Editing was simple. An editor named Betty
Steinberg was employed to cut the film, but Stanley would simply
tell her where he wanted the shots to go, then we'd go out and toss
a football around.'

The football routine, which many people remember as a feature
of Kubrick and Harris's brief period in Hollywood, along with
Kubrick's scorn of the show-business bible *Variety* and the other
'trades', and his insistence on reading no film magazine but the
heavyweight critical journal *Film Quarterly*, became the approved
means among young film-makers of indicating their scorn for Hollywood studio practice. For later generations football would be
replaced by jukeboxes, candy machines and video games in production offices, or organic meals in the commissary.

Hayden, who had been complimentary about the film on its first
screening, had second thoughts when his agent Bill Schifrin saw it.
Schifrin rang Harris and complained that the fragmentary structure
made nonsense of his client's performance. He implied that in taking
such a line they had damaged his client – the sort of remark that
paved the way for a lawsuit. Glumly, Kubrick moved in to Titra
and tried re-editing the film as a straight-line story. It didn't work.
In fact, the effort simply confirmed him in his belief that the structure
was what made the film superior to conventional thrillers. He and
Harris resolved to go with their original cut, and risk litigation.

Harris and Kubrick showed the first print of *The Killing* to
Youngstein, who accepted it with a shrug. Anxious to know if they
were heading in the right direction, Harris said, 'You have other
people who make films for you. Where would you rate us?'
Youngstein said, 'Not far from the bottom.' To render their opinion
self-fulfilling, UA opened *The Killing* in a cavernous New York
cinema, the hurried replacement for a film that had fallen out of
their schedule. It did poorly, so they put it out on general release
as a double bill with Richard Fleischer's *Bandido*, a Western starring
Robert Mitchum.

Time magazine praised *The Killing*: 'the camera watches the
whole shoddy show with the keen eye of a terrier stalking a pack
of rats,' it said. Kubrick, it went on, 'has shown more imagination
with dialogue and camera than Hollywood has seen since the
obstreperous Orson Welles went riding out of town'. Elsewhere,

however, the film was largely ignored. In England it played as the support to Sheldon Reynolds' *Foreign Intrigue* with Robert Mitchum, and while it never reached the West End's more prestigious cinemas, it was seen and admired by enough critics to launch Kubrick's reputation in Europe.

Harris, watching his and his father's investment wiped out almost overnight, was appalled. After two years, *The Killing* would only have earned $30,000, and Harris would sell his and Kubrick's 50 per cent share to UA in return for the money to acquire *Lolita*. 'And it's marvellous,' reminisces Harris sarcastically, 'how quickly the film went into profit after UA owned all of it.'

If the poor reaction to *The Killing* distressed Kubrick, Jim Thompson was even more anguished when he found his contribution described in the screen credits as 'Additional Dialogue'. 'My father nearly fell out of his chair when he saw that,' said Patricia Thompson. 'There were fireworks when he next saw Kubrick. He couldn't believe that Stanley would cheat him out of his credit.' Harris says defensively, 'We hired Thompson *because* of his dialogue. The structure of the story was already pretty much there, and we all contributed changes. Today of course he would get co-screenplay credit, but in those days "Dialogue by ..." or "Additional Dialogue by ..." were perfectly legitimate credits. He couldn't have been so disturbed about it, because he went on to write *Paths of Glory* for us and we commissioned a novel from him.'

Alex Singer is less certain that justice was done. 'Attribution of credit on a screenplay is frequently a central issue [of authorship in a film]. As directors get more recognition for their work, they are likely to be more generous with their attributions.' In Kubrick's case, this has not proved to be true: wrangles over credit for writing and music trail his films to the present day. Kubrick, through his lawyer, called Thompson's claims 'unfounded', and insists he 'doesn't have to defend himself'. However, Thompson's family maintain that, in a private deal with Kubrick, the writer agreed not to protest any further in return for a commission to script *Paths of Glory* at $500 a week. Deal or not, such an offer was made. Thompson accepted – he wasn't in a position to refuse – and left for Hollywood in June 1956.

*

After the grim experience of *The Killing*'s New York opening, Harris and Kubrick returned disconsolate to Hollywood in March 1956. Neither was accompanied by his wife. Harris's marriage failed during the production; and the friction over her future with Harris–Kubrick irreparably damaged Kubrick's relationship with Ruth, who went on a European tour with the New York City Ballet. David Vaughan, by then back in London, went to see her when the company performed in Paris. She tearfully confided that the marriage was in trouble.

Later in 1956, Vaughan, who had ambitions to become a full-time choreographer, returned to New York. 'I had no job, so I called Stanley and Ruth in Hollywood, and he said, "Come on out here. I'll find you something to do." I think Stanley had some idea that he'd set me up making movies. A friend happened to be driving out, so I went with them. And when I arrived, it was obvious that the relationship between Stanley and Ruth was on the rocks. Stanley would storm out of the apartment every morning on his way to the studio, and Ruth would be left weeping.'

Ronnie Lubin, who had handled the early negotiations with UA, offered to represent Harris–Kubrick in Los Angeles, and managed to get a copy of *The Killing* to Dore Schary, Louis B. Mayer's Head of Production at MGM. Schary liked the film so much that when Harris explained how badly it was being handled, he proposed that MGM buy it from UA and re-release it. Harris was delighted at the thought of recouping his investment, and was dashed when UA refused Schary's offer: selling the rights to films simply wasn't their policy. Schary, however, was unconcerned, and said, 'Well, what do you want to do now?'

Harris and Kubrick had been determined, if someone should offer them a deal after *The Killing*, not to be caught without a project as they had been after *Killer's Kiss*. They'd decided on a war – or anti-war – film. Kubrick told Harris about an obscure 1935 novel by Canadian screenwriter Humphrey Cobb, *Paths of Glory*, which he'd read at fourteen. It was long out of print, but Harris tracked down a lone copy in the New York Public Library. He wasn't allowed to take it away, so he settled down to read it right there, and was immediately gripped.

*

Humphrey Cobb was a Canadian screenwriter working in Holly-wood in 1934 when he read a *New York Times* report of a trial just concluded in France. The widows and families of five French enlisted men shot for mutiny in 1915 had sued the army for damages. The court agreed that they were unfairly executed, but awarded two of the widows a token one franc each. The others got nothing.

An indignant Cobb wrote a short novel based loosely on the case. In his book, a press release by the French army erroneously announces the capture of a notorious strongpoint in the line known as 'the Pimple'. Rather than risk an embarrassing disclosure, General de Guerville orders Assolant, an ambitious subordinate, to take the Pimple, and promises promotion if he does so.

Assolant is vain enough to think his exhausted troops will succeed under his leadership, but so heavy is the German fire that few even make it out of the trenches. Furious, he orders a section from each company to be shot. De Guerville coaxes him down to three men. Colonel Dax, a junior officer, protests, but in vain. Three men are chosen, supposedly by lot but actually from spite or prejudice. One man attacks the priest sent to hear their confessions and is beaten up by the guards. Still unconscious, he's shot with the others.

The book had no title when Cobb delivered it, so Viking, its American publishers, held a competition offering a cash prize. The winner suggested a line from Thomas Gray's 'Elegy Written in a Country Churchyard', 'The paths of glory lead but to the grave,' and the novel was published in June 1935 under the title *Paths of Glory*.

The book excited much interest in liberal intellectual circles, if not with the public. Sidney Howard, later the major screenwriter of *Gone with the Wind*, adapted it for the stage, and the play ran briefly on Broadway at the end of 1935. Hoping that college theatre groups might take it up, influencing the new generation against war, Howard stylised the settings, even suggesting that the whole play, which takes place mostly in the trenches, could be performed on a single symbolic set: perhaps around a cenotaph. The play wasn't a success, but theatre critic Brooks Atkinson was prescient when he wrote in the *New York Times*, 'Some day the screen will seize this ghastly tale and make a work of art from it.'

*

By 1956, Humphrey Cobb was dead, but his widow was more than happy to sell Harris–Kubrick the rights to *Paths of Glory* for $10,000. Harris was delighted. Although they had no script, here was a project they could table immediately for MGM.

Unfortunately, Schary wanted nothing to do with it.

'Not on your life,' he said. 'We just did *The Red Badge of Courage*. Enough with war films. They're death at the box office. Poison.' As chronicled in Lillian Ross's book *Picture*, the debacle of John Huston's adaptation of Stephen Crane's Civil War novella put Schary in fatal conflict with MGM's bosses, and was to lead to his downfall.

'But listen,' Schary went on, 'we have a room full of properties we own. There must be something in there you boys want to do.'

He offered them a forty-week development deal on a first-look basis; Harris–Kubrick would get office space and salaries in return for giving MGM first refusal of anything they found. Once approved, the film would need to be cast, shot and edited within the period of the contract. It seemed an impossible idea, but they accepted. At the same time, however, Harris contracted on the sly with Jim Thompson to write a script based on *Paths of Glory*.

MGM's Story Department was a graveyard of bad ideas and worse deals going back thirty years. Once-fashionable Broadway plays, *Saturday Evening Post* short stories and novels bought for their titles or to keep them from other studios, shared space with screenplays that had occupied the attention of half the most distinguished figures in world literature, from Arthur Schnitzler and Hermann Sudermann to Scott Fitzgerald and William Faulkner.

For Harris and Kubrick to sift them alone was impossible; it took them two weeks simply to go through the card index. Alex Singer came in to help, and Kubrick also hired Gavin Lambert. When reading old screenplays and treatments palled, Kubrick and Harris would play ping pong, or take over an executive screening room to look at old movies, a habit that drew a reprimand from the front office when they began to monopolise the preview theatres.

The search ended when Kubrick discovered Stefan Zweig's 1914 story '*Brennendes Geheimnis*' – 'Burning Secret'. Zweig, born in Vienna in 1881, had been one of Europe's best-known and most popular writers between the wars. A friend of Freud, Rilke, Hofmannstahl and Schnitzler, fluent in three languages, biographer of historical figures as diverse as Erasmus and Mary Queen of Scots, he dazzled not only Europe but the English-speaking world, throughout which his books were widely translated. Many of them had been filmed, particularly *Amok*, a fevered tale of a doctor's obsession with a pregnant woman in the jungles of Malaya, and *Brief einer Unbekannten – Letter from an Unknown Woman –* the best film made by Max Ophuls during his frustrating stay in Hollywood from 1941 to 1949.

MGM had bought 'Burning Secret' at the height of Zweig's fame. Slow but intensely cinematic, the story deals with a young Baron who spots an attractive Jewish woman at a mountain spa, and idly decides to seduce her. As a route to the mother, he befriends her twelve-year-old son, who grows increasingly resentful as he senses he's being used. After attacking the Baron when he thinks his mother is being menaced – the couple are actually embracing – the boy runs off to his grandmother's house, where his father arrives from Vienna to find out what's going on. The boy is about to explain when he sees his mother desperately put her finger to her lips. He lies, saving her reputation, and learning something about sexuality and dishonesty – an insight that will make him, like the Baron (and Zweig), an accomplished seducer.

When the Nazis marched into Vienna in 1938, Zweig was driven first from Austria, then from Europe. He settled in Brazil, but the loss of his beloved German language and the destruction of his hopes for a united and peaceful Europe, a cause for which he'd campaigned passionately throughout the thirties, depressed him. In February 1942, he and his mistress attended the carnival in Rio, then drove back to their home and took fatal overdoses of Veronal. 'Many men of feeling,' wrote André Maurois, 'must have meditated, the day when they learned of this double suicide . . . on the shame of a civilisation that can create a world in which Stefan Zweig cannot live.' 'Burning Secret' returned to MGM's vaults – until Kubrick found it.

'Stanley was very excited,' says Lambert. 'He was a great admirer of Max Ophuls, and we had agreed about his version of Zweig's *Letter from an Unknown Woman*. "Burning Secret" was the only thing he wanted to do at Metro. Nothing else was seriously considered.' Kubrick saw the story as a chance to combine a strong intellectual theme and faultless literary credentials with the appeal of a big-budget Hollywood film. MGM was also a pushover for literary adaptations if they had sex appeal. Gregory Peck and Ava Gardner had just starred in Robert Siodmak's *The Great Sinner*, an adaptation of Dostoevsky's *The Gambler*, and even though it flopped at the box office, the studio still regarded it, and films like it, with a certain pride.

Harris was baffled by Kubrick's enthusiasm for the Zweig story. However, he acquiesced in proposing it to Schary, who agreed to move on to a script. At Kubrick's urging they commissioned another of his enthusiasms, the little-known novelist Calder Willingham, to write it. The drawling, conceited but undeniably brilliant Willingham had been educated at The Citadel, South Carolina's tough military academy, and made his reputation with *End as a Man*, a novel and, later, play about sadism and homo-eroticism at such a school which had just been adapted into a film. Willingham knew the dark side of the military mind, though it was mixed in his work with a streak of farce. Critic Richard Dillard called him 'a comic chronicler of iniquity', and after his novels *Geraldine Bradshaw* and *To Eat a Peach*, the *New Yorker* would credit him with having 'inadvertently fathered black comedy'. Working later with Willingham on *Paths of Glory* encouraged in Kubrick the lunatic irony that led him to hire those other dark literary comedians Terry Southern, for *Dr Strangelove*, and Gustav Hasford, for *Full Metal Jacket*.

On the debit side, Willingham's regard, indeed reverence for the value of his prose, and a habit of wincing theatrically if he heard one of his lines rewritten, made him unwelcome on most sets. To get him off the film of *End as a Man*, which had been shooting in Florida, producer Sam Spiegel sent him to help out on another of his projects, David Lean's version of *The Bridge on the River Kwai*, shooting in Ceylon. From the start, this adaptation of Pierre Boulle's novel had suffered script problems, and despite the efforts of two of the best of Hollywood's blacklisted screenwriters, Carl Foreman and Michael Wilson, the difficulties persisted well into shooting. Willingham, unfortunately, didn't solve them. Lean loathed the stilted dialogue he wrote for Alec Guinness's stiff British Army Colonel, and was delighted when, after six weeks, the novelist was recalled to Hollywood and 'Burning Secret'.

Even while Willingham and Kubrick were busy adapting Zweig's story, Jimmy Harris's heart still belonged to *Paths of Glory*, and he kept Thompson at work on the draft screenplay. This arrangement, unstable from the start, was always headed for disaster. Kubrick, now committed mentally to 'Burning Secret', was impatient with *Paths of Glory*. After working with Willingham all day, he spent the evenings with Thompson arguing about it. 'They'd scream at each other until it drove me mad,' said Alberta, Thompson's wife, who'd come out to Hollywood with him.

Hollywood leaks information like a sieve, and before long MGM knew that Harris–Kubrick had two scripts going at once, in breach of their 'exclusive personal services' contract. Normally they would have turned a blind eye, but Schary was under attack from the studio hierarchy, and all his projects shared in his obloquy. An executive called in Harris and told him that, in view of the long delay in finishing the script for 'Burning Secret' and the fact that it would need rewriting, too little time remained on their contract to start production. Accordingly, they were terminating the deal. Harris rang Schary in New York to protest. Called out of a meeting with the east-coast executives who really controlled MGM, a distressed Schary muttered, 'Right now I've got problems of my own.' He was in fact being terminated as head of production, and could do nothing for Harris or Kubrick.

'Hiring Jim Thompson got us fired from MGM,' Harris admits. '"Burning Secret" went down the drain.' Harris didn't mind too much. 'I'd like to forget that one,' he says. 'It went out of my mind as soon as Metro dropped us. I breathed a sigh of relief when we could get into *Paths of Glory*.'

Chapter Seven

Kubrick in the Trenches

'We are born astride a grave.'

Samuel Beckett

Late in the summer of 1956, Jim Thompson had taken *Paths of Glory* as far as he could. He'd mainly transposed Cobb's bleak parable into film form, but had added, at Kubrick's urging, a happy ending, with the men reprieved at the last minute when Colonel Dax blackmails General de Guerville (now called Broulard) with the news that in the heat of battle Assolant (renamed Mireau) ordered the French artillery to fire on his own men. Dax gets Mireau's command, and he and Broulard stroll away, arm in arm.

Kirk Douglas, who was to play Dax, says he confronted Kubrick with this script and its sunny conclusion just before they started shooting, and asked, 'Stanley, did you write this?'

'Yes.'

'Stanley, why would you do that?'

'To make it commercial,' he said. 'I want to make money.'

We only have Douglas's testimony for this conversation, but there's no reason to disbelieve him, since Thompson's first draft screenplay bears him out. Richard Anderson, an old tennis buddy of Jimmy Harris's who was hired to coach the actors on *Paths of Glory* as well as to play the commanding General's toadying Adjutant, St Auban, insists that Max Youngstein, head of the film's eventual distributors, United Artists, agreed with Kubrick that the three must be saved from execution. In Anderson's recollection,

Harris and Kubrick accepted this as part of the price of the deal.

The second script, dated 26 November 1956, bears a shared credit to Kubrick, Thompson and Calder Willingham, whom Kubrick swung onto the project when 'Burning Secret' fell through. Drafts three and four still bear Thompson's name as one of the three collaborators, but Kubrick and Willingham alone worked on them, Thompson having returned to New York. These rewrites widened and deepened Cobb's story. In particular Dax emerged from relative anonymity into the blaze of drama and motivation that makes a star vehicle. Transformed into France's most brilliant criminal lawyer in civilian life, he defends the condemned men in a court martial that becomes, with the attempt to take the Pimple (renamed 'the Ant-hill'), one of the two pivots of the film.

After *The Killing*, Ruth remained in Los Angeles with Kubrick. David Vaughan moved to a nearby apartment and, in some anguish, watched the marriage collapsing. Hoping to find a project on which he and Ruth could collaborate, Kubrick approached *Village Voice* cartoonist Jules Feiffer, one of whose continuing characters was a barefoot modern dancer, but a plot based on her adventures failed to emerge. When the New York City Ballet went back into rehearsal, Kubrick paid for Ruth and Vaughan to return to New York. An increasingly distraught Ruth moved back into the 10th Street apartment.

According to Vaughan, someone had given Kubrick details of a sexual encounter said to have taken place between Ruth and another man during the time she and Vaughan shared the apartment. Though this preceded his relationship with Ruth, Kubrick was furious, and taxed her with it in a letter containing considerable circumstantial detail. They never lived together again.

When Kubrick went to Germany to film *Paths of Glory*, Ruth left ballet and started training as an actress. After she and Kubrick divorced in 1957, she again embarked on more disastrous relationships with young designers and actors. In 1967, at the age of forty-two, she died suddenly and mysteriously in a New York hospital of what David Vaughan suspects were complications from taking the then-untried birth control pill, though at least one source has hinted at suicide.

*

The history of *Paths of Glory* began by reprising that of *The Killing*. Again no studio would touch the story. Again Ronnie Lubin got the script to a backer, in this case Kirk Douglas. Douglas liked the story, but was committed to a play on Broadway, and couldn't make another film for at least eighteen months.

Kubrick and Harris talked to Richard Burton and James Mason as possible candidates to play Dax. The agents of many other stars refused even to show their clients so depressing and non-commercial a script. Then, unexpectedly, Kubrick received a call from director William Wyler, who had just made *Roman Holiday* with Gregory Peck and Audrey Hepburn, and was planning, he explained, a film called *How to Steal a Million* for the same pair. Hepburn would play the daughter of an art forger who's about to be found out, and Peck the high-class cracksman who falls for her and covers her father's crime by arranging an elaborate museum robbery.

Wyler had seen *The Killing*, and wondered if Kubrick could inculcate some of the same nervy atmosphere into his script. Harris and Kubrick met Wyler and Peck, and though Wyler eventually shelved *How to Steal a Million* until 1966, when Peter O'Toole starred in it opposite Hepburn, Peck became interested in *Paths of Glory*, and asked to see a script. He rang back with gratifying speed, saying he'd be delighted to play Dax – providing they waited eighteen months. The merry-go-round had come full circle.

But the relationship with Peck flourished. He planned a film about Confederate General John Singleton Mosby, leader of Mosby's Rangers, which inflicted vast damage behind the Union lines during the American Civil War, and offered the project, under the working title 'The 7th Virginia Cavalry Raider', to Harris and Kubrick for development. Reminded of Agee's *Mr Lincoln*, Kubrick thought of basing the film on Matthew Brady's evocative photographs of the war. He started work on a screenplay, but hadn't gone far before Kirk Douglas, who was being kept up to date with the latest revisions on *Paths of Glory* – the second and third drafts are among his papers – heard about Peck's offer. Early in 1957 he rang to tell Harris and Kubrick that his play was postponed. He could start work immediately on the film, subject to a deal with his company, Bryna Productions. With no money in sight and any collaboration with Peck more than a year down the line, the partners had little choice but to go with Douglas.

Harris recalls, 'We drove out to Palm Springs, where Kirk had his house. Ray Stark was his agent then. I think this might have been his last deal as an agent before he became a producer. And Stark killed us with that deal. He just *buried* us. He was a tough agent and we were desperate. They had no shame. It had to be a Bryna production. We had to sign for five pictures, of which Kirk would be in two, including *Paths of Glory*. He didn't have to be in the other three, but I had to produce them and Stanley had to direct.'

Douglas demanded $350,000 to play Dax, plus a percentage of the profits, first-class travel for himself and his family to Europe – Kubrick insisted on shooting as close to the site of the original incident as possible – and generous expenses. Harris winced. This would push the budget close to $1 million for the sixty-six-day shoot. No sooner had the deal been made than news reached Peck. He rang to say he'd reassessed his commitments and could find time to play Dax. But by then it was too late.

Initially, the relationship with Douglas promised much. He could be, as everyone who worked for him agreed, a juggernaut – once he had control of a project. Director Richard Fleischer, then preparing *The Vikings* for him, said, 'You couldn't ask for a better producer ... He was knowledgeable, creative, and passionately involved. There was no penny-pinching or cutting corners. Most importantly, I had his confidence and trust. It seemed too good to be true.'

It *was* too good to be true, but for the moment Harris and Kubrick felt the same optimism, especially after Douglas 'sledge-hammered the deal through UA', in Harris's words. Kirk had promised UA *The Vikings*, patently a money machine. Now he held over their head the alarming prospect that he might pull out of that deal if they didn't back *Paths of Glory*. Max Youngstein grudgingly agreed to invest $850,000 in Kubrick's film, plus or minus 10 per cent. Due to Harris's meticulous planning, the film came in for $954,000, though, once more, both he and Kubrick worked for a share of the profits alone.

1957 was the heyday of runaway production, and almost every capital in Europe could boast a studio complex for rent at low rates, together with military units eager to provide men and equipment for scenes of mass slaughter. Billancourt or Joinville studios near Paris would have been the logical places to shoot *Paths of Glory*, but even this early in the project it was obvious to both Harris and Kubrick that France would not welcome a film about one of the most discreditable incidents in its military history.

Douglas nominated the Geiselgasteig Studios near Munich, where he was also planning to film parts of *The Vikings*. Not only were the studios themselves spacious; within half an hour's drive there were locations suitable for the battlefield and the General's château headquarters where the court martial takes place. Kubrick and Harris were in no position to disagree. With Calder Willingham, their German-born production manager John Pommer and Richard Anderson, they flew to Munich to start pre-production.

Wrangling over the script and rewriting the lines continued with undiminished vigour. Well into the fourth, penultimate draft, the optimistic ending remained, even after everyone except Kubrick had reached the uneasy conclusion that a last-minute reprieve would not only negate the film's message, but would earn critical derision, without necessarily guaranteeing box-office success. In the end, Kubrick reluctantly agreed, and a fifth, final version of the script was written with the same final scene as the book: the men dead, tied to their posts, as the drunken Lieutenant Roget gives each the *coup de grâce*.

By contract, this major change required UA's agreement. Knowing that, if he confronted him, Youngstein would almost certainly reject the new version, Harris decided simply to hand over the final screenplay for formal approval, and not to draw attention to the changes: 'It was up to them to read it, but I knew they wouldn't. These guys are too busy to read scripts.' He returned to New York, delivered the script to UA and waited nervously for a call. None came, and the ending was shot as written. Nor, when the studio executives saw the completed film, did anyone comment on the change.

Harris returned to Munich on the same flight as Gerald Fried, who had again been contracted to write the music, to find that, in his absence, Kubrick had found what he believed was a way to end the film, if not happily, then on a heartening note. He had roughed out with Willingham a scene after the execution in which the men, drinking in a bar before going back to the trenches, are entertained by a German girl whom the owner goads into singing for them. As she launches nervously into the old folk song 'Der Treuer Husar' ('The Faithful Soldier'), the men fall silent, and begin to sing along, and to weep. Outside, Dax tells the Sergeant to give the men a few minutes more.

To play the girl, the only German seen in the film, Kubrick proposed Christiane Harlan, a twenty-four-year-old actress whom he'd seen on TV under the name Suzanne Christian. Harris quickly realised that her main recommendation was that, during his absence in America, she had become Kubrick's mistress.

Harris was furious. 'Are you fucking *crazy*?' he said. 'You want to put your girlfriend on the payroll?' He became further alarmed on discovering that she was related to Nazi film-maker Veidt Harlan, director of the notorious *Jud Süss*.

But Kubrick was convinced the scene demanded her presence. 'Try it, try it,' he urged. Harris reluctantly agreed – and was so moved that he ended up leading the men in singing.

Calder Willingham dissents angrily from this version of how the ending came to be written. He and not Kubrick invented the final scene, he claims, but when he tried to describe it, Kubrick resisted, only acquiescing when he outlined it in a memo. 'I can't resist your arguments when you put them in writing,' Kubrick is supposed to have told him. 'My circuits are overloaded and I blow a fuse and start agreeing with everything you say, like I am hypnotised.'

Willingham argued that the script of *Paths of Glory* was '99 per cent' his work. Aggrieved writers can appeal to the Writers' Guild for arbitration in an argument about credits, and in September 1957, before *Paths of Glory* was released, such a demand was made, presumably by Willingham (all Guild deliberations are confidential). On 24 September, the film's publicist Stan Marguiles wrote in an internal memo, 'Stanley Kubrick has just informed me that as a result of a recent Screen Writers' Guild decision, it will be necessary to change the screenplay credit on *Paths of Glory*. It should now read "Screenplay by Stanley Kubrick, Calder Willingham and Jim Thompson".'

Had Kubrick been of a mystical turn of mind, he would have found the choice of Geiselgasteig Studios significant, since it was there, two years before, that Max Ophuls had shot what was to be his last film,

Lola Montes. Ophuls showed the fabulous courtesan reduced at the end of her life to recreating her sensational career in a circus while horses and acrobats caper around her in the centre ring.

Kubrick, reminded of how the paths of artistic high hopes and bold creative ambition lead just as surely to the grave as those of military glory, wandered, respectful but chastened, among the peeling remains of Jean d'Aubonne's sets and the cracked leather harnesses in which dwarf trapeze artists had once swooped around the head of Martine Carol's Lola.

Ophuls's pleasure in following the characters with his camera, avoiding the obligatory Hollywood cuts to the sudden reactive close-ups which – the actor's eyes wide, the ears pricked up – he dismissed as 'rabbit shots', suggested to Kubrick the style of *Paths of Glory*. Though easily lulled by the flexibility of dolly and crane into a delirium of *art nouveau* glides and leaps, Ophuls could also use the mobile camera with discretion, quietly tracking with his performers so that their backgrounds were revealed along with their emotions. Kubrick planned his film as a series of such tracking shots. Close-ups are reserved for the major confrontations. 'I remember watching *Paths of Glory*,' Steven Spielberg has remarked, 'and realising how few tight close-ups there were, but when Kubrick used a close-up it meant something.' The trenches were built wider than in real life and floored with planks, so that George Krause's camera could travel with Mireau and St Auban as they tour the front line, rallying the troops for the assault. It tracks too with Dax and his men across no-man's land, and down the long alley of the château gardens to the stakes at which the three men are shot. In between such bravura movements, the camera prowls with everyone, especially with the general officers as they manoeuvre, plot and dissemble in the opulent salons of the château, weaving among Boulle cabinets and past larger-than-life portraits of eighteenth-century courtesans.

Ophuls inspired Kubrick in his treatment of characters too. As Peter Ustinov, who played the ringmaster in *Lola Montes*, said, 'Max loved officers of the *belle époque*, their utter uselessness, their obligations towards virility, their statutory quick temper over imagined slights, their generous ability to make room for younger men by eliminating each other on the field of honour. And yet his comments were never destructive, and he handled the objects of his attention like rare wines, as though the absurdity of years could be destroyed by an excessive movement of the bottle in which these rare essences were contained. He was a tender despot, more than a little in love with those things his intelligence most disliked.'

Similarly, Kubrick can't help but admire the villains of *Paths of Glory*, whom he invests with a suavity and aristocratic style they don't possess in the original novel. The British critic Adrian Turner said much later, '*Paths of Glory* is Kubrick's least interesting picture. Whilst those silky tracking shots tracing circles of corruption around the conniving generals are quite masterly in conception, the film is a stacked deck of liberal idealism which is never convincing. It's almost a Stanley Kramer picture. We know those hapless soldiers will be executed and, like Kubrick, we couldn't care less. They exist not as characters but as targets. Kubrick loves the generals who, like the Romans in *Spartacus*, have the best lines and give the best performances. Kubrick is enthralled by their control and their authority, for they demonstrate his theories of universal and inherited evil.'

Cobb's Assolant/Mireau is young and ambitious, a no-nonsense soldier who wears simple breeches and a second-hand tunic from stores, and affects to be just one of the rank-and-file. He's a Lawrence of Arabia figure, nicknamed 'General Insolent'. But Kubrick gave the part to George Macready, an actor nearing fifty, with a reputation for playing epicene villains in films like *Gilda* and *My Name is Julia Ross*, and a long scar across his right cheek, actually from a car crash but turned into a battlefield wound for this film by extra make-up and some faked stitches.

De Guerville/Broulard in the book is 'distinguished . . . mature, not in the least decrepit', and sounds something like David Niven, whereas the actor Kubrick chose, portly Adolphe Menjou, had been born in 1890, starred in Chaplin's *A Woman of Paris*, von Sternberg's *Morocco* and one of Kubrick's favourites, *Roxie Hart*, and would make only one more film after *Paths of Glory*.

Both men relish the luxuries of rank. 'I wish I had your taste in carpets and pictures,' Broulard tells Mireau enviously as he looks around his sumptuous *salon*. To emphasise that these are aristocrats, sensualists, dandies, with tailored uniforms and sensibilities to match, Kubrick shot their first meeting in a series of tracks, following them as they weave around columns, pause at fragile tables for a thimble of cognac, pose by a marquetry desk. These men *are* their setting, their clothing, their style. Kubrick filmed this scene well into the production, on 26 March 1957, characteristically obscuring its hidden agenda until he finished the day's work. Only then did he turn to Richard Anderson and murmur, 'Max Ophuls died today. This shot is in his honour.'

Once he was deep into *Paths of Glory*, Kubrick became so intimate with his camera that its movements became his. Increasingly, he operated it himself; the credited cameraman, George Krause, was, he claimed, an assistant to whom he gave a battlefield commission as director of photography on the understanding that he keep out of the way. As a result, the camera responds to incidents not as a dispassionate mechanism but as a human observer, man and machine locked in a voyeur's dance as intimate as any waltz.

Tracks begin a split second after the action and carry on a fraction after it halts, as if the camera watching Dax and his men advancing over no-man's land is another soldier. The effect, which Kubrick used again in *Full Metal Jacket*, is nowhere more evident than in a brief scene on the staircase of the château, where Dax is halted by a call from Mireau. After the two men chat on a landing, Dax turns to mount the next flight, only to be stopped by Mireau. Yet, though Dax doesn't climb the stairs, the camera starts to, moving a foot, then halting. The shot has no logic, but it's exactly right. The camera, representing us, the audience, has become a character in the drama.

For the battle scene, Kubrick set up six cameras one after another along the edge of no-man's land. Six hundred German policemen, each with three years' military training, played the French *poilus*. It took a lot of rehearsal to stop them behaving with stage heroics and to make them look as scared as they would have been in a real attack. The field of each camera was designated a 'dying zone', and numbered. Every extra was given a number, and instructed to die in the appropriate zone, ideally after a nearby explosion. Kubrick himself operated an Arriflex with a zoom, concentrating on Douglas. From then on, he routinely used a hand-held camera himself on his films, frustrating his directors of photography but imposing a distinctive mobile style that became one of his trademarks.

Kubrick peopled the film with what was becoming his stock company. Joseph Turkel and Timothy Carey play two of the soldiers.

Rather as he cast archetypal henchman Joe Sawyer against type as the kindly barman in *The Killing*, he mischievously used Emile Meyer, brutal cop or prison guard in countless Hollywood crime movies, as the priest who tries to bring solace to the prisoners. With equal sarcasm, Wayne Morris, a decorated flying ace during World War II, was cast as the cowardly Roget, described, in one of the completed film's few verifiable Jim Thompson lines, as 'a sneaky, boozed, guzzling, yellow-bellied rat with a bottle for a brain and a streak of spit where his spine ought to be.'

On *Spartacus*, Kubrick's next film, stills cameraman William Read Woodfield asked him why he cast people like Timothy Carey, 'who couldn't act at all'.

Kubrick replied, 'They bring a texture to the picture that a better actor wouldn't.'

'Are you sure, Stanley?' Woodfield pressed. 'Or is it that you don't really like good actors?'

'That may be,' Kubrick conceded.

What could Kubrick have against good actors? It's Woodfield's theory, borne out by Kubrick's later work, that he prefers performances which remove the film from reality. Given capable actors like George C. Scott or Jack Nicholson, Kubrick forced them by repeated takes to abandon naturalism for mannerism and hysteria. A protean actor like Peter Sellers, who stuffed half a dozen characters into a single film, and an abysmal one like Carey, who always played himself, gave the same distancing effect.

Kubrick had a soft spot for Carey, a New York contemporary of his, though from Brooklyn, not the Bronx. The gangling Carey bluffed his way into the Marines at fifteen and, after demobilisation, joined the thousands of dissatisfied young men milling around New York in search of artistic fulfilment. He took advantage of the GI Bill to study drama, and agent Walter Kohner got him bit parts in Billy Wilder's *The Big Carnival* and Laslo Benedek's *The Wild One*. These led to a role for Carey as the brothel bouncer Joe in Elia Kazan's version of *East of Eden* opposite James Dean.

None of this experience refined Carey's technique, which always hovered somewhere between Elvis Presley and Lon Chaney Jr. On *Paths of Glory*, he could never remember to tear into his last meal of roast duck the same way twice. 'Every take required an untouched duck,' says Kubrick. 'I think we used up sixty-eight or so ducks

before we got it right.' Kirk Douglas despised such unpro-
fessionalism, which may have been why Kubrick insisted on flying
Carey to Germany for the film. During the court-martial scene,
when Douglas was making his disgust at Carey's bad acting obvious,
Kubrick whispered, 'Make this a good one, 'cause Kirk doesn't like
it.'

In the original of *Paths of Glory*, Humphrey Cobb used his victims to confront readers with the moral dilemmas of capital punishment. Each of the men to be killed is chosen by a different method:
one by pure chance, by drawing lots; another in a naked piece of
chicanery, when Roget takes the opportunity to nominate the only
witness to his cowardice under fire; and the third systematically, on
the basis of the condemned's social value.

The Captain making this third choice narrows it down to two
men: Meyer, a syphilitic, drug-addicted child-murderer; and Ferol,
a mentally deficient alcoholic with a criminal past. Entering into
the spirit, his Adjutant points out that Meyer, with his infectious
disease, is the greater threat to society, but the Captain chooses
Ferol, for fear that shooting Meyer would revive memories of the
Dreyfus Affair, in which a Jewish officer was blamed for espionage
actually committed by a gentile with impeccable aristocratic connections. After this lapse, the mask slips to reveal even more prejudice,
as the Captain muses that he'd really like to choose 'a man in the
ranks who had high connections – really high, like GHQ, or who
was a deputy or something. I'd have picked him out of pure
mischief . . .' In war, all paths lead to the same insanity.

As an ironist, a fatalist and a chess player, Kubrick couldn't bring
himself to tell Cobb's story so schematically. To him, every narrative
plays out a game whose rules and limits are set before the first
move. People learn in the course of the game, but nobody can ever
learn enough to escape. In this sense, the happy ending he tried to
impose on *Paths of Glory* is entirely consistent with his philosophy:
live or die – it's all chance.

Kubrick had been flattered by critical comparisons between *The
Killing* and *Rashomon*, Akira Kurosawa's 1950 adaptation of
Ryonosuke Akutagawa's story 'In a Grove', which showed the rape
of a woman and the murder of her husband as seen in four conflict-
ing versions, including one offered by the dead man through a
medium.

Paths of Glory aims at the same non-deterministic story-telling. Unlike Cobb's book, the film blurs our sympathies. Mireau and Broulard, its villains, are the most interesting and attractive characters in the film, while the three victims are monosyllabic and unpleasant. Dax, far from being a hero, is an ineffectual armchair liberal who quotes Samuel Johnson on patriotism as 'the last refuge of the scoundrel' but, under pressure, acquiesces in the attack, assuring Mireau, not without an ironic reservation embedded in the remark, 'We'll take the Anthill. If any soldiers can, we can.' Cobb meant the executed men to be random victims of a soulless military aristocracy, but Kubrick implies that they were, as he'd told the *New York Times* interviewer, 'doomed from the start', like all soldiers. As Mireau passes along the trenches before the attack, stopping to mouth the same jovial inanities to his men, three of those with whom he speaks, apparently at random, are Paris, Ferol and Arnaud, the eventual scapegoats.

Such devices lifted *Paths of Glory* out of the Hollywood pattern. They served notice of the fact that Kubrick was aligned with neither the commercial film-making of Hollywood nor the art-house cinema of Europe. He would never cut himself off from the mass market represented by Hollywood, but equally, he refused to acquiesce in making the sort of film that market demanded. When he returned to Hollywood with the finished film late in 1957, he remained, mentally, in Europe. As a reminder, he had Christiane Harlan and Katharina, her three-year-old daughter from a previous marriage, with whom he settled down in Beverly Hills. The following year, after the divorce from Ruth, Christiane became his third wife.

In retrospect, *Paths of Glory* has proved more interesting as a technical exercise than as polemic. Winston Churchill would later observe that it came closer than any other film to catching the mood of World War I. It was a carefully diplomatic remark which, while acknowledging the film's skill, avoided commenting on its power as anti-war propaganda, which isn't that strong.

In its wake, some American directors tried to film the only similar incident in more recent US history, the sole American military execution of World War II for cowardice, that of Private Eddie Slovik; but no studio would fund a version of William Bradford Huie's account of the event, *The Execution of Private Slovik*. Carl

Foreman based an incident in his flaccid 1963 *The Victors* on Slovik, but almost everyone rightly excoriated as crass his decision to accompany the snowbound death by firing squad with 'Have Yourself a Merry Little Christmas'. Compared to such bludgeoning irony, *Paths of Glory* gradually came to be acknowledged everywhere as the American screen's most elegant and concise depiction of militarism unmediated by morality, if not a particularly passionate one, as well as the first film to show Stanley Kubrick as a master film-maker.

Chapter Eight

Kubrick and the Ten-Foot Kangaroo

> 'I beat the army by being declared psycho-neurotic.
> They thought I was crazy. When I filled in their forms,
> under "Race" I wrote: "Human." Under "Colour": "It
> varies." '
>
> Marlon Brando

In the early spring of 1957 director Richard Fleischer, on his way
to Bergen in Norway where he was preparing *The Vikings*, had
called at Geiselgasteig to see his producer and star Kirk Douglas.
Anxious to lift the film above the level of the average epic, Fleischer
had commissioned a script in modified blank verse which, he felt,
conveyed the heroic nature of Viking history better than the original
screenplay, adapted by Dale Wasserman from Edison Marshall's
novel. Fleischer recalled:

> The first night [in Munich] I had dinner with Kirk, Kubrick,
> James Harris ... and Calder Willingham ... They had all read
> the *Vikings* script. Their opinions were unanimous. The dialogue
> stank. Kubrick said that no actor could speak those lines, and
> they all agreed, including Kirk. I was dumbfounded.
>
> I argued my position throughout dinner that they were dead
> wrong, all of them. It was pointless, however. As far as Kirk
> was concerned it was a *fait accompli*. I hadn't actually realised
> that was so until he told me Calder Willingham was going to
> rewrite the dialogue. You know, get rid of the mystical crap,

make it more colloquial. Goodbye, semi-classic, hello comic book.

A few years before, Kubrick would probably have sided with Fleischer, but the punishing experience of making *The Killing* for United Artists and the mauling he and Harris endured at the hands of Ray Stark over *Paths of Glory* had forced him radically to revise his reverence for the cinema as Art. In any event, this had never been very deep. Profit always interested him, but independence interested him more. The ideal world was one in which he could have both.

This new perspective made him unsympathetic to people like Fleischer who harboured unrealistic expectations. After *Paths of Glory*, this perception followed Kubrick back to California, along with his new family and a small black Mercedes, the first of half a dozen high-performance German cars he was to own over the next three decades. He was ready for a decisive move into the next part of his career.

Paths of Glory opened in a Broadway cinema, without intentional irony, on Christmas Day 1957; all films did a little better over the holiday period, and UA thought this one needed all the help it could get. Kubrick had cut a few minutes since his first edit, removing details of how the three men were chosen, and abbreviating their arguments while waiting for death. If anything, the slight jerkiness imposed by the trimming added to the film's immediacy. We are not so much led to an inevitable dramatic climax as jolted down the road to execution like condemned men on a tumbril, an effect increased by Kubrick's pioneering use of overlapping sound, so that the clatter of a motorcycle or the boom of artillery fractionally precedes the scene it should accompany.

The film attracted welcoming if somewhat resentful reviews, as if Kubrick had no right to exhibit this spectre at the Christmas feast. With the three executed men more than ever ciphers after the last-minute cuts, most critics assumed the point of the film to be the cynicism of the French army high command rather than the insanity of war in general, and tut-tutted appropriately. In the *New York Herald Tribune*, Robert Zinsser agreed that, rather than condemning war, the film merely spotlit a lone atrocity. 'You may not believe that two such evil men [as Broulard and Mireau] could wield this power,' he wrote, 'or that French military justice could be so polluted. In this case, *Paths of Glory* will strike you as a narrow and unlikely drama.' The *New York Times*'s Bosley Crowther, a mouthpiece for Hollywood and never an admirer of Kubrick, wrote that the incident was 'so framed and isolated . . . that you are left with the feeling that you have been witness to nothing more than a horribly freakish accident'.

The French took a similar line, refusing to accept Kubrick's interpretation of the original episode, nor the implication that it typified their army command's battlefield behaviour in 1914–18. They were particularly incensed by Gerald Fried's ironic use of a stridently martial *Marseillaise* over the credits, the only tune in a score mainly consisting of drum ruffles and trumpet fanfares. Amid a predictable furore, the film was banned in France and Kubrick threatened, not very seriously, with criminal charges for having libelled the French high command and impugned the honour of France. It wasn't released there until 1976. The American Department of Defense also barred it from all US military bases.

During the European release, Kirk Douglas lunched with *Newsweek*'s film critic David Slavitt at the Four Seasons in New York. Douglas was furious that the French had pressured the Berlin Film Festival into refusing *Paths of Glory*, and continued to impede its Continental distribution. In his anger he crushed his wine glass. Blood spilled on the tablecloth. Slavitt reflected that everything Kubrick did seemed to raise passions.

Soon after the release of *Paths of Glory*, Harris and Kubrick were astonished to have a call from Marlon Brando, asking if they were interested in working with him.

Watching *The Killing*, Brando told the press after this episode had reached its bizarre conclusion, he'd been amazed that Kubrick 'could project such a completely distinctive style with so little previous film-making experience. Here was a typical, episodic detective story – nothing unusual in the plot – but Stanley made a series of bizarre and interesting choices which buttressed and embellished an ordinary story into an exciting film.'

Brando's approach to the partners disguised the fact that the star was in a state of near-panic. In the rush to climb on the bandwagon

with the independent producer/stars of runaway Hollywood, Paramount had given Brando's company Pennebaker Inc. a generous
mandate to find and develop projects. Instead, Brando ran up bills
for lavish restaurant meals and holidays with cronies like Carlo
Fiore, a drug addict whom he had met when they were both drama
students in New York. Fiore became his drinking and whoring
companion, as well as helping to satisfy Brando's taste for exotic-
looking women, usually actresses of mixed Asian, African-American
or Pacific Island blood. The fact that Brando was already married
to such a woman, the beautiful but incendiary Anna Kashfi, who
was pregnant with his child, was only a minor impediment.

By 1957, Paramount was weary of Brando's shenanigans, and
the IRS suspicious of his spending. Hurriedly he announced that
Pennebaker would back three films, all of them shot overseas,
though none starring him: *Shake Hands with the Devil*, with James
Cagney; *The Naked Edge*, a Hitchcockian mystery set in London
and destined to be Gary Cooper's last film; and *Paris Blues*, a story
about expatriate jazz musicians in Paris which Brando desultorily
considered starring in opposite Marilyn Monroe, but which was
made with Paul Newman, Joanne Woodward and Sidney Poitier.
Brando needed more projects, however, and Harris–Kubrick, young
and hungry, looked as if they might provide them.

Unaware of this subtext, the partners were flattered by Brando's
interest. He was among the world's most charismatic performers,
and as long as their relationship with Bryna was on hold while Kirk
Douglas shot *The Vikings*, there was no harm in talking.

For Kubrick, who until a few months before had moved from
one furnished room to another, carrying the box of books, the chess
set and the armful of clothes that were his only possessions, Brando's
275-square-metre Japanese-style hilltop house set in an acre of land
on Mulholland Drive, overlooking both Greater Los Angeles and
the San Fernando Valley, was a distinct step up. Once a trifle in the
multitudinous holdings of Howard Hughes, the house had been
refurnished to Brando's exotic taste, with highly polished hand-
fitted teak floors – all visitors had to remove their shoes – and
priceless furnishings from Tahiti, Japan and China. In the background Anna Kashfi smouldered, slamming doors on visitors and
looking for an excuse to escape from her marriage to Brando.

Any hopes that Harris and Kubrick might have harboured of

soon owning equally opulent houses themselves quickly foundered, however. Kubrick proposed a boxing picture, exploring the Terry Molloy character Brando created in *On the Waterfront* who 'coulda bin a contender'. Brando said he would prefer something more sensitive, and mentioned some books he'd bought, or that Paramount had bought for him. It quickly became clear that Brando had no idea what he wanted. By February 1958, meetings had receded to the level of occasional chats, and Harris and Kubrick were talking to Jim Thompson again about a new crime story.

After collecting rejections from a number of studios, Thompson had sent Kubrick his novel *The Getaway*. One of his best books, and destined to be filmed twice by Hollywood – once, notably, by Sam Peckinpah – *The Getaway*'s story of a wife who gets her husband out of prison by sleeping with a crooked lawman who wants him to pull off a robbery, and the couple's flight to Mexico after double-crossing and killing him, seemed to most studio readers flat and formulaic. Kubrick turned it down too.

Harris and Kubrick contemplated *The German Lieutenant*, a World War II film by Richard Addams as unsparing as *Paths of Glory*, but seen from the German side. However Brando was playing a similar role in the adaptation of Irwin Shaw's *The Young Lions*, and there was little enthusiasm from the studios. The same fate befell *The Last Parallel*, a novel of the Korean War by Martin Buss which they optioned. They even contemplated a TV comedy series starring Ernie Kovacs and based on the character he played in the film *Operation Mad Ball*, about the convoys of supply trucks that serviced the advancing Allied forces in Europe during World War II.

Meanwhile, another crime subject caught Kubrick's eye, though in this case the story, *I Stole $16,000,000* by Herbert Emerson Wilson, was true. Wilson was the archetype of the twenties gentleman safecracker. A former Baptist minister who emptied strongboxes and banks all over America, he'd had the *chutzpah* to take a course with the Mosler Safe Company before setting out to loot their products. Maintaining a lifestyle worthy of A. J. Raffles, Wilson always dressed for dinner and, when the police arrested him one Christmas in his mansion in Venice, California, was wearing a silk smoking jacket and reading Gibbon's *Decline and Fall of the Roman*

Empire while he waited for his staff to serve his turkey, chestnut stuffing and pudding.

UA agreed to underwrite *I Stole $16,000,000* if Bryna would take it under its wing, so Harris, after getting the green light from Kirk Douglas, visited Wilson, now retired in Mexico, where his companions included crime writers like the hard-drinking Georgiana Randolph, alias 'Craig Rice'. With the rights in his pocket, Harris commissioned a treatment from Lionel White, author of *Clean Break*. During the first half of 1958, Kubrick worked with White in turning this into a full screenplay called 'The Theft'. He showed it to Douglas, who didn't like it. Kubrick shrugged. 'I'll get Cary Grant,' he said. 'The Theft' remained on Bryna's books, however, a down-payment by Harris–Kubrick on what both partners glumly sensed could be a lifetime commitment to Douglas's swelling empire.

In May 1958, Brando unexpectedly rang Kubrick again. He asked for another meeting, this time without Harris. Over dinner, he pitched a new idea.

Almost two years before, in a mystical phase during which he would hand out copies of *Zen and the Art of Archery*, which he bought in bulk, he'd committed himself to doing a Western with Paramount. In 1956 he optioned a novel by frontier writer Louis L'Amour called *To Tame a Land*, and hired Niven Busch, author of *Duel in the Sun*, to write a script. Busch quickly realised that Brando hadn't read the book; he just liked its title, and the idea of an environmental Western, more about landscape than character. 'I think we ought to have . . . uh, the rivers and the woods,' Brando told Busch vaguely, rubbing his stomach under his shirt. 'The beautiful hills. And the wildlife.'

After three title changes – to 'Guns Up', 'Ride Comanchero' and 'A Burst of Vermilion' – 'To Tame a Land' had cost Paramount $500,000 and was no nearer to production. The project came to life again in 1957 when independent producer Frank P. Rosenberg read a review of a novel by Charles Neider, *The Authentic Death of Hendry Jones*, in the *New Yorker* and bought the rights for $25,000. After working with Rod Serling on an early draft, Rosenberg asked Sam Peckinpah, then an obscure TV director/writer, to script it.

A fanatic for the old West, Neider, who was born in Odessa, had intended to tell the story of gunfighter William 'Billy the Kid' Bonney and his death at the hands of his old confederate turned lawman, Pat Garrett. Garrett's own book, *The Authentic Life of Billy the Kid*, provided him with several incidents and even some dialogue. After months of research in New Mexico, Neider moved to Northern California, and was so impressed by its dramatic coastline that he decided to set the story there. His characters became 'Dad Longworth' and 'Hendry Jones', but in essence his legendary gunfighter, known simply as 'The Kid', is Bonney in all but name. The most original element of *The Authentic Death of Hendry Jones* is the setting, the rocky shores around Monterey.

The story of Billy the Kid and Pat Garrett fascinated Peckinpah as much as it did Neider, and he took the job for a meagre $3000. He spent six months restructuring and rewriting, and delivered the script in October 1957. Two days later, Rosenberg rang to tell a delighted Peckinpah that Brando was interested and wanted to meet him.

For three weeks Brando and Peckinpah met and talked over the script, and movie Westerns in general. 'Sam was as high as a kite,' said his wife. 'He really thought Brando could do a fantastic job with the character.' Rosenberg proposed a six-week rewrite, but Brando said the script was fine just as it was. After that, Peckinpah heard no more from Brando until March 1958, when the star rang and said he was now ready to buy the screenplay for $150,000. On 25 April, Pennebaker Inc. signed a deal with Rosenberg for a $1.8 million production – not including Brando's salary.

Behind all this was some ingenious double-dealing by Brando and his business manager Walter Seltzer. By acquiring a relatively cheap Western screenplay with a vague resemblance to *To Tame a Land*, they transformed the $500,000 already spent on the earlier project into script development money for 'Hendry Jones', thus placating Paramount. The studio was even happier when Brando suggested that the young and inexpensive director of *The Killing* and *Paths of Glory*, already well known for his economical methods, be placed in charge.

According to Carlo Fiore, his girl-finding crony, Brando had never heard of Kubrick, and it was Fiore who arranged the well-lubricated after-dinner screening of *The Killing* and *Paths of Glory* at the

Beverly Hills office of Brando's agency, MCA, which also fortuitously happened to represent Kubrick at the time. It was following this screening that Brando approached Kubrick with the offer to direct 'Hendry Jones'.

At his dinner with Kubrick, Brando described the project in an appealing light. He was committed to doing a Western with Paramount, and 'Hendry Jones' was as good a project as any other. If Kubrick would help him by getting it out of the way, the two could then develop something closer to their real interests.

Back at Mulholland Drive, Brando began to read out Peckinpah's script to him. After two pages, Kubrick stopped him and said he'd finish it at home. He called Harris as soon as he reached the end.

'I've just read this script,' he told him, 'and it's terrible. I don't know what to do about it. We don't want to rupture the relationship with Marlon. On the other hand, I can't do the script in its present form. So what do you think? Maybe what we can say is, "I'll do this, but only if you start over from scratch, with a new script."'

Kubrick saw that allying himself with Brando would give him the independence he craved as well as the clout of a major star at his back. It was the deal with Douglas on *Paths of Glory* all over again, but this time the star wanted *him*, not vice versa. True, it would mean ceding some independence to Brando. Nor would Harris be the film's producer. Harris acquiesced: 'We both agreed that it was good business for us to work with Marlon, but only if it was something Stanley was comfortable with.' Technically Harris–Kubrick was under exclusive contract to Bryna, but, as Harris is the first to point out, 'In Hollywood you can always make a deal.' Douglas, preoccupied with the European release of *Paths of Glory* and his preparations for *Spartacus*, agreed to release Kubrick to work with Brando, who rang Peckinpah at home on 12 May 1958 with the news.

Peckinpah's wife was there when he took the call. 'I went out of the room,' she said, 'and came back a little while later, and Sam was just sitting there on the bed, staring into space. I asked him what was wrong, and he said Kubrick had wanted to bring his own writer onto the project to do a rewrite of the script. Sam had been fired, just like that. It was over. He was devastated.'

Kubrick nominated Calder Willingham to rewrite 'Hendry Jones', encouraging him to rethink the story totally. Willingham joined the swelling meetings at the house on Mulholland Drive, where Kashfi still maintained a nervy presence. To mollify her, Brando suggested she play Dad Longworth's wife. Kubrick, whom Kashfi described as 'shy, taciturn [and] insecure', became, in her words, her 'watchdog. He followed me about for several days, taking notes on my actions and speech patterns. Only in the bathroom could I escape him.'

Kashfi fled to the pool, only to be driven away from it when Brando ordered his horsemaster Bill Gohl to provide ten horses for a street scene which Brando and Kubrick mocked up on the lawn to check camera angles. Rather than descend from the heights to Paramount's headquarters in the smog of Hollywood, Brando had costume designers visit the house for fittings. Under this pressure, and the knowledge of Brando's chronic philandering, the already unsteady Kashfi became hysterical and violent. Frank Rosenberg rented a small house near the corner of Gower and Melrose, and the meetings moved there.

Kubrick and Willingham tabled the new treatment, which, to Brando and Rosenberg, seemed full of holes. When Rosenberg voiced his concern, Willingham drawled, 'You gotta have faith in ma God-given gifts as a rahtah.' Unconvinced, Rosenberg persisted in his criticisms, until Brando took him aside and said, 'Why don't you give them a chance to see what they can do?'

Unused to film-making by committee, Kubrick was disoriented by events as they unfolded in the stuffy little house on Gower. To his surprise, Brando included Carl Fiore in the script discussions. Without directly giving credit to Fiore for having proposed Kubrick, Brando implied that his yes-man had played an important part in putting the film together. Kubrick didn't make an issue of it, except to tell Brando bluntly that he didn't want Fiore anywhere near the set once they started shooting. Brando was happy to agree, since he was increasingly unsure that he wanted to work under so assertive a director as Kubrick. He was no more enthusiastic about Calder Willingham, and was already rehearsing ways of replacing him with a more tractable and seasoned Hollywood writer.

At the end of one meeting, Fiore happened to pick up a pad on which Kubrick had been doodling all afternoon. He'd written, 'Carlo is a bright guy but he wastes a lot of time.' Fiore suspected

Kubrick had left it there on purpose. Despite this, he found Kubrick fascinating. 'He was always in motion,' he recalls, 'running his fingers through his hair, doodling on a pad, or diddling a loose bridge or shaky tooth at the back of his mouth. It was strange to see his New York pallor among the perpetual suntans of Hollywood; the Californians, synthetic and real, observed that his body had gone too long without exercise.'

'Hendry Jones' limped through the summer. Kubrick tried to keep his mind on it, but the second-hand nature of the material and the problems of working with the spiky Willingham and an indolent, evasive Brando didn't help.

In August, he became even more distracted when *Lolita*, Vladimir Nabokov's novel of a mild-mannered European professor's obsession with a twelve-year-old girl, was published in the United States.

Three years before, in the spring of 1955, publisher Maurice Girodias, working at the office of his Olympia Press in Rue de Nesle, a narrow sidestreet on Paris's Left Bank, had a call from literary agent Denise Clarouin. She wanted to drop around with a friend; they had something interesting for him. Clarouin arrived with a Russian woman, Doussia Ergaz. They had a book to sell, a novel by another Russian, Vladimir Nabokov, who lived in the United States and taught literature at Cornell University.

Girodias looked from one to the other. Perhaps Mme Clarouin, who specialised in selling French publication rights of prominent English-language authors, didn't realise that Girodias too was a specialist. He showed her his catalogue: *Amorous Exploits of a Young Rakehell* by Guillaume Apollinaire; Pauline Réage's sado-masochistic *The Story of O*; Henry Miller's *Sexus* and *Plexus*; the collected works of the Marquis de Sade. The names were often distinguished, but the content was erotic. Girodias was in the porn business.

The ladies smiled. Of course they knew M. Girodias's editorial policies. But this book was sure to interest him. Four American publishers had already turned it down, despite the fact that Nabokov (of whom Girodias had never heard) was widely published in Russian, German and English. And the theme, as he would see, was perfect for the Olympia Press.

Next morning, Girodias opened the first of the two typed volumes of Nabokov's manuscript. Idly he read the opening lines:

Lolita, light of my life, fire of my loins. My sin, my soul. Lo – lee – ta: the tip of the tongue taking a trip of three steps down the palate to tap, at three, on the teeth. Lo. Lee. Ta.
    She was Lo, plain Lo, in the morning, standing four feet ten in one sock. She was Lola in slacks. She was Dolly at school. She was Dolores on the dotted line. But in my arms she was always Lolita.

He began to get the drift. 'I evacuated all the papers surrounding my swivel chair and unplugged my telephone extension,' he recalled.
    Lolita purports to be the posthumously-published confessions of Humbert Humbert, who died in jail in 1952 while serving a term for murder and sexual offences involving a girl named Dolores Haze, whom Humbert christened 'Lolita'.
    Born in Paris in 1910 of a wealthy family and educated in the best schools, Humbert has the sexual tastes of any boy until, just before he turns thirteen, he falls in love with his slightly younger cousin Annabel. They never sleep together, and when Annabel dies a few months later, Humbert finds himself unable to forget her.
    The rest of the story has a tragic, though sweetly erotic, inevitability. After unsatisfying encounters with teenage prostitutes, Humbert gets a job in an American college, and rents a room in the house of the widowed Charlotte Haze and her daughter Dolores. Seeing Annabel reincarnated in Dolores, he marries Charlotte to be near her, and falls under the spell of this girl who seems to possess some mystic, almost diabolical power.
    In *Lolita*'s most crucial, but also most controversial passage, Humbert spells out his theory about such girls:

Between the age limits of nine and fourteen there occur maidens who, to certain bewitched travellers, twice or many times 9lder than they, reveal their true nature which is not human, but nymphic (that is, demoniac); and these chosen creatures I propose to designate as 'nymphets'.

Not all girls between nine and fourteen are nymphets, and there-fore fair game for Humberts. True nymphets, Humbert contends, are rare, and well aware of their power. It is they who do the seducing. And, having seduced, they move on complacently to charm other older men, as Lolita takes up with the writer Clare Quilty, whom Humbert jealously murders.

There was nothing new about the idea of pre-pubescent girls as seducers. Graham Greene for one had raised it in a 1937 review of a Shirley Temple film, *Wee Willie Winkie*. 'Infancy with her is a disguise,' he said of little Shirley, then just nine years old. 'Her appeal is more secret and more adult ... Watch the way she measures a man with agile studio eyes, with dimpled depravity. Adult emotions of love and grief glissade across the mask of child-hood, a childhood skin deep ... Her admirers, middle-aged men and clergymen, respond to her dubious coquetry, to the sight of her well-shaped and desirable little body, packed with enormous vital-ity, only because the safety curtain of story and dialogue drops between their intelligence and their desire.'

Twentieth Century-Fox sued for libel on Temple's behalf. They bankrupted the British weekly *Night and Day*, which published the review, and forced Greene, then a penniless novelist, to pay £1500 of the damages.

With *Lolita*, Nabokov raised Greene's 'safety curtain' with a vengeance, insinuating himself inside the kind of man who found Shirley Temple seductive. He spent pages describing the texture of Dolores' skin, her way of eating an apple, her by-play with a tennis racquet. Humbert almost faints when Lolita puts her legs across his, and has an orgasm when she, all unawares, plops briefly into his lap.

Lolita was hardly what the furtive tourist who bought other Girodias publications was looking for. The text was scattered with phrases in French, quotations from or tributes to James Joyce, T.S. Eliot and Edgar Allan Poe, references to butterflies (Nabokov was a collector and scholar of lepidoptera) and linguistic jokes: 'Vivian Darkbloom', for instance, Quilty's mistress, is an anagram of 'Vladimir Nabokov'. But Girodias decided there were enough steamy evocations of downy limbs and budding breasts to satisfy the punters. He'd taken flyers before, on Samuel Beckett and Henry Miller, and never regretted it.

Nabokov signed a contract in June 1955, and the book was published in September, in two paperback volumes, bound in the dark green card that had made the Olympia Press famous, or notorious, around the world. Once an inattentive US Customs Officer, apparently nonplussed by the book's elliptical language, had let through a copy stamped 'Passed for Publication in the USA', the Olympia Press *Lolita* was circulated in the United States, after which Putnam published a hardcover edition. The word 'nymphet' passed into the language, where it was widely misused as a synonym for any sexy young girl, a fact which was to cause problems for Harris and Kubrick.

Willingham was the first of the group to read *Lolita*, and he recommended it enthusiastically to Kubrick. Coincidentally, Harris had received notice of the novel through the *Kirkus Reviews* service, which circulates preliminary information on books likely to interest the media. He was halfway through the copy supplied by Putnam when Kubrick demanded to start reading it. Harris ripped the book in half and gave Kubrick the front section. Both found it fascinating, an interest that grew as the American press acclaimed it as an obvious masterpiece. If Harris noticed that the plot, of a seducer pursuing one member of a couple while actually interested in the other, bore a family resemblance to 'Burning Secret', he didn't mention it.

Nabokov, then teaching at Cornell, was represented in the US by Irving 'Swifty' Lazar, one of the canniest of agents. Shrewdly, Lazar set the rights at $150,000 for a two-year option, payable in two instalments. If, as he suspected, producers had trouble 'licking' the book, it could well be optioned three or four times. Once a producer did start shooting, however, the option became convertible to a downpayment to Nabokov against 15 per cent of the producers' profits.

By good luck, Harris and Kubrick, for the first time in their careers, could afford $75,000. *The Killing* had been quietly earning back Harris's investment and now stood at only $100,000 in the red. Assembling a package of films for television, United Artists asked if they could include it, even though, by contract, eighteen months remained of its cinema run. In return, UA were prepared to guarantee that, should the film fail to clear the outstanding $100,000, they would make up the shortfall. Harris was able to sell this promise, as negotiable as a banknote, for the down-payment on *Lolita*, which meanwhile had jumped from tenth position on the *New York Times* best-seller list to fourth.

For Nabokov, the movie sale not only represented his first chance of real money, but the fulfilment of a forty-year-old prophecy. In 1916 he'd inherited the fortune of his uncle Vasily, only to lose everything the next year during the Revolution. Nabokov claimed that his uncle appeared to him in a dream and told him, 'I shall come back to you as Harry and Kuvyrkin.' Nabokov always visualised 'Harry and Kuvyrkin' as a pair of circus clowns, but 'Harris and Kubrick' was so eerily like this phantom duo that he decided their offer was mystically endorsed.

Once they had the option on *Lolita*, Harris and Kubrick asked for a meeting with Geoffrey Shurlock, head of the Legion of Decency's Production Code Authority, Hollywood's self-censorship office. Without its approval, no film could be shown in the majority of American cinemas. Would the subject-matter of *Lolita*, they asked him, an older man having an affair with a twelve-year-old girl, fall under the Code's interdict of 'sex perversion or any inference of it'? Shurlock told them, 'Of course.'

Kubrick and Harris then, according to Shurlock's notes, 'countered with the suggestion that they would treat the novel so that the man was married to the girl in some state like Kentucky or Tennessee where such is legal. I agreed that this seemed to remove the element of perversion if this were a legal marriage. However, if the girl looked like a child, the effect might still be offensive to the point where we would not want to approve the picture.'

Harris and Kubrick assured Shurlock that the film wouldn't deal with the sexual relationship, 'but with the humour that arose from the problems of a mature man married to a gum-chewing teenager'. Shurlock remained uneasy. 'The novel itself seems to have aroused so much resentment and revulsion in so many quarters on account of its depravity,' he wrote in his notes on 18 March 1959, 'we felt there was a danger that no matter how well the rewrite was handled, a great deal of damage might be done to the industry and to the Code even before the film was released.' All this manoeuvring irritated, then depressed Kubrick. 'If I realised how severe the [censorship] limitations were going to be,' he said later, 'I probably wouldn't have made the film.'

*

During the *Lolita* negotiations, Kubrick and Willingham continued to wrangle with Brando over *The Authentic Death of Hendry Jones*, but with waning enthusiasm. When they got tired of discussing the script, the men played poker or dominoes. These games had more than recreational significance for Brando. Kubrick was being put through elaborate tests of *machismo* and expertise, not unlike those which he would impose on his own collaborators in later years. It was from Brando that he learned them.

One by-product of the poker games was the retitling of the script. It became *One-Eyed Jacks*, a Southern card-playing expression referring to the fact that the figures on some cards are full-face, others in profile. In some forms of poker, the one-eyed Jack becomes a 'wild' card, a clear reference to the shifting morality and renegade nature of the film's protagonists. 'You're a one-eyed jack around here,' Brando's character, renamed Rio, tells his rival Longworth, 'but I've seen the other side of your face.'

In September, Anna Kashfi left Brando, taking their son Christian, and filed for divorce. Gratefully, the star moved the script conferences to his now empty and peaceful house. Since he had to go barefoot to protect the floors, Kubrick opted for complete comfort and removed his trousers as well, habitually working in underpants, socks and shirt. Brando sat cross-legged on the floor, and when arguments became too heated, quietened everyone by hammering a giant Chinese gong.

There were plenty of opportunities for its use. By August 1958, only fifty-two pages of script were done, and everyone, Kubrick included, doubted that even those would work. Increasingly it was Brando's conception that dominated the film. Far from the edgy psychopath of Neider's book, Brando's character had become a plump, smouldering seducer in a Mexican *charro* costume, cutting a swathe through the bedrooms of the border country.

Jailed for five years after his pal Dad Longworth abandons him to the *rurales*, the Mexican police force, on a windswept hill in Death Valley following a robbery, Rio swears vengeance. Tracking him to Monterey, where he's married a Mexican widow and become Sheriff, Rio seduces Longworth's stepdaughter. After that, he's ready to go straight, but two confederates pull a robbery and Rio is blamed. Longworth flogs him publicly, smashes his gun hand with a rifle butt and drives him out of town. After a long recuperation by the crashing waves of a lonely beach, Rio rides back for a showdown.

Under pressure from Paramount, now $1.25 million in the red on the film, Brando announced that *One-Eyed Jacks* would start shooting in December 1958. Six months of wrangling had eroded what goodwill Willingham, Kubrick, Rosenberg and Brando once shared. With Fiore always voting with Brando, the balance of power shifted inexorably. Increasingly, Frank Rosenberg toadied to Brando. 'Now it was safe to show Kubrick how powerful he was,' said Fiore, 'and he did it by riding him in his strident voice at the story conferences.'

One such altercation ended with Rosenberg threatening to throw Kubrick out of the window.

'You're bigger and stronger than I am,' Kubrick said mildly, 'so if you want to fight, do you mind if I pick somebody to stand in for me – someone like Tim Carey?'

Brando laughed at the thought of Rosenberg squaring up to the hulking actor, who'd already been given a role in the film. He hammered his gong, and the moment passed.

Changes, however, were inevitable. Willingham was the first to be purged. Brando took him to dinner, fired him, and gave him as a parting gift the inlaid rosewood chess table on which they'd played so many games of poker at Paramount's expense.

To replace him, Rosenberg brought in Guy Trosper, an amiable old hand whom Brando recognised instantly as someone he could charm, and proceeded to do so. Kubrick and Fiore were less enthusiastic, not only because Trosper was plainly a journeyman with just a few routine gangster films and Westerns to his credit, but because, according to Fiore, he 'gave off a peculiar body odour, a sweet, sickly smell he himself was not aware of'. Nobody wanted to hurt Trosper's feelings by mentioning his problem, but Brando finally ordered him to buy some deodorant.

With the arrival of Trosper, Kubrick's position became untenable. Every decision, even relatively minor ones, escalated into a battle between the lone director and his increasingly hostile collaborators. One such disagreement erupted over publicity. Still in his heart a photographer, Kubrick suggested hiring Henri Cartier-Bresson to shoot a special series of stills on the film.

'Just think of all the publicity,' Kubrick coaxed. 'High-level stuff.

Cartier-Bresson on Brando. That kind of publicity is priceless. And it's all free. Can you imagine anything better?'

Brando refused. 'I want to feel free to tell a still photographer to split when I don't want to be photographed,' he told Fiore. 'I can't order an artist like Cartier-Bresson to stop snapping his shutter at me and get lost. It wouldn't be nice.'

Casting became the cracking point. Kubrick persuaded Brando to see some of his own favourites, including Slim Pickens, Ben Johnson, Tim Carey and Elisha Cook Jr, all of whom wound up in the film. However, Brando insisted on casting his co-stars, especially the women. Free of Kashfi, he prowled the ranks of Hispanic and Chinese performers, supposedly looking for exotic actresses to play Longworth's wife and daughter. He chose a frail, nervous Mexican named Pina Pellicer for the latter part, and was thinking of a few more old flames, including Kary Jurado and France Nuyen, for her mother. He finally chose Nuyen, and conveyed his decision to Kubrick, who was furious.

'She can't act!' he snapped. Brando shrugged his indifference; she was undeniably beautiful, and great in bed.

For Longworth, Kubrick suggested Spencer Tracy. Brando preferred the pedestrian character actor Karl Malden – who, he told an astonished Kubrick, had already accepted the part, and was drawing a salary. Kubrick suggested buying out his contract. Brando refused.

At this point, memories of events diverge, though everyone agrees that the final rift between Kubrick and Brando occurred during a conference at Brando's house in mid-November, with the start of shooting only a few weeks away.

According to Brando, Kubrick told him, 'Marlon, I don't know what this picture's about.'

Brando retorted, 'I'll tell you what it's about. It's about $300,000 that I've already paid Karl Malden.'

'Well,' Kubrick said, 'if that's what it's about, I'm in the wrong picture.'

At this point, Brando, according to Fiore, asked his crony, 'See if you can find out from Kubrick how he'd feel if he was fired.'

'I know damn well how he'd feel,' Fiore retorted, 'and so do you.'

'OK, but try to find out anyway.'

Fiore raised the question over dinner. 'Well, I don't know,'

Kubrick said thoughtfully. 'I guess I'd survive. I always have.' Brando took this as a green light.

Frank Rosenberg has a different account of the make-or-break decision, which he says took place during a script conference. 'Marlon kind of looked at me, and being the great actor he is – he doesn't do very much – he excused himself and went into the kitchen. The eye contact he made with me indicated he wanted me to follow him, so I did. We stood there in his long, narrow kitchen and he was patting his stomach. "We gotta get rid of Kubrick," he said. "I'd like to direct the picture myself."'

Brando's executive producer on the film, Walter Seltzer, has yet another version. According to him, Brando said of Kubrick, 'This guy is a fake,' and asked him to get rid of him. On 21 November Seltzer called Kubrick to the office of Pennebaker Inc. at Paramount and told him, 'This isn't working, Stanley.'

Fiore agrees the meeting took place, but says it was at MCA, and that Brando was also present. 'Stanley was so dumbfounded,' says Fiore, 'he could say nothing, and the silence stretched out into an embarrassed eternity, which Marlon broke.

'"This is like being in a room with a ten-foot kangaroo," he said. "Come on, let's get out of here."'

If Kubrick did appear astonished at being fired, it was probably a pose. He was too shrewd not to have seen this coming, with or without Fiore alerting him. He and Harris had formed a strong suspicion that Brando had meant the project to play out this way all along. Walter Seltzer agrees. 'My feeling, unsupported by anything but my gut, was that Marlon always intended to direct it.' Carlo Fiore later recounted a conversation in which Brando told him, 'This is *my* picture. *My* toy. And nobody's going to tell me who works in it and who doesn't. Nobody. I'm The Man.'

Kubrick accepted a reputed $100,000 to drop out. He would claim that his contract forbade him discussing the terms, and only issued a statement that he was leaving 'with deep regret because of my respect and admiration for one of the world's foremost artists, Marlon Brando'.

Once Kubrick was out of the project, Brando abruptly began to represent himself as infinitely malleable. He asked Henry Fonda if he'd be interested in playing Longworth. Not surprisingly, Fonda wasn't, and Malden came to seem the inevitable choice. He earned a whopping $400,000 for the role. In later years, the actor wryly described his luxurious West Los Angeles home as 'the house that *Jacks* built'.

Brando said he tried to persuade Elia Kazan, Sidney Lumet and four or five other directors to direct the film, but all refused. Only then, he said, did he decide to do it himself. But it's clear that Kubrick had never been more than Brando's stalking horse, a decoy to mask his true intentions. He might conceivably, if Kubrick had been willing to shut up and take orders, have made him technical advisor and co-director, but even that possibility is remote.

Brando's publicists later devoted a great deal of energy to depicting the star as a man forced to direct *One-Eyed Jacks* out of loyalty to the project. 'The decision to assume additional responsibilities was not easily arrived at,' said a press release. 'Fame or money alone has never meant anything to Brando; what has concerned him are the opportunities that this fame makes possible . . . "I have the obligation and the opportunity," he once said, "to try to communicate the things I think are important."'

Brando's decision perversely cheered Kubrick. He told Carlo Fiore he was 'relieved. If he had hired another director, it might have appeared that I was lacking in talent, or temperament, or something. But if Marlon directs it, it gets me off the hook.'

The excesses of *One-Eyed Jacks*, which wouldn't be released until 1961, became legendary. Brando's relish for scenes in which he's ritually mutilated and humiliated went back to *On the Waterfront*, and in *One-Eyed Jacks* he pulled out all the stops, offering $200 bonuses to extras for the most realistic reaction to his whipping. No longer constrained by anything but Brando's ego, Neider's monosyllabic teenage psychopath became a variation on the Napoleon who Brando had played in Henry Koster's version of Annemarie Selinko's bodice-ripper *Desirée* five years before. He'd always resented being forced to the margin of that story by co-stars Jean Simmons and Merle Oberon, but there was no such risk here. Rio is almost never off the screen.

Running 141 minutes, the $6 million film showcased VistaVision, Paramount's answer to Fox's CinemaScope. Since the film ran horizontally through the camera, giving a much wider frame which demanded less magnification, the system offered superior clarity and colour, encouraging the shooting of scenery for scenery's sake. Brando, seduced by his rushes, spent weeks by the Pacific with his crew on alert at $50,000 a day, waiting for sufficiently photogenic waves.

Charles Lang Jr's photography made *One-Eyed Jacks* a gorgeous visual experience, but its financial losses ended Brando's directorial ambitions for all time. No studio would ever again give him unlimited control of a feature budget. When, a few years later, he tried to turn Arthur Penn's *The Missouri Breaks* into a tract for his enthusiasm of the time, the plight of the Native American, Penn told him severely, 'Not at these prices, Marlon.' Content to become one of Hollywood's highest-paid performers, Brando abandoned the director's chair.

Of the five writers who worked on *One-Eyed Jacks*, only Guy Trosper and Calder Willingham receive screen credit. Sam Peckinpah recognised two scenes from his original script. 'Marlon screwed it up,' he said bitterly in the film's most cogent obituary. 'He's a hell of an actor, but in those days he had to end up as a hero, and that's not the point of the story. Billy the Kid was no hero. He was a gunfighter, a real killer.'

If it was any consolation to Peckinpah or Kubrick, Brando didn't remember his only film as director with any fondness. 'It was an ass-breaker,' he told *Rolling Stone* in 1975. 'You work yourself to death. You're the first one up in the morning . . . I mean, we shot that thing on the run, you know. You make up the dialogue the scene before, improvising, and your brain is going crazy.' He blamed the others, including Kubrick, who'd worked on the film. 'You get in a picture with six guys like that, it's like an old whore in a lumber camp who's been fucked till she can't see straight.'

Kubrick's separation from *One-Eyed Jacks* was fortuitous. On 27 January 1959, Kirk Douglas started shooting *Spartacus* in Death Valley under Anthony Mann. Six days later, Mann was fired, and Kubrick, with no script yet in sight for *Lolita*, agreed to replace him.

Chapter Nine

Kubrick in Chains

> 'The system under which writers work in Hollywood
> would sap the vitality of a Shakespeare. They are intelli-
> gent enough to know that they are writing trash, but
> they are not intelligent enough to do anything about it.'
>
> Dalton Trumbo

While Kubrick was finding his feet with *The Killing* and *Paths of Glory*, the landscape of international cinema had changed. By the end of the fifties, the test of a director, producer or star had become whether he could handle an epic. CinemaScope, launched in 1953 with *The Robe*, had in two senses flung wide the doors of Hollywood. Audiences became eager for its wraparound image and stereo sound, and American film-makers, aware that spectacle was one area where they could defeat TV, poured overseas in search of colourful settings and cheap facilities.

The epic's promise of huge returns would mesmerise Hollywood for almost a decade. It was a fascination Kubrick shared, and which has remained with him ever since. He knew he had the vision to make epics even before the means existed in Hollywood to do so. Every ambitious soldier is supposed to carry a field marshal's baton in his knapsack. Kubrick had an anamorphic lens.

During the gestation of *One-Eyed Jacks*, *The Vikings* had become a major hit for Bryna, grossing $15 million on its first release. Inspired, Kirk Douglas plunged boots and all into the epic business. He commissioned scripts for two more extravaganzas, *Montezuma* and *Spartacus*, with the latter, based on the 1952 novel by Communist writer Howard Fast about the gladiator who led a rebellion of slaves against Rome in 73 B.C., to be made first. In both cases, he would produce and star.

Douglas pitched *Spartacus* to United Artists, who told him they already had a film of Arthur Koestler's retelling of the Spartacus story, *The Gladiators*, in pre-production, with Yul Brynner and Anthony Quinn, under director Martin Ritt. Unstoppable as ever, Douglas took *Spartacus* to Universal, and persuaded them to invest in it so heavily that Ritt and UA realised their film would be eclipsed. They offered to amalgamate the productions, but Douglas refused. Brynner, humiliatingly, was required to wire Douglas his admission of defeat.

Bryna moved into one of the coveted 'bungalows' on the Universal lot, premises lip-smackingly described in a celebratory brochure as having 'five offices, thick carpets, oil paintings on the walls and two chic secretaries ... The executives sit behind large walnut desks, each with two phones and a name plate.'

Douglas himself had no office and no desk. 'Such things,' he said airily, 'impede creative accomplishment.' He had every reason to stay away from Universal, since *Spartacus* was in trouble from the start. Though he owned the rights to Fast's book, he had no screenplay. A script commissioned from Fast himself was, according to Douglas, 'a disaster – unusable. He hadn't used the dramatic elements he'd put in his own book. It was just characters spouting ideas; speeches on two legs.'

This could hardly have come as a surprise. Fast's book was a piece of Marxist historiography, contrasting the rival visions of mankind held by Spartacus, the unlettered immigrant slave, and therefore archetypal humanist, and his nemesis Crassus, the culti-vated, decadent and ambitious Roman general and potential dic-tator, to whom slaves are simply 'tools', just one remove from domestic animals. Much of what is good in the film would come from Arthur Koestler's more detailed and sophisticated account of the Spartacus story.

In his memoirs, Douglas has enshrined his version of how the screenplay of *Spartacus* was written. According to him, he decided the only person fit to do the script was Dalton Trumbo, most famous of the so-called 'Hollywood Ten', the group of left-wing writers and producers who had elected to go to jail for contempt of

Congress rather than respond to questions about their politics put
to them by the House UnAmerican Activities Committee during its
inquiry into alleged Communist influence on Hollywood.

Trumbo and the rest of the Ten, along with hundreds more
writers, directors, technicians and performers with real or fancied
left-wing sympathies, were covertly blacklisted by the film and TV
industry. Writers were more fortunate than performers or directors,
in that they could continue to work under pseudonyms or through
'fronts' who took credit for their scripts. Trumbo, once Hollywood's
highest-paid and most prolific scenarist, became also the busiest of
the blacklisted group, writing eighteen screenplays, including two
Oscar-winners, *The Brave One* and *Roman Holiday*, from Mexican
exile. He needed to. His fee had plummeted from $75,000 a picture
in 1949 to less than a quarter of that on the blacklist which, though
McCarthy had been publicly repudiated by President Eisenhower
in 1954 and died in 1957, was kept in force by a coalition of
right-wing ideologues who continued to threaten massive boycotts
of films which employed known Communists or their sympathisers.

Fast and Trumbo were as fundamentally opposed as only supporters of the same creed can be. Fast thought Trumbo a cocktail-
party Communist. Trumbo regarded Fast, who criticised him for not
holding classes on Marxism for his fellow prisoners while serving his
ten months in prison in Ashland, Kentucky, as a fanatic.

Knowing that Fast would pull out of the project once he heard
Trumbo was involved, Douglas ironically employed the strategies
of the blacklist and used his line producer Edward Lewis as a front,
telling Fast that Trumbo's script was by Lewis, but paying Trumbo
under the pen name 'Sam Jackson'. In Douglas's version, this subterfuge continued until, weary of the hypocrisy, he left a pass at the
front gate of Universal in Trumbo's name. 'Thanks, Kirk, for giving
me back my name,' Trumbo told him. 'The blacklist,' Douglas wrote
portentously, 'was broken.'

In truth, Trumbo's name appeared on *Spartacus* out of the most
cynical of manipulations. When Douglas launched Bryna in 1955,
his lawyer Sam Norton had urged him to make use of the black
market in scripts; it was good business. By March 1959 Bryna had
five prominent blacklisted writers on retainer at bargain rates: Ring
Lardner Jr, Paul Jarrico, John Howard Lawson, Mitch Lindemann
– and Trumbo.

Trumbo was never Douglas's first choice to write the film. Dreaming of a prestigious name, he approached Dudley Nichols, Lillian Hellman, Irwin Shaw and Maxwell Anderson, all unblacklisted but with impeccable liberal credentials. After they turned it down and the job passed to Trumbo, Douglas intended that one of them would still take the screen credit.

Douglas exploited his team of undercover writers still further by trading off their already reduced fees in return for the promise of legitimacy. As Trumbo explained, 'Someone had come up with the idea of suggesting to Douglas he use one of the black market people openly. He declared himself willing to do this. The idea would be that whoever broke away as the first writer [to get screen credit] would work practically for expenses – that is, for say $5000 or $7500 – for the concession that his name would appear on the screen. If, when the release date arrived, bankers or distributors caused too much trouble, the producing company would have the right to take the name off, but would compensate the author handsomely for the lost credit.'

Trumbo was proposed as guinea pig. Not on *Spartacus*, however; its $12 million budget didn't permit such a gamble. The film Douglas chose was a low-budget adaptation of Edward Abbey's *The Brave Cowboy*, to be called *Lonely are the Brave*, in which he would play a disaffected rodeo rider who makes a lone protest against the industrialisation of the West. Even if the film was boycotted by bastions of conservatism like the veterans' organisation the American Legion, any loss would be negligible.

This plan began to fall apart as *Spartacus* edged closer to production, and it became clear that it, and not the Abbey film, would be the first Trumbo script to go before the cameras for Bryna. Douglas's hand was further forced in March 1959 when Walter Winchell, a willing mouthpiece for anti-red propaganda, published the news of Trumbo's involvement in *Spartacus* in his column, even naming Trumbo's fee: $50,000. Bryna refused to admit that it was employing Trumbo, but it became increasingly difficult for them to deny him his credit.

Douglas claims that it was Edward Muhl's administration at Universal which decreed that the studio-appointed director Anthony Mann wasn't right to direct *Spartacus*, and demanded his firing. 'I balked,' wrote Douglas, 'not prepared for this sudden shift. I hated making a change when we were already shooting. A commitment is like a marriage; you try to make it work. You don't get a divorce immediately. I tried to keep him. Besides, who could I get to replace him? But they were adamant; they wanted him fired. On Friday 13, 1959 I sat down with Anthony Mann. It was not easy.'

In fact it was Douglas who most wanted Mann off the film. The fact that he was Universal's nominee was sufficient reason to dislike him, but the two men never got on. Douglas consistently bad-mouthed Mann. 'I like people who come up with ideas to make things better,' he said. 'Mann had very little to say. He seemed scared of the scope of the picture.'

The reality was exactly the reverse. Douglas preferred directors who said nothing and obeyed orders. Nor would Mann, who preferred understated performances, tolerate Douglas's overplayed acting. As for his supposed inability to handle epics, Mann later made *El Cid* and *The Fall of the Roman Empire*, regarded today as benchmarks of the genre for their visual style and understated playing.

Douglas had other reasons to resent Mann. He felt the director was too friendly with the film's imported British stars, all of whom were scornful of Douglas's star status and bridled at his hectoring manner. Laurence Olivier, who played Marcus Lucinius Crassus, had alarmed Douglas the year before by suggesting, when Douglas offered him the role in London, that he, Olivier, both direct the film and star as Spartacus. Charles Laughton, cast as Gracchus, the main opponent of Crassus on the benches of the Roman senate, was a self-pitying masochist who saw slights and insults in the least offensive situation, and recoiled from the bullying Douglas. His rivalry with Olivier was exacerbated by the inequality of their salaries. Laughton's $41,000 was embarrassingly closer to the $35,000 paid to newcomer Sabina Bethmann than to Olivier's whopping $250,000.

Most difficult of all for Douglas to deal with was Peter Ustinov. Playwright, director, novelist, linguist, *bon viveur* and inspired mimic, Ustinov, who had interrupted the US national tour of his play *Romanoff and Juliet* to appear in the film, was cast as Lentulus Bataitus, the *lanista* or gladiator entrepreneur who plucks Spartacus from the salt mines and trains him for the arena.

Word got back to Douglas of Ustinov joking at Hollywood parties that, on Douglas's pictures, 'You have to be careful not to act too well.' His favourite party piece was a description of the first read-through of the script at Douglas's home. Olivier wore his most comfortable Savile Row three-piece, Ustinov a loose cotton suit and Laughton, in a perfunctory gesture towards character, a bathrobe. All were astonished when Douglas threw open the door in full costume as Spartacus. While the three Britons sat under a lemon tree in the garden with their scripts, suppressing their giggles, Douglas bounded and sprang around in his abbreviated toga and sandals, waving a sword.

Douglas was furious at being mocked, but Ustinov, who relished the power game of the production – 'As full of intrigue,' he crowed, 'as a Balkan government in the good old days' – soon insinuated himself into the good graces not only of his fellow stars but also of Anthony Mann, to whom he proposed a few changes to his own role. Mann accepted most of them. 'He was taking every suggestion Peter made,' Douglas complained. 'The suggestions were good – for Peter, but not necessarily for the picture.'

Mann took Ustinov to meet Dalton Trumbo, then still cloaked as 'Sam Jackson', at his Pasadena home. Sitting in his bath with his typewriter on an improvised worktable, a glass of bourbon beside it and a parakeet on his shoulder, Trumbo made an engagingly baroque sight. After the meeting, Ustinov, who thought Bryna's 'masquerade [about screen credit] too ludicrous for words', began signing his memos to Douglas 'Stonewall Ustinov' – a sly reference to the Confederate General Thomas Jackson, who earned the nickname 'Stonewall' by his resistance to the Union forces at the battle of Bull Run. Douglas took this as further proof that his stars, led by Ustinov, were close to open revolt.

Trouble was not long in coming. Laughton's biographer Simon Callow claims that Douglas had assembled his cast by 'sending each [actor] a version of the script in which he, or she, appeared to have the largest, most interesting part'. There's no evidence of this. Rather, since the actors were contracted at different times and for different periods, each probably got the current version of a constantly changing script.

A few weeks before shooting was to begin, Laughton protested bitterly to Mann at what he saw as the erosion of his role. He was getting ready to play *King Lear* on stage in London for the first time, and was nervous about attempting this Everest in the career of any classical performer. His indecisiveness affected his view of Gracchus, whom he decided was too weak, and was becoming more so as Trumbo rewrote the script, shifting the weight of the story towards Crassus and Spartacus. Olivier, for his part, was using his role as Crassus to hone a forthcoming stage performance as Coriolanus, which made him more than usually commanding and peremptory.

Trumbo paid a courtesy call on Laughton at his home to discuss the problem, but found the actor difficult to deal with. It was Ustinov whom Mann finally asked to work with Laughton and Olivier on striking a better balance between their roles. Ustinov rewrote and rearranged some of their lines, making Douglas even more furious.

Shooting began on *Spartacus* with this time bomb waiting to explode. On the first day, Mann drew Douglas aside after an early take in which Spartacus mauls a fellow worker in the salt mines with his teeth, and told him he found his slavering animal intensity false.

'If you see him as a mongoloid idiot, a Neanderthal ape,' said Mann, 'how do you expect the audience to believe the slaves would follow you to the death? Play him with a spark of decency, of humanity.'

'I prefer to do it *now* like an ape,' said Douglas, 'and *later* like a human being.'

But Mann continued to criticise Douglas's performance for the rest of the first week.

After each day's filming an air-conditioned grey Lincoln Continental drove Douglas back to the Furnace Creek Inn where the stars stayed on location. At the end of the week, the star offered a ride to Ustinov and William Read Woodfield, the stills photographer who had been with him on *The Vikings*. Halfway back to the hotel, Douglas startled both by blurting out to them, 'I need a new director. It's not working out.'

Woodfield couldn't understand why Douglas wanted a change. 'The stuff we were shooting was pretty innocuous; Kirk chopping at stuff – he's supposed to be in a salt mine – and Peter going by on a mule, trying to buy slaves. Filming it, [Kirk and Mann] didn't seem to be fighting, or anything like that.'

Ustinov's emotions can only be imagined. With Mann gone, his position on the film would be seriously undermined. Like any actor in his position, he sought to cover himself by proposing replacement directors with whom he could get on.

'Peter seemed to understand Kirk's feelings,' said Woodfield. 'He brought up Carol Reed and David Lean.' The year before, Douglas had asked Lean to direct *Spartacus*, but he'd been too busy with *The Bridge on the River Kwai*. Now, according to Woodfield, Douglas said, 'I don't want a goddamn Englishman.'

Woodfield claims it was he who proposed Kubrick. 'Why don't you get the guy who directed the best picture you ever made?' he suggested. 'Kubrick.'

'Because he's an ingrate,' Douglas replied. 'I made that picture for him at a loss, and then I asked him to do something for me, and he refused.' Presumably he was referring to Kubrick's manifest lack of enthusiasm for doing more Bryna projects about which he felt no commitment. However, the idea grew on Douglas, and after firing Mann on Friday he rang Kubrick and asked if he could take over *Spartacus* from Monday. After a weekend of meetings, Kubrick agreed, for a fee of $150,000.

In part, Kubrick did *Spartacus* to extricate Harris–Kubrick from its commitment to Bryna. Jimmy Harris says:

> We'd already started negotiating [to leave Bryna], and we'd got to the point where Kirk might release us if we agreed to give him the lion's share of any films we made on our own. But our next film is going to be *Lolita*, which by this time has climbed to the top of the best-seller list – only to be bumped by *Dr Zhivago*. We had this top *top* best-seller in our pocket – and Kirk has our next picture. So when he asks Stanley to do *Spartacus*, we figure that here's a chance to get him to waive *Lolita*, and pick up some money too on a loan-out arrangement for Stanley.
>
> So I met with Kirk, and it was obvious he didn't think we'd ever get *Lolita* made. He was only too happy to waive any participation to get Stanley.

Kubrick in 1951, on location for his first feature, *Fear and Desire*, in the forests of northern California.

Fear and Desire (1953). *Clockwise:*
Kubrick and his first wife Toba on
location in California.
Virginia Leith, the film's female lead,
in a provocative publicity still taken
by Kubrick.
Joseph Burstyn's strident publicity for
the re-release of the film with Buñuel's
El Bruto.
The *Fear and Desire* unit: front row:
actors Kenneth Harp, Steve Coit, Paul
Mazursky and Frank Silvera; middle:
the anonymous Mexican grips;
standing: Chet Fabian, Herbert
Leibowitz, Steve Hahn and Stanley
and Toba Kubrick.

Jamie Smith and Frank Silvera battle amid the shop-window dummies in the action climax of *Killer's Kiss* (1955).

Right: A masked Sterling Hayden leads the racetrack robbery in *The Killing*.

Timothy Carey in the first of many appearances in Kubrick's films, as the marksman Nikki Arano in *The Killing* (1956).

Right: Kubrick (left) and his partner James B. Harris with Kirk Douglas during the shooting of the court-martial scene of *Paths of Glory* (1958).

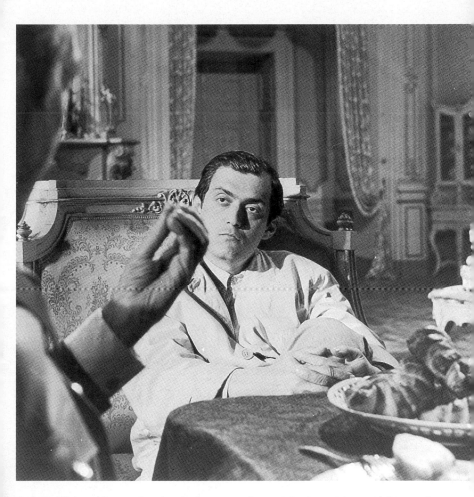

Left: Kubrick on the set of *Paths of Glory* with Kirk Douglas and actress Suzanne Christian, *née* Christiane Harlan, later his second wife.

Above: Kubrick receiving, with his usual impassivity, Adolphe Menjou's complaints about his role as General Broulard.

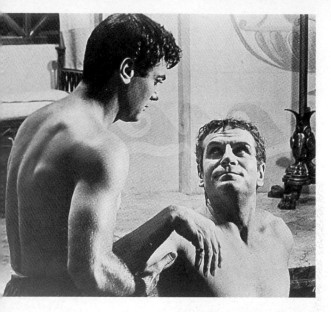

'Snails or oysters; it's just a matter of taste.' Laurence Olivier as Crassus propositions his body slave Antoninus (Tony Curtis) in the sequence deleted from *Spartacus* (1960).

'Stanley Kubrick is a talented shit.' Producer/star Kirk Douglas tries without success to talk Kubrick round to his vision of *Spartacus*.

Once his hands were free, Harris felt able to put more projects into the pipeline. Saul Bellow had just published his novel *Henderson the Rain King*, and Kubrick thought this story of a white man who becomes chief of an African tribe might make a good film, but Gavin Lambert talked him out of it. While Kubrick was busy on *Spartacus*, Harris hired Jim Thompson in May 1959 for twenty weeks at $300 a week to rewrite Lionel White's script of *I Stole $16,000,000*. Working at his usual furious rate, Thompson finished in three weeks, and delivered the screenplay on 1 June. Kubrick suggested some changes, and Thompson started on them, only to collapse with a stroke. Harris–Kubrick continued to pay him throughout his illness. However, it was clear that not only would he probably never write again, but that *I Stole $16,000,000* too greatly resembled *The Killing* to interest either Kubrick or a Hollywood obsessed with epics.

Towards the end of a stifling July, Vladimir and Vera Nabokov arrived in Los Angeles, where Harris had checked them into the Beverly Hills Hotel. Kubrick was too busy to spend much time with them, but Harris raised the idea of Nabokov writing the screenplay of *Lolita*. He refused. He had begun to see that bringing his novel to the screen through a Hollywood company would involve drastic reorganisation and compromise, neither of which appealed to him. Once the Nabokovs left for the cooler air of Lake Tahoe, Calder Willingham was hired to write a script.

As if to immediately establish Kubrick's secondary function on *Spartacus*, Douglas chose to introduce him to the unit on the set of Ustinov's gladiator school, where almost all the cast was gathered. From their dais overlooking the arena, Olivier, Ustinov, John Dall, Nina Foch and Joanna Barnes, all playing thrill-seeking Romans, looked down sceptically at their new director. 'It was a funny scene,' Douglas recalled. 'Here was Kubrick with his wide eyes and his pants hiked up looking like a kid of seventeen. You should have seen the look on their faces. It was as if they were asking, "Is this some kind of joke?"' It was a strategy that rebounded on Douglas, since Kubrick was soon taking charge of any part of the film that wasn't nailed down.

Concerned that middle-aged men dominated *Spartacus*, Dalton Trumbo had written in the role of Antoninus, a young slave who becomes the friend and confidant of Spartacus; current romantic heart-throb Tony Curtis, who still had one film to make at Universal under an old contract, got the role. Varinia, Spartacus's wife, was being played by a twenty-seven-year-old German blonde, Sabina Bethmann, in her first film, after Ingrid Bergman, Jeanne Moreau, Elsa Martinelli and Jean Simmons had turned the part down. Making up the rest was a legion of character performers battle-scarred in the Hollywood wars: John Ireland and Harold J. Stone as gladiators, Charles McGraw as the overseer of Ustinov's school, and John Gavin as a wooden young Julius Caesar. The only surprise among this group was Woody Strode, the commandingly tall black actor whose duel with Douglas is one of the high points of the film.

Changing the director didn't disguise the major problem of *Spartacus*. 'It had everything but a good story,' Kubrick decided. Since the total known facts about the slave revolt scarcely filled ten pages, there was a great temptation to fall back on invented sub-plots. The first third of the film is the strongest. Toughened by the salt mines of Libya, Spàrtacus is taken to Capua, trained as a killer by Batiatus, and even given a woman, Varinia, with whom he falls in love. When a group of patrician Romans drop by at the school, they ask to see a fight to the death. Spartacus is matched against the giant Ethiopian, Draba, who refuses to kill him when he has him netted. Instead Draba attacks the dais where the guests sit, and one of them, Crassus, kills him. Angered, the slaves revolt, and take to the slopes of Mount Vesuvius, where they are soon joined by ninety thousand more, a mob which Spartacus, a natural general, turns into an army.

After this, the focus of the film moves to Rome, where Crassus demands the position of dictator in return for crushing Spartacus. Gracchus, a liberal senator representing the Roman in the street, and standing for the traditional balance of power between army and state, opposes him.

Trumbo's socialism takes over once more when Spartacus decides to fight his way to the sea and leave Italy with his army. He makes a deal with some Cilician pirates through their slippery representative, Tigranes, but is double-crossed when Crassus, who needs to defeat Spartacus in order to establish his claim to power, bribes the pirates to renege, stranding the slave army with its back to the sea. In the ensuing battle, all but six thousand of the slaves are killed. Crassus crucifies the survivors along the Appian Way between Rome and Capua.

Spartacus is captured but not identified. All the slaves who survive loyally claim to be him. Crassus decides to confirm his suspicions by forcing Douglas into a fight to the death with Curtis; surely the faithful lieutenant won't kill his leader. Even then Spartacus retains his incognito, until Crassus tells him that Varinia and his son are in his house, and Spartacus reveals himself. Antoninus lets his friend kill him, and Spartacus, his identity carefully disguised by Crassus, who prefers his fate to be left in doubt, is crucified with the rest. Varinia, fleeing Rome, pauses at the foot of Spartacus's cross to surreptitiously show him their child, after which she goes into safety and exile under the protection of Gracchus, a final gesture of triumph by the old liberal, who has committed suicide rather than live under the tyranny of Crassus.

From the start, Douglas and Trumbo were at cross-purposes on the thrust of the film. Douglas, a passionate supporter of Zionism and Israeli independence, wanted what film historian Derek Elley calls 'a Roman variation on the let-my-people-go theme'. Trumbo preferred to manufacture agitprop for his own socialism. He played down Spartacus and emphasised Crassus, whom he used to parody the American military-industrial complex. Politically powerful, militarily distinguished and privately wealthy, Crassus mouths the rabble-rousing rhetoric of the American far right with suave assurance. 'One day I shall cleanse this Rome which my fathers bequeathed me,' Crassus promises. To the remark 'Rome is the mob,' he responds fiercely, 'No, Rome is an eternal thought in the mind of God.'

The character of Crassus, as Olivier plays him, recalls Patton, MacArthur, even Joe Kennedy. 'The enemies of the state are known,' he informs Gracchus silkily at their midnight confrontation after his *putsch*. 'Arrests are in progress. The prisons begin to fill. In every city and province, lists of the disloyal have been compiled.' *I have in my hand the names of fifty-seven card-carrying Communists* . . .

Trumbo omitted from his adaptation anything that didn't accord with this vision. The historical revolt, which in the film appears to be a mass popular uprising that lasts for years, actually had limited support and was over in two. Spartacus led the revolt of the Capua school in 73 B.C., and was defeated in 71 B.C. Nor was he the plaster saint of the film. He slaughtered three hundred prisoners as revenge for the killing of his friend Crixus, and, to show his men what awaited them if they were captured, crucified a Roman soldier between the armies before a battle. Twice he led his army to the borders of Italy, and could easily have escaped. Each time, however, he turned them back to continue looting and destroying.

The script maligns Crassus correspondingly. He never schemed to take over the government. He was simply a wealthy ex-general when he defeated Spartacus, and never became dictator of Rome or anywhere else. Gracchus, a conflation of various members of the Gracchi family, didn't exist; the last of the Gracchi to lead the Roman plebeians died fifty years before the revolt. The greatest historical error of *Spartacus*, however, is the strong implication as the film opens that Spartacus laid the foundation for 'a new society' of Christianity – with, it is implied, no slavery. Slavery, of course, flourished in the Christian era, and in many parts of the world flourishes still.

Trumbo's deletions include elements of which Howard Fast made great play in his book. Some were true; for instance that Spartacus's body was never found. Others were fabrications, like the rumour that Crassus, true to his conviction that a slave was only a 'tool', sold the corpses of the crucified rebels for sausages. Trumbo replaced these with ideas cribbed from Arthur Koestler, including the device of Spartacus trying to embark his army on pirate ships, which appears only in *The Gladiators*.

An expert at having his cake and eating it, Douglas, at the urging of Universal, boasted to the press that *Spartacus*, which promised to be the most expensive film ever made, would stem the tide of runaway productions by shooting almost entirely in America. Only the battle scenes would be done in Spain. In fact he originally intended to shoot the whole picture in Italy, where the government film studio Cinecittà offered lucrative incentives. The first job of producer Edward Lewis had been to visit Rome and check out possible locations, but Universal's Ed Muhl made it one of the conditions of its involvement that the film be shot in Hollywood. Patriotism didn't come into it. He wanted his technicians and studio

KUBRICK IN CHAINS 135

facilities employed as much as possible, even if Bryna had to take pressure off his costume store and prop warehouse by importing statues, weapons, uniforms and aluminium armour from Rome. Muhl also insisted that *Spartacus* respect the Universal studio style, a bland plastic polish which characterised its feature films, TV episodes, even the trailers and advertising.

Throughout the spring of 1959, the second unit under Irving Lerner moved around California, picking up scenes in quasi-Roman locations. William Randolph Hearst's San Simeon doubled for Crassus's villa. Kubrick remained in Hollywood to shoot scenes like Varinia's recognition of Spartacus among a line of crucified men. Thousand Oaks stood in for the Appian Way. To make room for Rome, Universal bulldozed the old sets on which it had shot its money-spinners of the forties and fifties. The gladiator school was built on the site of the house occupied by Marjorie Main and Percy Kilbride, who played the hillbilly couple Ma and Pa Kettle in a series of cheap comedies, and the Forum shoved aside the streets where Abbott and Costello had clowned.

Kubrick later told American critic Gene Phillips, 'The script could have been improved during shooting, but it wasn't. Kirk was executive producer. He and Dalton Trumbo and Edward Lewis had it their way with the script and the casting.' The reality was that, as they worked, everyone, including Kubrick, tinkered with the script, by then into its seventh draft. Kubrick angered Douglas by cutting all but two of his lines from the first thirty minutes. 'We fought about that one,' Kubrick said, 'but I won.'

Despite the revelations in Walter Winchell's column of the year before that Trumbo had written *Spartacus*, Bryna stuck with the pretence that he had nothing to do with a film on which, he later estimated, he wrote a quarter of a million words. Kubrick did suggest at one point that, if they didn't want to credit Trumbo, they could attribute both direction and script to him. Douglas commented sententiously, 'Stanley's eagerness to use Dalton revolted us.' The bickering continued until, in January 1960, while *Spartacus* was still being edited, Otto Preminger stole what remained of the thunder Bryna might have gained from giving Trumbo credit by announcing that the writer's name would appear on screen in the credits of the forthcoming *Exodus*, to be released two months before *Spartacus*. Hollywood nervously awaited the American Legion's threatened national boycott of *Exodus*, but the protests were negligible. By the time Trumbo's name appeared on *Spartacus*, the parade had long since moved on.

One of Kubrick's first acts as director was to fire Sabina Bethmann, even though her costumes had already been fitted and she'd posed in them for stills with the other stars. Such peremptory dismissals were a feature of the big-time movie business. They represented a ritual marking-out of territory, a gesture, like the Roman slaughter of captured enemies in the Circus Maximus, signifying the destruction of the old order and its replacement by another. Whether Bethmann was a good actress or not was beside the point, but Douglas and Lewis did make mild demurs, mostly about the cost of replacing her. Kubrick agreed that, rather than dismiss her outright, they might discover if she had any talent by doing an improvisation.

'What sort of improvisation?' Douglas asked.

'We'll tell her she's just lost a part in a movie,' Kubrick said, straight-faced. 'Eddie can play the producer and you can be the film's star and executive producer.'

Lewis refused to co-operate, and left the room. Douglas stayed, though declining to play the role Kubrick suggested for him. In the event, he wasn't needed. Faced with the disaster Kubrick outlined, Bethmann froze. Jean Simmons, an earlier contender for the part, replaced her in a role which needed no more than the poised patrician primness in which she specialised. (Ironically, Bethmann's firing from *Spartacus*, richer by $35,000, persuaded *Life* magazine to run a feature story on her non-existent Hollywood career, a distinction it had never contemplated giving her when she was just another unknown.)

Uneasily, Douglas began to understand that Kubrick was not the tractable and grateful protégé he'd hoped for. This conviction hardened when he showed some rushes to Howard Fast. The novelist was delighted. How fortunate for Douglas to have found such a fine director on such short notice! Douglas was livid. *Spartacus* wasn't Kubrick's film; it was *his*. From then on, the tone of his remarks about Kubrick, even to the press for publication, was snide. Decades later, he was still grouching. 'Kubrick was never a big fan of this movie, which I resented. He never accepted it with any enthusiasm. He was someone used to having his own way, but this wasn't something initiated by Kubrick . . . the ship was sailing.'

Once *Spartacus* got rolling, Kubrick relaxed into his role, like a child, as Orson Welles had described directing, with the world's biggest and best train set at his disposal. Among his ambitions, he wanted to make this the most realistic of all epics, and a worthy successor to *Paths of Glory* in its unromantic vision of war. Make-up man Bud Westmore was given a free hand to invent the goriest effects. According to film historian Bill Warren, special effects technicians Rick Baker and Dick Smith asked Westmore what had been his most difficult job: 'Westmore surprised them by citing *Spartacus*. He said that Kubrick had wanted the film to be as grue-somely brutal as possible, in an attempt to turn people off war. Westmore said that he'd hired people with limbs missing, even one guy with part of his head missing, and made them up with the parts in place. The guy with the side of his head missing was slammed with a morning star or a mace, spilling calf brains down the side of his face. A guy with some kind of problem with his lower torso had a new one built, filled with real animal guts, which spilled out when he was slashed.'

The rate of shooting slowed as he began to lavish on each scene the visual imagination for which he was to become famous. Russell Metty, the director of photography supplied by Universal, fumed.

So did Douglas, who had to stand by as the director he had hand-picked made a gift of the film to his co-stars. The skirmishing between Crassus and Gracchus illustrated Kubrick's belief in the abiding evil at the heart of all power, and he missed no opportunity to explore it. He was helped by the continuing friction between Olivier and Laughton. Laughton found Olivier bombastic and aggressive. For his part, Olivier thought Laughton discourteous. When the time came to shoot the close-ups for their big scene, in which Crassus, by dead of night in a dimly-lit senate chamber, offers Gracchus his life in return for collaborating with his administration, Olivier asked Kubrick that someone other than Laughton feed him his lines.

Used to working on stage or on a smaller screen, Ustinov, Olivier and Laughton collaborated enthusiastically with Kubrick in most scenes, which they knew favoured their style. Kubrick said, 'I discussed this point with Olivier and Ustinov, and they both said that their powers were just drifting off into space when they were working out of doors. Their minds weren't sharp and their concentration seemed to evaporate. They preferred that kind of focusing-in that happens in a studio with the lights pointing at them and the sets around them. Whereas outside everything faded away, inside there is a kind of inner focusing of psychical energy.' Kubrick even introduced the practice, used in silent films, of playing 'mood' music on the set to stimulate the actors. Douglas, who was no music lover, and whose powers, far from drifting away outdoors, worked far better there, sensed – probably with justice – that Kubrick was intriguing against him with the other stars, and was furious.

Laughton, Olivier and Ustinov were all busy men, much in demand, and their commitments complicated the scheduling of *Spartacus*. Laughton could only spare three weeks, and Olivier had to be back in London by June. On top of this, bad health, accidents and tantrums dogged the production. Jean Simmons needed emergency surgery, and Tony Curtis was in plaster for weeks after he split an Achilles tendon playing tennis with Douglas, so a commitment of three weeks turned into nine months, during which he had time to make two other films. Ustinov squeezed in both the Los Angeles and San Francisco runs of *Romanoff and Juliet*, and completed a novel. He liked to joke that, when his son asked him what he did for a living, he told him '*Spartacus*.' Douglas himself, often late on the set, caught a virus that put him in bed for ten days. He also took Kubrick to see his psychoanalyst, in the hope that it would improve their relationship. It didn't.

Olivier's role was to become the most contentious in the film, mainly because of a scene in which Crassus, being soaped by Antoninus in his bath, reveals his bisexuality with a cumbersome metaphor about a preference for snails not necessarily debarring the appreciation of oysters. When he turns to what he hopes will be a complaisant sexual partner, the slave is long gone.

Olivier played up to his character with some camp behaviour on the set. According to his biographer Donald Spoto, the actor had only recently terminated a ten-year romantic relationship with Danny Kaye, part of a restructuring of his life during which he also sold his beloved home, Notley Hall, divorced Vivien Leigh and married Joan Plowright. One person on the *Spartacus* unit remembered, 'He wore this little skirt that he was always playing with, crossing his legs, pulling down his tunic and saying coquettishly, "A girl must keep her skirt down." He never made a pass at me, but he did clown around with some of the extras. In particular he became very friendly with a young black extra and spent a lot of time with him. Here was the greatest actor in the world, making absolutely no pretence at all, not masking the fact that he was at least bisexual.'

Olivier's inclinations amused the other stars. During the bath scene he asked Curtis, 'Tony, where do you get arms like that?'

Curtis said, 'Come with me,' led him behind the dressing rooms and told him, 'Get down on your face.'

Intrigued, Olivier acquiesced. Standing over him, Curtis grinned. 'You were worried, right?' he said, then got down beside Olivier and demonstrated the secret of his powerful biceps: push-ups.

Once Geoffrey Shurlock of the censorship authority saw the script, he questioned the bath scene. The Code's rules against 'sexual perversion' covered homosexuality, and Shurlock had already commented after reading the script, 'Any suggestion that Crassus finds a sexual attraction in Antoninus will have to be avoided ... The reason for Antoninus's frantic escape should be something other than the fact that he is repelled by Crassus's suggestive approach to him.'

Kubrick shot it as an overtly homosexual advance, but after a long argument in post-production, during which Shurlock suggested, bafflingly, that the scene might be acceptable if truffles and artichokes were substituted for the presumably more suggestive oysters and snails, it was dropped altogether, less for moral reasons than because it contributed nothing to the story and might, moreover, have produced giggles in the audience. (The bath scene remained in the print seen and approved by the British censor and previewed to the London press, but disappeared before general release.)

It was far easier to paint Crassus as someone with a mildly romantic interest in women who got his real sexual stimulation through the manipulation of power. To show that he has a heterosexual side, Trumbo included a long scene in which, having sheltered Varinia in his house, he unaccountably falls in love and dances attendance on her, draping her in jewels and serving her squab and melon on his gold dinner service. She responds, understandably, with disdain. The scene is deeply embarrassing, and absurdly out of character.

Late in the summer of 1959, the unit moved to Spain for six weeks to shoot the battle scenes, which Kubrick supervised, rather than leaving them to second-unit director Irving Lerner. Spartacus's forces had been essentially guerrillas, and Trumbo's script included no formal battle, only a surreal evocation of the final slaughter, with helmets floating down a stream, and distant thunder. Kubrick, however, persuaded Douglas that audiences would feel cheated without a set-piece showdown.

Calder Willingham was called in to script it, and found inspiration in the *Roman History* of Appian of Alexandria, the Greek-born historian who wrote during the reign of Marcus Aurelius. 'He fell upon them unexpectedly and continually,' Appian said of Spartacus attacking the Roman positions, 'threw bundles of faggots into the ditch'and set them on fire and made their labour difficult.'

On this brief description, Willingham and Kubrick erected a climactic confrontation in which the Roman phalanx (actually eight thousand soldiers of the Spanish army, made to look like sixteen thousand by Universal's special effects department and Lerner with cameraman Clifford Stine), is briefly scattered as flaming cylinders of brushwood are rolled into its midst. Saul Bass, the specialist in credit sequences who did those for *Spartacus*, with their multiple dissolves of increasingly smashed and defaced Roman busts, had been retained as visual consultant, and helped design many sets, including the gladiators' school. For the battle, he helped choreograph the movements of chess-like precision with which the Romans triumph.

The battle itself is awkwardly directed, with some clumsy stunt action and a plethora of improbable horse falls. Inevitably Douglas is at the centre of what fighting there is. Kubrick, however, reserves his punch for the sunset that follows, and the shot of the battlefield littered with corpses as Crassus and Julius Caesar stroll among the fallen, looking for Spartacus, and find Varinia and her child.

It was this shot, made at great expense at Universal after earlier attempts to shoot it in the open, which brought Kubrick into conflict with cameraman Russell Metty and the Universal hierarchy, and first established his stubbornness in pursuit of a personal vision.

The fact that Universal backed down was proof that the studio system could be bluffed and beaten. The realisation would dominate the rest of his career.

Chapter Ten

Kubrick in Love

'I'm looking for a girl with a beautiful body and a sick mind.'

Arthur Fellig, aka 'Weegee', to Peter Sellers on the set of *Dr Strangelove*

Once he had finished the battle scenes of *Spartacus* and was back in Hollywood, Kubrick started to assemble the film, initially with the help of Irving Lerner, and then, after the two fell out, with Lerner's assistant Robert Lawrence, who edited most of it. He also had time to read Willingham's screenplay for *Lolita*. As he and Harris had promised Shurlock, Humbert and Lolita married at the end, a conclusion Kubrick disliked even more when he saw it on paper.

Nabokov, now in his favourite summer hideaway, the Grand Hotel in Lugano, Switzerland, was no happier. Kubrick cabled him: CONVINCED YOU WERE CORRECT DISLIKE MARRIAGE STOP BOOK A MASTERPIECE AND SHOULD BE FOLLOWED EVEN IF LEGION AND CODE DISAPPROVE STOP STILL BELIEVE YOU ARE ONLY ONE FOR SCREENPLAY STOP IF FINANCIAL DETAILS CAN BE AGREED WOULD YOU BE AVAILABLE. Nabokov, more at ease in Lugano than he had been in Los Angeles, said he'd think about it. In February 1960 he agreed. He and Vera returned to Hollywood, and in March they rented a house on Mandeville Canyon Road.

Every fortnight or so he met Kubrick in his office at Universal to discuss his slow progress. Occasionally Kubrick took him to parties, at one of which he got into conversation with a tall, quietly-spoken gentleman.

'What do you do for a living?' Nabokov asked.

'I'm in pictures,' said John Wayne.

From the start, there was no chance that *Lolita* would be filmed intact. Not until *Taxi Driver* in 1976 and *Pretty Baby* in 1978 would Hollywood find credibly sensual teenage actresses in Jodie Foster and Brooke Shields, and even then their presence on screen outraged many. Harris and Kubrick never believed that their *Lolita* could deal with underage sex. Harris says:

> We decided that this was a bizarre love story, and that we were not going to deal with [Humbert's] predilection for little girls. We're not interested in a pervert.
>
> The great love stories are usually about the inability of the lovers to get together. In the old days they'd alienate themselves from society by religious differences, by class differences, by colour differences. All of those things have been done before. But what hadn't been done was the age difference. If we could make him the most innocent guy in the piece and her a little brat, and he just singled her out as someone to fall in love with – let people put their own interpretation on it.
>
> We knew we must make her a sex object. She can't be childlike. If we made her a sex object, where everyone in the audience could understand why everyone would want to jump on her, and you make him attractive, it's gonna work.

Kubrick put an equally good face on their decision. *Lolita*, he insisted, conformed perfectly to the political and social interests of his other films. 'It concerns the outsider who is passionately committed to action against the social order. I mean the outsider in the Colin Wilson sense – the criminal, maniac, poet, lover, revolutionary. The protagonists of *Paths of Glory*, *The Killing*, *Spartacus* and . . . *Lolita* are all outsiders fighting to do some impossible thing, whether it's pulling a perfect robbery or saving innocent men from execution by a militaristic state or carrying on a love affair with a twelve-year-old girl.'

In 1968, however, he acknowledged that this was said simply for the record. The film 'should have had as much erotic weight as the novel had. As it was, it had the psychology of the characters and the mood of the story ... but it certainly didn't have as much of the erotic as you could put into it now. It would have made it more true to the novel, and it would have been more popular. The film was successful, but there's no question that people expected to see some of the things that they had read in the book – or *hoped* they might see those parts, anyway.'

Something different might have been made of *Lolita* had Kubrick discovered a cinematic equivalent to Nabokov's allusive, playful text, but there was neither the time nor the encouragement for such experiment. Instead, like Elia Kazan, who revamped the nymphet of Tennessee Williams's play *Twenty-Seven Wagon Loads of Cotton* into the thumb-sucking twenty-five-year-old Carroll Baker of *Baby Doll*, Kubrick transformed Dolores Haze from predatory infant to teenage sexpot. 'The gap between the ages of Nabokov's Lolita (twelve and a half) and Kubrick's (say, fourteen and a half) ... marks a crucial change from novel to film,' critic Richard Corliss has pointed out. 'The book is about child abuse; the movie is about the wiles a teenage girl might have learned in those two years: an awareness of her power over men.'

Once Harris and Kubrick decided to abandon pre-teen sexuality, the choice of an actress for Lolita became less difficult. Kubrick's first suggestion was Tuesday Weld. At seventeen, she had already played in eight or nine films, and had survived alcoholism, drug addiction, a series of liaisons and one suicide attempt. Kubrick introduced her to Nabokov, who saw a girl sensual and knowing beyond her years. 'A graceful ingenue,' he agreed courteously, 'but not my idea of Lolita.' (Weld herself claims she was offered the role but turned it down.)

For his own reasons, Nabokov shrank from making the screen Lolita too real, or too pretty, and concurred with Harris and Kubrick that the film shouldn't delve too deeply into her appeal. In the book, Humbert and Quilty are excited not by Lo's looks but by her precocious sexuality, her hoydenish ability to manipulate her ageing admirers. Nabokovian nymphets aren't placid victims but calculating demons, human versions of the nymphs of the insect world, the half-formed immature larvae-like forms of mosquitoes and dragonflies. 'Humbert thinks Lolita irredeemably vulgar and trite,' remarks Nabokov's biographer Brian Boyd, 'endowed with nymphet magic and grace thanks to his discerning eye but otherwise without special interest.'

Nabokov was alarmed when people transposed his creation into the real world. *Lolita*, he said, was purely fictional, unreal and unrealisable; any film performance would be at best an approximation. He'd insisted that there be no picture of a little girl on the cover of the book's American edition, and was horrified at Halloween when a child appeared at his door, trick-or-treating for candy, with a tennis racquet, a ponytail and the word 'Lolita' on a sign. What the role demanded, he told Kubrick, wasn't a real teenager but someone who combined the physical nature of a child with the sophistication of an adult – perhaps 'a dwarfess'. Flinching at this thought, Kubrick started collecting photographs of young models and actresses. Over a year, he accumulated eight hundred. Harris checked out Broadway and monitored TV plays and commercials, as well as the hopefuls sent by casting agents. Whoever they eventually chose, though, would almost certainly be little-known, and since no studio would invest in *Lolita* without a major star, the most pressing problem became finding Humbert.

The search occupied Harris and Kubrick throughout 1960. According to the mythology, their first choice was the English playwright and actor Noël Coward, but Harris denies that he was ever considered: 'I don't even know what Noël Coward *looks* like,' he says.

From the start, despite – or perhaps because of – his shopworn, hangdog image, James Mason, once considered for Dax in *Paths of Glory*, was their first choice. At fifty-two, the British actor feared he had come to the end of his years as a leading man. Trapped in a declining marriage about to end in an acrimonious and financially disastrous divorce, he was secretly involved with a young actress. His attempts to be both producer and actor in films like *Bigger than Life* had failed, nor had he done much to launch the career of his daughter Portland, a famous wild child after whom he'd named his company, Portland Productions.

Mason had resigned himself to ending his career in character roles, and even to disappearing entirely. During one of his last films as producer, *Hero's Island*, in which he'd played a pirate, he became morbidly fascinated with a minor character named Enoch Gates. Shortly after, he began to accept tiny roles in TV Westerns under this pseudonym, and fantasised about living out his old age as Gates in the hand-to-mouth world of the extras.

Kubrick approached Mason, only to be told that he couldn't do *Lolita* because he was about to star in his first Broadway musical, adapted by Howard Dietz and Arthur Schwartz from *The Affairs of Anatol*, Arthur Schnitzler's stories of *fin-de-siècle* Vienna. Though his drawling speaking voice was famous, and already a butt for mimics, Mason was no singer – 'But then neither was Rex Harrison,' he reminded Harris, 'and look at *My Fair Lady*.' Anyway, he was taking singing lessons, and had invested too much effort to give up now. 'Kubrick sounded a little surprised,' recalled Mason, 'but made no effort to dissuade me.' In the meantime, he proposed his wayward daughter Portland as Lolita. Kubrick promised to think about it.

The first year of the option on *Lolita* was ending, and unless they soon found a star and a backer, Harris and Kubrick would be forced either to pay the second $75,000 or relinquish the rights. While *Spartacus* was still shooting, Kubrick audaciously offered Humbert to Laurence Olivier. Olivier seemed interested, had lunch in the partners' bungalow to discuss it, and, to their delight, agreed, subject to the approval of his agents, MCA, who then also represented Harris–Kubrick, since Ronnie Lubin had joined them.

That afternoon, however, Olivier sidled up to Kubrick and whispered that he'd changed his mind. Harris was dashed. 'I'll never forgive MCA for that,' he says. 'It was a big blow for us. Having him leave the lunch saying yes, and then . . . I'm sure they said to him, "Sir Laurence Olivier cannot do Humbert Humbert!" We at that point didn't say anything to MCA, but in our minds we had discharged them. I mean, if that's the way the game is played, fuck you!'

Once Olivier was back in London, the idea continued to tantalise him. He was enjoying a lively affair with Sarah Miles, his co-star in his next film, *Term of Trial*, and more than twenty years his junior. Speculation about and reconstructions of what Lo and Hum got up to became a feature of their pillow talk.

With both Mason and Olivier apparently out of the running, Kubrick thought of Peter Ustinov, but rejected him. Ustinov could play Humbert almost too well; no hope of eradicating the eye-rolling, lip-smacking nympholept relish from *his* performance.

Harris then persuaded Kubrick, who was doubtful, to try David Niven – who accepted. Warily, however, they waited a few days before making an announcement, which was just as well, since within a week they were summoned to a panic meeting at the William Morris Agency, where Abe Lastfogel, its head, flanked by a platoon of flunkies, explained that, while Niven would love to play Humbert, his partners in the TV show *Four Star Theater*, Charles Boyer, Ida Lupino and Robert Coote, weren't sure the sponsors would stand for it. So, reluctantly . . .

Harris was in despair when the phone rang in their office. It was James Mason. 'Is that part still open, by any chance?' he asked.

'Just wait right there,' Harris said, reaching for a contract.

Mason never explained why he changed his mind. Perhaps his voice needed more than a few lessons to bring it up to Broadway level. He was right to do so, however. *The Gay Life*, as Dietz and Schwartz called their show, was no *My Fair Lady*. It went on Broadway in 1960 with Italian actor Walter Chiari in the main role, and made no particular splash.

Throughout this period, Kubrick was completing the post-production of *Spartacus*. Counting the final pick-ups and retakes, he had shot for 167 working days. In addition, Anthony Mann had filmed for a week on the salt mine locations in Death Valley, and his footage was so effective that Kubrick included it in the film. Organising the massive amount of material taxed his devotion to the art of editing. Even with the most drastic cuts, the film ran 196 minutes, extended by an orchestral overture, a convention of the time, that ran for five minutes over the drawn curtains before the film, and a further five minutes of music to introduce the second half. Alex North, who had never written the score for an epic before (and who would do only one more, *Cleopatra* – not counting his unused music for *2001: A Space Odyssey*), laboriously researched the period but, since little was known of Roman music, made a stab at its feel by dusting off exotic instruments like the dulcimer and the *ondioline*. Coaxed by Kubrick into studying Prokofiev's *Alexander Nevsky*, North used mainly brass and drums for the rest, withholding the syrup until the arrival of the film's love story, when the track blossomed with oboe and *cor anglais*.

Over the next six months, Kubrick and Robert Lawrence pared

the film down to 184 minutes. To emphasise the *gemütlich* nature of life in the slave army, and to suggest parallels with the flight out of Egypt, Douglas had insisted on some sentimental cutaways worthy of Cecil B. DeMille: frolicking children, affectionate old-sters, young lovers, family picnics and freed gladiators exercising traditional crafts. Kubrick removed them. John Gavin as Julius Caesar had been inflicted on him by Universal, and Laughton was the least co-operative of his stars, so Kubrick had no compunction in deleting a sequence of Gracchus and Caesar touring the slums of Rome to buy votes, part of Caesar's political education. Crassus's homosexual overture to Antoninus disappeared too.

Preview audiences were so disgusted by the scenes using maimed extras that all but one were removed. Geoffrey Shurlock also fretted about the moment when Varinia, standing at the feet of the crucified Spartacus, begs him to die. It smacked too much of suicide, or euthanasia. This was one of the last scenes to be cut, Kubrick snip-ping it, plus the shot of Woody Strode's blood spurting into Olivier's face and Douglas hacking off a man's arm, between the trade pre-view on 6 October and the New York premiere a few days later. Most of the scenes were lost, though a few would be restored when Jimmy Harris supervised a reissue of the 'director's cut' in 1994.

Spartacus shone against an otherwise lacklustre Universal slate. Of the eleven other movies the studio released in the same year, two would be hits (*Pillow Talk*, *Imitation of Life*) and the rest either break-evens or flops. Everyone in the Universal front office was impressed with the way Kubrick had taken over a limping project and, despite its cantankerous stars, delivered a smooth and assured epic which, they decided, had every chance of being as big a box-office success as *The Vikings*.

MCA, looking for ways to guarantee work to its clients, had been acquiring an interest in Universal with a view to taking it over. Ed Muhl, the studio president, was desperate to maximise profits in order to keep the share price high. In this state of mind he was prepared to take any kind of chance, and rumours circulated that, in the honeymoon period before the release of *Spartacus*, he offered Kubrick a job as head of production. Kubrick told Billy Woodfield about the suggestion, and they discussed the possibility of Wood-field, later to become a successful TV producer, heading the studio's

TV division. Their first production would have been *Dr Brilliant*, from an original idea by Ian Fleming, about the world's greatest criminologist. Woodfield, who had done a book of comic photographs with Ustinov, went as far as to offer the role to the actor, who accepted. Before anything could come of the plan, however, MCA bought Decca Records, acquiring that company's large interest in Universal, and in 1962 took it over totally, installing Lew Wasserman as head and abandoning management completely in favour of film and TV production. In the change of power, any future Kubrick may have had as an executive evaporated.

The experience of *Spartacus* profoundly affected Kubrick. If he could take on so ill-starred a production and make something out of it, he could, he believed, do anything. Any discipline might be mastered by consulting the right people, reading the right books.

From someone who had never read for pleasure, he now became the ultimate autodidact, an information addict. Intrigued by gambling, he read up on poker so omnivorously that he and Jimmy Harris were able to hold their own in Hollywood's $500-ante games with notorious high-stakes gamblers like director Martin Ritt. Kubrick handed out copies of Yardley's *Education of a Poker Player* to friends like Vince Edwards, and urged them to use its tables of when to bet and when to fold. In the same spirit, he studied the stock market. He and Harris became speculators, sometimes arriving at their brokers' office at 6.30 a.m. to snap up profits on shifts between the British and US exchanges. Always ready to take a flutter, Kubrick bought five hundred MGM shares in February 1968, just before the studio released his *2001: A Space Odyssey*.

Kubrick has always guarded details of his wealth, another advantage of living in Britain with its close-mouthed attitude to money, but by the eighties it undoubtedly ran into millions of dollars. His brother-in-law Jan Harlan is fully occupied as his resident financial adviser, acting as comptroller of his films – he usually receives Executive Producer credit – and also custodian of his personal fortune, most of it stashed in Switzerland as gold.

This aspect of Kubrick was to both bemuse and irritate his collaborators. During the time she was writing *The Shining*, Diane Johnson found that Kubrick was 'very into gold. As it turned out, though, it was the wrong time to buy.' In the nineties Brian Aldiss was slaving at Childwick Bury over the screenplay of his unmade science fiction film 'A.I.' when Kubrick stuck his head round the door and brusquely advised, 'The Dow Jones is down. Buy gold!' Only wishing he could, Aldiss gritted his teeth and typed on.

The search for a Lolita moved into high gear once Harris and Kubrick were certain of James Mason as Humbert. In June 1960 Kubrick said to Harris, 'We saw a girl a few days ago. I didn't think she was right, but I saw her last night on a *Loretta Young Show*, and she was good. Maybe we should see her again.'

Sue Lyon was a strawberry blonde from Davenport, Iowa. She was fourteen and had been acting for a year in TV and commercials when Pat Holmes of the Glenn Shaw agency brought her to the *Lolita* casting director. After a second look, Kubrick included her photograph in his collection, which he showed to Nabokov. Sifting through them, the writer pointed to Lyon's picture and said, 'No doubt about it; she is the one.' Harris–Kubrick promptly signed her to a seven-year contract.

After that, it was an easy matter to assemble the rest of the cast. Shelley Winters, a plump sensualist succumbing to terminal flab, was cast – by mail – as Lolita's mother, Charlotte. Nabokov insisted on vetting everyone in the film, so Kubrick sent Winters to see him at the Sherry Netherland Hotel in New York during a break in her main activity of the period, travelling in John Kennedy's campaign entourage. Nabokov approved.

Meanwhile Rome was hosting that year's Olympics. Kirk Douglas contemplated holding a gala premiere of *Spartacus* in the Baths of Caracalla when the Games closed in September, but decided instead to wait until October, giving Universal time to plan lavish advertising and publicity stunts which emphasised their belief that this was a special film. The studio staged a charity premiere for Cedars of Lebanon Hospital on 19 October at the venerable Pantages on Hollywood Boulevard, some seats of which had to be torn out to accommodate a new curved screen for SuperTechnirama – 70mm made even wider by Panavision lenses. So great was the pre-publicity that when Universal asked for its traditional block of free tickets, Douglas twisted the knife by not only making them pay full rates, but extracting a hefty cash premium as well. Elsewhere, promotion was just as intensive. Throughout its first reserved-seat engagement in Times Square, usherettes wore robes copied from one worn in the film by Jean Simmons.

The feared furore over Dalton Trumbo's credit failed to eventuate. A few hard-line supporters of the old studio regime had their say. 'I happen to think *Spartacus* was one of the worst pictures I have ever seen,' shrilled columnist Hedda Hopper, 'and the script was written by Dalton Trumbo.' The American Legion warned its seventeen thousand members to avoid *Spartacus*. Neither action appeared to affect ticket sales.

Spartacus cost $12 million, and even after its worldwide run and sale to TV it grossed only $14.6 million, though that was no mean achievement: MGM's *Mutiny on the Bounty* and UA's *The Greatest Story Ever Told* (on budgets of $20 million each), *My Fair Lady* (which cost $17 million) and *Cleopatra* ($37 million) all lost money. The critics were as ungenerous as ever to epics, though *Variety* singled out the director for praise. 'At thirty-two, with only six [sic] pix behind him, Kubrick has out DeMilled the old master in spectacle, without ever permitting the story or the people who are the core of the drama to become lost in the shuffle.' In a break with tradition, under which presidents normally viewed movies at private White House screenings, John F. Kennedy visited a Washington DC cinema unannounced to see *Spartacus*, a public relations gesture to support Universal's initiative against 'runaway' productions, filmed abroad.

Kubrick didn't by any means disown *Spartacus* at the time, though he was to do so later. 'I think the film will be a contender for awards,' he told the *Los Angeles Times*. 'It's just as good as *Paths of Glory* and certainly there's as much of myself in it. I don't mean to minimise the contributions of others involved, but the director is the only one who can authentically impose his personality onto a picture, and the result is his responsibility – partly because he's the one who's always there.' Faced with this implied slur on his frequent absences from the set, Douglas snarled of Kubrick, 'He'll be a fine director some day, if he falls flat on his face just once. It might teach him how to compromise.'

Work continued on the script for *Lolita*. Nabokov had delivered a four-hundred-page manuscript which Kubrick was whittling down to a manageable length. Meanwhile, with commitments from Nabokov, Lyon, Winters and Mason (who wouldn't, however, sign a contract until September 1960, the same month that a final screenplay was agreed), Harris and Kubrick shopped *Lolita* around the studios. There was little enthusiasm, even with the book still a best-seller.

Most executives asked how they hoped to get around the film's sexual theme without offending the censors. Nabokov recalled wryly to Kubrick and Harris that when the book was first circulated among American publishers before Girodias accepted it, some had suggested it might be more acceptable if Lolita was turned into a boy – which seemed equally true of its prospects as a film.

Warner Brothers, however, were prepared to advance Harris and Kubrick $1 million, and even allow them a share of the profits, providing they could guarantee that the film would receive a Code seal of approval. The banks had already warned all studios that without a guarantee, they would refuse funding. Harris recounted their conversation with Geoffrey Shurlock about marrying off Lolita and Humbert. He didn't mention that neither Nabokov nor Kubrick liked this device. Warners warily offered their $1 million in increments: so much on delivery of a screenplay, so much on the first day of shooting. The contracts were sent to Kubrick and Harris's lawyer, Louis Blau, and they arrived at his office to sign them. Reading them over, they were astonished by a restriction written into almost every clause. 'There shall be mutual approval, but in the event of a disagreement, Warner Brothers shall have final control.' It gave the studio the say over even the musical score. Warners wouldn't budge, so the partners refused to sign. 'Now we were *really* nowhere,' Harris says.

He left for New York, en route to Europe and a schedule of appointments at Cinecittà in Rome and studios in London and Paris, where *Lolita* might conceivably be made on a shoestring. Ironically, the director of the 'anti-runaway' *Spartacus* would be forced by circumstances to become a runaway himself. In New York, he lunched with an old school friend, Kenneth Hyman, who like him had gone into film distribution with his father Elliot, as Associated Artists. Harris explained his predicament.

'We're financing film production in England,' Hyman said. 'Maybe we can find the money for you.'

They returned to Associated Artists' office. Elliot Hyman was no believer in haggling. He listened to Harris's pitch, then said, 'Whaddaya need, kid?'

Harris swallowed hard and said, 'A million dollars.'

'Ya got it,' growled Hyman. The meeting was over. Louis Blau flew to New York, drew up the contracts, and Harris left for Europe with *Lolita* almost fully funded. Even more reassuring were the terms of the contract. It guaranteed Kubrick an absolute right to the final cut: not one foot of film could be deleted without his express agreement. It also gave Harris–Kubrick, in the event of a sale to a distributor of which they didn't approve, the right to a sixty-day delay in which to find an alternative buyer, or buy out the other's share themselves.

In Britain, Associated Artists had gone into business as Seven Arts UK with two of the most active independents: Woodfall, built around the new talents emerging from theatre, like Tony Richardson, Lindsay Anderson and Albert Finney; and Bryanston, which consolidated the remnants of the old Ealing Studios team. Seven Arts's first British production, *The Roman Spring of Mrs Stone*, set in Italy, with an American director, Jose Quintero, a British screenwriter (Kubrick's old friend Gavin Lambert), and a mixed cast of British (Vivien Leigh), American (Warren Beatty) and Continental European (Lotte Lenya) performers, showed what could be done in England, especially with help from the Eady Fund, which funnelled a tax on cinema seats into local productions.

Harris knew that, since James Mason had kept his British passport, *Lolita* would be eligible for Eady money, but a second British performer would make the underwriting even more certain. Of the main roles, the only one uncast was Clare Quilty, Humbert's rival in nympholepsy. The two men compete for Lo, but, like men playing chess by mail, seldom meet. Instead Humbert has to track Quilty down from clues, like the playful pen names under which he registers with Lolita in motels. The character of Quilty didn't suggest any actor in particular. It was Kenneth Hyman who proposed Peter Sellers.

At thirty-six, Sellers was on the verge of becoming an international star, a giddy prospect for a boy who'd left school at fourteen and worked his way up in show business from running errands at the variety theatre in which his father was a musician. He and

Kubrick had a lot in common. Both left school young, played jazz drums, loved photography and as boys spent more time in the darkroom than in the sun.

Sellers became sufficiently expert on drums to spend his military service in Malaya as a musician with the RAF's Gang Show. Demobbed in London, he drifted into radio, where his ability to mimic famous voices and invent new ones made him an instant star. The BBC's *Goon Show* launched him into films, of which, by 1960, he'd made sixteen. Four of them were showing in New York when he'd visited America the previous April on a promotional tour: *I'm All Right, Jack*, in which he played a pompous middle-aged union official in a factory; *Man in a Cocked Hat*, the American retitling of *Carleton-Brown of the F.O.*, where Sellers was the seedy Prime Minister of a Caribbean island; *Battle of the Sexes*, an adaptation of James Thurber's story 'The Catbird Seat' with Sellers as an elderly Scot who tries to protect his job from a new woman boss by plotting her murder; and his first colour film with an international cast, *The Mouse that Roared*, playing three roles, including the dowager Duchess of the tiny European principality of Grand Fenwick and the bumbling General who leads an invasion force on New York.

Sellers's chameleon ability fascinated Hollywood. The press hailed him as the successor to Alec Guinness, who had also played multiple roles in films like *Kind Hearts and Coronets*. The comparison delighted Sellers, who was famously unsure of himself, and proud of a tenuous friendship with the aloof Guinness that began when they appeared together in *The Ladykillers* in 1955. But during his American visit, the English critic Kenneth Tynan made the mistake of introducing Sellers to some New York humorists like Mike Nichols, on whom Sellers failed to make any impression. 'Nothing that Peter said amused Mike,' Tynan recalled, 'nothing that Mike said amused Peter; and the giggly facetious whimsical fantastic Goon-jokes of Sellers seemed merely embarrassing to Mike. I've never been more conscious of the abyss that separates British humour from the specialised world of Jewish Manhattan.'

After this humiliation, Sellers was eager for projects that promised intellectual legitimacy. *Lolita* could not have come at a better time. Unfortunately he was heavily committed. In the US he'd been offered twenty-five roles. He'd just shot Bernard Shaw's *The Millionairess*, playing an Indian doctor opposite Sophia Loren, with whom he'd had an obsessive affair in real life, then gone on to another comedy, *Two Way Stretch*, after which he was signed for an adaptation of Jean Anouilh's *Waltz of the Toreadors* and a film of John Mortimer's play *Dock Brief*. However, a fourteen-day window of opportunity existed around Christmas 1960, and if Kubrick shot all his scenes in that time, Sellers could do it.

Sellers was then living with his wife Anne and their two children in an enormous house at Chipperfield, on the edge of London. Kubrick and Harris were often guests there during the production of *Lolita*, Kubrick with his Rollei facing off with Sellers behind his 16mm Bell & Howell. The opulence of Sellers's lifestyle, with half a dozen servants, acres of barbered lawn and a dining room the size of a ballroom, impressed Kubrick, even if the evident unhappiness of Anne Sellers (they would separate within a year) and the actor's relative coolness to his son and daughter did not. If Sellers could live in Britain and still have an international film career, why couldn't Kubrick?

Now boasting a star cast, *Lolita* was a more solid prospect than it had been six months before, and Seven Arts upped the budget to $1.75 million. The risk of censorship still loomed, however. Kubrick asked the opinion of John Trevelyan, urbane chairman of Britain's board of film censors, who replied that he'd read the book and felt that only one passage, Humbert's soliliquy about the appeal of nymphets, might cause a problem. In the event it wasn't included in the film, and *Lolita* received a lenient local X certificate without cuts.

At the urging of Kenneth Hyman, Harris–Kubrick also retained Martin Quigley to guarantee a US Production Code seal. Quigley, the millionaire Catholic publisher of *Photoplay* magazine, had been one of the prime movers towards the formulation of a Hollywood self-censorship code in the thirties, believing, like many in the film business, that it was better for the industry to 'clean house' than hand over censorship, as in Britain and many other countries, to a government body. A pedant for propriety whose shrill voice and silver cigarette holder were unwelcome presences at most high-level film events, Quigley had meddled in the administration of the Code ever since, and had thoroughly worn out his welcome with the Legion of Decency. The slightest infraction drew his lengthy and sarcastic criticism, which simply became more acid as the Legion protested that times were changing and artists had to be allowed more latitude.

To regain his privileged position, Quigley offered his services to producers 'to act as a guide and advocate', as a censor of the time, Jack Vizzard, put it, 'in shepherding the property through the Code'.

While *Lolita* was in pre-production, Quigley rang Geoffrey Shurlock.

'Look, Geoffrey,' he told him bluntly, 'this picture is going to be made, come what may. Would you just want to turn the producers loose, to make it their way? Or would you rather settle for a silk purse from a sow's ear?'

Shurlock was furious. 'For God's sake, Martin, this's what we've been saying over the years, and you've sneered at us for it. Now that you're on the other side of the fence, it's suddenly all right.'

Quigley promised Shurlock a preliminary look at the completed screenplay. When he hung up, Shurlock told Vizzard, 'The pious prick. When he comes to us with that picture, it better be clean, or I'm going to rub his nose in it.'

Kubrick's arrival in Britain in August 1960 to start planning *Lolita* was greeted with respect and, in some quarters, awe. Lindsay Anderson, underwhelmed by *Paths of Glory*, had written dismissively to Gavin Lambert, 'A bit *cold*, isn't he?' Most of the people Kubrick met, however, were warm. Joseph Losey, Britain's ranking expatriate, told American journalist Dwight Macdonald that he was 'almost the only director of the youngest generation whose work I respect'.

British technicians lined up to work with him. Anthony Harvey, who would cut *Lolita* and *Dr Strangelove*, and would go on to become a highly regarded director, had seen *Paths of Glory* a number of times and wrote to Kubrick, asking if he could cut *Lolita*. Kubrick gave him a grilling. 'He invited me to see him and I had at least four or five interviews. He gave me the MI5 treatment: "What kind of hours do you work? What time do you go to bed? Are you married? Do you go on holidays?" He wanted somebody who was going to be there seven days a week, twenty-two hours a day, and indeed I did work very long hours for him. But, my God, what an experience! He's a fascinating, funny, brilliant, eccentric fellow. I wouldn't have missed working with him for the world.'

To shoot the film, Kubrick hired Oswald Morris, famous for his expertise in atmospheric black and white photography. Here the chemistry didn't work, however, Morris resenting Kubrick's relentless second-guessing of his lighting choices.

> He'd say, 'Now I want this scene lit as though there's just one lightbulb in the middle of the set.'
> Fifteen minutes later he'd come back and say, 'What are all those lights? I told you just one lightbulb.'
> I said, 'It's basically and faithfully lit as if with one lightbulb.'
> . . . It all got a bit boring, inquest after inquest about the lighting.

Later in the shoot, when a tabloid newspaper got hold of some shots of Lyon, whose identity was jealously guarded, Kubrick accused Morris of leaking them, and demanded he account for every frame of film.

Kubrick decided the film needed footage of real American settings, and hired Bob Gaffney, the cameraman he'd met in the course of Jimmy Harris and Alex Singer's Signal Corps short, to film freeways and motels for use as back projections. Once principal photography was finished, Kubrick returned to New York and went on the road with Gaffney and Christiane, personally shooting further material with the hand-held Eyemo. In neither case did he inform Morris, a major breach of professional etiquette that rankled with the cinematographer for the rest of his career.

The *Lolita* which Kubrick began shooting at the ABPC studios outside London in October 1960 opened with Humbert Humbert driving through the mist towards a large country house in which Clare Quilty is asleep amid the ruins of a huge party. Nabokov had written such a scene, but its placement at the start of the film was Kubrick's idea. It put Quilty – and Sellers – at the heart of the story, which became more a tale of the rivalry between the two men than, as in the book, of Lolita and Humbert's mutual seduction.

Reeling around the chaotic house, draped in a toga-like sheet ('I am Spartacus,' he drunkenly informs Humbert. 'Have you come to free the slaves or sump'n?'), Quilty, unfazed by the gun in Humbert's hand, challenges him to a game of 'Roman ping pong' – 'Like a pair of senators,' he says, continuing the Spartacus theme. At Humbert's insistence, he reads a poem Humbert has written about Quilty's seduction of Lolita (interpolating a few literary criticisms), then bolts upstairs and hides behind a Gainsborough-type portrait of a lady, through which Humbert shoots him.

Kubrick delighted in working with Sellers, who was so adaptable, so vulnerable, so *hungry*. Alexander Walker describes Kubrick feeding him the oxygen of encouragement to make his invention burn hotter. He had Quilty impersonate Dr Zempf, a school psychologist supposedly suspicious of Humbert's relationship with Lolita, and a nameless American who accosts Humbert at the motel where she finally instigates their affair. Quilty also plays two versions of himself: the hungover clown of the opening, and the suave TV writer who turns up at the Ramsdale high school prom in white dinner jacket and horn-rims, a parody of New York cool. When Sellers ran through his repertoire of American accents, Harris thought one resembled the voice of jazz entrepreneur Norman Granz, then retired in Switzerland. He sent a script to Granz and asked him to tape a few scenes in his nasal twang, which Sellers copied.

Not everyone shared Kubrick's satisfaction with Sellers. Shelley Winters, like many people with whom he worked, found him colourless, almost transparent: 'He seemed to be acting on a different planet.' As the writer Bruce Jay Friedman remarked, 'There *was* no Peter Sellers. He was close to panic as himself and came alive only when he was impersonating someone else.'

Sue Lyon proved eager, competent and professional – almost too professional. 'She knew the script back to front, and front to back,' said James Mason, 'but really needed to be induced to think of the lines in a particular scene as something that came out of the feeling of the character in that scene. So we started improvising during rehearsals – forgot the lines we'd learned and got to grips with the situation instead . . . Sue Lyon made a considerable contribution to many of the scenes because she spoke the same language as the character she was playing.' Sellers needed no encouragement to join in.

This was a very different approach to acting from the one Kubrick had used on his earlier films, and which he had learned from the Russians. He'd begun to understand that not every performance could be created in the cutting room. From now on, a period of intensive rehearsal before every film would come to characterise

Kubrick's working methods. During these rehearsals the actors would be encouraged, even required, to come up with new lines, new 'business', sometimes entirely new characterisations.

Mason was so furious at this unprofessional behaviour that he stalked off the set more than once. But the ease with which actors could be persuaded thus to create a large part of the film encouraged Kubrick to believe that he no longer needed scriptwriters. If you could improvise a performance from the bare bones of a character, you could make a film directly from a novel, without a screenplay. This delusion, common among directors who pride themselves on their visual sense, was to prove as troublesome to Kubrick as it did to another famous victim, Federico Fellini. After *Lolita*, conflicts with writers would characterise Kubrick's career as he tried to dispense with them, at the same time fighting the suspicion that without the sustaining logic and intellectual structure of a screenplay, his films would never be totally coherent.

In time, he arrived at a compromise. Films, he believed, depended on a small group of 'non-submersible' sequences – five or six scenes which supported the whole argument of the film. Once these were constructed and anchored in place, the gaps between them could be disguised with brief narrative links, or a voice-over. Scripting films for Kubrick became a process, usually carried on over months of exhausting argument, involving the questioning and discarding of innumerable ideas, of finding and refining these key sequences – a frustrating search which was to wear out any number of good writers.

In general, *Lolita* follows Nabokov's screenplay as adapted by Kubrick. After the confrontation with Quilty in the mansion, Humbert, in flashback, described in Mason's urbane drawl, arrives in Ramsdale, New Hampshire, for a few months' rest before he begins teaching French poetry at Beardsley College in Ohio. He searches for lodgings, and rejects Charlotte Haze's house, her baking – and Charlotte herself – as Suburban Phoney until he sees Lolita sunning herself on the back lawn. 'What made you change your mind?' Charlotte asks. 'It must have been your cherry pies,' says Humbert, purring in expectation.

By expunging Lolita's pimples, her chewing gum, her skinned knees, Kubrick created an archetype sufficiently elastic to accommodate half a generation. Sue Lyon, by then fifteen, lounging in a flowered bikini and wide feathered hat, bopping silently to the music on her portable radio as she assesses Humbert slumbrously over heart-shaped sunglasses, was, as Richard Corliss says, 'not a "potential" anything; she was already there'.

The rest of *Lolita* is more a dark comedy of manners than the sexual pursuit of the novel. Kubrick repeatedly scores easy points against Charlotte: her hunger for 'cul-cha', represented by framed Impressionist prints and misused French, and her horny itching after Mason, with the occasional nod towards 'the late Mr Haze', whose ashes and photograph repose in a bedroom shrine. Humbert's true concerns are elegantly dramatised when, as Charlotte draws him down onto her doughy body, he fixes his eyes and his imagination on the photo of Lolita by the bed.

Kubrick rockets through the rest of the story, culminating in Humbert's rediscovery of the adult Lolita as a pregnant *hausfrau* living in a cheap suburban bungalow. She refuses to leave her husband and return to him, and a postscript informs us that she dies a few months later in childbirth.

Few films of 153 minutes move with such pace and assurance as *Lolita*. Charlotte's discovery through a furtive reading of Humbert's diary of his obsession with her daughter is followed by a bravura scene in which Humbert, hurrying downstairs to try to convince her she's mistaken, is interrupted by a phone call which informs him she's just been knocked down and killed by a car outside the house.

His puzzled scrutiny of her corpse on the road segues into a scene of numbed drunken comedy as he soaks in a bath, the most recent of numerous large Scotches floating a few centimetres from his chin, being visited by a series of friends and the father of the driver who made him a widower.

'You've been so understanding,' the man says in relief when Humbert tells him he isn't going to sue. 'I was about to suggest that maybe you'll allow me to pay the funeral expenses.' He is startled when Humbert agrees. Nabokov, who was always generous about the film and endorsed it enthusiastically to the press, said that this scene was one invention of Kubrick's he wished he'd thought of himself.

He was less sure about Lolita's motel seduction of Humbert,

which follows some comic by-play with a folding bed which col-lapses under him. ('An Experience that has Happened to Every-body!' cried the film's publicity booklet, relieved to have found something to promote that didn't directly mention sex.) Geoffrey Shurlock fidgeted in particular about this scene, the only one in the script that the Legion found 'unapprovable'. 'Our only suggestion at the moment is that the seduction must be done by suggestion, without any pointed dialogue, and certainly not on a bed,' he said. Harris responded, 'Wouldn't it be more offensive if we implied that such a thing happened on the floor or some other place?' He promised that Lolita would wear a heavy flannel nightdress and Humbert pyjamas and a robe, but conceded no more than that. 'We are never forgetting for one minute how crucial this scene is in relation to censorship, but we ask that you try to realise how crucial this scene is relative to our story.'

True to their promise, Kubrick made the scene a model of probity. Lolita's murmuring description of the 'games' learned at summer camp, and her offer to teach some of them to Humbert, is done with such low-key flirtatiousness on Lyon's part, and such well-bred interest on Mason's, that she might well be talking about Parchesi or Monopoly rather than the sex shared with a girlfriend and the camp's lone male which Nabokov describes in the book.

After considering Bernard Herrmann, who scored *Citizen Kane* and *Psycho*, Harris and Kubrick, admirers of Frank Sinatra and his album *In the Wee Small Hours*, commissioned the arranger for those sessions, Nelson Riddle, to write the music, lacquering the story with a Hollywood gloss. Harris's brother Bob added a Love Theme, and the British firm Chambers & Partners shot a cutely provocative credit sequence of a man's hand delicately enamelling the toenails of a plump female foot. A poster featuring a soft-focus close-up of Lyon with her heart-shaped glasses and lollipop, plus the discreet slogan, 'How Did They Ever Make a Movie of *Lolita*?', completed the repackaging of Nabokov's erotic masterpiece as what *Newsweek* called 'a January–May romance'.

The end of shooting coincided with the award of the previous year's Oscars in March 1961. Hedda Hopper warned, 'If Dalton Trumbo gets an Oscar for either *Exodus* or *Spartacus*, the roof may blow off the Santa Monica Auditorium from boos and hisses.' In the event, Trumbo didn't figure even in the nominations. Nor did Kubrick, Douglas or *Spartacus* as a whole, though some well-co-ordinated block voting by Universal employees ensured that its art direction, photography, editing and costume design were all nominated, as was Ustinov for best supporting actor. He won, as did Russell Metty for the photography he didn't do, and J. Arlington Valles and Bill Thomas for costumes mostly imported from Rome. Only the art direction, by Eric Orbom, Russell A. Gausman and Julia Heron, under Alexander Golitzen, truly earned its statuette.

Before he left Britain after shooting *Lolita*, Kubrick took Christiane on holiday. For five days, they had his idea of a good time – touring the Normandy bunkers and the battlefields of World War II. He wouldn't take another vacation for a decade. 'Telling me to take a vacation from film-making,' he said, 'is like telling a child to take a vacation from playing.'

Some months later, Martin Quigley screened the completed *Lolita* for Geoffrey Shurlock. Jack Vizzard was there. 'Martin assumed the guise of a protective father, hovering over Jimmy [Harris] in a commanding way, and referring with skittish joviality to "this young fellow". He took pains to tell us how "this young fellow" had made changes that were edifying in order to bring the picture in line with the requirements of decency, and that "this young fellow" was quite aware of his responsibilities, and that, all in all, Jimmy was a good guy, and had landed on his feet with a pretty good picture.'

Harris returned to Quigley's room at the Beverly Hills Hotel to await the Legion's verdict. When he was gone, Shurlock solicited opinions from everyone in the room as to whether the film violated the Code. As might be expected from a group which aimed to represent all shades of conservative opinion, from nuns and priests of the Catholic Church to schoolteachers and psychologists, the range of reactions was absurdly broad. Once every opinion had been canvassed, Shurlock, Vizzard and his inner circle got down to horse-trading with Quigley.

Many people had been concerned about the scene where Humbert, in bed with Charlotte, fixes his eyes on the portrait of Lolita on the bedside table.

'We take it to mean,' said Shurlock to Quigley, 'that the man is fucking Lolita in his imagination while he is having the mother.'

Quigley leapt to his feet. 'That's grotesque,' he said. 'You're just *looking* for trouble in this picture!'

Shurlock let him rage on for a minute, then cut him off. 'It's yours,' he said off-handedly. 'The scene's yours. You can have it.'

(Despite Shurlock's agreement, however, the scene was changed, since Winters had not been comfortable doing even a semi-nude scene with Mason, and refused to appear even with her back briefly naked. In the finished film, Charlotte and Humbert are lying on the bed, she fully clothed, he in a robe. Though Humbert gazes at Lolita's portrait, they argue, and Charlotte leaves the bed, flouncing into the bathroom, where she discovers the incriminating diary with its revelations of his lust for Lo.)

After dealing with this scene, Shurlock raised Lolita's seduction of Humbert. He insisted that she whisper the details of her 'games', not describe them audibly. And after that, the scene must speedily fade.

'It can't be any shorter and convey the idea,' protested Quigley.

'Martin,' sighed Shurlock, relishing his moment, 'now you sound exactly like all the rest of the producers. This is how they argue. Now you see how we pass all the stuff we've passed over the years.'

To complete his triumph, Shurlock insisted on bypassing Quigley and ringing Harris personally at the hotel to tell him that, subject to minor changes, the film would be given a certificate. When Quigley returned with the amended film, Shurlock's people put him over the jumps again, 'demanding,' wrote Vizzard, 'that he scrub here and sandpaper there'. Focus groups of priests, nuns and lay Catholics dictated scores of nitpicking cavils. Words, phrases, even pauses had to be changed. Someone took exception to the juxtaposition of Mr Haze's ashes with a crucifix in Charlotte's bedroom shrine. Kubrick tried to blur out the crucifix, then replaced it with a triptych of Our Lady of Perpetual Succour, a Byzantine image that probably looked sufficiently exotic to count as Jewish or Middle European. The Legion also demanded that the phrase 'Over 18' appear prominently on all the advertising. Quigley's reputation as a negotiator never recovered, and he declined into a querulous nitpicker on the fringes of Hollywood self-censorship – which was, in any event, soon to collapse in the liberalism of the sixties.

*

Seven Arts had done so well with its production programme in collaboration with British companies that it negotiated a major distribution contract with MGM. Elliot Hyman brought in Ray Stark, Kirk Douglas's ex-agent, to run the company, and Stark now summoned Harris and Kubrick to a meeting. As the first film in its MGM deal, Stark wanted to give them *Lolita*. However, under the terms of their contract, he couldn't sell it without their approval.

Harris, remembering how Stark had screwed them on *Paths of Glory*, made it clear that they had every intention of exercising their right to find another buyer, so Stark, who knew when he was beaten, sued for peace and bought them out. The partners extracted not only a hefty sum in cash, but Stark's guarantee that not a foot of film would be cut. Seven Arts also agreed to finance another Harris–Kubrick film. Leaving the meeting, Harris reflected, 'What goes around, comes around.' To complete the partners' triumph, MGM submitted *Lolita* to the Venice Film Festival as the official US entry, the first major acknowledgement of a Kubrick film.

Having made *Lolita* through a Swiss corporation, Anya Productions (named after Kubrick and Christiane's first daughter, Anya Renata, born on 6 April 1959), Harris and Kubrick were able to take their profits at an advantageous rate of tax, making each financially secure for life.

With money to spend, Kubrick bought the thing he wanted most in the world: independence. In the autumn of 1961, Louis Blau negotiated an end to the deal with Bryna, and on 15 December, with yet another show of false generosity, Kirk Douglas let Harris–Kubrick buy out the balance of their contract. Now the partners were free to do what they pleased – which turned out to be splitting up.

Chapter Eleven

Kubrick Destroys the World

> 'Gentlemen, you can't fight in here! This is the War Room.'
>
> President Merkin Muffley to General Buck Turgidson, in *Dr Strangelove*

In retrospect, the termination of Harris–Kubrick was inevitable.

Throughout 1960 and 1961, Kubrick, even with an apartment on Central Park West at 84th Street, and a happy home life with Christiane and his new family, became increasingly disillusioned with America. He'd experienced enough of working in Los Angeles to know he could never make his home there. 'You read books, see films that depict people being corrupted by Hollywood,' he said, 'but it isn't that. It's this tremendous sense of insecurity. A lot of destructive competitiveness. I think it's good to just do the work and insulate yourself from that undercurrent of low-level malevolence.'

The hunger for such insulation strengthened a resolve to leave. So did his satisfaction at having become a father. Anya had been followed on 5 August 1960, just before the release of *Spartacus*, by Vivian Vanessa, and the well-being of the girls and Christiane increasingly filled his life. In a rare display of emotion, comparable to his bursting into tears at the screening of *Fear and Desire*, Kubrick said, 'When you get right down to it, the family is the most primitive and visceral and vital unit in our society. You may stand outside your wife's hospital room during childbirth muttering, "My God, what a responsibility! Is it right to take on this terrible obligation? What am I really doing here?" and then you go in and look down at the face of your child and – zap! – that ancient programming takes over and your response is one of wonder and joy and pride.'

Christiane, despite having been brought up in wartime Germany and survived its post-war desolation, was alarmed by life in New York. 'I began to get used to seeing the streets white with smashed Coke bottles, to seeing police taking the children to schools. In the shops, roughs would just slouch and sprawl across the doorways and you'd have to step over them as if it was quite normal. The women were harsh too. You just got elbowed out of the way by them. The terrible danger was going home and taking it out on somebody weaker, like a child. Just like the animal kingdom. New York did something to me. Before we went there we thought that Americans who complained about the schools and the atmosphere were just right-wing creeps, but of course they had a point.'

Kubrick, like most people in the West, feared nuclear war. In 1960, Khrushchev sabotaged the Paris summit with revelations of American U2 spy flights over the Soviet Union. 1961 brought the Bay of Pigs and the Berlin Wall, 1962 the Cuban missile crisis. Europe, at least in theory, looked safer than the United States as a place to live, and he was increasingly drawn to move there, especially since London and Hollywood were the only two places in the world where he felt he could pursue a career as a film-maker.

Kubrick, however, also found the mechanics of destruction intellectually fascinating. He read intensively on modern warfare. By 1963 he'd collected seventy or eighty books on nuclear strategy, like *On Thermonuclear War* by Rand Corporation strategist Herman Kahn. He also subscribed to technical journals about military weaponry. On his desk, his German Computerised Chess Opponent, with a plate indicating 'Grand Master Level' – 'I have perfected my endgame,' he told a startled Terry Southern later, 'to such a degree that I can now elude the stratagems of this so-called opponent' – that sat next to a pocket-sized Nuclear Bomb Effects Computer.

At first, Kubrick said, his interest was motivated by 'a kind of primitive concern for survival. Then, gradually I became aware of the almost wholly paradoxical nature of deterrence ... If you are weak, you may invite a first strike. If you are becoming too strong, you may provoke a pre-emptive strike. If you try to maintain the delicate balance, it's almost impossible to do so because secrecy prevents you from knowing what the other side is doing, and vice versa, *ad infinitum.*'

His fears were legitimate, but they also smacked of the paranoia that would increasingly characterise his life and work. Even as a child he was obsessive, and in adulthood this modified into a highly developed, even morbid rationality. Kubrick would do nothing without examining every aspect, probing every possibility. And because he so distrusted his own mental mechanism, he came to distrust machines also. His films, always preoccupied with systems that fail and plans that don't succeed, increasingly dealt with the same problems but on a global or cosmic scale, as if even the universal order could no longer be relied on.

Kubrick resembled a man trying to play chess on a rowing boat in the middle of a choppy sea. On the board, the rules are clear, the game a model of logic. But every few seconds a wave threatens to wash the pieces away, or a lurch of the boat send them tumbling. Over the next few years, he would do everything in his power to steady the board. Potential disturbances would be damped down. He would install himself and his family in a walled mansion and see almost nobody. He became hyper-sensitive about infections, and sent home anyone on his unit who had a cold. He kept guns and, when he was working with Arthur C. Clarke in New York on the script of *2001* in 1966, carried a large hunting knife in his briefcase.

He would become reluctant to drive, and demand that no car in which he was a passenger travel at more than thirty-five miles an hour. (Cab drivers were told he had a badly sprained back, and asked to drive at a crawl even in New York.) On *Lolita* he surprised even the British by commuting from one part of the studio to another by bicycle.

He would also refuse to fly, for reasons he explained to designer Ken Adam, a fellow pilot. 'He was learning to fly,' says Adam, 'and on his first solo trip he staggered into the air because he didn't have enough power, and was completely horrified. He just managed to complete a circuit and land, and what apparently had happened [was that] we have two magnetos on the engine, and he'd forgotten to switch on the second magneto. So he was taking off on half power. He was lucky ever to get back. I think this must have influenced him on not wanting to fly again.' In Kubrick's version, the switch stuck rather than being forgotten, but he has never denied the shock the incident gave his confidence.

This near-disaster, which may have taken place, as Adam asserts, during Kubrick's first solo flight in the mid-fifties but probably dates from 1958 or 1959, started Kubrick fretting about pilot error. Reading up on commercial flying accidents destroyed what faith he still had in aviation. By the time he flew back from Spain after *Spartacus*, he was close to being a white-knuckle flier. The PanAm flight he and Harris caught to London in August 1960 to begin *Lolita* was Kubrick's last. After he took up residence permanently in Britain, he made his infrequent transatlantic trips by boat.

Kubrick also became a compulsive note-taker, always on the 10 x 15cm cards or slips of paper he'd become convinced were the ideal dimensions for memos. On *Dr Strangelove*, Terry Southern watched, bemused, as Kubrick prowled stationery stores, buying up notebooks, planners, diaries. This metamorphosed into an intricate system of annotation and documentation. Jeremy Bernstein, a physicist friend and chess opponent who visited him on the set of *2001* to write a profile for the *New Yorker* magazine, noticed that Kubrick had 'just ordered a sample sheet of every type of notebook paper made by a prominent paper firm – about a hundred varieties – which were spread out on a large table'. Once Kubrick made his choice, small notebooks were produced to his order.

He explained: 'I'm distrustful of delegating authority and my distrust is usually well-founded. I especially don't trust people who don't write things down. With those who do write things down, I'm very interested in what they write things in. If it's one of those chic little Fifth Avenue notebooks with those expensive gold pencils, I'm more suspicious than ever. Many people feel it's beneath their dignity to take notes, and try instead to trust their memories. I don't work with them.'

After finishing a film, Kubrick transferred the information in his notebooks to a cross-referenced system in his home. 'He was fascinated with flat storage,' recalled Diane Johnson, his writer on *The Shining*. 'There were cabinets everywhere, filled with who-knows-what.' Malcolm McDowell, summoned to the house to audition for *A Clockwork Orange*, was shown into a drawing room the walls of which were draped with towels to hide Kubrick's files. When he returned some months later, the material had been transferred to the carousel-like German Definitiv filing system which dominated the room.

'Ask me anything about the film,' Kubrick coaxed, anxious to show off his new toy. 'Anything you like. Want to see the stills for your parents' apartment?'

He spun the carousel, plucked out a folder, and opened it triumphantly under McDowell's nose. It was empty. Furious, he flipped the switch on his intercom and yelled for production secretary Margaret Adams.

'That's what Stanley can never understand,' grins McDowell. 'It's the human element. If only he could eliminate that, he could make the perfect movie.'

On 14 February 1962 (Valentine's Day, obviously by design) MGM issued a press release announcing it had 'acquired' Seven Arts's *Lolita*, which had been 'approved by the Production Code Administration' of the MPAA and 'submitted' to the National League of Decency, which, it assured exhibitors, would not give it a 'Condemned' rating. Cinema owners and managers all over the country could now book the film, confident that the local priest or bishop would not fulminate against it from the pulpit, nor would Watch Committees and Citizens' Groups picket screenings.

The national opening on 24 June brought modest box office and mildly approving reviews. Most people concurred with Bosley Crowther in the *New York Times* that the film was good family entertainment, and Lyon no more a child than Marilyn Monroe had been at eighteen. The film grossed $3.7 million in America – respectable, if not in the same league as the year's other hits, *Lawrence of Arabia* ($17 million gross) and *How the West was Won* ($21 million).

Seven Arts put Sue Lyon into one of its first films under its MGM deal, John Huston's adaptation of Tennessee Williams's *Night of the Iguana*, but her career never took off. In the seventies, retired and all but forgotten, she complained that playing Lolita had ruined her life. Like many people, she had the sense that Kubrick had merely used her. During *Lolita*, she had gone riding every day. Kubrick told her, 'If you get thrown, roll over. Don't hurt your face.' Lyon remarked, 'It's not that he wasn't interested in you personally. He was. But for him the film was the important thing.'

Peter Sellers's interest in his young co-star, on the other hand, was entirely non-professional. James Mason recalls that, on a post-filming visit to their house while promoting the film, Sellers spent the whole time lying on the floor taking pictures of Lyon.

Kubrick's immediate inspiration for making a film about nuclear war came from Alastair Buchan, head of the London-based think-tank the Institute of Strategic Studies. On his recommendation, Kubrick had read a 1958 novel called *Two Hours to Doom* in which 'Peter Bryant', actually Peter George, an ex-RAF flight lieutenant and an active member of the Campaign for Nuclear Disarmament, drew on his inside knowledge of the nuclear stand-off to describe an all-too-credible scenario. USAF General Quinten, commanding a Strategic Air Command Base in Sonora, New Mexico, succumbs to terminal depression over his fatal illness and launches forty atomic-armed B52s at Soviet targets under an emergency procedure which permits such drastic decisions in the event of a sneak attack. After urging Washington to follow his lead and obliterate the Soviet Union, Quinten seals the base, warning his men to resist the infil-trators who will attack with the intention of discovering the recall code only he knows.

In the War Room under the Pentagon, the American President and his Chiefs of Staff first entertain, then reject, Quinten's plan, and instead negotiate a compromise under which they help the Russians to shoot down the rogue planes, then agree that, if a Soviet city is bombed, SAC will itself bomb Atlantic City, New Jersey. In the event no such drastic gesture is needed, since the one American bomb which does get through the Russian defences explodes in open country. The book ends optimistically, with American and Russian leaders pledging themselves to avoid such risks in the future.

Both Harris and Kubrick recognised the cinematic possibilities of the book. Harris checked with George's agent, Scott Meredith, to find he'd sold the movie option for $1000 in 1959, since when it had passed through three or four different hands before lapsing. Harris bought it for $3500 – comically low by comparison with *Lolita*'s $150,000 – and persuaded a dubious Elliot Hyman to accept it as their next project for Seven Arts. George, a troubled man morbidly preoccupied with the growing threat of an accidentally-triggered nuclear war, came to New York, where he and Kubrick, working in the Central Park West apartment, wrote a screenplay.

Kubrick shared George's horror of nuclear war, but there was much about the idea of atomic holocaust that fascinated and even amused the war-lover within him. He was both too enamoured of high technology and too politically neutral to be interested in a simple polemic. Though many people co-opted *Paths of Glory* as a pacifist film, Cobb's book had attracted Kubrick more as an illustration of the dynamics of a political decision than an assault on the military mind.

The script he wrote with George proposed to stand back from nuclear destruction. The end of mankind would be seen from the perspective of history; in early drafts, the observers are aliens, and the film part of a documentary series, 'Dead Worlds of Antiquity' – an idea that may have been suggested by 'Scientists and Tramp', James Agee's aborted project for Charlie Chaplin, which also began with a view of the earth from outer space.

Kubrick and Harris, however, getting together in the evenings over a beer, couldn't help seeing the funny side. What if the Cold Warriors in the War Room got hungry and sent out for pizza? Someone would arrive with a pile of white cardboard boxes and start handing them out: 'Who's for the pepperoni?' 'Hey, I said no anchovies . . .' Next morning, solemnity – and Peter George – returned, but Kubrick regretted losing the jokes. 'I found myself tossing away what seemed to me to be very truthful insights because I was afraid the audience would laugh. After a few weeks of this, I realised that these incongruous bits of reality were closer to the truth than anything else I was able to imagine.' Groping for a new approach, Kubrick asked Jules Feiffer to write a version; 'but,' recalls the cartoonist, 'my idea of an anti-nuclear satire and Stanley's were miles apart.'

'Two Hours to Doom' might have stayed mired in reality had Kubrick not met Texas-born writer Terry Southern. A wayward and eccentric prose stylist with a surrealistic sense of humour not then blunted by his taste for booze and drugs, Southern had lived in Paris, where he and fellow expatriate Mason Hoffenberg wrote the porn satire *Candy* for Girodias's Olympia Press.

Back in New York, Southern drifted into the circle that assembled at the East River apartment of George Plimpton, editor of *Paris*

Review, a group that included Norman Mailer, Kenneth Tynan and Jonathan Miller, then a young English satirist appearing in the Cambridge Footlights' *Beyond the Fringe*. In 1962 Southern was making a precarious living freelancing for magazines as various as *Esquire*, *Evergreen Review*, the *Nation* and *Glamour*, while working on a new novel, *The Hipsters*.

His first, *The Magic Christian* (1959), about a playful millionaire named Guy Grand who enjoys elaborate practical jokes, already had an underground reputation. Grand buys up prints of Hollywood movies like *Mrs Miniver* and inserts brief shots which subliminally suggest that Walter Pidgeon plans to murder Greer Garson, or sets up a vat of boiling sewage on a vacant lot, strews the surface with money and stands back while people risk death to grab the banknotes.

On Peter Sellers's visit to New York in 1962, Jonathan Miller gave him a copy of *The Magic Christian*. Tickled by the book, and anxious to be seen as 'hip', Sellers bought dozens of copies and sent them as Christmas and birthday gifts. Kubrick received one, and liked its anarchic humour.

Hearing of this, Southern suggested profiling Kubrick. There was immediate interest from the *Paris Review*, the *Atlantic* and *Esquire*, which finally gave him the job, and the two men met in New York; but, as Southern put it, 'Somehow or other we get into this rather heavy rap – about *death*, and *infinity*, and the *origin of time* – you know the sort of thing. We never got through with the interview, but the point is we met a few times, had a few laughs, and some groovy rap ... and then about three months later, he called from London, and asked me to come over and work on *Strangelove*.'

Through the autumn of 1962, Kubrick and George continued to polish the screenplay of 'Two Hours to Doom', still at this point a straightforward adaptation of the book. Because Seven Arts were putting up the money, the film would be shot, like *Lolita*, in Britain. Shooting was scheduled to start in October at Shepperton, and Christiane had already rented a house in Kensington, one of London's smartest suburbs.

Everyone involved knew that the film's theme wasn't especially original, but Kubrick never set much store by originality of plot. His virtuosity emerged in the making, not the conception. Working well-trodden ground had its drawbacks, however. The projected 'Napoleon', 'A.I.' and 'Wartime Lies', as well as *Full Metal Jacket*, would all suffer from or be aborted as a result of the existence of one or more similar films in production, and 'Two Hours to Doom' was no exception. Half a dozen other nuclear or post-nuclear dramas were either in preparation or already circulating. In particular there was *On the Beach*, Stanley Kramer's worthy but uninspired version of Nevil Shute's best-selling novel. It had done its best to evoke the reality of nuclear war by showing fallout inexorably obliterating all life until only a handful of survivors remained in Melbourne, Australia, but the film's release in December 1959 was greeted with general indifference. Not even its all-star cast of Gregory Peck, Ava Gardner and Fred Astaire won audiences. Having been confused with Kramer earlier in his career, Kubrick could imagine the sarcastic parallels some critics were certain to draw between 'Two Hours to Doom' and *On the Beach*. Nevertheless, he was too heavily committed to stop now.

With Harris, Kubrick began assembling a cast. For the B52 pilot he wanted John Wayne, who refused almost immediately. Kubrick saw George C. Scott as Shylock in *The Merchant of Venice* in Central Park and made a deal with him to play the USAF Chief of Staff. Young black actor James Earl Jones had the small role of the Duke of Morocco in the same production, and Kubrick, on impulse, cast him as Lothar Zogg, one of the crewmen in the atomic bomber. Sterling Hayden accepted the part of Quinten, the unbalanced General who instigates the nuclear strike.

It was at this point that Kubrick told Harris he wanted to end their partnership. Most books attribute the dissolution of Harris–Kubrick to a conflict over the direction of 'Two Hours to Doom'. Harris, it's assumed, quarrelled with Kubrick's plan to take the film in the direction of 'nightmare comedy', which would produce *Dr Strangelove*. Some weight is given to this by Harris's decision to launch his own directorial career shortly after with *The Bedford Incident*, a story of Cold War brinksmanship with many echoes of George's book. (He also used Gil Taylor, Kubrick's cameraman on *Strangelove*.) Unfortunately for this theory, the dates don't match. When Harris–Kubrick was dissolved in 1962, Kubrick still intended to shoot 'Two Hours to Doom' much as he and George had written it.

Harris also strenuously denies that he and Kubrick fell out, over differences in their views of nuclear war or anything else. For years, he says, Kubrick had urged him to start directing himself: 'There is no pleasure on earth like seeing your own rushes,' he told him. The director's chair certainly tugged at Harris, but he had lacked the incentive to make the move. Both he and Kubrick deny vehemently that there was any tension or rivalry in the split, though Harris does acknowledge being galled by the constant attribution of their success to Kubrick alone.

Harris had helped his friend as much as he could, often to the cost of his own career. It made sense to split now, before the distance between them became wide enough to engender animosity. While having no desire himself to move to Britain, Harris understood Kubrick's need to relocate, to cut himself off from the mainstream of the film industry. Shrewdly, he saw Kubrick as being an artist closer to a musician than a film-maker, but also as the sort of performer sufficiently protean to find an audience without pandering to it. Such people could live and work anywhere. Kubrick, he felt, had affinities with Frank Sinatra: 'The jazz people love him and the mainstream Top 40 people love him. I think Stanley's in that class. He does pictures His Way.'

To replace Harris–Kubrick, Kubrick formed Hawk Films, which would become the holding company for all his films from *Strangelove* on. Each new film would be produced by a subsidiary of Hawk Films which was usually folded after it had served its purpose. These companies all took their names from varieties of falcon. *Barry Lyndon* and *The Shining* were Peregrine Productions, *Full Metal Jacket* a Harrier Film, the projected 'Wartime Lies' a Hobby Production – the hobby being a small falcon. Vivian's documentary *Making The Shining* was an Eagle Film.

One result of folding Harris–Kubrick Productions was the loss of the Seven Arts connection. After the difficulties of *Lolita*, neither Elliot Hyman nor Ray Stark was anxious to take on another Kubrick project, especially without the steadying influence of Harris. 'Two Hours to Doom' finally found a home at Columbia, but only at the cost of severe restrictions on budget and casting. Among other things, Columbia were convinced that the success of *Lolita*, which was well on the way to becoming a *succès d'estime* in Europe, was attributable to Sellers. As a condition of their involvement, they insisted not only that he feature in the new film, but also that he play multiple roles.

Kubrick, installed in London and deep into pre-production, was forced to court Sellers as the price of getting his film made. Fuming that 'what we are dealing with is film by fiat, film by frenzy,' he besieged the actor, who was, as usual, in the midst of a domestic crisis. His wife Anne having left him, Sellers had started an affair with ex-child actress and archetypal English rose Janette Scott, whom he'd installed in a Chelsea flat while the lawyers worked out a divorce settlement. Fortunately for Kubrick, this meant that the actor, for both legal and emotional reasons, had to remain in Great Britain. Kubrick took to turning up unannounced at Sellers's American-style Hampstead penthouse and waiting for him to stagger home in the early hours of the morning. In his weakened state the actor was in no condition to resist, and agreed – for $1 million plus a variety of perks, including a suite at the Dorchester during the production – to star in the film.

A further complication arose with the publication of *Fail-Safe*, a novel by political scientist Harvey Wheeler and Eugene Burdick, author of *The Ugly American*, which became an instant best-seller. Peter George detected so many parallels to *Two Hours to Doom*, renamed *Red Alert* for American publication, that he sued for plagiarism, and won an out-of-court settlement. Nevertheless *Fail-Safe* was optioned by Hollywood, and there was a real risk that the film might be in the cinemas before Kubrick's. (Sidney Lumet's version wasn't in fact released until 1964.)

Driven by a new sense of urgency, Kubrick began shooting his and George's original script of 'Two Hours to Doom' at Shepperton in October 1962. Terry Southern told his biographer Lee Hill that the shooting was 'very tentative'. Obviously it didn't involve any of the principals, and may only have been in the nature of costume and camera tests. Kubrick called a halt almost immediately, however, while he searched for a new vision. The casting of Sellers and the risk of *Fail-Safe* stealing any thunder 'Two Hours to Doom' might still possess drove him to a radical reassessment of the whole project. Remembering his conversations with Harris about pizza in the War Room, he gambled on a new approach which would turn Sellers to advantage and definitively separate his film from every other project of the same kind.

In December 1962 Terry Southern in New York received an unexpected phone call from Kubrick. 'He said he had thought of the story as "a straightforward melodrama" until this morning,' recalled Southern, 'when he "woke up and realised that nuclear war was too outrageous, too fantastic to be treated in any conventional manner". He said he could only see it now as "some kind of hideous joke". He told me that he had read a book of mine [*The Magic Christian*] which contained, as he put it, "certain indications" that I might be able to help him with the script.'

Southern, flat broke, couldn't refuse Kubrick's offer of $2000 for a month's work. He spiked his *Esquire* profile of Kubrick, and flew to London.

To design the film, Kubrick had chosen the relatively untried German-born Ken Adam, who had just won his reputation with the sets of *Dr No*, the first James Bond film, directed by Terence Young. In particular Kubrick liked the evil scientist's laboratory, dominated by four inward-tilted concrete struts which, carried on at right angles, became the roof beams – structures that recalled the buttresses of the play area at Taft High School, but also the pre-World War II style of German futuristic romances like *F.P.1 Anwortet Nicht* and *Gelt*, which, like the studios in which they were filmed, featured vast halls with gleaming floors, dominated by humming machines.

Kubrick and Adam met at the Connaught Hotel, the sort of staid English *milieu* Kubrick found increasingly attractive. Adam says:

He told me about the Peter George book, but Stanley was never the sort of person who would send you a script, because he felt that it was unwise to give one to too many people. But I was taken in by his charm. He has incredible charm. And his intelligence. Which is very deceptive. When you first meet him, he seems like a young boy, full of enthusiasm. Then, as you got to know him more, you found out what an incredible brain he has, and basically was interested in every detail and aspect.

We had a very good first meeting, and I started work on the designs. He seemed to like my first scribbles, in particular for the War Room. It was a sort of two-level control room, with a mezzanine, loosely based on NORAD and places which I'd researched. He seemed to be very thrilled by that, so I started working drawings.

But after three weeks, he said, 'Ken, this second level is going to be a nuisance. Who's going to be up there? I'm going to have to fill it with extras and so on. I think you'd better come up with a different concept.' I was really taken aback at that. I didn't have the experience to adjust so quickly. My art department was in the old house at Shepperton. There was a lovely park outside, and I just walked for about an hour, trying to calm down.

So I started scribbling away again, and Stanley, as he often did, was standing behind me. And he said, 'Oh, I quite like this triangular shape. Isn't the triangle one of the strongest geometrical forms?' I agreed. Then he said, 'How would you treat the walls?' And I suggested reinforced concrete. 'Like a gigantic bomb shelter?' And that convinced him.

Adam had designed a variation on his *Dr No* set – which Kubrick had wanted all along. But neither ever commented on the similarity.

Each morning from mid-November 1962 to just after Christmas, when *Strangelove* began shooting again with the rewritten script, Kubrick's chauffeured Bentley collected him from his Kensington house at 4.30 a.m., then, once Southern had arrived in London, picked the writer up at his nearby hotel. During their journey to Shepperton, always in the dark – Kubrick lowered the curtains as the sun rose – they worked on the script.

At first Kubrick told Southern he only wanted him to 'add some decoration to the cake', but on the long, slow drives the collaboration widened. Although he had never written a screenplay before, Southern's contribution to 'Two Hours to Doom' was crucial, beginning with its retitling as *Dr Strangelove or How I Learned to Stop Worrying and Love the Bomb*, an adaptation of the facetious mock-Edwardian titles pioneered in *Esquire* and quickly picked up by Hollywood.

Kubrick and Southern inked in Sellers for four roles: an RAF group captain on secondment to Burpleson Air Force Base as Adjutant to Sterling Hayden's crazed General Ripper; the inept President of the United States; his sinister German security adviser; and the Texan pilot of the rogue B52 bomber. The other roles were cast in

Britain. American expatriates Ed Bishop and Shane Rimmer made up part of the B52's crew. Peter Bull, a specialist in stocky and apoplectic authority figures, was a perfect Russian ambassador. For the only woman in the film, General Buck Turgidson's secretary, an ex-centrefold girl who's glimpsed posing as 'Miss Foreign Affairs' wearing nothing but a copy of the staid *Review of Foreign Affairs*, Kubrick had wanted Adrienne Corri, a willowy redhead who'd worked for Jean Renoir and Federico Fellini. When she wasn't available, he cast Tracy, daughter of director Carol Reed.

Southern brought to the film a uniquely sixties black humour, redolent of stand-up comedian Lenny Bruce, cartoonist Jules Feiffer and New York's satirical magazines. His additions to the script recalled *Evergreen Review*, Paul Krassner's acerbic *Realist* and Harvey Kurtzman's magazines *Mad* and *Help*, with their comic-book parodies of Hollywood clichés. Names that appear in Southern's novels – Guy Grand, Candy Christian, Professor Mephesto, Dr Irving Krankeit, Jack Katt, Pete Uspy – are echoed in the film. General Quinten became Jack D. Ripper, and his Adjutant Lionel Mandrake. Air Force Chief of Staff General Franklin was now Buck Turgidson; General Keppler, charged with retaking the base with ground troops, became General Faceman; and his subordinate, Andrew Mackenzie, was reborn as 'Bat' Guano. The President is Merkin Muffley, the Russian Ambassador DeSadesky, the Russian head of state Dmitri Kissoff.

The last surviving B52 in the wing, *Alabama Angel*, became *Leper Colony*, lifted from Henry King's 1949 World War II flying drama *Twelve O'Clock High*, in which the losers and slackers of Gregory Peck's squadron are relegated to a plane with this name. Its commander, Clint Brown, became Colonel T.J. 'King' Kong. Guano's accusation that Mandrake is 'some sort of deviated prevert' who has tried to take over the base is also *echt* Southern (though Kubrick must have enjoyed the resonances with Geoffrey Shurlock and the Legion of Decency). So, surely, is the image of Kong riding the bomb down to his target, whooping like a rodeo rider.

It's less sure who invented Dr Merkwürdigichliebe, aka Strangelove. Nobody like him appears in George's novel, but as early as May 1962, while he and George were still working on the script in New York, Kubrick announced that the film would be 'a slightly irreverential story [of] an American college professor who rises to power in sex and politics by becoming a nuclear wise man.' A German-born security specialist, Dr Walter Groteschele, plays a central role in the novel *Fail-Safe*, advising the Chiefs of Staff on nuclear scenarios, and it seems likely that Kubrick and Southern borrowed him as the basis of Strangelove.

It is often assumed that the model for Strangelove is Henry Kissinger. Certainly Southern and Kubrick lifted much of the doctor's dialogue from a report of Kissinger's on nuclear strike capability, but it's highly unlikely that they copied his voice and physical appearance. In 1962, Kissinger was still mainly known as a Harvard theorist. He had taken his first steps onto the national stage in February 1961, when the Kennedy White House retained him as a part-time security adviser, but he wouldn't become a familiar public figure until Richard Nixon's election in 1969.

Once the script was written, Southern and Kubrick often drove to the studio in Ken Adam's sleek crimson E-type Jaguar – though still at thirty-five miles an hour. Kubrick quizzed Adam about his career as a World War II RAF pilot and Southern about his life in France and New York, in particular the worlds of Paris pornography and New York underground literature and film.

Kubrick's relentless questioning wore down Adam as it had worn down others, leading some years later to the collapse of their collaboration. Adrienne Corri says, 'Stanley is like a vampire of people's brains. He draws out whatever he thinks anybody knows. He just goes on and on in that rather flat voice to get out what people know. He doesn't necessarily listen. He just wants to see what they know.'

Both Adam and Southern, having exhausted their stock of stories, began inventing. Southern, though chronically shy, was so enthusiastic about porn – which many intellectuals, including Kenneth Tynan, saw as the cutting edge of libertarian artistic progress – that Kubrick arranged to screen a hard-core film at his home. The event became the seed of his later flirtation with making Hollywood's first big-budget porn feature, *Blue Movie*.

On these drives, the intellectual and physical similarity of Adam, Southern and Kubrick became more apparent. All three preferred severe black clothing and a conversational style of reticent understatement. All shared the same dark hair, heavy eyebrows and hawklike profile, as did Peter Sellers; visitors to the set said that Kubrick, Southern and Sellers might have been brothers. Adam in particular became emotionally attached to Kubrick. 'I think I fell in love with him,' he said. 'It was like a marriage. I became part of the family.' He was less enamoured of Southern, especially when the writer, after his first look at the giant War Room set in January 1963, drawled, 'It looks great, Ken – but will it dress?'

The shared journeys hastened the polarisation of the film's personnel. Kubrick, Southern, Adam and Sellers constituted the A-Team. Anyone else was fodder, doomed to be manipulated, bullied or made a victim of Kubrick's taste for games. This included the director of photography, Gilbert Taylor. Fiftyish, balding, Taylor had flown on raids over Germany as a World War II combat photographer and filmed Belsen and Buchenwald before going on to a workmanlike career in British cinema. He had handled low-level aerial shooting for films like *The Dam Busters*. This made him ideal for *Strangelove*, which required extensive film of Arctic wastes as back-projection footage for the B52 flight that occupies much of the last half of the film.

Even Taylor's war experiences hadn't prepared him for the painstaking Kubrick. 'He interviewed me [for the job] with a copy of [the technical magazine] *American Cinematographer* in his hand,' complained Taylor, 'and he was asking me how processes like the travelling matte worked, with him looking at it and asking me questions to see whether I was right or wrong, and whether I was technically good enough to do his film. I suppose that was a unique conversation. No one else has ever dared do that.'

'Nothing good comes out of tension with the director,' Taylor says. 'Everybody was under tension on *Dr Strangelove*.' Peter George suffered more than most. Though he wrote a novelisation of the screenplay which outsold his novel (and which he dedicated to Kubrick), he detested the film's facetiousness. After publishing another novel, *Commander-1*, about the struggle to survive after an atomic war, he shot himself on 1 June 1966 at the age of forty-one while working on a novel called *Nuclear Survivors*.

While the War Room was being built, Kubrick began shooting the sequence in which General Ripper despatches his bombers, then seals off Burpelson Air Force Base. The army unit sent to break in and arrest Ripper has to fight off resistance from their own men, who have been told that the soldiers trying to enter the base are Russian infiltrators. For most of the battle scenes outside the base, Kubrick personally operated a hand-held Arriflex.

Sellers had no trouble with the character of Group Captain Mandrake. As long ago as his days in the RAF Gang Show in Malaya he'd enjoyed putting on a false moustache and pretending to be an officer. Essentially Mandrake plays straight man to Sterling Hayden's Ripper, a paranoid whom Kubrick and Southern garnished with another fashionable right-wing obsession of the period, fluoridation of the public water supply, which some of the more volatile elements of the idiot fringe regarded as a Communist plot to poison America. Ripper drinks only grain alcohol and rainwater, and is convinced that his waning sexual potency – 'I do not avoid women, but I do deny them my essence' – is caused by pollution of his 'vital bodily fluids'.

Sterling Hayden hadn't worked on a film for six years. Harried by tax liens, he lived in Paris on a houseboat, mostly writing. It took him some time to work his way into the character of Ripper. 'On the first day of shooting, I found that I just couldn't handle the technical jargon in my lines. I was utterly humiliated. Stanley told me, "The terror on your face may yield just the quality we want, and if it doesn't, the hell with it, we'll shoot the whole thing over. You and I both know that this is something that can happen to anyone." He was beautiful. A lot of directors like to see actors wallow. Stanley isn't one of them.'

George C. Scott's Buck Turgidson was a caricature of the cigar-chomping, war-loving head of the Strategic Air Command in the fifties, General Curtis LeMay. During the Bay of Pigs crisis in 1962 LeMay had advised President Kennedy to obliterate the Russian missiles based on Cuba without warning, and then to invade. In 1957 he told two members of a Congressional inquiry that, at the threat of a Soviet attack, he would 'knock the shit out of them before they got off the ground'. When the Commissioners reminded him that a pre-emptive strike was not US national policy, he retorted, 'No, but it's *my* policy.' In 1968 LeMay ran for President on the same ticket as Governor George Wallace of Alabama. Asked for his solution to the Vietnam problem, he suggested that America should 'bomb North Vietnam back into the Stone Age'.

News of Kubrick's satiric intentions quickly reached the United States government, who voiced their concern to Columbia. Southern was alone in the office one day when Mo Rothman, the executive designated by the studio to oversee the production, rang. 'Just tell Stanley,' he informed Southern, 'that New York does *not* see anything *funny* about the end of the world as we know it.' Hoping to placate Rothman, a keen golfer, Kubrick had Abercrombie and Fitch, New York's premier sporting goods store, deliver a state-of-the-art electric golf buggy to him at the Westchester Country Club with his compliments. Rothman refused the gift. 'He said it would be "bad form",' Kubrick irritatedly told Southern.

The US Air Force refused access to one of its B52s to help in the building of *Leper Colony*, and even declined to supply photographs of the instrument panel. Ken Adam found all he needed in technical magazines like *Flight*, which Kubrick now collected, and which routinely published minute specifications and illustrations of the latest weapons of mass destruction. American servicemen who visited the *Strangelove* set on a publicity junket looked at the reconstructed B52 flight deck with awe, astonished that Adam had been able to discover so much. One element, however, stumped both Adam and Kubrick. Nobody had up-to-date shots of atomic bombs, so Adam had to use his imagination. In one respect, though, the Pentagon had the last laugh. Once the film was finished, it prevailed on Columbia to add an on-screen statement giving the official American government view that such were the checks and balances built into SAC's fail-safe system that an incident like the one in the film could never take place.

The War Room set which Adam built inside Stage B at Shepperton, and which was destined to become one of the most distinctive and evocative examples of contemporary film decor, was the front line of the battle to make *Strangelove*. The temperature inside became blistering. In the centre of twelve hundred square metres of gleaming black floor, under a ring of lights, thirty actors, mostly in heavy wool military uniforms but all incongruously wearing felt overshoes to protect the floor, sweated at a circular table seven metres across, the top covered in green baize like a billiard table. Above their heads a ring of shaded lamps directed a blaze of heat and light onto their heads.

The walls were dominated by illuminated maps ten metres high showing the Soviet Union, the United States, Europe and Asia. Without cities or frontiers, the continents had the stripped-down simplicity of a board game, an effect accentuated, in the case of the Soviet Union, by forty glowing arrows that inched towards scores of dots scattered across the map: each arrow represented an American aircraft armed with nuclear weapons, each dot a target.

The system posed major logistical problems for Ken Adam:

I liked the idea of accentuating the size of these displays or maps, and I also felt that inclining these surfaces would give a feeling of claustrophobia. As we built it, and added the black floor, one could feel this sense increasing. It was an eerie sensation. We had plenty of problems. The first was that big shiny floor. They had already prefabricated eight-by-four-foot sheets of hardboard faced with shiny black material, but when they had laid about two-thirds of the floor, it looked like a seascape, because the floor at Shepperton, which is an old studio, wasn't that perfect. And we'd used quarter-inch rather than three-quarter-inch material, which was too thin. We had to do the whole floor again.

We designed those big maps in the art department and drew them out to four feet by three, then blew them up photographically, glued them to plywood and covered the whole thing in perspex. Stanley and I had investigated the possibility of projecting the symbols onto the maps, but it meant that we needed something like twenty or thirty 16mm projectors, so we decided it would be better if we simply cut out the symbols from the plywood on which we mounted the photographic blow-ups, and put 75-watt photofloods behind them on a switch circuit, and do it mechanically.

Well, the first thing that happened was the heat generated was so enormous that the photographs lifted from the plywood, even with the perspex to hold them down. We had to install a complete air conditioning plant behind them to prevent the whole stage from burning.

We had similar problems with the circular light fitting over the table, which Stanley liked. We decided this would be his main source lighting for all the actors sitting around this poker table. We spent hours in my office with photofloods at various heights, above myself or above him, until he was satisfied that the angle was right and the intensity was right.

There never was an establishing shot of the War Room with the lights on, so that one could see its size. Stanley did this intentionally. He didn't want it to be like a Bond movie, where you have a chance to admire the set. He didn't want any sense of geographical boundaries to this claustrophobic bomb shelter. He made sure that all the ceilings were nailed down, so that the cameraman couldn't light it from overhead. I was upset at the time, but I think he was absolutely right.

The War Room's sepulchral solemnity awed everyone who worked on it. Its slanting roof beams, so much a feature of the *Dr No* set which inspired it, are almost invisible in the gloom above the ring of lights that illuminate the conference table, but a sense of them survives, suggesting the weight of concrete they support. When Strangelove at the climax of the film coos to the awed generals of descending even deeper, into mineshafts, taking with them the most beautiful and fertile women, his tone is lubricious, redolent of a claustrophilic love of the warm dark places where the masters of war make their homes.

This sense of oppression, emphasised by Kubrick's monosyllabic, expressionless style of direction, soon made itself felt on the production team. 'A camera crew is very much a tight bunch,' says Gil Taylor, 'and they all felt they were being stifled. [Kubrick's] got no sense of humour whatsoever. Nobody could laugh because he'd just glare at you.' No one was exempt from this strict regime. 'His wife used to come and sit on the set,' says Taylor, 'and he'd never speak to her.'

Apparently indifferent to his cast's discomfort, Kubrick, always in a jacket and often with a tie, prowled the shadows beyond the ring of light, a cigar regularly clamped in the corner of his mouth. He stared at the sloping ceiling and peered at the maps through his foot-long viewfinder. From habit he now almost automatically saw the world framed in its hair lines.

Dogging his steps, also with a cigar wedged in his mouth, giant Speed Graphic camera always poised, was the gnome-like figure of Arthur Fellig, 'Weegee', Kubrick's hero from his days at *Look*.

As a result of Jules Dassin's 1948 film loosely based on his book *Naked City*, Fellig had become a celebrity of sorts, and persuaded an American publisher to finance a trip to France, where he hoped to compile *Naked Paris*, a companion to *Naked City*. From there he moved to London, and in March 1960 he signed a contract with the *Daily Mirror* for $500 a week to photograph royalty and the famous. Checking into the Mapleton Hotel on Piccadilly Circus, as close to the heart of London as he could get, he converted his bathroom into a darkroom and began covering high and low society. Kubrick saw his pictures – of Princess Margaret and Prime Minister Harold Macmillan, of tramps and Soho strippers, and remembered his idea of hiring Henri Cartier-Bresson as stills photographer for *One-Eyed Jacks*. Weegee joined the crew of *Strangelove* on special assignment.

Perversely, Peter Sellers found the atmosphere on the War Room set as inspirational as others felt it oppressive. Much of this had to do with his growing respect for Kubrick. 'Kubrick is a god as far as I am concerned,' he said later. He would arrive from the Dorchester each morning in near-torpor, saying very little, looking depressed, tired and ill. Only when Kubrick began to set up the cameras – of which he always used at least three for any Sellers scene – did he begin to revive. By the afternoon, coaxed by Kubrick, he would have hit his stride, ripping off improvisations which reached what Kubrick called 'a state of comic ecstasy' before his energy tailed off again into silence and despair.

But by the evening he had come to life once more. With Janette Scott as his hostess, he threw dinner parties at Hampstead for Kubrick and his co-stars, George C. Scott and Sterling Hayden, greeting his guests at the elevator, cigar in mouth, with a lordly, 'Well, man, how d'ya like the pad?' Sharing Kubrick's delight in electronics, he'd fitted the apartment with a battery of gadgets which dimmed lights, opened curtains and controlled an elaborate stereo system that murmured jazz by the Modern Jazz Quartet and Stan Getz.

But Sellers's good humour could be shattered. Sometimes he railed against the problems of playing four roles. In particular he had trouble with the Texas accent of B52 pilot T.J. 'King' Kong, and surreptitiously coveted Hayden's effortless drawl. For his part, Hayden – 'as dense as his character,' according to Janette Scott –

tried to seduce Scott, not realising she was Sellers's mistress.

A week into production, Sellers sent Kubrick a wire in which he told him, 'I am very sorry to tell you that I am having serious difficulty with the various roles. Now hear this; there is no way, repeat, *no way* I can play the Texas pilot, Major King Kong. I have a complete block against that accent.' A letter from his agent backed him up.

Kubrick, undeterred, argued that Alec Guinness had played eight roles in *Kind Hearts and Coronets*, so why not Sellers? Sellers was tempted by the comparison with his idol. 'I was going to do them *all*,' he said in a later interview. 'Stanley was convinced I could. I could do no wrong, you see. Some days, Stanley used to be sitting outside my front door saying, "What about Buck Schmuck Turgidson? You've *got* to play Buck Schmuck." And I'd say, "I physically can't do it! I don't like the role anyway, Stan. And I'll try to do the ['King' Kong] thing, but I mean I think that's *enough*."'

Terry Southern, who was born in Alvarado, Texas, recorded Kong's dialogue, and Sellers listened to the tape every morning, but he still couldn't – or wouldn't – master the twang. Even after Kubrick shot a sequence with him piloting the bomber, Sellers's resistance persisted, though his long-time driver and valet Bert Mortimer believes the supposed accent problem was really a subterfuge to avoid the difficult scene of Kong balancing on the bomb, which needed to be shot three metres above the studio floor: 'He didn't fancy dropping out on the bomb.'

By contrast, Sellers relished the colourless President Muffley. The script called for him to arrive at the War Room table from below on a hydraulic lift, like a jack-in-a-box, and suffering with a bad cold. Sellers played the scene with such vigour, popping up with a whoop and making great play throughout with an inhaler, that a whole afternoon's shooting had to be scrapped, and the scene dropped, because everyone was laughing so much. Finally Kubrick decided he preferred Muffley to be the one sane man in the room, so Sellers forgot the comic sniffles and played him as a staid combination of Dwight D. Eisenhower and presidential hopeful Adlai Stevenson, the archetypal intellectual 'egghead'. Kubrick also shot a scene of Muffley consulting a computer – actually an IBM 7090, the same sort of machine which calculated the precise point of John Glenn's splashdown after the first American orbital flight. The scene was cut, but the idea of a super-intelligent computer remained, to metamorphose into HAL 9000 in *2001*.

The character of Strangelove himself posed more problems for both Sellers and Kubrick. Physicist Edward Teller and rocket scientist Wernher von Braun contributed to his appearance. Remembering the scientist Rotwang in Fritz Lang's 1926 *Metropolis*, the maimed technocratic genius behind the future city, Kubrick added the black-gloved artificial arm which Rudolph Kleine-Rogge had assumed for the role. The arm having a mind of its own, making Nazi salutes, refusing to relinquish a slide rule and going for its owner's throat, sprang from one of Sellers's improvisations. For the voice he borrowed Arthur Fellig's strangled New York-ese, crossing it with stage German.

Kubrick was no less demanding of other actors. Peter Bull's entire role as Ambassador DeSadesky was taped by a Russian-speaker in both Russian and heavily accented English. Bull was required to learn both. He also complained that in his characterisation Kubrick encouraged the most extravagant overacting. 'The rest of my perf[ormance],' he said, 'was, in my opinion, amateur, heavy-handed and plain ham.'

George C. Scott made the same complaint. From dozens of takes, Kubrick selected only the most manic moments of each, often cutting away at the moment of maximum emotional output. As a result, Scott comes over like a gibbering idiot, spasmodically chewing gum, interjecting, frowning, grimacing, miming a B52 in low-level flight so that he resembles a gangling buzzard hovering over the War Room table.

Kubrick controlled Scott by engaging him in games of chess, leaving the actor to chew over a difficult move while he got on with another scene. The continual defeats of Scott, whom Kubrick quickly identified from his days hustling chess in Greenwich Village as a *potzer*, a weak player who deludes himself as to his ability, had the effect, believes physicist Jeremy Bernstein, a friend who spent some time on the set, of 'all but hypnotis[ing]' the actor into giving an inspired performance.

Nobody agrees about when Kubrick and Southern came up with the idea of Major Kong riding the bomb down to its target. Whoever made it, and whenever it was made, the decision caused Ken Adam major problems:

I'd built the B52, which was a huge, huge set, without bomb doors, or at least not practical bomb doors. We had an old special effects man whom I was very fond of, named Wally Veevers, and whenever I had problems I'd go to Wally, and he'd help me out. Wally said, 'Give me overnight to think about it.' And then he came up with a solution, as he always did.

We took a still of the bomb bay, an eight by ten, and cut the bomb doors out of the still. We had [Kong] get into the bomb bay and mount the bomb. Then we cut away to him on the bomb outside the plane, with a back projection of the photo behind him. And it worked perfectly. Stanley was fascinated by this little bit of trickery. I think it started his interest in special effects.

Sellers's nervousness about playing Kong culminated in a fortuitous accident. He had a large imported Buick with left-hand drive, which often caused problems in London's narrow streets. He was alighting in Panton Street in the West End when he tripped, and shouted to his driver that he'd broken his leg. A few hours later, he appeared at Shepperton with his ankle in plaster and a doctor's certificate swearing he had a hairline fracture. 'The completion bond people know about Peter's injury and the physical demands of the Major Kong role,' Victor Lyndon, the line producer, told Kubrick. 'They say they'll pull out if he plays the part.'

So absolute was Kubrick's commitment to Sellers that he couldn't consider casting anyone else in the role. 'We can't replace him with another *actor*,' he said. 'We've got to get an authentic character from life, someone whose acting career is secondary – a real-life cowboy.' This story gains credibility from the fact that Kubrick did almost the same thing on *2001: A Space Odyssey*, where the Mission Controller, seen only in TV reports from Houston, is a real USAF Traffic Controller, Franklin W. Miller, and on *Full Metal Jacket*, where Lee Ermey, the Marine drill instructor hired to coach the actors playing recruits, replaced the actor originally cast to play the role.

Southern suggested Dan Blocker, bulky star of TV's *Bonanza*, but Blocker's agent rejected the script as 'too pinko for Dan – or anyone else we know for that matter'. At this point Kubrick remembered Slim Pickens, who had shown up at an open call for

One-Eyed Jacks. Pickens (whose real name was Louis Bert Lindley) was a Texas cowhand who competed on the rodeo circuit, then drifted into movie stunt work. Both Kubrick and Brando were so impressed by the lanky Pickens's lazy drawl and shit-kicking manner that he was cast in *One-Eyed Jacks* as Lon Dedrick, the bullying deputy sheriff blown out of his boots during Rio's jail escape.

Pickens took Kubrick's call on his horse farm near Fresno, drove to town to apply for a passport – his first; he'd never left the US before – and flew to London. The next morning, baffled members of the production unit told Terry Southern of his arrival, adding 'He's come in costume!' But Pickens was just wearing what he always did: Justin boots, jeans, cowboy shirt and his giant Stetson.

Southern offered Slim an eye-opener of Wild Turkey bourbon and asked how he liked his hotel.

'Wal, it's like this old friend of mine from Oklahoma says,' Pickens drawled. 'Jest gimme a pair of loose-fittin' shoes, some tight pussy, an' a warm place to shit, an' ah'll be all right.'

Kubrick refused to show Pickens any footage already shot: 'Play it as straight as you can and it'll be fine.' He introduced him to the other members of the bomber crew, including the black actor James Earl Jones and Canadian Shane Rimmer. To make conversation, Jones asked Pickens what it had been like to work with Brando on *One-Eyed Jacks*.

'Wal,' said Pickens, 'you know ah worked with Bud Brando for right near a full year, an' durin' that time ah never seen him do one thing that wudn't *all man* an' *all white*.'

Jones caught Southern's eye. Both men were having a hard time keeping a straight face.

The film was meant to end on a scene of utter insanity as the assembled brass in the War Room batter one another into exhaustion with cream pies from the buffet. Originally Kubrick and Southern didn't intend to parody international thermonuclear war, but rather the battle between branches of the armed forces over their slice of the appropriation pie.

This metamorphosed as Southern hit his stride. The fight as shot began when DeSadesky, trying to avoid a body search for recording equipment, throws a pie at Turgidson. He ducks, and it hits the President, who faints. Turgidson says, 'Gentlemen, the President has been struck down, in the prime of his life and his presidency. I say – massive retaliation!'

The scuffle degenerates into a free-for-all, with more than thirty men in uniform pitching pies made of shaving cream. 'We threw a thousand pies a day for a week,' says George C. Scott. Peter Bull recalled that 'the corridors, lavatories and dressing rooms looked quite extraordinary, as if some creature from outer space, constructed rather loosely from a lot of vegetables, had been cruising around.'

Terry Southern has described how the scene ended.

At about the time that the first pie is thrown, Dr Strangelove raises himself from his wheelchair. Then, looking rather wild-eyed, he shouts, '*Mein Führer*, I can valk!'

He takes a triumphant step forward and pitches flat on his face. He immediately tries to regain the wheelchair, snaking his way across the floor, which is so highly polished and slippery that the wheelchair scoots out of reach as soon as Strangelove touches it. We intercut between the pie fight and Strangelove's snakelike movements . . .

Strangelove, exhausted and dejected, pulls himself up so that he is sitting on the floor . . . Then, unobserved by him, his right hand slowly rises, moves to the inner pocket of his jacket and, with considerable stealth, withdraws a German Luger pistol and moves the barrel towards his right temple. The hand holding the pistol is seized at the last minute by the free hand, and both grapple for its control . . .

The gun explodes, stopping the pie fight dead.

'Gentlemen,' Strangelove calls to them. 'Enough of these childish games. Vee hab vork to do. Azzemble here pleese!'

Turgidson is the first to respond. He helps the doctor back into his chair and wheels him across the War Room. They pass the President and the Russian Ambassador sitting on the floor, building a sandcastle of cream and singing 'For he's a Jolly Good Fellow' in Strangelove's honour.

'Ach, their minds have snapped under the strain,' says Strangelove. 'Perhaps they will have to be insti*chew*shunalised.'

'Well, boys,' says Turgidson, 'it looks like the future of this great land of ours is going to be in the hands of people like Dr

Strangelove here. So let's hear three for the good doctor!'

The men cheer and, as Turgidson leads them out, pushing Strange-love, Vera Lynn's 'We'll Meet Again' fills the empty War Room.

Many people, including George C. Scott, believe that the assassination of President John F. Kennedy on 22 November, two months before *Dr Strangelove* opened, persuaded Kubrick to delete the pie sequence. In fact the film was finished long before then, and the scene was never in the final cut. Southern told an audience at Yale in July 1995 that Kubrick cut it because everyone was having too good a time: 'He believed that watching people have fun is never funny.' Dismissing the supporting cast, Kubrick cleaned up the War Room and shot a new ending focusing mainly on Scott, Sellers and Peter Bull, in which Strangelove describes how the military and political elite can hide out in mineshafts for the hundred years it will take the fallout to clear. As Kong's bomb triggers the Soviet 'Doomsday Machine', an automated system of nuclear reprisal which will make the earth uninhabitable except deep underground, and Strangelove prepares to lead the surviving members of the American military and government into the bowels of the earth, Turgidson solemnly urges that the US avoid 'a mineshaft gap'.

In order to shoot the revised ending, all the costumes used in the pie sequence had to be cleaned and pressed. The wardrobe department at Shepperton, unable to handle such a job, took them to the nearest large dry-cleaner. Faced with the mountain of blue serge liberally slathered with shaving cream and pastry, the owner jumped to the wrong conclusion. Looking around surreptitiously for the hidden film crew, he muttered, 'This is for *Candid Camera*, right?'

Kubrick finished shooting on 23 April 1963, after fifteen weeks of principal photography. His first look at the completed film appalled him with the apparent incomprehensibility and unevenness of tone. 'As with all first cuts,' said editor Anthony Harvey, 'you want to slit your throat, and everyone runs off in different directions looking for a knife! The balance from one scene to another is such a delicate thing that sometimes it can't really be put on paper.' The final cost of *Strangelove* would be $2 million, much of it attributable to the eight months Kubrick was to spend editing.

However, many of the film's most memorable images evolved during post-production, including the opening, where a bomber refuels from a tanker in mid-air to the strains of 'Try a Little Tenderness'. As more than one critic remarked, the proboscis of the tanker trembling flexibly over the B47's entry port recalled mayflies mating. The playful tone was echoed in the blackboard credits, lettered in white chalk, elongated or compressed as the mood took designer Pablo Ferro. Nor did Kubrick waste Gil Taylor's harrowing flights above the Arctic circle to gather back-projection footage for the final scenes of *Leper Colony* approaching its target. They counterpoint the unhurried efficiency of Kong and his crew inside the plane and the growing mania in the War Room, an effect further underlined by a martial version of 'When Johnny Comes Marching Home', credited, like the rest of the film's music, to Laurie Johnson, but reminiscent of Gerald Fried's *Marseillaise* over the opening of *Paths of Glory*.

Columbia elected to have no preview screenings of *Strangelove*. To qualify it for nomination in the Oscars, the film was given a brief New York release in December 1963, then withdrawn out of sensitivity over the assassination of Kennedy and for some minor alterations. Kong's comment to his crew, 'A guy could have a great weekend in Dallas with this,' as he lists the contents – condoms, cash, nylons – of the survival kit was changed to 'a great weekend in Vegas'.

Strangelove went on general US release on 30 January 1964, to the classic mixed reviews, but an improving box office. 'A true satire,' said the *Saturday Review*, 'with the whole human race as the ultimate target. I'm inclined to say that this mordant young director Kubrick has carried American comedy to a new high ground.' Bosley Crowther in the *New York Times* harrumphed, 'I am troubled by the feeling which runs all through the film, of discredit and even contempt for our whole military establishment.' The *Washington Post* concurred: 'No Communist could dream of a more effective anti-American film to spread abroad than this one.'

In September 1964 *Fail-Safe* opened, and showed that Kubrick had been right not to shoot Peter George's novel straight. Coming from a background in TV, Sidney Lumet gave his film the character of early TV drama, with contrasted blacks, flaring whites and lots of back projection. Walter Matthau was the government mouthpiece, talking casually about the Balance of Terror. Dan O'Herlihy played the General who has nightmares of being in a bullfight and, having to drop a bomb on New York in retaliation for one which has obliterated Moscow, realises the bull in the dream is himself. As had been the case with *On the Beach*, the dour subject imposed a sense of the classroom lecture or the Sunday sermon which left audiences bored and indifferent.

Fail-Safe was no serious competition for *Strangelove*. It was forgotten, while Kubrick's film flourished, particularly after the Writers Guild of America honoured its scenario as the Best-Written American Screenplay. The New York Film Critics recognised Kubrick as Best Director, passing over George Cukor whose *My Fair Lady* swept up most of the year's awards, including the Oscars, of which it collected those for Best Picture, Best Director, Best Actor, Colour Photography, Set Decoration in Colour, Sound, Music Score and Colour Costume Design; almost everything else went to either *Mary Poppins* or *Zorba the Greek*. *Strangelove* received nominations for Best Director and Best Film, Sellers for Best Actor, and the screenplay for Best Adaptation. It won none, but Kubrick was mollified by the fact that the film took $5 million in domestic US rentals, making it Columbia's top box-office success of the year.

The question of who wrote *Dr Strangelove*, the screenplay of which was credited to Kubrick, Southern and George, from George's novel, continued to fester for years. When, on 9 August 1964, producer Martin Ransohoff took a full-page ad in the *New York Times* to announce that Terry Southern, 'the writer of *Dr Strangelove*', was about to collaborate with Tony Richardson, 'the director of *Tom Jones*', on an adaptation of Evelyn Waugh's novel *The Loved One*, Kubrick fired off a letter insisting that Southern had come onto *Strangelove* when a 'completed script' already existed, and that 'many substantial changes were made in the script by myself and/ or Peter George', not just by Southern. Other additions, he went on, resulted from improvisations with the actors, in particular Sellers. 'Mr Southern took no part in these activities,' insisted Kubrick, 'nor did he receive any further employment, nor did he serve in any consulting role. The most accurate way for me to sum up Southern's contribution to the film is to say that I am glad he worked on the script, and that his screenplay credit in third place is completely fitting and proportionate to his contribution.' To Diane Johnson, Kubrick summarised Southern's contribution as, 'Terry would drive by in a cab and toss out a few pages.' Asked why he gave him credit at all if his contribution was so minor, he told her, 'I guess I was being generous ... but I thought it might help him get more work, if he wanted it.'

Peter George backed up Kubrick's claim, but Southern was derisive. 'Stan may be long on "generosity" (ha-ha), but I'm afraid he's a bit short on humour (not to mention memory). And what he neglected to say about his "completed script" is quite simple; *it wasn't funny*!'

It's untrue that Southern merely polished the *Strangelove* script and had 'no consulting role' thereafter. Once *Strangelove* began shooting, the writer brought his wife and son to London and became a regular guest at the Kubrick home. Often on the set during shooting, he's remembered by many of the production team as informal greeter and sounding-board for Kubrick's frequent outbursts against Columbia, Sellers or his technicians.

Southern's assertion that the first script of *Strangelove* 'wasn't funny' rings more than true. Kubrick is not noted as a generator of laughs. Gil Taylor says, 'I love to work with a sense of humour, but if he saw anyone laughing the associate producer would come around and say, "Stanley doesn't like it when people are laughing," so you worked in sheer bloody misery.' Gavin Lambert is one of the few people to credit Kubrick with any sense of humour at all: 'I liked his dry, ironic view of life,' he says circumspectly. George C. Scott called him 'an incredibly, depressingly serious man, with a wild sense of humour. But paranoid.' Brian Aldiss, who worked with Kubrick on the aborted 'A.I.' project in the eighties and nineties, agrees that he's funny, but mainly remembers his racist gibes, so acid he couldn't repeat them.

Southern was also responsible for involving Kubrick in the most outrageous project of his career, *Blue Movie*.

The dismal quality of the porn made on the fringes of mainstream American cinema disguises the fact that many Hollywood film-makers, especially in the sixties, were eager to plunge into 'adult' cinema, had they, or the studios, found the courage to rise above their innate conservatism. During the making of *Dr Strangelove*, Southern arranged a screening of a hard-core porn film at Kubrick's home. Kubrick watched only part of the not-very-sophisticated movie, but later he mused to Southern, 'It would be great if someone made a movie like that under studio conditions.'

When Southern returned to the US in mid-1963, he was inspired to start writing *Blue Movie*, a novel about the attempt of top art-house director Boris Adrian to make *The Faces of Love*, Hollywood's first big-budget porn film, with stars visibly indulging in full penetrative sex, without doubles.

Adrian, 'the best in the biz', is clearly meant to be Kubrick. 'The genius, beauty (and hard-ticket appeal) of his work,' wrote Southern, 'was so striking and undeniable that it had finally penetrated even the bone bugbrow of Hollywood itself . . . Except that by now he was very tired. He had seen too much, though he was only thirty-four, and yet he had not seen what he was looking for. He had made twenty pictures – all of them dealing with the three things no one understood . . . *Death* . . . *Infinity* . . . and the *Origin of Time*.'

Southern said, 'I thought Kubrick would be the ideal person to direct such a movie. I would send him pieces [from the novel] from time to time. I still have a great telegram from him saying, "You have written the definitive blow job!" in the scene with the Jeanne Moreau type, Arabella.'

Contemplating *Blue Movie* was a step in the right direction for Kubrick. Whatever he chose as his next film in the role of Fabulous Exile, it had to be spectacular and original. With *Blue Movie* he would have been taking a discredited genre and reintroducing it to the world. But he rightly decided that he had neither the temperament for porn nor the patience to subjugate his invention to the rigid demands of erotic ritual. Porn maker and porn consumer fitted together in a closed system as hermetic as sex itself. There was no place for him.

Once he decided to settle in England, Kubrick bought Abbots Mead, a large house fourteen miles north of London, conveniently close to the film studios of Borehamwood. A piece of stockbroker Georgian, not unlike Peter Sellers's Chipperfield house, with good-sized grounds, a high wall and heavy metal gates, it turned an almost blank façade to the road but offered, from the back, a striking view over a wooded valley. A busy stretch of road ran outside, but opposite were empty fields and a wood. It wasn't the house of someone who had decided to embrace a new way of life, but rather of a person seeking security and isolation. In the course of 1964 Christiane and the girls were installed there, and Christiane returned to the painting that was to become a second career.

As if to underline his divided allegiance, Kubrick kept his old apartment on New York's Central Park West. He was wise to do so. The British film industry happened to be riding high, as American film-makers flooded into the country, attracted by cheap facilities, government assistance and a pool of skilled performers whose salaries were a fraction of Hollywood's. But there had been false dawns before: in the thirties, when the United Kingdom government forced American studios to invest locally part of their profits from the films they exhibited to British audiences, and a decade later, during World War II, when a slowdown in American production encouraged local producers. Each time, the balance soon tipped back towards Hollywood and British studios went dark once more.

Nor, historically, did American film-makers flourish in Europe. Many had tried, starting with Rex Ingram, who set up in Nice in the twenties with his wife and star, Alice Terry. The last influx had been of left-wingers blacklisted in Hollywood who relocated in Paris and London. Jules Dassin, Cy Endfield and Joseph Losey all enjoyed some success, but it was hand-to-mouth work, and dependent on American companies accepting their films for distribution. Kubrick didn't have the temperament to make art-house dramas like Losey, the all-star international thrillers of Dassin, or epics of lost empire like Endfield. Equally he could no longer stomach the life of a hired Hollywood hand, the 'film by fiat, film by frenzy' of which he'd complained to Terry Southern.

Continental Europe was being swept by the New Wave, as the French, with a guerrilla cinema that used 16mm cameras and lightweight tape recorders like machine guns, attacked an imperial Hollywood which, paradoxically, they deeply admired and were fundamentally influenced by. An aficionado of independent cinema and hand-held technique, Kubrick, who would conquer the Everest of hand-holding by shouldering, with considerable help, the bulky 70mm camera for the shot of Floyd and his party descending into the Tycho excavation in *2001: A Space Odyssey*, should have found the *nouvelle vague* inspiring, or at least interesting. But, like most Hollywood film-makers, he wanted no part of it, nor of any school or movement. In 1964, the French magazine *Cinéma* asked his opinion of its influence. Kubrick told them:

> Good directors, when there's a certain number of them, give the illusion that a 'school' exists. But I don't know what that 'school' can stand for. It is evident that Truffaut and Godard always make interesting films; sometimes they make marvellous films. But I can't really say if they have an influence in America. These days, a great many people know how to use a camera and a tape recorder, so we have an outpouring of 'first films'. The documentary technique often used in the films of the New Wave is the most practical one for making a film on a limited budget.
>
> But outside that, I don't believe we've seen any real innovations since *Intolerance* by Griffith, for example. There's perhaps one exception, and that's the use of non-continuity – when a scene moves into a room, for example, without caring about physical continuity, or about a dissolve. I don't know who exactly invented that, but we certainly have a debt to news cameramen.

Writing for Hollywood in the thirties, William Faulkner asked his studio if he could work at home. 'Go ahead, Bill,' they said, thinking he meant Beverly Hills, but Faulkner was thinking about his home town of Oxford, Mississippi. Kubrick's strategy was similar. As far as the studios were concerned, he was still a Hollywood director, working from home. Home, however, happened to be Hertfordshire.

Though he used British technicians and performers, Kubrick's funds came from the United States, and his films made most of their money there. By sleeping through the British day, he could be awake and working when it was light in North America. His new existence evoked the character of the names he'd chosen for his companies: the hawk, hovering, untouchable; the Minotaur in his labyrinth; Polaris, the North Star, one fixed point in the heavens by which all navigate. In particular he would become Odysseus, the mythic traveller, at home nowhere. With Tennyson's Ulysses, he could say,

'I am become a name.' Equally, however, he could identify himself, as Odysseus did to escape the blinded Polyphemus, as 'No Man'.

And what better film to announce his new independence from both American and European film-making, his status as a genuinely new kind of film-maker, the next stage in the development of cinema, than one that took place somewhere other than earth and dealt with 'the three things no one understood . . . *Death* . . . *Infinity* . . . and the *Origin of Time*'?

Chapter Twelve

Kubrick Beyond the Infinite

'There are some things man is not meant to know.'

Standard line in Hollywood science fiction films

'To untangle a can of worms,' runs a piece of good advice, 'start with one worm.' One such worm in the tangle that is the genesis of *2001: A Space Odyssey* is a story told by Alexander Walker, critic for the London *Evening Standard* and Kubrick confidant. Walker recalls visiting Kubrick in New York – around 1957, he thinks; certainly after *The Killing* but before *Paths of Glory*. Kubrick was living in an apartment on the Lower East Side of Manhattan that

> was being cannibalised into the one next door. The debris forced us out. We ate at a restaurant with an Austrian bias to its menu, drank many steins of beer and talked until midnight. I went up to the apartment to collect my overcoat and as I left – it was now about 12.30 a.m. – bright tin cans of film were off-loaded out of a delivery van into the elevator. I squinted at their titles. They were in Japanese. But one or two had English words – just enough to give me a clue to their content.
> 'Are you going to make a film about Outer Space?' I asked.
> Even now I can see the dark suspicious glance I got.
> '*Please,*' said Stanley, '*be careful what you write.*'

There's a superficial logic to Kubrick being interested in science fiction as early as 1957. In 1956 MGM released *Forbidden Planet*, the first modern science fiction film to be made by a major studio.

Traditionally, hand-to-mouth independent producers dominated the field. Cheap settings, cheesy special effects, tenth-rate talent and flashy salesmanship characterised even the relatively ambitious *Destination Moon* and *The Conquest of Space*.

Forbidden Planet was exceptional. Shot in CinemaScope and directed by Fred McLeod Wilcox, who made *Lassie Come Home*, it had the same solidity as that film and, in Walter Pidgeon, a leading man of reputation, supported by the cream of MGM's young contract players: Anne Francis, Leslie Nielsen, and Jimmy Harris's tennis partner Richard Anderson, who would be in *Paths of Glory*. For a change, a science fiction film was made with no expense spared. To perfect the special effects, MGM borrowed Disney's Joshua Meador, who did the volcano work for the *Rite of Spring* episode of *Fantasia*. An original score was commissioned from Louis and Bebe Barron, early experimenters in electronic music. Kubrick undoubtedly saw *Forbidden Planet*, as he saw everything. Its technique would have impressed him, as would the fact that MGM financed it. They would finance *2001: A Space Odyssey* too.

The mid-fifties also ushered in the *Kaiju Eiga* genre: Japanese science fiction adventures in which men in monster suits lumbered knee-deep through Tokyo until halted by either the might of the Self Defence Forces or someone in an even bulkier suit. Inoshiro Honda launched the cycle in 1954 with *Gojira*, better known under its anglicised release title *Godzilla*. Gojira begat Rodan, Gigantis, the Mysterians and, in *The Mysterious Satellite*, alias *The Cosmic Man Appears in Tokyo*, *The Space Men Appear in Tokyo*, *Warning from Space* and *Unknown Satellite over Tokyo*, nameless two-metre-tall black starfish with a single central eye who walk *en pointe* like ballet dancers.

Though it was never worth their while to improve on their pulp plots, *Kaiju Eiga* producers quickly gained technical assurance. Between the clumsy model sequences, the films were often well-photographed in colour and CinemaScope around Japanese beauty spots, and their dismal dialogue was delivered in well-designed and well-lit sets. Hollywood distributors with an eye for a quick profit bought the best of them, added new scenes with second-string American actors, and released them in the US under new names.

Also released in 1957 was the British-made *Satellite in the Sky*. An experimental bomb clung to the space vehicle designated to test it, and the crew, including the bomb's inventor, struggled to nudge it loose. The effects, including the launching of a spaceship on a railroad-like track that zooms up a mountain, were by Wally Veevers. A year later, in December 1958, BBC TV broadcast Nigel Kneale's six-part *Quatermass and the Pit*, in which radical scientist Bernard Quatermass investigates an apparent unexploded World War II bomb under London, and discovers instead a spaceship with the remains of its alien crew inside. Scattered around the ship are the skeletons of ape-like humanoids who have been genetically altered to increase their intelligence. Quatermass develops the unpalatable theory that mankind is descended from hominids who were interfered with by aliens millions of years ago.

Satellite in the Sky and *Quatermass and the Pit* were both examples of that rarity, the British science fiction film, and bore the mark of Britain's undemonstrative scientific visionaries. The rocket launch by rail, though adopted by George Pal for *When Worlds Collide*, had been developed by British writer Arthur C. Clarke for his novel *Prelude to Space*, and was illustrated on the cover of the book's first edition. Clarke would write *2001: A Space Odyssey* and Veevers would work on the special effects. The parallels between *Quatermass and the Pit* and *2001: A Space Odyssey* also seem obvious. Did Clarke, Veevers, MGM, Nigel Kneale and *Kaiju Eiga* plant the idea for the film in Kubrick's fertile brain ten years before it was made?

Well, perhaps. Though Walker does have his dates wrong: Kubrick didn't move into the New York apartment until the mid-sixties; many friends remember the renovations taking place at almost the same time as he and Arthur C. Clarke were writing the screenplay in 1964. But there's enough circumstantial evidence to suggest that *2001: A Space Odyssey* had an earlier gestation than previously suspected.

The traditional starting date of *2001* is February 1964, and the departure point Trader Vic's restaurant in the Plaza Hotel in New York, where Kubrick, in town for the national release of *Dr Strangelove*, was lunching with Roger Caras, the Columbia publicist assigned to the film.

Caras asked what he was doing next. 'Don't laugh,' Kubrick said, 'but I'm fascinated with the possibility of extra-terrestrials.'

If a film like *2001* had to have an incubator, Kubrick could hardly have chosen one more appropriate than Trader Vic's, a chain for which he has always shown a perverse affection. For the man who never travels and prefers always to eat and sleep in familiar surroundings, these ersatz Polynesian eateries, franchised solely to Hilton Hotels, offer, with their Disneyland decor and fanciful food, the perfect combination of the exotic and the familiar. One can cross the world and find oneself sipping the same soupy blue and yellow cocktails festooned with paper parasols and hedged with flowers and slices of fruit, digging into the same dishes of giant shrimp or frozen crab doused in coconut and pineapple and more often than not served in flames. Not surprisingly, the franchise on hotel accommodation on Kubrick's space station circling the earth in *2001* would also be in the hands of Hilton Hotels.

The immediate inspiration for *2001* wasn't, however, science fiction, but the American West. In 1962 MGM released its Western epic *How the West was Won*. 162 minutes long, with four directors, it purported to tell the story of America's westward expansion in four episodes spanning almost a century. Flanking these dramatic sections were slabs of documentary footage, bound insecurely to the drama by a mucilage of narration from Spencer Tracy.

MGM shot the film in three-panel Cinerama, the biggest yet of the big formats, so large that, to fill its enormous screen, the film had to be shot on three cameras side by side and projected by three projectors, a method which left two fuzzy vertical lines where the images met. Despite this trifling technical difficulty and the fact that it could only be shown in a handful of cinemas, *How the West was Won* took $21 million at the US box office and was nominated for three Oscars, winning one of them, for James Webb's screenplay. All over the world, entrepreneurs who, with studio encouragement, had built or rebuilt cinemas to accommodate Cinerama, demanded films to show in them. Kubrick would sell *2001: A Space Odyssey* to MGM as part of that product. The first press release reassured everyone that it would be filmed 'in the Cinerama process', and as a working title Kubrick used 'How the Solar System was Won'.

Having decided to make a science fiction film, Kubrick, systematic as ever, had an assistant draw up a list of the most highly regarded writers in the field, and set out to read at least one work by each of them.

'Why waste your time reading everyone else?' Caras demanded at Trader Vic's. 'Why not just start with the best?'

'Who?'

'Arthur C. Clarke.'

'But I understand he's a recluse,' Kubrick said, 'a nut who lives in a tree in India someplace.'

Caras, who was an intimate of Clarke's, explained that the writer, while not without eccentricities, was an amiable Englishman in his forties who, though born in Somerset, lived in Ceylon because of its pleasant climate, both physical and moral, and because his long-time companion Mike Wilson ran a skindiving business there. Clarke travelled a great deal, and would be in New York within a few weeks for the opening of the World's Fair.

After lunch, Caras cabled Clarke in Ceylon: STANLEY KUBRICK DR STRANGELOVE PATHS OF GLORY ETC INTERESTED IN DOING FILM ON ETS STOP INTERESTED IN YOU STOP ARE YOU INTERESTED QUERY THOUGHT YOU WERE RECLUSE STOP

Clarke hadn't seen *Dr Strangelove*, but he had liked *Lolita*. With the effusiveness typical of him, he cabled Caras: FRIGHTFULLY INTERESTED IN WORKING WITH ENFANT TERRIBLE STOP CONTACT MY AGENT STOP WHAT MAKES KUBRICK THINK IM A RECLUSE QUERY

Had Caras suggested Isaac Asimov, Robert A. Heinlein, Ray Bradbury or any one of half a dozen other successful science fiction writers, *2001: A Space Odyssey* would have been very different. But Clarke and Kubrick made a match. Both were solitaries by nature. Both had a streak of homoeroticism that favoured the sort of film *2001* would become: sleek, sexless, preoccupied with style. Both were opinionated and conceited – Clarke's nickname was 'Ego' – and Caras rightly saw that the two would work better with each other than with a weaker partner, whom the stronger would quickly bulldoze.

Caras was also doing Clarke a favour. Whatever Caras told Kubrick, his friend was far from the world's best science fiction writer. 'His literary abilities are traditional and his prose workaday,' said writer and historian of science fiction Brian Aldiss, who himself would later collaborate, unhappily, with Kubrick. On the other hand, Aldiss acknowledged that, 'More than any other sf author,

Clarke has been faithful to a boyhood vision of science as saviour of mankind, and of mankind as a race of potential gods destined for the stars.'

Clarke's appeal had always been largely in the British market, and though he had a reputation for scientific extrapolation, based on his early interest in rocketry and a lucky guess about the use of synchronous satellites in worldwide communications, other speculations, like horizontally-launched rockets, a Mars that resembled the Sahara desert, and whales being farmed like cows, were more often wrong. Most recently, his 1961 novel *A Fall of Moondust* had speculated that the moon was covered so deeply in talcum-fine dust that vehicles could be engulfed in its drifts.

Working with Kubrick would be the making of Clarke. It elevated him from the front rank of second-rate science fiction writers to someone who, as a speaker put it in welcoming him to a 1976 MIT symposium, 'is the only person I know who can be unambiguously introduced by a four-digit number – 2001'.

In March 1964, Kubrick wrote to Clarke, formally outlining his ambitions. 'He wanted to do the proverbial "really good" science fiction movie,' Clarke told friends. The themes would be: '(1) The reasons for believing in the existence of intelligent extra-terrestrial life. (2) The impact (and perhaps even lack of impact in some quarters) such discovery would have on Earth in the near future.' It would, Kubrick hoped, be 'a film of mythic grandeur'.

While waiting for Clarke to arrive in New York, Kubrick read some of his work. One book immediately caught his attention. The 1954 *Childhood's End* was among Clarke's better efforts, deeply rooted in the work of Olaf Stapledon, the British visionary whose novels *Last and First Men* and *Starmaker* inspired a generation of writers with a conception of mankind developing over millennia against the starry immensity of the universe.

As *2001: A Space Odyssey* was to do, *Childhood's End* covered a century, discarding characters along the way: the real protagonist wasn't a man, but Man. The theme was the same as that of the eventual *2001*: the first contact between humans and an alien race. So was the payoff: the revelation that Man has come to the end of this stage in his evolution, and must be consumed by a holocaust from which New Man will emerge. The characters of the last section of the book are the final generation of mankind as we know it.

Their children go on to a new and higher state; all redolent of *2001: A Space Odyssey*, with its final image of the Star Child reborn in space.

Like many science fiction writers, Clarke was represented by the Scott Meredith agency. When Kubrick checked with them on *Childhood's End*, they told him that Abraham Polonsky, left-wing screenwriter and director of *Force of Evil*, had optioned and scripted the book, but so far had not found a backer. Kubrick kept reading, but it was *Childhood's End* that remained in his mind.

Meanwhile Clarke wrote to him suggesting that his ends might be served by a short story he'd written in 1948 for a BBC competition. It didn't win – it didn't even make the shortlist – but 'The Sentinel' found a place in subsequent collections and was widely anthologised.

There wasn't much to 'The Sentinel'. The seismologist with a 1996 moon expedition spots an unexpected glint high on a mountain at the edge of the Mare Crisium – the Sea of Crises. He finds a plateau a hundred feet across sheered from the mountain. In the centre is 'a glittering, roughly pyramidial structure, twice as high as a man . . . set in the rock like a gigantic many-faceted jewel'. It takes twenty years and a great deal of force for earth's engineers to penetrate the pyramid. They can make nothing of the mechanism inside – and realise they aren't meant to. The object is an alarm, and they have triggered it. Now the aliens who planted it there will come to see if Man is ready for the stars.

Clarke arrived in New York in April 1964. Passing through London, he'd seen and been impressed by *Dr Strangelove*. He met Kubrick at his favourite Trader Vic's, and they began talking science fiction. Eight hours later, they were still at it. The discussions continued for six weeks. By day, Clarke worked on editing a book he'd written for Time-Life. At night, he and Kubrick beachcombed the shore of technology, picking up the prettier stones and bits of driftwood.

Among the documents they discussed was a Rand Corporation report on the possibility of life on other planets which Kubrick had read during his research on nuclear warfare, and which had already contributed to the framing 'documentary by aliens' device planned for *Dr Strangelove*. 'Stanley was in some danger of believing in flying saucers,' said Clarke. 'I felt I had arrived just in time to save him from this gruesome fate.'

Kubrick and Clarke visited the New York World's Fair, and were so impressed by NASA's contribution, a documentary called *To the Moon and Beyond*, that they hired the production company, Graphic Films, to do preliminary work on *2001: A Space Odyssey*. Once Kubrick decided to move the production to Britain, one of the technicians who made the NASA film persuaded him his skills were needed in London. The man, Douglas Trumbull, was hired in a minor capacity. *2001* would launch him on a major career in special effects that would come full circle years later. Hoping, by repeated exposure, to equal what Trumbull called the 'awesome simplicity' of *2001*, Steven Spielberg screened Kubrick's film often before and during the making of another production on which Trumbull did the effects, *Close Encounters of the Third Kind*.

Roger Caras, who became *2001*'s director of publicity, was asked to acquire every book on space travel – still feasible in 1964, when the field was not as crowded as it has since become. He found hundreds, all of which, he insists, Kubrick read. Kubrick and Clarke also screened a lot of sf movies from all periods and countries – the cans Alexander Walker saw. Clarke was still enough of a fan to have an uncomplicated enthusiasm for even the cheesiest of them. He could enjoy *Attack of the Fifty-Foot Woman*; Kubrick burrowed into his newspaper.

A film which did make Kubrick take notice was, improbably, a black and white documentary made in the Montreal studios of the National Film Board of Canada in 1959. Special effects man Wally Gentleman had been assigned to a documentary called *Universe*, which would explain the latest thinking in cosmology and cosmogeny to the Canadian public. Among Gentleman's tasks was to show, without colour or a big budget, the spawning of nebulae and star clusters from the mass of cosmic dust.

Musing over a cup of coffee in the NFBC's commissary, Gentleman noticed that sunlight glancing from the surface of the cup where a whorl of cream was dissolving projected onto the ceiling a revolving pinwheel of light that resembled the great nebula Messier 31 in Andromeda. From this insight – that movements of incandescent gas millions of light years across could be duplicated in blobs of ink crawling in oil on a tiny metal plate – grew the award-winning effects of *Universe*.

Kubrick tried to hire *Universe*'s production team of Gentleman, Colin Low and Con Pederson for *2001*. Long before the start of principal photography, Gentleman supervised the shooting in New York of what Kubrick christened for security purposes 'The Manhattan Project', that being the codename for America's wartime development of the atomic bomb. In a gutted warehouse, an incendiary charge was exploded and filmed in super-slow motion to duplicate the forming of a supernova. Upgrading his *Universe* experiments to colour and 65mm, Gentleman also used microphotography of dyes, inks and drops of coconut oil to create the striking sequences of *2001* in which Bowman watches universes forming. He had no stomach for the pressures of big-time filmmaking, however, and when his health began to suffer he retreated gratefully to Canada; but Pederson remained to become one of the film's ten credited special effects supervisors.

Realising that using Cinerama would demand razor-sharp special effects, Kubrick had also rung Wally Veevers from New York and offered him the job of special effects supervisor. After *Dr Strangelove*, Veevers had suffered a heart attack. He was also technically under contract to Shepperton. But Kubrick, who had visited Veevers in hospital and, according to Ken Adam, 'thought the world of him', persuaded the studio to release Veevers for three months, a secondment that stretched to three years, during which the ailing technician created the crowning achievement of his career.

Science fiction's trashy image has not discouraged serious writers from trying their hand at it. H.G. Wells, Karel Čapek, William Morris and Jack London all wrote visionary novels or plays. On film, it had its classics: the 1926 *Metropolis*, which Kubrick had seen and admired, and William Cameron Menzies's *Things to Come* (1936), based on a book by H.G. Wells, and partly scripted by him, which Kubrick had not seen until Clarke screened it for him, and which he loathed. 'What are you trying to do to me?' he wailed at Clarke. 'I'll never see anything you recommend again!'

Though he never said so, what probably irked Kubrick about *Things to Come* (on which Wally Veevers had worked as an apprentice) was its Englishness. The first third is filled with hand-wringing about the possibility of mass bombing wiping out London, a disaster which, for all the agonising, takes place promptly on schedule. The centre section is occupied by an elaborately evoked post-war Home Counties racked with plague, while the last shows Britons heading into space with all the proselytising passion of Victorians sent to subdue the fuzzy-wuzzies.

'Oh, God,' moans Edward Chapman's archetypal stay-at-home as the first expedition heads for the moon, 'is there ever to be any age of happiness? Is there never to be any rest?'

Raymond Massey, with a profile like Progress on one of Albert Speer's Nazi monuments, intones the great technocratic prayer which must have inspired thousands of young Britons to switch from the humanities to science: 'Rest enough for the individual man – too much, and too soon, and we call it Death. But for Man, no rest and no ending. He must go on, conquest beyond conquest. First this little planet with its winds and ways, and then all the laws of mind and matter that restrain him. Then the planets about him, and at last out across immensity to the stars. And when he has conquered all the deeps of space and all the mysteries of time, still he will be beginning ... All the universe – or Nothingness. Which shall it be?'

For all that Kubrick disliked their rhetoric, films such as *Things to Come* had their effect on *2001*. The future envisaged by H.G. Wells was the sort of future Kubrick wished for, both in his life and for the film: uncluttered, single-minded, and – saving the serpent that always lurks in such Edens – safe. Managed by bureaucrats, its astronauts near-automatons, their philosophy of space as functional as a Ford production-line worker's thoughts about clutch assemblies, its most interesting individual would be the computer HAL 9000. HAL, novelist Clancy Sigal decided when he visited the set, 'is far, far more human, more humorous and conceivably decent than anything else that may emerge from this far-seeing enterprise'. He was right. It was this construct of pure reason, a disembodied voice and a single blood-red eye, with which we, and Kubrick, would most identify: Polyphemus, staring at Ulysses/No Man over a chessboard.

On 17 May, Arthur C. Clarke shook hands with Kubrick on a deal to write the story and/or script of 'How the Solar System was Won'.

Stepping out onto the penthouse patio of Kubrick's New York apartment about 9 p.m., both men saw a bright object crossing the sky. Clarke said it must be a satellite, but the *New York Times* noted no pass by an orbiting satellite that night. It turned out to be Echo 1, a thirty-metre metallised balloon used for high-atmosphere research. Clarke said later that his first thought had been that *They* had decided to intervene to make sure the film never took place.

Clarke quickly realised that Kubrick didn't want to make a science fiction melodrama at all, but what he called a 'mythological documentary' with dramatic inserts – like *How the West was Won*. It would probably have a voice-over, and should include experts on extra-terrestrial life and space travel outlining the possibilities and problems man faced in going into space. Interviews would be filmed with distinguished astronomers, physicists, religious leaders and experts in extra-terrestrial biology for a prologue. For these scenes Clarke persuaded Kubrick to hire Frederick Ordway, an astrophysicist friend, as scientific adviser.

After the interviews, the 'story' would develop, with two themes, both well-worn, predominating. The first was 'We are Property', exemplified by *Quatermass and the Pit* and *Childhood's End*. In the film, mankind has been under the benign supervision of an alien race for millennia, the vehicle of its intervention a black monolith which can act as an alarm, as in 'The Sentinel', but can also influence and educate: in early versions of the script, the ape men see a sort of documentary film about hunting inside the block. The second, and related, theme, also familiar, in particular from *Childhood's End*, is 'Men are Gods'. Our supervisors are only waiting for us to work the kinks out of our system before promoting us to higher levels of consciousness.

True to Kubrick's distrust of technology, however, and reflecting his conviction that the more complex the plan, the more likely it is to fail, Man's elevation to Superman would involve complications and indeed violence. In *Childhood's End*, the children, now superminds, cause the earth they have deserted simply to evaporate. In early versions of *2001: A Space Odyssey*, the Star Child detonates a ring of atomic satellites orbiting the globe, an early prefiguring of Ronald Reagan's 'Star Wars' initiative. One representative of mankind, however, would get the point, and become the avatar of the new consciousness. This mystical sense of man as a God-in-waiting would permeate the film. Kubrick wasn't entirely joking when he said, 'MGM don't know it yet, but they've just footed the bill for the first six-million-dollar religious film.'

If Kubrick couldn't have *Childhood's End*, at least he could have some of the stories which had contributed to it. On 20 May 1964 he optioned six Clarke short stories for $10,000, including 'The Sentinel'. The others were 'Breaking Strain', 'Out of the Cradle, Endlessly Orbiting . . .', 'Who's There?', 'Into the Comet' and 'Before Eden'. Some had potential relevance to the film – the sentient Martian vegetation of 'Before Eden', for instance, wiped out when the first space traveller leaves behind his germs with his debris – but the unexplained disturbance in a spaceship of 'Who's There?', revealed to be kittens, clearly didn't. Buying them all camouflaged Kubrick's real interest in 'The Sentinel', since by 28 May Clarke had signed a deal to write a treatment of that story alone for $30,000, plus a further $30,000, payable half on the start of principal photography and the rest on its conclusion. A year later, Kubrick sold him back the other five stories.

Before Clarke could start on the treatment, Kubrick told him he'd changed his mind. Instead of a treatment, he proposed that he and Clarke write a novel which would become the basis of the screenplay. The script would be credited to Kubrick and Clarke, the novel to Clarke and Kubrick.

Had Kubrick always planned such a strategy? Given the war of nerves he'd fought with all his previous writers, and his fear of someone discovering his plans and getting in ahead of him, it's likely he'd been thinking long and hard about ways to protect his investment. He was also influenced by the fact that Clarke had never written a screenplay.

Clarke worked in the Central Park West apartment for a while, then checked into the run-down but easy-going Chelsea Hotel, which the novelist Nathanael West had once managed and where the likes of William Burroughs still lurked. He aimed to finish the novel in six months, and publish it well before the release of the film in two years' time. He would have done well to recall the old joke, 'If you want to see God laugh, tell him your plans.'

*

The knowing gaze of Dolores Haze, aka Lolita, as first glimpsed by Humbert Humbert in Kubrick's 1962 adaptation of Vladimir Nabokov's novel.

Kubrick with fourteen-year-old Sue Lyon, his choice to star in *Lolita*.

Hollywood censors particularly objected to this scene in *Lolita* where Humbert Humbert (James Mason), grappling with Charlotte Haze (Shelley Winters), gazes longingly at the photograph of his stepdaughter.

Dr Strangelove, or How I Learned to Stop Worrying and Love the Bomb (1964). *Left*: Kubrick and director of photography Gilbert Taylor line up a shot in Ken Adam's War Room set. *Above*: one of Arthur Fellig's shots of the film's deleted pie-fight climax: Russian Ambassador DeSadesky (Peter Bull) and President Merkin Muffley (Peter Sellers) play 'mud pies' in the debris (*Estate of Arthur Fellig; Weegee the Famous/International Center for Photography, New York*). *Below*: Kubrick directs Sellers as the sinister Dr Strangelove.

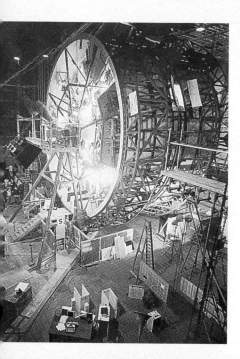

'The first $6,000,000 religious film': *2001: A Space Odyssey* (1968). *Above:* Frank Poole (Gary Lockwood) and Dave Bowman (Keir Dullea) hide out in a pod to plot against the homicidal computer HAL 9000. *Above right:* Poole, en route to Jupiter, jogs round the living quarters of the *Discovery*, past three other frozen members of the crew. *Right:* Kubrick shooting the sequence, and *left:* the exterior of the $750,000 Vickers-Armstrong centrifuge in which it was set. *Below:* Heywood Floyd and his party descend into the excavation in Tycho where the monolith was unearthed. Kubrick personally hand-carried the giant 70mm camera for this shot.

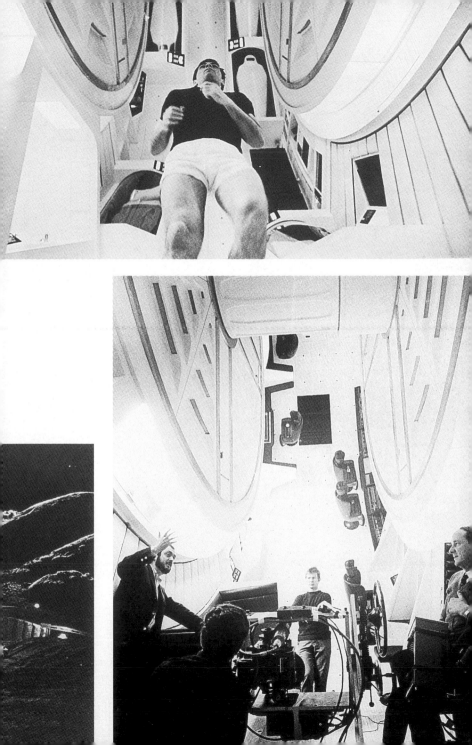

'This is my picture. My toy. I'm the Man.' Marlon Brando, in costume as the gunfighter Rio, with Karl Malden as his Freudian antagonist 'Dad' Longworth in *One-Eyed Jacks* (1961), which Kubrick prepared but Brando directed.

By the end of 1964, Kubrick and Clarke had completed a 130-page summary of the film. Its 'chapter headings', which would appear in the completed film – 'The Dawn of Man', 'Jupiter Mission: Eighteen Months Later' and 'Jupiter and Beyond the Infinite' signposted the 'non-submersible' sequences on which it was based. Louis Blau, who increasingly functioned as Kubrick's agent, lawyer, spokesman and business manager, delivered a copy to Robert O'Brien, who had taken over as president of MGM two years earlier. Starting as he meant to go on, Kubrick told O'Brien he had three days to make up his mind before the project was offered to other studios.

O'Brien, an Irishman with a love of movies and a respect for its greatest directors, among whom he numbered Kubrick, was receptive to the idea of *2001*, but embattled. The chickens – more like turkeys – of the epic fad were coming home to roost. *Mutiny on the Bounty* and *The VIPs* with Elizabeth Taylor and Richard Burton had put MGM $17.5 million in the red, and now David Lean was proving ominously liberal with funds on location for *Dr Zhivago*. It was small comfort that other studios were doing no better. The Burton/Taylor *Cleopatra* had bankrupted Twentieth Century-Fox. Costs on Samuel Bronston's *The Fall of the Roman Empire*, shooting in Spain, were about to top $20 million.

On the other hand, Hollywood had recorded its greatest profits that year since the arrival of television. Foreign markets were booming: since 1956, studios had been earning more overseas than domestically. Cinerama operators were still crying out for material. And with the Beatles' first film, *A Hard Day's Night*, just out, Tony Richardson's *Tom Jones* cleaning up and the new James Bond film *Goldfinger* showing the route to medium-budget, high-profit comedy thrillers, Britain was *the* hot place to make movies. O'Brien also calculated that *2001: A Space Odyssey* could soak up some of the overhead on its underused studios at Borehamwood.

How the West was Won would be the last film shot in three-strip Cinerama. Camera engineer Robert Gottschalk had developed a new spherical lens that answered the optical problems of shooting with extra-wide-angle lenses. A film shot on an anamorphic system with a Super-Panavision lens and released in 70mm, with 5mm of the film reserved for a stereo soundtrack, filled the Cinerama screen without needing three projectors. Stanley Kramer had filmed his maniac comedy *It's a Mad, Mad, Mad, Mad World* in this process, and Cinerama cinema owners had been delighted to find that audiences flocked to it. Most were in the middle of long runs of the Kramer movie, and were eager to know what MGM would offer them to follow. *2001* was the logical choice.

On 23 February 1965 MGM issued a two-page release announcing 'Stanley Kubrick to Film "Journey Beyond the Stars" in Cinerama for MGM.' Like most such documents, it was a confection of half-truths, bad guesses, pious wishes, misquotations and bullshit.

The film, it said, would start shooting on 16 August (it actually began on 29 December). It would be based on a novel to be published in winter 1965 (the book emerged in July 1968). It would use MGM's studios near London (Borehamwood proved too small for many things, so larger sets like the excavated monolith in Tycho were built at Shepperton). It would be filmed on location in Britain, Switzerland, Africa, Germany and the United States (in the end, everything but a few front-projection transparencies of Africa was shot in Britain, almost all of it in a studio).

The estimated cost of *2001* wasn't mentioned in the press release. MGM initially allocated $4.5 million, but this quickly rose to $6 million – roughly the amount finally spent on special effects alone. The total bill was $10.5 million, setting MGM the task of grossing between three and five times that sum before it saw a profit. Fortunately it grossed $21.5 million in the US domestic market alone in its first outing, more than justifying MGM's confidence.

O'Brien gave nothing away about the story, except to assure journalists: 'One thing is certain. It won't be a Buck Rogers kind of space epic.' The release was also cagey about performers ('a cast of international importance'), but this vagueness reflected Kubrick's relative lack of interest in stars. As Kingsley Amis said of science fiction, 'The plot is the hero.' Even so, neither Clarke nor Kubrick were any more forthcoming about the plot. Privately, they had already agreed that it would follow, more or less, the action of 'The Sentinel', with some additions from *Childhood's End*. At the start, an expedition to the moon would discover an alien artefact which, as it was investigated, emitted a piercing signal in the direction of Saturn. A two-man expedition to investigate is aborted when the spaceship's on-board computer goes mad and kills all but one of the astronauts. The survivor, arriving near Saturn, is subjected to a battery of bizarre phenomena, at the end of which he is transformed into a Star Child, the avatar of the next stage in human development. As his first act, he detonates the earth's ring of atomic satellites. Retrospectively, Clarke and Kubrick added two prologues: one in which an earlier, primitive form of man is seen being given basic intelligence by another alien artefact, and another in which contemporary experts in astronautics and xenographics speculate about the possible nature of alien life and the impact on man of his first contact with a cosmic overmind.

In April 1965, 'Journey Beyond the Stars' officially became *2001: A Space Odyssey*. For the next year, Kubrick was almost entirely occupied in gathering and assessing material, and Clarke with rewriting the novel to keep up. The pace of scientific change under the forced draught of the space race was dizzying. When Kubrick began shooting, Luna 1 had just become the first spacecraft to escape from earth's gravity. In 1968, the year the film was released, Apollo 8 put three Americans into moon orbit.

Computer technology, spacesuit design, rocketry and cryogenics all accelerated. The production team fidgeted when Alexei Leonov became the first man to walk in space on 18 March 1965, spending twelve minutes nine seconds outside the Voskhod 2. Ranger 9 went live on TV, sending back 5814 photographs of the moon's surface, then crashing into it. The only damage was to Clarke's moondust theory. Ed White matched Leonov for America on 3 June. After Mariner IV sent back the closest pictures yet of Mars on 14 June, Kubrick facetiously asked Lloyds to quote him on insurance against Martians being discovered. It was too expensive.

Given the flimsy nature of the film's story, strong characters were extraneous, and powerful performances more so. The few good actors approached to appear in the film turned it down on the grounds that there was nothing for them to do. Even Keir Dullea, who played Bowman, one of the astronauts, complained that there was little enough for him to start with, and by the end there was even less. British actor Robert Shaw always claimed that Kubrick offered him a role, and that he accepted, until he found he was being cast as Moonwatcher, the ape leader, but this is probably apocryphal.

Dullea, best known for his role as a disturbed boy in Frank Perry's *David and Lisa* who has an affair with an equally dysfunctional

Janet Margolin, his fellow patient in a mental hospital, was glad to escape from typecasting as a tormented teenager. Gary Lockwood, who started in movies as a stunt man and doubled Anthony Perkins before getting second roles in films like *Tall Story*, was simply glad to have even as thankless a role as that of Frank Poole, the other astronaut.

The rest of the cast Kubrick picked up in London, including North American expatriates Robert Beatty and Ed Bishop. William Sylvester, a Californian who'd settled in Britain, played Heywood Floyd, the bureaucrat whom we follow on his trip through the space station to Clavius Base on the moon, and the triggering of the monolith's signal. Along the way Floyd meets British actors Norman Rossiter and Margaret Tyzack, transformed into improbable Russians. The only other character of note, Floyd's daughter, whom he sees only on a TV screen, and who asks for a bush baby for her birthday, was Kubrick's five-year-old daughter Vivian. Kubrick shot a scene in which someone buys the furry animal for her at *2001*'s equivalent of Harrods, but this, like much else, ended up on the cutting-room floor. So did the souvenir shop selling chunks of moon rock and the sign pointing to 'Howard Johnson's Earthlight Room'.

More effort went into the voice of the HAL 9000 than into finding actors. At one point called 'Athena' and given a female personality, HAL later acquired the voice of British actor Nigel Davenport, then of the American Martin Balsam, until Kubrick decided he put too much personality into it. Returning to one of his initial inspirations, *Universe*, he hired Douglas Rain, who read the commentaries for many Canadian National Film Board documentaries. Rain was originally retained to read the commentary Clarke planned for *2001*, but his supremely calm and rational mid-Atlantic voice became that of HAL.

Clarke used HAL to insert some personal jokes into the film. The machine is made in Urbana, Illinois, because an old college professor of Clarke's became a faculty member of the University of Illinois in Urbana. 'Daisy' was chosen as HAL's party piece because some other friends at the Bell laboratory taught a computer the same song. Both Clarke and Kubrick deny that, since the three letters H, A and L fall, alphabetically, immediately before I, B and M, calling the computer HAL was a slur on IBM. 'HAL' equals '*H*euristically Programmed *Al*gorithmic Computer', and no more, they insist. But many thought the fact that Kubrick inspected the IBM 7090 during *Dr Strangelove* was more than a coincidence. Anthony Burgess believed that Kubrick's interest in codes led him to 'create relationships without knowing it – like in *2001*, where the name of HAL was associated with IBM. He was totally unaware of it.'

HAL developed so intriguing a personality that his relative unimportance to the story became an increasing embarrassment. The idea that he should crack up and kill off most of the expedition came relatively late in development, and the rationale later still. Filmgoers wouldn't discover the reason until the sequel *2010*, directed by Peter Hyams in 1984. In his script for that film, Clarke explained that HAL possessed full details of the monolith's signal but was ordered to withhold them from Poole and Bowman for reasons of security. Forced to lie, the over-refined intelligence, unused to ethical dilemmas, has a nervous breakdown.

This theme does surface briefly in *2001*, in the scene where HAL asks Bowman if he is having doubts about the mission, and if he was disturbed by rumours of a monolith on the moon which preceded the expedition's hurried departure. Bowman assumes the computer is writing a routine psychological report on the crew's state of mind, though it's likely, in the context of the larger story, that HAL's questions are symptoms of a growing paranoia.

In the original script, Bowman quizzes HAL, suggesting that there is 'something about this mission that we weren't told. Something the rest of the crew know and that you know. We would like to know whether this is true.'

'I'm sorry, Dave,' HAL replies smugly, 'but I don't think I can answer that question without knowing everything that all of you know.'

These conversations and much else were lost when Kubrick, at the last minute, decided to emphasise the visual qualities of the film and toss out most of its talk. Frederick Ordway protested at the loss of 'several pages of superb and absolutely required dialogue, without which nothing that happens later can make much sense'. He was right to do so; without this exposition, the story is disjointed. But Kubrick had sensed that the film would not make its most direct appeal on the rational level. *2001: A Space Odyssey* aspired not to the condition of a science fiction novel, but to that of music.

*

Kubrick started shooting on 29 December 1965. Geoffrey Unsworth was the cameraman, assisted by John Alcott, who would eventually replace him. Tony Masters shared Production Designer credit with Ernie Archer, a veteran of the business, and Harry Lange, an ex-Wernher von Braun engineer who supervised much of the space vehicle design. Ray Lovejoy, a young editor who had been David Lean's first assistant editor on *Lawrence of Arabia*, would cut the film, launching a relationship that was to end explosively on *The Shining*.

Meanwhile, Clarke wrote the last chapters of the novel and pressed Kubrick to approve its text so that Scott Meredith could negotiate with publishers. Having devoted most of the last two years to the project, he was running short of money. Kubrick, however, insisted that the book still needed work, though he was vague about just *what* work. Visiting the set towards the end of the year, Clancy Sigal noted, 'Clarke is going up the pole, trying to meet with Kubrick to put the end together.' Andrew Birkin, then a nineteen-year-old assistant runner whose job had been to ferry tea and coffee to the set and to operate one of Kubrick's new toys, an early and cranky version of the Xerox machine which kept overheating and gushing smoke, remembers Clarke moping around the studio 'like a spare prick at a wedding', with plenty of time on his hands to chat with a film-struck teenager, and to speculate for his benefit about the future course of communications technology. One day, Clarke suggested, all this technology would be superseded by chips implanted in our brains, to which our audiovisual requirements would be beamed direct. Chips? Birkin wondered what he was talking about.

The first scene to be shot showed Floyd, Beatty and other scientists examining the monolith in the Tycho excavation. The demands of film-making had imposed sweeping changes on the original story. From a black tetrahedron – it looked too much like a pyramid – the object on the moon became a transparent cube. But nobody could cast perspex of the necessary purity, so it metamorphosed into a simple black slab faced in well-rubbed pencil graphite.

The spaceship Discovery which would track the alien emission from the moon back to its source was originally going to Saturn, until the artists had trouble with the rings. The destination became Jupiter. The ship's configuration posed problems too. The radio-active power plant and living quarters of such a craft would need to be as far from one another as possible, which didn't make for graceful design. After some preliminary guesses at an awkward turkey-in-flight configuration – tiny head stuck out in front on a flimsy neck, and a bulky body with a tuft of rocket exhausts at the rear – Harry Lange and his team developed the matchstick-like Discovery. Once the basic shape had been sculpted in wood and Styrofoam, teams went to work 'detailing' the exterior with moulded plastic parts from Airfix kits of World War II German planes. Credit for much of the well-engineered look of the spacecraft in *2001* belongs rightly to Dornier and Messerschmitt.

The design team under Tony Masters had an easier job creating a credible future. Many regard Masters as the unsung co-creator of *2001: A Space Odyssey*. The white-bread blandness of his PanAm Orion shuttle, staffed by polyester stewardesses in bubble helmets like mini-busbies, and the cream lobby of the space station Hilton with its cerise armchairs, remain in the mind when flashier elements of the film have been forgotten. The art department, however, could never work fast enough for Kubrick, who, convinced that its members spent most of their time chatting and drinking tea, briefly contemplated setting up hidden TV surveillance cameras to spy on them, until others on the unit more acquainted with British union rules advised him that even to contemplate such a move would result in an immediate strike.

Visualising the future offered less of a challenge than recreating the distant past. The apes whose consciousness is raised by the monolith, in particular Moonwatcher, the prototypical warrior/leader and first of his kind to use a bone as a club, needed personality and character beyond even the best-trained chimp. Nonetheless, they mustn't look like men in hairy suits. Aside from two baby chimps, all the apes in *2001* were actors or mimes, chosen for their slim build and thin arms which wouldn't bulk out the suits. All wore helmet-like masks so closely tailored that their own face muscles could be used to activate the apes' eyes and mouths. A pipe had to be wedged between the teeth between takes to stop the jaws from closing and cutting off their breathing. Baby chimps were trained to suckle on the false teats.

The scene of Moonwatcher demolishing the tapir's skeleton, then flinging his bone club into the air, was the only one shot outside a studio. Kubrick set it up on the Borehamwood backlot, on a raised platform which framed out the red double-decker buses passing on the nearby high street. After watching the shoot, he and Clarke walked back to the studio. Kubrick had a piece of broomstick which he tossed repeatedly into the air, studying the effect. Not long after, he suggested the film's most famous jump cut, a three-million-year transition from Moonwatcher's weapon to a bone-white orbiting atomic bomb.

Kubrick's distaste for travel hardened during this production into an absolute refusal to work further than ten miles from home. At the very least, he wanted to find every location within the British Isles. Initially Tony Masters tried to recreate prehistoric Africa on a stage at Shepperton, but when the art department unveiled it for Kubrick one morning, he wasn't convinced. 'I can't believe there isn't a desert in England somewhere,' he complained.

Andrew Birkin, who had just delivered the coffee, saw a golden opportunity to improve his position on the unit. Recklessly he volunteered that he knew of just such a location. Kubrick, delighted at a chance to show up his team, told Birkin to bring him details the next day.

Once outside, Birkin confessed to his friend John Alcott that he'd been bluffing. He had no idea if a desert existed in the British Isles. But a quick search of his school geography books produced a murky photograph of dunes just outside Liverpool. Coached by Alcott on how to write up a location report, and armed with another of Kubrick's techno-toys, a Polaroid camera, Birkin took a train to Liverpool, and had a cab drive him to the site. Arriving just as the sun went down, he shot a panoramic view on Polaroid, avoiding the nuclear power station and the block of flats that marred the view, took a hotel room where he pasted the pictures to boards and typed out his report, then caught the milk train back to London and, arriving at Borehamwood at dawn, persuaded a security guard to let him into Kubrick's production suite in Building 53. After depositing his report on Kubrick's desk, he took a train back to Liverpool, and arrived just as the phone was ringing. It was Victor Lyndon, the film's line producer.

'I don't know what you've done,' Lyndon said, 'but Stanley's just told me to put up your salary. What are you getting at the moment?'

'Eight pounds a week,' Birkin told him.

'As of today,' Lyndon said, 'you're on thirty. And we're going to get you a union card.'

The next day, Kubrick convened a meeting of the art department and produced Birkin's report. With the discomfited ex-runner at his side, he demanded of the assembled designers, 'How is it that you people spent eight months and £50,000 trying to create a desert, when this tea boy, in twenty-four hours and for the price of £8, finds one?'

Thereafter Birkin flourished in the *2001* unit. For the rest of the summer he scouted other possible desert locations in Britain, but as production was put back to the winter Kubrick delegated him to the special effects department as a co-ordinator, working with another newcomer, Ivor Powell, in keeping Kubrick informed day by day of progress. 'I didn't have a private life in those days,' Birkin recalled, 'so I could work until two in the morning. And I learned a lot.'

Technical problems continued to plague the 'Dawn of Man' sequence. No British desert looked quite right, and while the Namib Desert in German South-West Africa, now Namibia, was suitably bleak, it proved impossible to use film of it as back projection, since even the most translucent back projection screen proved too murky for SuperPanavision.

Since nothing needed to move in the background of the sequence, Kubrick decided to use instead 25 x 20cm glass transparencies, projected not from behind the performers, but in front. This system, called Sinar, was invented independently in both the US and France during the Second World War. It used a 27 x 12 metre screen of the optically polarised material developed by the 3M company for motorway 'cats' eyes'. Light hitting the surface was reflected at exactly the same angle, and with almost no diminution. Kubrick delighted Clarke by striking a match fifteen metres from the screen; the light came back with almost undiminished intensity. Any object placed in front of such a projection masked its own shadow. The only time one senses its use in *2001: A Space Odyssey* is when the leopard crouching by the dead zebra (actually a horse with painted stripes) turns to the camera, and its eyes flash with unnatural brightness.

However, so hot were the projectors necessary for this system that a draught or even a breath could crack the glass. The operators' facemasks started a rumour that Kubrick had a Howard Hughes-like terror of infections, just as his habit of wearing a hard hat while at work inside the centrifuge set launched the legend that he habitually wore a crash helmet.

Andrew Birkin went to Africa to shoot 35mm stills of deserts, from which Kubrick selected his backgrounds. Then a number of photographers were sent out to rephotograph them on glass plates with the Sinar camera. The job skyrocketed Birkin into the heart of big-time film-making. When Kubrick told him he liked one location but wanted a gaunt, photogenic but strictly protected two-hundred-year-old kookabong tree from another location placed in the foreground, Birkin bribed park rangers, laid on a midnight truck convoy, cut down half a dozen trees and, braving everything from savage wasps to helicopter patrols, hauled them to Stanley's favoured location for an appearance of a few seconds. Today, Birkin shrugs off the risks. 'If you didn't get the trees, Stanley would find someone who would. He just didn't recognise the word no.'

While engineers under Harry Lange were building and rebuilding models of the spacecraft, construction crews on Shepperton's Stage #3 created their full-sized interiors: the leisure spaces of the main space station in orbit, a hundred metres long and twelve high; the flight deck and cabins of the shuttle that carries passengers there from earth; an eighteenth-century apartment, but with futuristic walls and floor, for Bowman's final prison; and a dozen others.

Never entirely happy with a technologically 'pure' vision of the future, Kubrick continued to tinker with the look of the film, mixing details of decor from many periods, even on occasion trying to incorporate actual eighteenth- or nineteenth-century elements into those of the twenty-first. The gardens of the English stately home Luton Hoo, later to be a setting for *Eyes Wide Shut* in 1997, were taken over for a scene of children, including Anya Kubrick, painting around a decorative pond which Kubrick, by blocking out the house itself, hoped to insert into the space station scenes with front projection, a sequence first reshot in one of Masters' futuristic sets, then abandoned entirely.

The main set of *2001*, however, was to become one of the most admired and discussed creations in the history of cinema. Representing the living quarters of the Discovery, it was a drum with an interior twelve metres in diameter and two metres wide, built by aircraft manufacturers Vickers-Armstrong to revolve on its axis at five kilometres per hour. Strategically placed doors allowed Unsworth to shoot inside, but the camera could also be mounted in a groove running down the centre of the floor, making it possible to film travelling shots as the drum revolved. The set's capacities were little-used, considering the $750,000 it cost, but it contributed one of the most striking scenes in the film, and the one most characteristic of Kubrick: a track with Frank Poole as he jogged around the cylinder, shadow-boxing with the camera.

In every shot of the future, Kubrick aimed for symmetry of composition and shadowless light; what cameramen call 'high key against white'. Ray Bradbury bemoaned the effect: 'The freezing touch of Antonioni, whose ghost haunts Kubrick, has turned everything here to ice.' But one has no sense in the film of either heat or cold, simply an airy ease as neat, soft-spoken people move through bone-pale interiors – the calm of a rational world.

The effect wasn't achieved without some pain. To burn out every shadow, cameraman Geoffrey Unsworth and his assistant John Alcott (who took over after six months' shooting when Unsworth, like many other members of the crew, had to go onto another film, *The Battle of Britain*), poured enormous amounts of light into the set. Even then, Kubrick wasn't satisfied, and often relit the set, making it brighter but also hotter. Gil Taylor, called in to do some additional shooting, was proudly shown the centrifuge. Feeling the heat from the 5000-watt lamps inside the wooden and plastic structure, Taylor warned, 'You're going to have a fire with those lamps. What are you going to do? Have the fire brigade standing by?'

According to Taylor, Kubrick replied, 'Well, I'm not just thinking about lighting. I've got to think about the publicity too.'

Taylor was right to be worried. As would happen, more catastrophically, on *The Shining*, the sets on *2001* did catch fire, though fortunately while they were largely unoccupied; it took four minutes to evacuate the centrifuge.

By May 1966 Kubrick had shot most of the actors' scenes and sent Dullea and Lockwood back to the United States. For the space scenes they were replaced by stunt men dangling on wires from the roof of the studio, or by foot-tall articulated models. Before the two actors left, Kubrick admitted a few press people to the set. Clancy

Sigal found a unit in nervous equilibrium, with satellites revolving in disturbed orbit around a preternaturally calm Kubrick.

The dedication of the unit surprised Sigal, accustomed to the rivalries and petty jealousies of Hollywood. 'Everybody on this film I've met is tremendously responsible; all work and exist as if under the shadow of a great, looming bomb. It causes publicity people to talk like presidential candidates, assistant directors to walk like trappist monks and the art and science people involved to wear expressions of bemused, satisfied contentment that I had always associated with drier and more corporate enterprises, such as NASA and General Motors. This isn't a picture so much as an adventure.' The adventurer, everyone agreed, was Kubrick. 'Stanley will make it work if anyone can,' a reverent helper told Sigal.

Nothing gave more trouble than the last third of the film, when Bowman, the only surviving crewman of Discovery after HAL 9000 has cracked and killed not only Poole but the three in cryogenic storage, finds a giant version of the monolith floating around Jupiter, and is sucked through a Star Gate into the universe of its makers.

Clarke wrote numerous variations on the climax of *Childhood's End* without finding one sufficiently different and, more to the point, sufficiently visually striking to impress the Cinerama audience. One of Cinerama's primary claims to novelty was the fact that the curved screen filled even peripheral vision, so that one had the illusion of being right in the picture. Most Cinerama films had rollercoaster conclusions, with the camera tilting vertiginously on a runaway train or a boat plunging through rapids.

Brian Loftus, working with a cumbersome Bipack camera of the sort that had been used to make the earliest three-colour Technicolor films, provided a clue when he showed Kubrick how, by manipulating the three black and white masters it produced, one could give an almost infinite range of colour effects to the most ordinary images. Bob Gaffney was hired in the US to take aerial shots of desert areas in Arizona, and Andrew Birkin was despatched to the Outer Hebrides with a helicopter fitted with a 65mm camera. Reprocessed through Loftus's camera, this footage emerged as the alien landscape over which Bowman rushes after plunging through the Star Gate beyond Jupiter.

Douglas Trumbull plundered the work of experimental American film-makers to give Kubrick the Star Gate effect itself, a sense of rushing down a corridor of infinite width between walls scrawled with vivid patterns of light. Essentially an optical printer, the slit-scan camera photographed a slowly moving roll of artwork through a vertical slit, tracking from as close as two or three centimetres to as far away as five metres. Once photographed, the images – architectural drawings, op-art paintings, wiring diagrams, computer schematics – were projected at high speed above and below the horizon line of the image to create an effect more dizzying than any rollercoaster.

This device (the only part of the film on which Trumbull worked) was one of those gadgets thrown up by an American, and particularly Californian, culture preoccupied with attaining new states of consciousness and duplicating their effects in other media. It belonged to the same family as the gaudy improvisations of film-makers like John Whitney and Jordan Belson, whose Vortex Concerts splashed vivid patterns across the walls of San Francisco's Morrison Planetarium. Bennie Van Meter in San Francisco and in Los Angeles Pat O'Neill, Burton Gershfield and the Single Wing Turquoise Bird group attached to the studio of painter Sam Francis were all playing with colour separations and visual abstraction. The ecumenicalism of experiment made odd bedfellows. The ending of *2001: A Space Odyssey* would coincide eerily with the final sequence of *Behind the Green Door*, the 1975 pornographic classic made by Jim and Artie Mitchell in San Francisco, in which gouts of semen leap in multi-coloured slow motion.

2001: A Space Odyssey is a primer of the non-digital special effects of which Wally Veevers was a master. Instead of shooting models against a blue screen (which photographs clear on colour film), then adding the background from another negative, the so-called 'travelling matte' system, Kubrick insisted on returning to methods developed in the days of silent movies. Technicians meticulously built up each shot from dozens of elements, winding back the film repeatedly to re-expose the negative. Ironically, the futuristic world of *2001* would be as hand-crafted as a macramé plantholder. Stars were spattered onto backdrops by toothbrushes loaded with white pigment. Dozens of students methodically blocked out portions of the starfield by painting the shape of a spaceship on thousands of acetate sheets. To achieve the depth of field for the space sequences, cameras were stopped down to f22, and each frame exposed for between four and seven seconds.

'Wally Veevers was responsible for 85 per cent of the effects on *2001: A Space Odyssey*,' says Ken Adam. 'There were no computers and digital stuff. Wally did it all with worm gears [moving the camera millimetre by millimetre], the old-fashioned way. He was a brilliant person and rose to the challenge.' As Veevers explained to critic John Brosnan, 'The models had to move absolutely smoothly. When you consider that the model of the space station was nine feet across, and we were only moving three-eighths of an inch a minute while shooting it rotating, you can appreciate why it had to be smooth. The same applied to the model of the Discovery, which was fifty-four feet long and moved along a track 150 feet in length. It took four and a half hours to reach the end of the track, and each time we shot it it had to travel at exactly the same speed.'

Ken Adam didn't work on *2001* himself. He and Kubrick discussed the possibility in New York in 1965 while Adam was *en route* to Florida for the James Bond adventure *Thunderball*, but the designer, accustomed to conceiving the total look of a production, wasn't prepared to be just one talent among dozens, integrating speculative models of space vehicles, scientific hardware, futuristic hotel interiors, recreations of Pleistocene Africa, Louis XVI bedrooms, twenty-first-century business suits and non-gravity toilets into a coherent visual style. In essence, Kubrick created the equivalents of a studio's special effects, design and costume departments. Final decisions, however, rested only with Kubrick, who conceived the look of every aspect of the film, from the opening 'Dawn of Man' sequence to that of the Star Child at the finale.

Towards the end of shooting, Kubrick received a surprise call from MGM. Worried about delays and budget overruns, Robert O'Brien and a group of Metro brass were coming to London to check on progress.

Kubrick called Birkin and Ivor Powell into his office. 'We're going to need graphs,' he told them. 'Make them up.'

'Graphs of what?'

'Doesn't matter. Use lots of coloured tape. Fill the boardroom with them. It doesn't matter what they mean, just so long as they look important.'

Birkin and Powell worked furiously to dress the Borehamwood conference room. Kubrick and Victor Lyndon returned with their guests from lunch in the only decent restaurant in the town, and ten minutes later Birkin and Powell were called in. O'Brien proceeded to do exactly what Kubrick had promised would never happen, and ask what the graphs meant. Fortunately, the two assistants knew Kubrick well enough to have made contingency plans. Between them, they managed to spout enough gobbledegook to convince the men from MGM that the film was on course and in safe hands.

By this time, the *2001* unit was fraying at the edges. For every person who regarded Kubrick as a genius and the film as a potential masterpiece, there were half a dozen who couldn't wait to escape. It didn't help that Kubrick clearly scorned the nine-to-five serious-ness of the highly unionised British technicians. He enjoyed screech-ing to a halt outside the sound stage in his white Mercedes and piling out with the current favourites among his entourage, giggling, 'Gee, guys, it's a raid!' Many members of the crew looked on envi-ously at two other films being made on the Borehamwood lot, Roman Polanski's *The Fearless Vampire Killers* and Robert Ald-rich's *The Dirty Dozen*. '*That's* the real movies,' they told one another, 'not this . . .' When Tony Masters's contract came to an end and he left to work on Lewis Gilbert's glossy version of Harold Robbins's *The Adventurers*, Kubrick tried to hold on to him by claiming he hadn't designed everything he needed – the landing site at Clavius Base, for instance. The designer grabbed a pad from Kubrick's desk, quickly sketched a hexagonal landing pad, and left. Many went with him.

Music had always been in the forefront of Kubrick's mind as he conceived *2001*. He 'intended the film to be an intensely subjective experience', he said, 'that reaches the viewer at an inner level of consciousness, just as music does'. Screening some early footage for MGM, he played Mendelssohn and Vaughan Williams as accom-paniment. For inspiration while writing the script, he and Clarke had listened to the German composer Carl Orff's romping transcrip-tion of thirteenth-century sacred and secular songs, *Carmina Burana*. They even considered commissioning a score from Orff, who had written a fantasy opera, *Der Mond* (The Moon) but, at seventy-two he was too old for such a demanding job. Frank

Cordell, a minor composer best known for his work on Fred Zinnemann's *The Sundowners*, was briefly retained, and recorded some extracts from Mahler's Third Symphony for possible use in the film.

There are rival explanations of the final decision to use pre-recorded classical music for *2001* rather than a composed score. Kubrick himself claimed that he always had such a scheme in the back of his mind. Like most directors, he says, he compiled a 'temporary track' for the film to test the effect of different sorts of music. Some directors use pieces or, occasionally, an entire score, from other movies, but Kubrick used records.

As well as Mahler's Third, Kubrick says he intended to have the scherzo from Mendelssohn's *A Midsummer Night's Dream* accompany the shuttle with Floyd on board docking with the space station, but changed his mind when Christiane insisted he listen to a new recording of Johann Strauss's *Blue Danube* waltz, with Herbert von Karajan conducting the Berlin Philharmonic. She took the record to the cutting room and put it on the record player. Thinking that Kubrick had changed his mind about the music for the sequence, the cutting room staff said enthusiastically 'That's great, Stanley,' so Kubrick kept it.

Andrew Birkin remembers things differently:

> We spent hours in the screening room looking at rushes of the space sequences. It was very boring; there was one old technician who always went to sleep. You could hear him snoring.
>
> In the projection box, there was a pile of scratched old classical records that they played for preview audiences. The projectionist played these through the sound system while we were watching the rushes.
>
> On about the fourth day, we were looking at a shot of a space ship and the scratched old copy of the *Blue Danube* came on. After a few moments, Stanley said, 'Would it be crazy or a stroke of genius to use this music in the film?'

Wherever the idea came from, it took root and flourished in Kubrick's mind. According to Birkin, a *Time-Life* TV series about World War I which was running on the BBC at the time used Richard Strauss's *Also Sprach Zarathustra* as a theme, and suggested

Kubrick's use of its shouting fanfare to open *2001*. Turning to more modern composers, Kubrick chose *Atmospheres*, *Lux Aeterna* and *Requiem* by the contemporary Hungarian composer György Ligeti, whose shimmering writing for wordless choral voices evoked the mystery of the monolith, while the tedium of the long star voyage was underlined by the *Gayaneh* ballet music of Khatchaturian.

At the final preview screening for O'Brien and the MGM brass in Hollywood, Kubrick broke the news that he proposed to use recorded music on the film. The idea was instantly rejected. Anything less than a full score by a major composer would be inconsistent with the strategy of making each Cinerama release an event. The meeting broke up with Alex North, who had composed the music for *Cleopatra* and had worked with Kubrick on *Spartacus*, formally attached to the film as its composer.

North was living at New York's Chelsea Hotel, where Arthur C. Clarke had written the film's script. He'd just finished a tedious score for the dialogue-bound *Who's Afraid of Virginia Woolf?* and jumped at the offer of *2001*. Early in December 1967 he flew to London, where Kubrick ran his rough cut with the temporary tracks, some of which, he said, he wanted to retain. North protested. 'I felt I could compose music that had the ingredients and essence of what Kubrick wanted,' he said, 'and give it a consistency and homogeneity and contemporary feel.' Kubrick acquiesced.

Installed in a Thames-side Chelsea apartment on Christmas Eve 1967, North spent the next two weeks furiously composing forty minutes of music which his orchestrator, Henry Brandt, scored while the ink was still wet. Writing so large a score in so short a time almost wrecked North's fragile health, and he came down with stress-related muscle spasms and back trouble. Kubrick, however, seemed satisfied with the music, even suggesting some minor changes. For eleven days North waited to hear if more was needed, but in early February Kubrick said he would use only sound effects for the rest of the film, and gave the go-ahead for the score to be recorded. An exhausted North had to be taken to recording sessions by ambulance. With the music safely taped he returned to Hollywood, confident he'd done a good job under difficult circumstances.

Meanwhile, Arthur C. Clarke, back in Ceylon, continued to wrangle with Kubrick about the novel, the final text of which the director still refused to approve. Each time Clarke felt sure the script and book were set, Kubrick would cable him for some more dialogue or a new scene, none of which, Clarke claimed, ever found their way into the film. Clarke says, 'I asked [Kubrick] if he were deliberately delaying publication of the book until the film was out, so it would not appear that the film was based on the book. He made a genuine protestation that he was not up to that. He said he believed that the book needed further work, and he did not then have the time to read it. He also explained that the general release of the film would not be until late in 1967 or even 1968. And when it did first open, it would be running only in a few Cinerama houses, which would give us some breathing space.'

Scott Meredith negotiated a deal with American publishers Delacorte for a $160,000 advance for the novel, subject to delivery of a manuscript approved by both Clarke and Kubrick. They intended to issue the hardcover well before the movie came out, then to bring out the paperback as the film opened. Anticipating Kubrick's agreement, Delacorte set the book in type, even producing a few proof copies. Kubrick continued, however, to withhold his endorsement of the manuscript. He didn't give it until a few weeks before the film's release. 'Not a word had been changed,' said Clarke glumly when he read the approved text. By that time Delacorte had lost interest, broken up the type and binned the contract. Clarke, $50,000 in debt, did a deal with New English Library for a $130,000 advance, hardly imagining that this would represent only a fraction of the money he would ultimately make from the novel's many editions, translations, sequels and spin-offs.

Kubrick almost certainly did delay the book in order to protect the film. The film took on its own life as it was being made, and Clarke became increasingly irrelevant. Kubrick could probably have shot *2001* from a treatment, since most of what Clarke wrote, in particular some windy voice-overs which explained the level of intelligence reached by the ape men, the geological state of the world at the Dawn of Man, the problems of life on the Discovery and much more, was discarded during the last days of editing, along with the explanation of HAL's breakdown. So were all references in the dialogue to worldly politics and to the atomic bombs trained on the earth, making nonsense of the cut from Moonwatcher's spinning bone weapon to its twenty-first-century equivalent, the orbiting bomb. The fact that generations of filmgoers have found the film eminently watchable without this logical underpinning justifies Kubrick's decision. As William Kloman was to write in the *New York Times*, 'Space Odyssey is poetry. It asks for groovin', not understanding.'

In March 1968 MGM began previewing the film in Washington DC, New York and Los Angeles, prior to a New York premiere on 4 April. Kubrick and his family had come over from England by boat, fitting an extra cabin with a Steenbeck editing table so he could keep editing during the trip. With the family deposited in a rambling mansion on Long Island, Kubrick threw himself into the pre-release of the film. He attended every preview, prowling the aisles, noting when people began to squirm with boredom. The Washington presentation, which Robert O'Brien attended, received an ominously muted response. According to producer David Brown, 'the word that night was that [O'Brien] was out of a job. At the end of the preview, marked by scattered applause, mostly from MGM executives, word also came that Lyndon Johnson would not run for re-election, whereupon the chief publicity officer of MGM gathered some of his group around him and said solemnly, "Gentlemen, tonight we have lost two presidents."' O'Brien survived, but after this screening Kubrick ditched the interviews with real-life authorities on space, alien life and religion which were originally intended to open the film.

The first New York preview took place on 1 April. MGM turned it into a social event for celebrities of science and show business. They included Alex North, who was shattered to discover that Kubrick had discarded his score totally, and restored his pre-recorded classics. He had been told nothing about the change – presumably because he would have complained to MGM, causing a confrontation with the studio. *Paths of Glory* had taught Kubrick to keep his production partners as much in the dark as possible.

North's disgruntlement at the fate of his work was mirrored by the reaction of many in the cinema that night. 'I have never seen an audience so restless,' said Kubrick, who watched from the projection box. Most of the guests were aged between thirty-five and sixty. 'By the end of the film some of these were already leaving,' Kubrick recalled, 'and I will never forget my irritation at watching the sight of the Star Child's enormous eyes gazing at their backs as they headed up the aisles towards the exit.' It seemed that his greatest gamble would also be his most monumental flop.

Chapter Thirteen

Kubrick Among the Thugs

'Yarbles, bolshy great yarblockos to thee and thine!'

Alex Burgess, aka Alex DeLarge, in *A Clockwork Orange*

MGM opened *2001: A Space Odyssey* on 4 April at a single cinema, Manhattan's only Cinerama venue, Loew's Capitol, at Broadway and 51st Street, and two days later at the Cinerama Dome in Los Angeles. Critics and audience were instantly polarised.

Of the reviewers in the daily papers, Charles Champlin in the *Los Angeles Times* found 'deliberate obscurantism' in the ending, but agreed that the film was likely to sweep the Oscars for technical inventiveness. Renata Adler in the *New York Times* felt, like many, that the intellectual content didn't match the skill of the special effects. The film's 'uncompromising slowness', however, impressed her, even though it encouraged people to talk throughout screenings as their attention wandered. 'The movie is so completely absorbed in its own problems,' Adler wrote, 'its use of colour and space, its fanatical devotion to science-fiction detail, that it is somewhere between hypnotic and immensely boring.' The comment was meant kindly, and made up part of a largely favourable, if somewhat baffled, review, but it and other such notices irritated Kubrick, who snapped that demanding a coherent opinion from someone within a few hours of seeing so complex a film was absurd.

Some of the criticisms bit, however. The next morning, Kubrick arrived at the basement cutting rooms of the MGM building on 6th Avenue and set about removing nineteen of *2001*'s 161 minutes. Vivian scampered around the cutting room, demanding chocolate donuts, which a gofer fetched from the Sixth Avenue Deli opposite. Kubrick refused to patronise them. They couldn't, in his opinion, make a decent sandwich to go – just another frustration of life in New York.

Kubrick's cuts had little effect on the film's sense, though they did speed up its pace. In the first version, Poole jogged around the centrifuge, shadow-boxing, eleven times. Before he cut the film, it also showed every step of each attempt by the astronauts to replace the apparently faulty AE53 unit, following both Poole and Bowman out of the Discovery's antenna and back inside, all in laborious slow motion and without dialogue.

MGM, at Kubrick's insistence, kept the publicity for 2001 low-key. The first poster, used only for the Capitol, showed Floyd chatting to a group of Russian scientists in the lobby of the space station hotel under the slogan 'New at the Hilton for the Year 2001'. Below was a small red-tinted shot of Dullea in his helmet, and a visualisation, soon to become famous, by Robert McCall, of the PanAm shuttle being launched from the landing port at the station's axis. For the general US release, the studio experimented with two 3-D posters using McCall's artwork, then settled on the most common graphic, the Star Child against a space background. Once the film reached neighbourhood theatres in 35mm, the advertising became more strident. 'A shrieking monolith buried by an alien intelligence!' yammered the trailer, 'and a talking computer known as HAL!' To enliven the trailer, publicists scrounged from out-takes a few shots of meteorites bowling past the camera, to imply that the film contained this most hoary of space-movie menaces.

Despite little pre-publicity, 2001 broke the first-day record for the Capitol. And by the end of the week, magazine critics, with less demanding deadlines than their newspaper colleagues, had given the film a more measured assessment. It was these second looks which began to build 2001's reputation. The *Village Voice*'s Andrew Sarris, doyen of intellectual film critics, initially panned it, but was persuaded to go again 'under the influence of a smoked substance ... somewhat stronger and more authentic than oregano'. It must have been great grass, because he reversed his position and reviewed the film favourably the next week.

It became fashionable to attend 2001 while stoned. Author Michael Herr, then just back from Vietnam and later to write *Full*

Metal Jacket for Kubrick, recalls seeing the film in a cinema 'pungent with pot smoke – some of it my own'. As the Star Gate sequence approached, people began gravitating towards the front of the cinema, lying down in front of the first row of seats to accentuate the vertiginous effect of the images. After an employee posted in the lobby to survey the kind of people buying tickets reported they were 'mostly Negroes and people with beads', MGM began offering discreet encouragement to the hallucinating classes. In particular, Louise Sweeney's comment in the *Christian Science Monitor* that '*2001* is the ultimate trip' figured prominently in many later ads.

Kubrick denied ever using LSD himself, but he'd discussed it with acid-head friends and anticipated its widespread use within a few years. A conviction that 'mind-enhancing perception-enhancing drugs are going to be part of man's future', as computers assumed more of the functions of our survival, would fuel his decision to film the novel *A Clockwork Orange*. He could readily imagine Anthony Burgess's street gangs high on 'Milk Plus' spiked with 'vellocet, synthemesc and drencom', and was more amused than alarmed by acid's potential for social disruption. On the set of *2001*, when Clancy Sigal mentioned his problems in plotting a political thriller, Kubrick excitedly suggested a possible scenario. 'Just imagine; this innocent-looking Puerto Rican bus-boy in the White House, but he's turned on. He slips an LSD sugar cube into President Johnson's coffee, and blammo!'

By 1972, *2001: A Space Odyssey* would rack up a respectable $31 million gross worldwide, more than satisfying MGM. Critic David Denby, wryly commenting on Kubrick's extraordinary sense of the *zeitgeist*, would later compare him to the black slab of the film – 'a force of supernatural intelligence, appearing at great intervals amid high-pitched shrieks, who gives the world a violent kick up the next rung of the evolutionary ladder'.

Even Arthur Clarke, who had sworn off films after *2001*, buried his resentment sufficiently to offer Kubrick his next project, 'The Songs of Distant Earth'. Set in a future where the sun has gone nova and only a single giant ship with a million frozen inhabitants has escaped, it is set mainly on the Tahiti-like planet of Oceania, where the natives live an idyllic existence unsullied by earthly concepts of civilisation. The ship pauses there to replenish the shield of ice which protects it while entering the atmosphere, and has the same impact on the locals as the first visit to earth's Pacific islands by Europeans. After discovering that the seas harbour intelligent giant squid which may give the Oceanians a run for their evolutionary money, the earthmen push off, leaving the two races to fight it out.

Not only did the story give Clarke a chance to ride his hobby horses of ocean farming and Pacific Rim culture; it was also his first novel to include a homosexual – or, more accurately, bisexual – relationship. Kubrick rejected the treatment as 'not his cup of tea'. (Ironically, the man who had got Clarke involved in 2001, Roger Caras, had by then left MGM to manage Kubrick's own company, Hawk Films.)

Clarke was not alone in hoping to capitalise on the success of 2001. The sets so impressed William Read Woodfield, Kubrick's stills cameraman on *Spartacus* and later the producer of TV series like *Mission: Impossible*, that he pitched to MGM *Earth II*, set on 2001's space station and using the miniatures created for the film. ABC liked the idea, and MGM asked for everything connected with the production to be shipped to them. Braced for an avalanche, they received a single roll of drawings and the two-foot-tall models of Poole and Bowman used for the space scenes. Everything else had been destroyed, they were told. A disappointed Woodfield produced and co-wrote a pilot for *Earth II* with Gary Lockwood and Anthony Franciosa, but the series never got off the ground, and the pilot was released as a TV movie in 1971.

Legends persisted of a warehouse near London filled with the props and impedimenta of 2001. Editor Gordon Stainforth recalls that as late as 1978, a storage area at Elstree next to where he was cutting Vivian Kubrick's documentary about the making of *The Shining* was crammed with props and artwork from Kubrick's films, including 2001. 'He's a jackdaw,' Adrienne Corri confirms. 'He saves *everything*.' One group of props at least was easily located. To make cryogenic coffins for the astronauts, the design staff modified three deep freezes. After the film Kubrick moved them into his house, where they became frozen food lockers.

On 14 April 1968 the Academy Awards, predictably, snubbed *2001: A Space Odyssey*. Despite the film's sweeping success in the youth market, which turned *Also Sprach Zarathustra* into a top-ten album hit, the predominantly middle-aged voters on the Academy stuck with old-fashioned studio movies: *Funny Girl, The Lion in Winter, Oliver!, Rachel Rachel* and Franco Zeffirelli's opulent but vapid *Romeo and Juliet. 2001* was nominated for Best Direction, Original Story and Screenplay, Art Direction and Special Effects. Astonishingly, despite the level of creativity achieved by make-up man Stuart Freeborn and his team, *2001* wasn't even nominated for an award for costume design, though the vastly inferior *Planet of the Apes* was.

Kubrick had jokingly told Anthony Harvey after editing *Lolita*, 'You know, Tony, you've become quite impossible. You've become the Peter Sellers of the cutting room. You'd better get out and direct before you drive me mad.' Harvey took his advice, and ended up nominated as Best Director next to Kubrick for *The Lion in Winter*. Both lost, however, to Carol Reed for *Oliver!*

2001 won only for Special Effects, setting the tone for Hollywood's treatment of *Star Wars, Close Encounters of the Third Kind* and *E.T.: The Extraterrestrial*, all of which would be fobbed off with technical awards. Normally each of the four special effects supervisors would have received Oscars, but it was Academy policy at the time never to give out more than three statuettes for a single award. Accordingly, Kubrick, who took screen credit for designing the effects, got the film's sole Oscar. Most of the film's technical team didn't begrudge it. However skilful their technical innovations, it was Kubrick's vision which appeared on the screen.

Nobody who has ever filmed an epic quite forgets the thrill of commanding vast forces and spending millions. Kubrick was no exception. However much he bad-mouthed *Spartacus*, he relished the glimpse it had given of how it must feel to lead an army. As both the actor Malcolm McDowell and Kubrick's closest colleague at the Warner Brothers office in London, Julian Senior, would comment a few years later, Kubrick in another life would have been a general, not a film-maker.

Late in 1967, Kubrick summoned Andrew Birkin, his inventive assistant on *2001*, to Borehamwood. Birkin found him installed in the same Building 53 from which he'd directed that film, his staff reduced to its editor, Ray Lovejoy, who remained on the payroll as a glorified personal assistant. He was shortly to be joined, however, by Bob Gaffney, whom Kubrick had persuaded to relocate to London with his family to work on a new project.

'Stanley really levelled with me,' says Birkin. 'He told me, if not exactly in those words, "I've got MGM eating out of the palm of my hand. This is my chance to make the one film I've always wanted to make, the life of Napoleon."'

Napoleon was a man after Kubrick's own rational heart. 'Different subjects and affairs are arranged in my head as in a cupboard,' the Emperor had said. 'When I wish to interrupt one train of thought I shut that drawer and open another. Do I wish to sleep? I simply close all the drawers and there I am – asleep.'

Malcolm McDowell was surprised at the way Kubrick ate – a mouthful of dessert, a piece of steak, another bite of dessert. 'What's the difference?' Kubrick said. 'It's all food.' Then the clincher: 'This is how Napoleon used to eat.' Napoleon also shared Kubrick's habit of assailing everyone he met with a barrage of questions, often asked with little interest in the answers, but simply as a means of reducing his interlocutors to exhausted acquiescence. Later, Kubrick confessed that he had adopted another technique of Napoleon's. Both kept a mental roster of the people on their personal staff, and subtly rotated them in and out of favour. A man praised one week would find himself progressively less valued, until even his most energetic efforts were rewarded with nothing but icy stares. Soon after, however, he would be elevated abruptly to a favoured position again. The system kept subordinates subtly off-balance, and too busy competing for their leader's favour to waste time or intrigue against him.

Kubrick's initial plans for the film were grandiose. He outlined them to the critic Joseph Gelmis in a rare interview in 1968. Shooting would start in the winter of 1969, he said. Location work would be finished in three months, with four months in the studio to follow. He expected to use 'a maximum of forty thousand infantry and ten thousand cavalry for the big battles, which means that we have to find a country which will hire out its armed forces to us – you can just imagine the cost of fifty thousand extras over an extended period of time.'

Anyone who still regarded Kubrick as anti-war would have been taken aback by his description of how he proposed to film the battles. 'Napoleonic battles are so beautiful, like vast lethal ballets

... They all have an aesthetic brilliance that doesn't require a military mind to appreciate ... It's almost like a great piece of music, or the purity of a mathematical formula. It's this quality I want to bring across, as well as the sordid reality of battle. You know, there's a weird disparity between the sheer visual and organisational beauty of the historical battles sufficiently far in the past, and their human consequences. It's rather like watching two golden eagles soaring through the sky from a distance; they may be tearing a dove to pieces, but if you are far enough away the scene is beautiful.'

Andrew Birkin had proved his courage and enterprise on *2001*. Additionally, he knew the Sinar system, to which Kubrick was now completely converted. He believed he could make 'Napoleon' for very little money by front-projecting all the static settings, reserving his money for the battles and scenes of pomp, which would be shot somewhere like Romania, with its armed forces standing in for the Grande Armée. Bob Gaffney, acting as advance man, had already made the deal; the Romanians were even prepared to draft more conscripts to make up the numbers Kubrick demanded. News that Italian producer Dino de Laurentiis was planning his own massive production of *Waterloo*, to be directed by John Huston and starring Peter O'Toole as Napoleon, didn't worry Kubrick. Anything de Laurentiis and Huston could do, he could do incomparably better.

Kubrick put Birkin in charge of researching 'Napoleon'. 'Wherever Napoleon went,' he ordered, 'I want you to go. And if you find a few trinkets, buy them up.' In May 1968, at the height of the student riots that littered Paris's streets with barricades and burned-out cars, Birkin found himself in the French capital with a two-man film crew and a letter from Minister of Culture André Malraux authorising their entry into any and all of the nation's great monuments. Meanwhile, Kubrick hired Felix Markham, Britain's leading Napoleon expert, as historical advisor. By June, twenty students from Oxford were at work summarising every Napoleon biography. Material about Bonaparte accumulated at Borehamwood: books, props, battle plans, sketches of locations and interiors – five thousand illustrations.

In July, MGM and Kubrick jointly announced the project – an extraordinary one for the studio, which had lost heavily on a series of expensive misfires. Corporate sharks were already eyeing MGM's real estate and library of films, the value of which its share price failed to reflect.

If Kubrick was aware of MGM's fragility, he proceeded as if it made no difference. He screened all the surviving Napoleon films, from Abel Gance's silent 1927 epic, still then existing largely in fragments, to Daniel Taradash's 1954 version of Annemarie Selinko's best-seller *Desirée*, with a pouting Marlon Brando as Bonaparte. His film would offer a new vision of the man, he said, one which played down his heroics and stressed his human fallibility. He told the American Jesuit film critic Gene Phillips, 'It is difficult to make a film about a historical figure that presents the necessary historical information and at the same time conveys a sense of the day-to-day reality of the characters' lives. Most people don't realise, for example, that Napoleon spent most of his time on the eve of battle immersed in paperwork. You want the audience to get the feeling of what it was like to be with Napoleon.' He spent weeks trying to unravel some of Napoleon's more puzzling actions, such as his and Josephine's snatching the crown jewels on the night before his coronation.

The technical problems of filming the eighteenth and early nineteenth centuries fascinated Kubrick as much as had recreating the twenty-first. With John Alcott, the assistant cameraman on *2001* who was eventually to shoot *Barry Lyndon*, he had long discussions about the possibility of shooting by candlelight, and the relative resolution of negative over reversal stock: Kubrick favoured reversal. To design costumes he hired John Mollo, an expert on military uniforms and regalia, and ballet and opera designer David Walker, who Adrienne Corri, an expert on the painter Thomas Gainsborough, believes 'knows more about eighteenth-century costume than anyone I have ever met, being able to date a cuff or a lace cap in a picture practically to the day'. After three exhausting months doing costume sketches for 'Napoleon', however, Walker, according to Corri, 'gave up. He told me, "I'm not going to spend any more time doing pornographic drawings for Stanley Kubrick." Stanley had him doing sketches of ladies in these Empire line dresses, with their tits falling out. Stanley has a fixation about tits.' Kubrick's plans for balletic battles and historical insight were rapidly becoming submerged in a fascination with Napoleon's love life, which Kubrick had called 'worthy of Arthur Schnitzler'.

After a protracted argument about whether rhododendrons had been introduced to Britain from India in Napoleonic times – they hadn't – stage designer Carl Toms also cracked, and resigned, as did Mollo. Kubrick offered to double, then triple his salary, but Toms had had enough. 'Stanley's quite an ignorant man in many ways,' says Corri. 'He's not a curious man either. But he's a vampire on people's brains. All this note-taking is just a way of accumulating what other people know.'

At the end of 1968, Andrew Birkin returned from the last of his research trips around Europe. Such was the power of Kubrick's reputation and Malraux's letter that the holiest of holies, the cabinets of the Hôtel des Invalides containing the Emperor's most intimate treasures, including his ring and his portable field chair, had been flung open for him. Birkin tried on the ring but couldn't get it off, while the camera assistant sat on the chair and broke it. At Fontainebleau he'd unearthed Napoleon's personal lavatory, now a broom cupboard, and, under the floorboards of her apartments, Josephine's sunken bath. At Waterloo he took samples of earth so that Kubrick's recreation would match the original. Birkin also acquired a bronze facsimile of Napoleon's deathmask, which he presented to Kubrick as a Christmas present. 'He looked at it with what seemed a sense of foreboding,' Birkin says. 'I think he'd already heard what had happened at MGM, and that O'Brien had been given his marching orders.'

In October 1968, Robert O'Brien had come under attack from MGM's board. In January 1969 he would be replaced by Louis F. 'Bo' Polk, an executive with a background in the cereal industry. O'Brien's fall paved the way for hotelier Kirk Kerkorian to start acquiring the shares that, by August 1969, had made him owner of MGM, with an agenda that foreshadowed the company's virtual extinction as a producer of movies.

At the end of 1968, unable to persuade MGM to finance the film, Kubrick fired all his researchers from 'Napoleon'. Stubbornly, however, he persisted with the project, writing a full screenplay which he delivered to MGM in September 1969. He had the advantage of knowing what was in *Waterloo*, since the resourceful Birkin had managed to acquire a copy of its screenplay while researching in Rome. De Laurentiis's film dealt only with the 'hundred days' between Napoleon's escape from Elba and his defeat by

Wellington, so Kubrick resolved to cover the whole of Napoleon's life.

Though Kubrick told the British press that he was considering British actors David Hemmings and Ian Holm to play Napoleon, his final choice was the American Jack Nicholson. Having just made a small reputation as the drunken liberal lawyer in *Easy Rider* after years playing in horror and biker films, Nicholson was exactly the sort of performer Kubrick preferred: up-and-coming, ambitious and therefore malleable. Ten days after seeing *Easy Rider*, Kubrick wrote to Nicholson that 'you alone have the quality that cannot be acted as an actor. The director cannot create intelligence within a characterisation for an actor and you have it tremendously. It permeates your work.'

Nicholson liked the idea, but before Kubrick could progress past his initial screenplay, the cinema, having largely ignored Napoleon for three decades, suddenly began to take an interest. Eli Wallach played the Emperor in Jerzy Skolimowski's *The Adventures of Gerard*, released in 1970, and Kenneth Haigh starred in Fielder Cook's 1971 *Eagle in a Cage*. After trying for years to raise $20 million to make *Waterloo* with Peter O'Toole under Huston, Dino de Laurentiis persuaded the Russians to put up the money, their army and *War and Peace* director Sergei Bondarchuk for a four-hour epic starring Rod Steiger as Napoleon. None of these films made money, however, and the chances of anyone funding Kubrick's epic became even more remote. He turned his mind to other more realisable projects.

It was at this point, towards the end of 1969, that Terry Southern in New York, to his surprise, had a call from Kubrick.

'You remember that book of Anthony Burgess that you showed me?' Kubrick asked.

Southern remembered it well. During the filming of *Dr Strangelove* he'd been deeply impressed by *A Clockwork Orange*, and had given Kubrick a copy. Set in a Britain of the near future, the novel described a London where twentieth-century technology co-exists with eighteenth-century squalor. At large in it, raping, murdering and robbing with impunity, are small gangs of elaborately dressed teenagers like the Roaring Boys of Regency days, who 'sharpen themselves up' on drug-spiked Milk Plus before their excursions.

One gang is led by Alex Burgess, an intelligent fourteen-year-old with a love of Beethoven who adopts the self-aggrandising nickname 'Alex DeLarge'. After a vicious attack on a middle-class couple, the government use Alex in an experiment with the 'Ludovico Technique' of aversion therapy. It causes him to become nauseous when tempted to inflict violence on anyone, but has the accidental side-effect of making him loathe Beethoven. Back on the streets, he's attacked by the tramps he once beat up, then victimised by his old friends, who are now policemen, and finally imprisoned by the husband of the woman he fatally raped, who plays Beethoven's Ninth Symphony until Alex throws himself out of the window. His case arouses widespread indignation, and the government hurriedly reverses the conditioning.

Burgess based the book's sexual violence on an incident in his own life. In 1944, while he was serving in the army in Gibraltar, four GI deserters beat up and robbed his wife in London. As a result she lost the baby she was carrying. Burgess also believed her later ill-health, mental and physical, stemmed from the attack. More directly, Alex and his gang were inspired by the street gangs of Leningrad, which Burgess had observed on a Russian visit, and by the British Teddy Boys of the late fifties, who affected modified Edwardian clothes. Burgess's gang members, though, are much younger – no more than fourteen.

He meant the story to take place around 1972, but, to avoid the book dating too much, invented a new clothing style and a private language for the gangs, a pidgin version of Russian. He called it 'nadsat' – the Russian equivalent to 'teen' (e.g. *pyatnadsat* = 'fifteen') – and Alex uses it to narrate the story. Breasts became 'groodies', from *grud*, hands or arms 'rookers' (*ruka*), legs or feet 'noga'. 'Litso' was face, 'rot' mouth, 'glazzies' eyes. A person was a 'veck', from *chellovek*. 'Horrorshow' (*horosho*) was the ultimate expression of enthusiasm. Burgess added scores more words of his own coining: 'cancers' were cigarettes, 'Pretty Polly' (lolly) was money. The 'gulliver', with a nod to Jonathan Swift, was one's head. The whole was garnished with literary references. When they roam London, Alex and his gang wear the masks of Henry VIII, Disraeli, Elvis Presley and 'Peebee' Shelley. There are streets called Kingsley (after Amis, or Charles) and Priestley (for J.B.).

The meaning of the phrase 'clockwork orange' itself was vague.

According to Burgess, who had a prodigious ear for argot in the half-dozen languages he spoke, 'as queer as a clockwork orange' was Cockney slang for very strange indeed – though not 'queer' in the homosexual sense. The phrase wasn't in common currency, but others of similar sense were, like 'as silly as a two-bob watch', and many people suspected that Burgess coined the term itself. Once the film was made, Warners made a brave stab at explaining that Alex's conditioning left him 'a clockwork orange – healthy and whole on the outside, but crippled within by reflex mechanisms beyond his control'. Others, with memories of *Dr Strangelove*, suggested the term could be a metaphor for a bomb: a smooth exterior, but filled with ticking mechanisms.

When he first read it, the linguistic inventiveness of Burgess's novel had been a turn-off for Kubrick. 'It didn't appeal to him at all,' recalled Southern. 'Stanley said, "Nobody can understand that language." That was that. The whole exchange occupied a day.' Despite Kubrick's lack of enthusiasm for it, Southern had taken out a six-month option on the novel, written a screenplay with photographer Michael Cooper, and showed it around. British producer David Puttnam saw its possibilities, but suggested Southern and Cooper check their script's acceptability with the British film censor. The censor returned it unopened, saying, according to Southern, 'I know the book and there's no point in reading this script because it involves youthful defiance of authority and we're not doing that.'

After renewing the option once, Southern let it lapse. His lawyer Si Litvinoff, who'd produced some plays off-Broadway and had ambitions to break into movies, picked it up, thinking it would make a vehicle for the Rolling Stones, with Alex played by Mick Jagger, an enthusiast for the novel. A screenplay was commissioned from Burgess. British critic Adrian Turner saw a copy. 'It was about three hundred pages long,' he recalls, 'and unreadable, Burgess having simply transferred the book, lock, stock and paragraph.'

In any event, the Stones could never find time in their schedule to make a film, so this project too lapsed, though Litvinoff and his partner Max Raab retained the film rights to the novel, which continued to hold a particular fascination for the new London glitterati. Photographer David Bailey considered filming it and, years later, rock singer Elvis Costello built up an eccentric collection consisting entirely of scores of copies of the novel's British first edition, which by the nineties could fetch £500 each. Paul Cook, drummer of the Sex Pistols, said, 'I hate reading. I only ever read two books. One was about the Kray brothers. And *A Clockwork Orange*.'

In 1969, Southern explained to Kubrick that Litvinoff and Raab now owned the property.

'Find out how much it is,' Kubrick said, 'but don't tell him I'm interested.'

'I tried to do that,' said Southern later, 'but Cindy Decker, the wife of Sterling Lord, my agent at the time, found out about this enquiry of Kubrick's, so she passed the word on to Litvinoff and his friend, Max Raab ... He and Raab sold it to Kubrick and charged a pretty penny for it.' In fact, Warner paid $200,000 for the rights, plus 5 per cent of the profits.

It's not hard to understand Kubrick's sudden interest in *A Clockwork Orange*. During 1969 and 1970 there had been a major shift in Hollywood towards 'youth cinema'. In the wake of *Easy Rider*'s $16 million gross on a $400,000 budget, studios plunged on cheap movies with young directors. Almost overnight, the power of the Legion of Decency, such a thorn in Kubrick's and Harris's side during *Lolita*, evaporated, swept away by the new network of art cinemas and independents which could afford to thumb their noses at even a condemnation by the Bishop of Boston.

Full-frontal nudity, profanity, sacrilege and political protest were the common currency of the new American cinema. Kubrick, at forty, looked like a dinosaur. The sense that he was out of date, a back number, stung. If he couldn't make 'Napoleon', he could make a youth film that would outrage the best of them. Adrienne Corri also believes that he wanted to show the opposite side of *2001*: 'That was what we might have got; this was what we were going to get.'

With MGM no longer funding anything, Kubrick needed to look elsewhere for money to make *A Clockwork Orange*. He tried Francis Ford Coppola's newly formed American Zoëtrope, the San Francisco-based mini-studio to which Coppola summoned the greatest talents of cinema – Jean-Luc Godard, Michael Powell, Wim

Wenders – to make films free of the interference that characterised big studios. When Zoëtrope was being formed in 1969, Kubrick was among the people who'd contacted Coppola, but the company never really got off the ground. Two years later, when Coppola needed major names to bolster his tottering enterprise, he complained that Kubrick wouldn't answer his calls.

Kubrick eventually found his way to his old partners Seven Arts, who had funded *Lolita*. In July 1967 the company had merged with Warner Brothers, and Elliot Hyman became chairman of the new Warners. In 1969 they were taken over themselves, this time by the energetic Kinney Group. Kinney had been morticians until the owner's ambitious son-in-law, Steve Ross, decided that money could be made from the firm's limousines by renting them out at night. From there Kinney moved into car parks, which became the basis of its fortune.

Tall, smooth, silver-haired, Ross had enough charm to run ten companies. Moving into the Mafia-dominated car rental business, he'd smoothly made his accommodation with organised crime. He did the same with Warner Brothers, charming the company's major shareholder, Louis 'Uncle Lou' Chesler, an old acquaintance of mob figure Meyer Lansky, into relinquishing control. Once behind the wheel, Ross installed an administration as fleet-footed and persuasive as himself. The chairman of the board was Ted Ashley, once one of Hollywood's hottest talent agents. John Calley was in charge of production. Youth affairs were handled by Fred Weintraub, an entrepreneur who'd made his name with a chain of campus coffee shops and the marketing of clothing and entertainment to the college crowd.

The swansong of the old Warners' British operation had been *Performance*, a sulphurous story of swinging London, directed by Nicolas Roeg and Donald Cammell. Mick Jagger played a burned-out rock star who lurks in a crumbling mansion with two mistresses. Gangster James Fox, on the run, hangs out there and is sucked into the bizarre milieu of group sex, drugs and cross-dressing. So traumatic was *Performance* for Fox that he joined a religious community and dropped out of showbusiness for over a decade. *Performance* also horrified the staid Warners management, which shelved it for three years. The film even split the board of the renamed Warner Communications, but enough of them liked it to agree that it must be released. Steve Ross took this as a good omen, and the company began to invest judiciously in films likely to raise the company's profile and attract a young audience increasingly hungry for the sensation denied it on television.

Among the films they funded or bought were *Woodstock*, Michael Wadleigh's documentary about the rock concert; Alan Pakula's unconventional detective story *Klute*, with a monosyllabic black-clad detective from the American heartland, Donald Sutherland, investigating a New York murder and falling in love with prostitute Jane Fonda; *Billy Jack*, by redneck radical Tom Laughlin; George Lucas's apprentice film *THX 1138*; Visconti's *Death in Venice*; and Ken Russell's outrageous *The Devils*.

They also signed a three-film deal with Kubrick, the first to be *A Clockwork Orange*. Since it seemed likely that its sex and violence would earn *Orange* an X certificate in both Britain and the US, severely limiting its profits, Warners wouldn't invest more than $2 million. The discreet announcement of their involvement came in February 1970. The parsimonious budget wasn't mentioned. So little was known about Burgess's book that the *New York Times*, announcing the project, had to quote its own review of 1963. Kubrick was described only as 'a forty-one-year-old New Yorker who has been living and working in England during the last few years'. The only film cited was *2001: A Space Odyssey*, though the report did explain that, after *A Clockwork Orange*, Kubrick would return to 'the epic-scale treatment of Napoleon's career on which he has been working since July 1968'.

Despite this low-key beginning, Kubrick's relationship with Warners would be the most durable of his life. Apart from simply enjoying their company, Steve Ross regarded high-profile stars and directors as his armour against opponents on his board. For the next decade, at crucial moments in his corporate career, he would call on Clint Eastwood or Steven Spielberg to rally the stockholders and head off boardroom revolt. The relationship with Kubrick was never this close, but his presence on the Warner Communication Industries roster did no harm. All Kubrick's films from *A Clockwork Orange* on would be produced by Warners under a unique agreement. The studio funded the purchase and development of projects which they understood would not reach the screen for years, if at all. Kubrick received 40 per cent of the profits and the guarantee of the final cut, even if this meant the film would be released with an uncommercial X certificate. Only Francis Ford Coppola was accorded the same right. The London office of Warners became Kubrick's embassy to the world, especially when Julian Senior, who'd worked for Roger Caras on *2001* as a junior publicist, was appointed head of European publicity. Senior lived in Borehamwood, and was a regular guest at Kubrick's house. He soon metamorphosed into Kubrick's spokesman, and the gatekeeper everyone had to pass in order to reach him. Warners' contract with Kubrick sounded more like a marriage than a deal. 'We are emotionally committed to Stanley Kubrick since 1970,' said Senior in 1996, 'and financially committed to him for the same time ... I would wish one [film] every year, but I will take one every seven years with a smile and a gleeful shout of triumph.'

Kubrick paid so much for the rights to *A Clockwork Orange* that he had to skimp on almost everything else, in particular casting. By the time the Warners deal was signed, he had already cast Malcolm McDowell as Alex. The rest of the characters are caricatures, though played by the cream of Britain's actors: Patrick Magee, Adrienne Corri, Michael Bryant, Anthony Smart. An exception is David Prowse as Julian, the body-building nurse to a crippled Patrick Magee. He was demonstrating exercise equipment in Harrods when Kubrick spotted him. The film launched a career as one of the most-seen but least-recognised of all movie stars. Designer John Barry recommended him to George Lucas when he was hired to design *Star Wars*. Unrecognisable under a mask and cloak, and with James Earl Jones's voice dubbed in, Prowse became Darth Vader.

Casting McDowell shifted the film's focus dramatically. The *droogs* of Burgess's book are teenage juvenile delinquents who squash pets, smash windows and seduce pimply teenage girls. They find the old disgusting, and only prey on them if they're weak and unprotected. Kubrick's Alex is an adult, and most of the attacks in the film are on other adults. Since Alex is the only attractive character in the film, we identify with him in his anarchic assaults. It's this above all that makes *A Clockwork Orange* so uniquely disturbing.

Kubrick first noticed McDowell in Lindsay Anderson's 1968 *If* .... He played a public schoolboy who, revolting against the ancient traditions of snobbery, stodgy teaching and corporal punishment, takes a machine gun onto the school roof with his working-class girlfriend and mows down the authors of his misery. Kubrick admired McDowell's ability to shift from schoolboy innocence to insolence and, if needed, violence. Though McDowell was the son of a pub-owner in the Midlands, the offhand accent of the British aristocracy, always a little too quick and too loud, came naturally to him. When an American reporter asked him, 'Who is the real Malcolm McDowell?', he snapped with perfect Harrow/Cowes/ Ascot arrogance, 'Madam, you've got two hours to find out. Why should I do your bloody work for you?' Kubrick pushed McDowell to use this tone as Alex – autocratic when he bossed his boys, respectful and obliging when dealing with superiors. This was no yob but a young man of intelligence and almost aristocratic bearing. Kubrick's closest comparison for Alex's marriage of command and protean manipulativeness was Richard III. McDowell also had the body that went with the voice. *If* ... had been the first major British film to include full frontal nudity, and he had handled it with aplomb. He also played sex scenes with equanimity. The fact that, at nearly twenty-eight, he was almost twice the age of Burgess's Alex, made no difference. 'If Malcolm hadn't been available,' Kubrick said, 'I probably wouldn't have made the film.'

Kubrick's small budget also made a high-priced screenplay unaffordable. Terry Southern offered the script he'd written with Michael Cooper, but received only a terse letter from a subordinate that 'Mr Kubrick has decided to try his own hand.'

Early in 1970, Anthony Burgess, *en route* to Australia and the United States for a series of festival appearances and residencies at various universities, heard that Kubrick was to film his book. He remembered:

> I did not altogether believe this and I did not much care: there would be no money in it for me, since the production company that had originally bought the rights for a few hundred dollars did not consider that I had a claim to part of their own profit when they sold those rights to Warner Brothers. That profit was, of course, considerable ...
>
> Stanley Kubrick was sending urgent cables about the need to see me in London on some matter of the script – and I feared,

justly as it turned out, that there would be frontal nudity and overt rape ... Some of the films of the new American wave considered themselves antiquated and reactionary if they did not use 'fuck' and show fucking. I foresaw a dangerous situation for myself and I was right to do so.

In 1970, Terry Southern published the novel of *Blue Movie*. He dedicated it to 'the great *Stanley K*', and hoped that seeing the book in print might revive Kubrick's interest in filming the comic tale of Hollywood's first big-budget porn pic. But Kubrick blew cool on the idea. 'It turned out he has an ultra-conservative attitude to things sexual,' said a disappointed Southern.

But, as *A Clockwork Orange* was to show, Kubrick didn't lack sexual imagination. The film revealed the sensual side of him which, until then, had appeared only fitfully on the screen.

Anyone who worked with Kubrick was aware of his more than usually active libido. 'He called me and Ivor Powell into his office one day on *2001*,' recalls Andrew Birkin. 'He had all these international model directories, and he'd gone through them, marking up all these girls.

'"We could get them in," he said, "for an audition."'

Birkin and Powell looked blank. 'For what?'

'We could always say we have to shoot one of those 16mm docking sequences,' Kubrick mused. (The films of sports and news that appeared on TV screens in the PanAm shuttle sequences were all back-projected 16mm.)

'But it was all a fantasy,' Birkin says. 'He never did it. He also had an obsession about meeting Julie Christie. He was always trying to work out some sort of scheme whereby he could audition her. I knew her a little, and I said, "I'm sure she'd come up if you just called her." But he didn't want to do that. It all had to go through the Fantasy Department.'

The Fantasy Department ruled Kubrick's sexual attitudes. Sex in Kubrick's films is never between loving couples. Rather he explores, as did Mickey Spillane, the furtive and violent side alleys of the sexual experience: voyeurism, domination, bondage and rape. *Lolita*, despite the eroticism of Nabokov's novel, is almost his least sensual film. One sees more of his predilections in the fate of the peasant girl in *Fear and Desire* and Gloria in *Killer's Kiss,* both bound and terrorised by groups of men; Davy watching Gloria through her window in *Killer's Kiss* and fondling her underwear; the post-coital tearfulness of Fay in *The Killing* and Sherry's death on the bed in the same film; Varinia and Spartacus spied on in their cell; Tracy Reed in bikini and high heels on Buck Turgidson's bed in *Dr Strangelove*; group sex and rape in *A Clockwork Orange*; Lady Lyndon in her bath in *Barry Lyndon* and Barry consorting with a gaggle of whores; the ghostly bathroom embrace of Jack and the nude phantom in *The Shining*; the flagrant Vietnamese prostitute of *Full Metal Jacket*, played by the unforgettably named Papillon Soo Soo.

One can only speculate on what he might have included in *Blue Movie*. There are hints, however, in *A Clockwork Orange*, which, from the opening in the Korova milkbar, where Alex and his gang drink their Milk Plus amid models of nude women, is suffused with sex.

Burgess's novel was imprecise about the decor of the Korova, but Kubrick and the young John Barry, whom he'd chosen to design the film, saw it as a temple to sexual consumerism. London pop artist Allen Jones had just caused a furore with three pieces of sculptural 'furniture' based on life-size mannequins of women in bondage harness. A fibreglass figure on all fours with a sheet of glass on her back became a coffee table, another an armchair, and the same figure upright, arms outstretched, a hat-stand.

Kubrick asked Jones if he could use the pieces in *A Clockwork Orange*.

Jones asked, 'How much?'

Kubrick temporised. 'Once people see them in my film,' he said, 'you'll be rich.'

Jones declined, so Kubrick hired Liz Jones, the pretty twenty-seven-year-old sculptress of the Star Child for *2001*, and asked her to create something in the same style as Jones's figures – based on her own body perhaps. When she refused to model as well as design, John Barry shot stills of a nude dancer braced face-up on hands and feet, in the reverse of Jones's 'Table' pose. He also shot her kneeling, breasts thrust forward. Modelled life-sized in fibreglass, the braced figures became tables, while the kneeling mannequins were converted into milk dispensers, with Milk Plus feeding through their nipples. (The real milk with which Kubrick insisted they be filled curdled under the lights, and the figures had to be emptied, washed and refilled every hour.)

A Clockwork Orange is also powerfully homoerotic. Whether preening as he prowls around his parents' flat in his Y-fronts, touching his toes to accommodate the rectal examination of Michael Bates, or accepting with *faux naïve* innocence the sexual approaches of his 'post-corrective adviser' Deltoid (Aubrey Morris) and two fellow prisoners, or Godfrey Quigley's prison chaplain, Alex, with his pale face, one eye made up with doll-like false eyelashes, his bulging codpiece and his indolent self-regard, belongs at the heart of gay iconography, brother to those lonely sailors Poole and Bowman in *2001*.

Roaming the town, Alex and his friends encounter the gang of their rival Billyboy, who are stripping a girl naked on the stage of a derelict theatre, and drive them off after a brawl. Stealing a car, they roar into the stockbroker belt, bluff their way into the house of a writer and his wife, the Alexanders, beating him and raping her. Alex goes home to his parents' high-rise flat in suburban Poplar. The next day, after rejecting the advances of Deltoid, Alex invites two girls home for a romp. That night he breaks into the remote house of the Cat Lady (Miriam Karlin), an exercise instructor who has decorated her home with erotic statuary and paintings, including a giant set of male genitals in white plastic which rocks suggestively when disturbed. Alex uses it to smash in her face, killing her.

Weary of Alex's arrogance, his *droogs* turn on him, leaving him semi-conscious at the scene of the crime, screaming that he's been blinded. At the police station he's beaten up by a group that includes a young Steven Berkoff as a policeman, and Deltoid, who drops by to taunt him and spit in his face. In prison he becomes the prey of homosexual prisoners and the prison chaplain. Sexual fantasies – being under the gallows as a woman is hanged; scourging Christ; hacking enemies in a Biblical battle, and relaxing afterwards with three naked women – divert him, but after experiencing the aversion therapy of the experimental Ludovico Technique, Alex is unable to function when a semi-nude girl is offered to him as part of a show for politicians and the press. The Ludovico treatment takes his mind off sex for the last two reels, but once the treatment is reversed, he's seen back in the saddle for the Ascot sequence which closes the film, fantasising about rolling in the sawdust with a beautiful half-naked girl while a well-dressed racecourse crowd looks on and applauds.

Most of the cast, and particularly the women, are fodder to Alex's sado-masochistic fantasies; this is the film in which Kubrick's admiration for Mickey Spillane's attention-grabbing techniques is allowed free rein. Adrienne Corri played the upper-class writer's wife:

The casting director told me, 'Adrienne, he's asking practically every actress in London to go into this little office with a hidden video camera and take off their blouse and bra so that he can look at their tits.' And I said, 'The hell with that,' and went to do an Iris Murdoch play at Greenwich. Another woman got the role, but after two days working on the scene she had torn some stomach muscles, so the casting director rang me.

Stanley asked me to audition semi-nude for the role, but I refused. 'But suppose we don't like the tits, Corri?'

I told him, 'Tough.'

Few of the auditions were wasted: Katya Wyeth appears bare-breasted as the model whom Alex tries, and fails, to rape; the two girls Alex picks up in the record shop and takes back to his parents' flat; three more who play wives and concubines in his Biblical fantasy; the girl stripped by Billyboy's gang; another gang-raped in the film shown as part of the Ludovico brainwashing; and the one with whom Alex has sex at the end; even the nurse looking after him in the hospital emerges naked to the waist from behind a screen where she's been necking with a doctor.

At Kubrick's suggestion, stills photographer Ken Bray did a special photo session with Katya Wyeth. When Bray returned, he told Kubrick, 'She's really very intelligent, you know' – thinking he might be persuaded to give her more to do in the film. But all Kubrick said was, 'Nice tits.'

With only $2 million to spend, *A Clockwork Orange* had to be made mostly on locations, and with 'live' sound and no post-synched dialogue. The film used all the equipment developed by new wave directors and perfected by TV documentary makers: lapel and necklace mikes for live sound recording, lightweight cameras, lamps that could be plugged into normal light fittings, lenses so fast and wide that one could shoot with them in normal domestic interiors. For all his scorn of *nouvelle vague* technique, Kubrick was happy to use it when it fitted the subject. Cinematographer Haskell Wexler had just written, shot and directed *Medium Cool*, a film about a news cameraman desensitised by the violence he has been forced to record. Impressed by the photography, Kubrick borrowed a fixed-lens camera Wexler had used for low-light shooting and used it extensively for *Clockwork Orange*. He also developed his own equipment. For smooth low-angle tracking shots in tight corners, he tried sitting in a wheelchair with an adjustable seat. It worked perfectly, and became a common option for camera operators.

A Clockwork Orange also marked Kubrick's definitive abandonment of CinemaScope. There was simply too much variation between individual cinemas in masking, screen sizes, and projection and sound equipment to guarantee that his films would look even remotely the same wherever they were shown. Kubrick had also been appalled by the excesses of TV presentation, and the 'pan-and-scan' technique, in which only half the image appears on screen and a 'technician' – notionally at least – tracks the significant detail from one side to the other. Alternatively, the film was simply run as if it had been made in a more square format, leading, as one critic joked, to 'talking fireplaces, and conversations between noses in empty rooms'. When *2001* was sold to TV, Kubrick attempted to prevent the use of pan-and-scan by urging that the film be shown in 'letterbox' format, with a black area at the top and bottom. The BBC protested that while this worked well enough for dialogue sequences, viewers became confused when the scene shifted to outer space. For the first BBC TV presentation, fake stars were added to the black areas above and below the picture area. This disastrous experiment, bitterly opposed by Kubrick, was never repeated.

Though his preference was for the 1.33:1 screen format used by Hollywood for decades, Kubrick decided that the 1.66:1 'widescreen' format offered an acceptable compromise between spectacle and intimacy. Even when slightly cropped at the edges, it preserved the essentials of the image. Wide-screen also favoured his rigorously symmetrical framing and, if anything, increased the beauty of his compositions. The effect of the new more square format, together with his growing dislike of dialogue, his penchant for tracking shots and painterly lighting, was to make his films even more evocative of the silent cinema he admired.

Kubrick bought ten years of back numbers of architectural magazines, and he and John Barry leafed through them, tearing out the pages with interesting buildings and cataloguing them in Kubrick's newest toy, the Definitiv filing system. Early-seventies London had no shortage of bleak concrete landscapes in which to shoot. Subways and high-rise apartment blocks in Wandsworth and the 'new suburb' of Thamesmead needed little in the way of special lighting to appear as grim as anything Burgess had imagined. The recently-built Brunel (later West London) University became the Ludovico Medical Facility, and the glitzy shopping complex, all coloured plastic and sheet steel, where Alex picks up the girls was exactly that – the American Drug Store in King's Road, Chelsea. Barry built only four sets – the Korova milkbar, the prison admission room, the entrance hall of the Alexander house, and its bathroom. The first three were constructed in a warehouse just a few minutes from Borehamwood, and the fourth mocked up in a tent pitched in the back garden of the house used for the Alexanders' place, ironically called, on its illuminated sign, simply 'Home'.

So much effort was later expended on attacking *A Clockwork Orange* for its supposed incitement to violence that few people noticed how much more time Kubrick spent on its visual style. *Time*'s art critic Robert Hughes said admiringly, 'No movie of the last decade (perhaps in the history of film) has made such exquisitely chilling predictions about the future role of cultural artefacts – paintings, buildings, sculpture, music – in society, or extrapolated them from so undeceived a view of our present culture.'

Today, the film looks like an anthology of the prevailing fashion in graphics in late sixties London, pop art. In 1957, Richard Hamilton, avatar of the movement towards art derived from popular culture, had written a definition which could serve for *A Clockwork Orange* as well. 'Pop art is Popular (designed for a mass audience), Expendable (easily forgotten), Low-cost, Mass produced, Young (aimed at youth), Witty, Sexy, Gimmicky, Glamorous and Big business.' Hamilton's 1956 collage *Just What is it that Makes Today's Homes so Different, so Appealing?* anticipates the juxtaposition of nudity and decorative objects in *A Clockwork Orange*. A near-naked body-builder stands in the centre of a middle-class apartment on the couch of which a nude stripper reclines, holding out heavy breasts. On the wall is a framed cover from a *Young Romance* comic. A TV set shows a girl on the phone, while a cinema marquee fills the picture window. A canned ham on the coffee table, a tape recorder on the floor and a Ford emblem turned into a lamp complete the decoration. Mass-marketing has rendered everything in the picture an object of desire, but the effect, far from denigrating the process, is one of celebration.

Autocratic regimes – Nazi Germany, Soviet Russia – also attracted pop artists because of the emphasis they placed on iconography, and the uniformity they imposed on daily life. 'I want everyone to think alike,' said Andy Warhol. 'Russia is doing it under government. It's happening here all by itself.' Kubrick, who has admitted, 'I share the widespread fascination with the horror of the Nazi period,' turned *A Clockwork Orange*, as he did *2001*, into a hymn to that uniformity. Alex and the gang dress in identical white trousers, shirts, codpieces and heavy paratroopers' boots. Any variations are minor: belts rather than braces, a top hat or beret instead of a bowler. In prison, everyone wears the same grey serge. All the prison officers are in military blue, the doctors who condition Alex, then cure him of his conditioning, in white.

Kubrick liked pop art's broad appeal and grounding in popular culture. As he told the French critic Michel Ciment, who wrote an authorised study of his work in 1980, 'I think modern art's almost total preoccupation with subjectivism has led to anarchy and sterility in the arts. The notion that reality exists only in the mind, and that the thing which simpler souls had for so long believed to be reality is only an illusion, was initially an invigorating force, but it eventually led to a lot of highly original, very personal but extremely uninteresting work.' He may have been influenced in this view by Christiane, whose work, some of which appears in the Alexanders' house, was, and has remained, strongly figurative. Pop art, and especially pop erotica, was the perfect visual motif for *A Clockwork Orange*. 'The erotic decor in the film suggests a slightly futuristic period for the story,' Kubrick told Ciment. 'The assumption being that erotic art will eventually become popular art, and just as you now buy African wildlife paintings in Woolworth's, you may one day buy erotica.'

The film's glossy, playful erotica, in particular the paintings and giant penis of the Cat Lady and the group of four ceramic Christs, nude and dancing like a chorus line, in Alex's room – all pieces by the Dutch brothers Herman and Cornelius Makkink – offered a visual Rosetta Stone through which contemporary and future audiences would achieve instant access to *A Clockwork Orange*'s world. Where almost every other film of the youth boom faded as quickly as the fashion for tie-dyed T-shirts, flared jeans with patches, beads, bongs and Joan Baez, Kubrick's vision survived and flourished. Ken Bray's close-up image of Alex leering satyr-like into the camera, the brow of his single made-up eye arched, joined the most instantly recognisable images of modern advertising.

During the making of *A Clockwork Orange*, nobody fretted much about its violence. The attacks aren't shown in excessive detail, especially not by comparison with American films like those of Sam Peckinpah, who was at the time finishing his own *Straw Dogs* in Britain, or Ken Russell, then preparing *The Devils*, his unsparing depiction of religious hysteria.

The worst cruelty in the film is that inflicted on Alex, not by him. He's beaten by police, by a gang of old men and by his ex-*droogs*. Escaping from Magee's house, he jumps out of the window – an effect achieved with typical Kubrick directness by dropping a £1000 camera into a paved yard. For the conditioning sessions, his eyes are held open by surgical 'lid locks', which clip over the lids and can only be endured under local anaesthetic. McDowell later complained to Kirk Douglas, 'That son of a bitch. I scratched the cornea of my left eye. It hurt. I couldn't see. Kubrick said, "Let's go on with the scene. I'll favour your other eye."' McDowell also suffered cracked ribs when the actor who attacks him in the staged demonstration of his new tractability stamped too hard. (This meant he was in considerable pain during the Magee/Corri sequence, which was shot later.) He had nearly drowned when breathing apparatus failed while his head was held in a horse trough for two minutes; he never forgot the taste of the meat extract used to colour the water. To top it off, Kubrick, knowing that McDowell was frightened of reptiles, greeted him cheerily one morning with, 'I got a snake for you, Malc.' He presented him with a python, which Alex keeps in a drawer and sleeps with on his bed.

By comparison with *Straw Dogs*, however, the violence of *A Clockwork Orange* looked tame. Peckinpah's film promised to be at least as bloody as *The Wild Bunch*, his 1969 Western about the last bloody exploits of the frontier's most ruthless bandit gang. Kubrick was insistent that he 'didn't want to do a Peckinpah'. He told the actors to imagine the violence was 'seen through a window on the opposite side of the street' – the voyeur's ideal. 'The film doesn't celebrate violence,' said Gavin Lambert, 'but *communicates* the celebration of violence, which it must do. That's what these kids get off on.'

Alex's devotion to Beethoven set the musical tone of *A Clockwork Orange*, so, to follow the classical motif while sustaining the 'pop' elements, Kubrick commissioned new electronic versions of Beethoven's Ninth Symphony, Rossini's *William Tell* overture and Purcell's *Music for the Funeral of Queen Mary* from pop composer Walter Carlos, loathed by purists for using the Moog synthesiser, which he helped develop, to record the hit album *Switched On Bach*. Carlos already knew Burgess's book, and news of the film inspired him to write a piece called *Timesteps* and send a tape to Kubrick's lawyer Louis Blau for transmission to the director. Carlos and his collaborator Rachel Elkind were summoned to England, and their twanging take on Ludwig van, *Beethoviana*, became the music for *A Clockwork Orange*. It was augmented by some tunes Kubrick happened to hear on the radio by an obscure American trio of 'New Age' musicians, Sunforest. To the group's surprise, Kubrick used their instrumental 'Overture to the Sun' and, more memorably, a jingly number called 'I Want to Marry a Lighthouse Keeper', composed and sung by Erika Eigen – their only moment of fame.

Anthony Burgess knew nothing about Walter (later – after a sex change – Wendy) Carlos, nor of the score, even though Carlos was writing it in Princeton at the same time that Burgess was lecturing there. His first experience of it, at a London screening hosted by Kubrick, was a shock. Both his wife and agent wanted to leave after ten minutes, but Burgess insisted they stick it out – from a courtesy greater, he implied, than Kubrick had shown him.

Little as Burgess liked the music, the film itself angered him more. He'd intended the novel, one of five he'd written in 1961 when he thought he was about to die of a brain tumour and needed to provide for his wife, to bear a complex moral message. It was to be 'a theological dissertation on the way the state messes up free will. I am a believer in original sin and this shows that man must fall to be regenerated. In the beginning one sees Alex's infantilism. He is still in a stage of impotence. He is still drinking milk. Then he is conditioned to respond, not to himself but to outside signals. Later, when he tries to commit suicide by jumping out the window, that represents the fall of man. Now regeneration will come, but it will not come through the state. It will come through man himself and his ability to recognise the value of choice.'

The British edition of the book ends with Alex, back on the street with a new gang and free to do pretty much what he pleases, finding that he's lost the urge to destroy. He becomes sentimental about children and old people, and decides he wants to have a family and settle down. 'Tomorrow is all like sweet flowers and the turning vonny earth and the stars and the old Luna up there and your old droog Alex all on his oddy knocky seeking like a mate.'

Eric Swenson, Burgess's editor at his American publishers W.W. Norton, felt the story ended naturally with Alex's restoration to society. 'I had a feeling he had dashed off the book in about ten days,' said Swenson. 'He never really came to grips with the subject. He has a marvellous mind, but he works much too fast.' When he suggested they drop the last chapter, Burgess, according to Swenson, 'said it was a marvellous idea. He told me he only wrote the happy ending at the request of his London publisher and never really liked it.' Whether this is true or not, Burgess didn't protest at the changes to a novel which, since he'd discovered that he had no tumour, he now felt carried a whiff of the potboiler. He had no idea that, ten years later, it would become his best-known and most influential work.

Kubrick insists he only heard about the original optimistic ending after working on the film for four months. He decided, like Swenson, that it was 'completely out of tone with the rest of the book', and forgot about it. As a result, the film ends on an endorsement of Alex's vicious way of life, a fact that was to have far-reaching effects.

Burgess chose not to make a fuss. Besides, he and Kubrick were enjoying one another's company. Visiting Kubrick at Abbots Mead, Burgess amused him by demonstrating on the piano the harmonic affinities between 'Singing in the Rain', the cheerful Nacio Herb Brown/Arthur Freed number from the twenties which Kubrick was using in *A Clockwork Orange*, and the film's other musical high point, the 'Ode to Joy' from the end of Beethoven's Ninth Symphony.

The two men shared an enthusiasm for Napoleon, and when Burgess told Kubrick he had been contemplating a novel written in imitation of musical form, based on a Mozart symphony, the idea of writing such a book about Napoleon based on Beethoven's *Eroica* began to coalesce. He returned to Rome, having agreed to write *Napoleon Symphony* in the hope that Kubrick would use it as the basis of his film. He also felt sufficiently emboldened to sue Warners for part of the profits from *A Clockwork Orange*. The studio did everything possible to delay settlement of the case, knowing that, should it go to trial, most judges would agree with Burgess that his share in the film's profits was derisory. Eventually they settled out of court, assigning him a minute percentage of the film's net income – a smaller share, as it turned out, than that Litvinoff and Raab received for doing nothing but picking up the unowned option.

Working without a screenplay on *2001* had persuaded Kubrick to make this his standard method of filming. Scenes for *A Clockwork Orange* were created day by day, taking passages from the book and improvising action with the performers. 'The filming sessions were conducted like university seminars, in which my book was the text,' complained Burgess. ' "Page 59. How shall we do it?" A day of rehearsal, a single take at day's end, the typing up of the improvised dialogue, a script credit for Kubrick.'

The attack on Corri and Patrick Magee culminating in the fatal gang-rape of Corri was created by this wearing method. While rain poured down outside and the rest of the cast and crew, banished by Kubrick, sheltered in the tent in the garden, he and the performers spent ten days turning three pages of Burgess's book into the film's most controversial scene.

Burgess's description of the incident is brief. The gang bluff their way into the house of Alexander, an author working on a book called *A Clockwork Orange*. (Kubrick insisted on an authentic library with the sort of books a writer might own.) They rip up the manuscript, smash the furniture, raid the kitchen, then beat up the husband and rape the wife. Dim, one of the gang, urinates on the remains of the novel. He's about to defecate on them as well –

'there being plenty of paper', Alex/Burgess comments puckishly –
when Alex orders the gang back on the road.

Most of these details were discarded, to be replaced by baroque
erotica: Alex kicking Magee rhythmically as he sings and dances,
snipping out circles from Corri's crimson jumpsuit to expose her
breasts, tearing off the rest before he rapes her in her red socks.
Corri recalls:

> We'd been sitting there for days, discussing whether there should
> be dialogue or whether the whole thing should be done silent,
> to increase the sense of menace, when Kubrick suddenly asked
> Malcolm, 'Can you sing?'
>   Malcolm said, 'I only know one song,' and started to do 'Sing-
> ing in the Rain'.

'Singing in the Rain' had been written for a movie called *The
Hollywood Revue of 1929*, in which it had been sung in the reedy
tenor and to the ukulele accompaniment of 'Ukulele Ike' Edwards,
who was to have his brief moment of fame as the voice of Jiminy
Cricket in Walt Disney's cartoon *Pinocchio*. After *Hollywood
Revue*, the song kicked around in a few more movies until Arthur
Freed, by then a producer at MGM, revived it as both the title and
theme song of Stanley Donen's musical about the early days of
Hollywood sound cinema, starring Gene Kelly and Debbie
Reynolds.

Adrienne Corri continues: 'Kubrick just got up and left the room
with Malcolm. We looked at one another and said, "Where's he
gone?"'

'What he was doing, it turned out, was driving back to Abbots
Mead, ringing Warners in Hollywood and asking if they could
get the rights to "Singing in the Rain". He came back an hour
later and said to me "You're playing the Debbie Reynolds part,
Corri."'

Stanley Donen was in London, so Kubrick also asked for his
opinion of this new use of the song. Donen raised no objection.

Everyone involved in this scene conceded that Kubrick shaped
their joint creative endeavour, but his taking credit for writing the
screenplay angered both Burgess and McDowell. The actor was also
infuriated that Kubrick's name was credited above the title, before

the stars. 'I mean, you don't exactly *see* any other name, do ya?' he snarled to American journalists. How appropriate, remarked Burgess to a friend, that Kubrick should have chosen as his music for the fight with Billyboy's gang Rossini's overture to *The Thieving Magpie*.

Warners had an option on Kubrick's next project, and in April 1971, while *A Clockwork Orange* was still months away from release, Warners executive John Calley announced briefly that it would be an adaptation of *Traumnovelle* ('A Dream Novel') by Arthur Schnitzler – mis-spelled 'Schnitsler' in the release – which would begin filming in the late autumn under the title 'Rhapsody'.

Schnitzler, who died in 1931, was a Viennese doctor whose ironic stories of sexual decadence made use of the pioneering work of Freud and Jung. He had come to believe that even the most romantic feelings could be traced back to sexual fantasies dictated by the lovers' mutual personal obsessions, which remain immutable even as the partners change. There is no true love; just a giddy dance in which we grab someone, whirl them for a time, then move on.

Kubrick first encountered Schnitzler's jaded view in Max Ophuls's *La Ronde* (1950), based on his 1900 play *Reigen*. As seen by its cynical narrator, played by Anton Walbrook, a series of couples resolve themselves into restless predators: A beds B, who beds C, who beds D, who beds E, until, down the line, K finds himself in bed with A, and the ring is complete. Ophuls's fluid camera style delighted Kubrick, but he found the film's unromantic vision of human relationships equally attractive.

Traumnovelle was first translated into English as *Rhapsody: A Dream Novel*, and quickly went into four printings. It tells a typical Schnitzler story. Fridolin, apparently happily married to Albertina, with whom he has a young child, is a successful and highly social Viennese doctor. The couple frequent the city's many masked balls, and are discussing one held the previous night when the novel begins. They play a sexual game by exaggerating the degree of attraction they felt for their anonymous partners, but

soon their light conversation about the trifling matters of the night before changed into a more serious discussion of those hidden, scarcely suspected wishes which can produce dangerous whirlpools even in the serenest and purest soul. They spoke of those mysterious regions of which they were hardly conscious but towards which the incomprehensible wind of fate might some day drive them, even if only in their dreams.

Fridolin recalls a Polish woman he danced with, but whom he never saw without her mask. Albertina confesses that on the day Fridolin proposed to her, she was so ready to give up her virginity that she would have done so to the first man who asked her.

Fridolin is intrigued, but before he can explore this idea he's called to the deathbed of an old man whom he's been treating with morphine, a drug that becomes a motif of the novel. The dead man's daughter, worn out from nursing him, falls to her knees and clutches Fridolin. He realises that she would let him have sex with her without protest, and retreats, confused but aroused. He wanders into the brothel quarter, and finds himself in the room of an attractive young prostitute, who displays herself semi-nude and offers herself for nothing. He's tempted, but refuses again.

In a café he meets an old student friend, Nachtigall, a brilliant pianist. Nachtigall tells him that he's waiting for a coach to take him to perform for the second time at a private masked *soirée*. He has to play with his eyes bandaged and his back to the dancers, all of whom dress as monks and nuns, but he confides to Fridolin that he can see things in a mirror. Extraordinary things.

'Impatiently and contemptuously,' writes Schnitzler, 'but feeling strangely excited', Fridolin says, 'In other words, naked females.'

'You never saw such women,' his friend replies.

Fridolin persuades Nachtigall to smuggle him into the ball, and the action becomes fevered and disjointed, confirming that Fridolin's narrative is at least partly a fantasy. At the height of the ball, the women – all as beautiful as Nachtigall had claimed – strip naked except for their masks, and dance with the fully clothed men.

Fridolin is spotted, and is about to be punished when one of the women offers to 'redeem' him.

'You know what you are taking upon yourself in doing this?' asks one of the men.

'I know,' says the woman, and Fridolin is released.

The next day, at the medical school, Fridolin is asked to examine the body of a woman who has been dragged from the river. She appears to have died of a morphine overdose. The woman who 'redeemed' him? Fridolin can't say. Nor is it important.

It did not matter to him whether the woman – now lying in the hospital morgue – was the same one he had held naked in his arms twenty-four hours before, to the wild tunes of Nachtigall's playing. It was immaterial whether this corpse was some other unknown woman, a perfect stranger whom he had never seen before. Even if the woman he had sought, desired and perhaps loved for an hour were still alive, he knew that the body lying in the arched room – in the light of the flickering gas-flames, a shadow among shadows, dark, without meaning and mystery as the shadows themselves – could only be to him the pale corpse of the preceding night, doomed to irrevocable decay.

Fridolin returns home to find Albertina sleeping, but with the mask he wore at the *soirée* on the pillow next to her. How much of what happened was a dream, how much a consensual fantasy shared by Fridolin and Albertina? Was she, and not the morphine addict in the morgue, the woman who 'redeemed' him? If there is a secret, she keeps it. In the book's last conversation she says, 'I think we ought to be grateful that we have come unharmed out of all our adventures, whether they were real or only a dream.'

Also in 1971, English novelist Frederic Raphael, an Oscar-winning scenarist for *Darling*, published *Who Were You With Last Night?* – a question Albertina might have asked Fridolin, and vice versa. A departure for Raphael, who specialised in lapidary and ironic examinations of middle-class Britain, the novel was a stream-of-consciousness story owing much to the *nouvelle roman* pioneered in France by Alain Robbe-Grillet and Michel Butor. Its main character, Charlie Hanson, is an ex-sailor who left the sea fourteen years before to marry Lola, an attractive redhead whom he made pregnant the first time they had sex. Feeling trapped by circumstances, he works as a salesman, spending his time on the road fantasising about Lola and how he might murder her in order to spend more time with Jean, the sexually inventive colleague with whom he's having an affair.

Jean and Charlie are together in the office one night when a stranger bursts in and menaces them with a gun. Is he Jean's husband, or lover? We never find out, because Charlie overpowers him, then lets him go. Back home, Lola, supposedly unaware of this incident, and of Charlie's affair, says she feels they are 'happier now than we've ever been', and Charlie agrees, still retaining, however, his homicidal fantasies. As Raphael puts it in the novel's blurb: 'Conspiracy [. . .] is the inevitable partner of permanence; we share our beds with strangers.'

Who Were You With Last Night? updates *Traumnovelle*, with Charlie as the fantasising Fridolin, Lola as Albertina, apparently unknowing but perhaps more involved than anyone imagines, and Jean, nude in an office armchair, smoking a cigar, replacing the naked nuns. The parallels may have struck Kubrick, since in 1995 he would announce a production of *Traumnovelle* with a script by Raphael, but not before the film had been widely rumoured as a version not of the Schnitzler but of *Who Were You With Last Night?* However Frederic Raphael denies he and Kubrick ever discussed the book.

What Warner Bros thought of the 'Rhapsody' idea in 1971 can only be imagined. It's quite likely that neither they nor Kubrick thought the film would ever be made. The announcement may have been a formality by Kubrick to satisfy their demand for a new project under their option. All his creative energies remained focused on 'Napoleon', which he still hoped and believed would be his next film.

Late in 1971, Burgess delivered to Kubrick the manuscript of *Napoleon Symphony*, structured in four movements. True to his revisionist view of the Emperor, this Napoleon is a bureaucrat with dyspepsia who thinks about his digestion more than about women. He catnaps, works a twenty-hour day, scribbling notes at the table, at the opera, in bed. He reads voraciously, endures piles and bladder trouble, flies into tearing rages. 'Ambition,' he believes, 'is the main driving force in man.'

Prevailed on by one mistress to make love to her, Burgess's Napoleon, with half an ear for the band playing outside, is already thinking about the evening's negotiations. 'He used the nudes on the wall to prime a distracted appetite and then, full dressed *en general* except for the lowered breeches, took her. She had better go back to that husband of hers, now they were divorced, and was he still alive for that matter? Raising his breeches, he worked out who would go with him . . . Monge? Berthollet? Berthier? Yes, those for a beginning. He must get some paper and make a list.'

Burgess's conception was closer to Kubrick's than most other versions of Napoleon's life, but in September 1971 the film project suffered a mortal blow when MGM announced it was scaling down movie production to concentrate on television. Its film library was sold off to balance the books, accelerating the slide that would put it out of business within the decade. Kubrick never quite shelved 'Napoleon', but he did start looking elsewhere for a project worthy of his standing.

Warners released *A Clockwork Orange* in New York just before Christmas 1971. Julian Senior, newly appointed to the London office, had his first taste of Kubrick's meticulous methods when the director called to say he'd like to visit him to discuss the film's promotion. He asked Senior to reserve him a parking space. Senior told him there was always plenty of room. 'And he replied – it's become almost a keynote of our relationship – that it's just when one puts one's trust in past experience than the unexpected happens. "It's so easy," he added, "to reserve a place. Why not do it?"'

Senior did it, and they spent six and a half hours going over the promotion plans in minute detail. From this meeting they drew up a thirty-page 'memory-jogger' covering every contingency: Did all cinemas have the correct 1.66:1 aperture mask? How many trailers and prints should be made? What sort of stills and explanatory text did newspapers require? Since Kubrick had refused to have either a stills photographer or a unit publicist for the film, stills were produced from frame blow-ups, and press releases were hurriedly compiled. Five major US critics, Joseph Gelmis (*Newsday*), Hollis Alpert (*Saturday Review*), Judith Crist (*New York*), Paul Zimmerman (*Newsweek*) and Jay Cocks (*Time*) were offered a preliminary screening of the rough cut if they flew to London. Fifteen marketing previews followed – 'the largest and most concentrated number in history', according to *Variety*.

One thing neither Kubrick nor Warners counted on was the coincidental US release of *Straw Dogs* in the same week. The two films were reviewed in the same issue of *Time* and *Newsweek*, each of which featured *A Clockwork Orange* on its cover, but while there was some mild criticism of the level of violence, most people seemed ready to accept *Orange* as valid satirical comment. In any event it had an X certificate, barring minors.

The real furore began in Britain, where *Straw Dogs* was released late in November 1971. The British censor, Stephen Murphy, who had been in the job for only two months, gave Peckinpah's film an X certificate, ordering only two small cuts. But the fact that the film's action took place in a cottage in rural England and not, like Peckinpah's other movies, in the American West, infuriated right-wing British opinion, always alert for a pretext to attack the increasing liberalism of Hollywood. The film became a *cause célèbre*. Thirteen critics wrote to *The Times* complaining about the increase in sex and violence on British screens. Just as many from the liberal press weighed in with their support of Peckinpah. Members of Parliament also had their say.

This was the climate into which, on 13 January 1972, Warners released *A Clockwork Orange* in Britain. John Trevelyan, whom Murphy had succeeded as censor, wrote later that he saw more good than harm in the film: 'I think it is perhaps the most brilliant piece of cinematic art that I have seen . . . In an age in which violence is on the increase Kubrick was challenging us to think about it and analyse it. He was trying to shock us out of our complacency and acceptance of violence; yet, although the violence in the film is horrifying, it is stylised, so it presents an intellectual argument rather than a sadistic spectacle.'

But, as Trevelyan acknowledged, 'not everyone sees the film in this way'. Among those who didn't was Labour MP Maurice Edelman, who wrote in the *Evening News* on 27 January that, according to the paper's headline, 'Clockwork Oranges are Ticking Bombs', forecasting that 'when *A Clockwork Orange* is generally released it will lead to a clockwork cult which will magnify teenage violence.' Though the censor had already passed the film, the Conservative Home Secretary, Reginald Maudling, demanded, in an unprecedented move, to see it for himself and, if necessary, cut it. In the event it was released without cuts, and proceeded to rack up the international audiences that would finally turn it into a $15.4 million hit for Warners.

It remained, however, a scandal. Everywhere it was shown, the issue of violence was raised. On 11 March the trade paper *Cinema/ TV Today* headlined its front page 'Murphy Must Go!', urging the censor's dismissal because he *hadn't* banned a film – a startling *volte face*. The term '*A Clockwork Orange*' became shorthand for any street crime involving young people.

Warners were delighted at the free publicity, and it seems more than likely that Kubrick was equally pleased, though he said almost nothing about the film in public. Instead, Corri, McDowell and Burgess were manoeuvred into becoming its apologists. Burgess, on his way to the United States to discuss a possible stage musical based on *Cyrano de Bergerac*, was told at Rome airport that he'd been bumped up to first class, and that the cost would be borne by Warners – providing he did some interviews about *A Clockwork Orange*.

In New York, he joined McDowell and Corri. As the most memorable victim of Alex's violence, Corri, who was articulate and multi-lingual, had been put on salary and sent on the promotion trail all over the United States. At each stop, Kubrick tracked her down and demanded tapes of every interview and clippings of each article. He himself, however, never left England. 'Since Kubrick went on paring his nails in Borehamwood,' growled Burgess, '[the trip] seemed designed to glorify an invisible divinity.'

Burgess was to have his first inkling of the growing controversy when friends rang him with reports of riots during New York screenings and street violence afterwards. He tried to see the film at a public screening, but the theatre staff, fearing for the safety of someone so 'old', attempted to refuse him entry. Burgess found the experience 'really quite frightening, because the cinema was full of blacks standing up and shouting, "Right on, man!" because they refused to see anything beyond a glorification of violence.'

Kubrick's intimate control of his film could instil a sense of paranoia in the most well-balanced person. As McDowell sat down to be interviewed in New York by the *Village Voice*'s Arthur Bell, he said, 'Our mentor, Stanley Kubrick, is watching our every move. He just switched a button in his headquarters and a satellite picked us up.'

A Kubrick legend grew around a Sunday preview screening of *Orange* at New York's Cinema 1. The day before, Kubrick rang Richard Lederer, then vice-president of advertising and publicity for Warners, to ask if they still projected onto a white cement wall at that cinema. If so, would someone paint the border round the screen area matte black before the screening. In some versions of this story, the owner of the cinema, Sid Rugoff, obliged. In others, he said it was impossible to get a painter on a Saturday, so Kubrick looked one up in the New York phone book, phoned him and told him to get down there and paint the wall.

On Sunday morning, Kubrick rang Lederer again to check the work. Joe Hyams, Lederer's assistant, went to have a look. An hour later he called Lederer. 'Good thing you sent me over. The directions got confused. They were painting the matte neon orange.' When the film was shown, however, the wall was black as ordered.

For the French release of *Orange Mécanique*, Warners retained a young publicist, Bertrand Tavernier, to promote the film. A true *cinéaste*, with an encyclopedic memory which he would later build into a distinguished career as a director (*Coup de Torchon*, *Round Midnight*), Tavernier was delighted to be working for a director he admired so much. But a barrage of nitpicking phone calls, cables and contradictory directions wore down even his equable temperament, and he cabled Kubrick c/o Warners Hollywood: I RESIGN STOP AS A FILMMAKER YOU ARE A GENIUS BUT AS AN EMPLOYER YOU ARE AN IMBECILE.

A few hours later he had a call from Joe Hyams.

'I got your cable,' Hyams said.

Tavernier braced himself for a bollocking.

'It's on my wall,' Hyams went on. '*Framed*. And listen, Bertrand. I know you're a film collector. Just name any movie in our vaults and a new 16mm print's yours.'

Chapter Fourteen

Kubrick in the Age of Enlightenment

> *'I like* Barry Lyndon, *but for me it was like going through the Prado without lunch.'*
>
> Steven Spielberg, *Sight and Sound*, Spring 1977

For more than a year after its release, *A Clockwork Orange* continued to excite comment and controversy on both sides of the Atlantic. Newspapers everywhere reported the crimes it had supposedly inspired, in particular the attack on a nun in Poughkeepsie, NY, though the rapists were later discovered not to have seen the film.

Britain's papers and courts cited *Clockwork Orange* as a convenient symbol of youth street violence, although the evidence that it encouraged teenage crime was flimsy. As Andrew Sarris remarked in *Village Voice*, 'Movies have always made a splendidly superficial target for our lazier moralists.' Writing in *The Times*, critic Tony Parsons said, 'The cases of rape, murder and beatings attributed to the film's influence are too numerous to be dismissed as tabloid hyperbole. Tramps were killed, girls were assaulted and beatings were dished out as Kubrick's symphony of violence rang in the heads of the perpetrators.'

Even as he wrote, however, Parsons had reservations. 'Whether these crimes would have been committed without the prompting of *A Clockwork Orange* is another question,' he acknowledged. He had seen boys in white suits and bowlers walking across Leicester Square when the film was playing in London, but the connection between a dress fad and an urge to rape and murder was tenuous. 'This is the cult that never was,' Parsons wrote. 'After the film disappeared, so did these white-suited droogs.' How to explain the fact that they never appeared in other countries? 'Britain has a different relationship to *A Clockwork Orange* from the rest of the world,' he suggested unconvincingly.

As late as November 1973, a seventeen-year-old Dutch girl was raped in Lancashire by a gang who were said to have chanted 'Singing in the Rain' as they did so, but no reliable witness ever came forward. When a fifty-year-old firewood seller was killed in May 1973, the *Daily Mail* based its claim that a '*Clockwork Orange* gang' was responsible on the fact that the film had closed in the area the day before, and that some local kids had been seen buying the sort of clothes and make-up worn in the film. Malcolm McDowell pointed out the absurdity of this: 'If they did do that, if they dressed like Alex, the police would know where to find them. I mean, in a codpiece and a bowler?'

It emerged in court that the boy who kicked the man to death hadn't seen the film, which was restricted to adults over sixteen. He *had* read the book, his mother said, but she insisted it had no effect on him. This didn't deter the defence, nor the psychiatrist called as an expert witness, who testified that the boy was 'acting a part which seemed very similar to the characterisation given by *A Clockwork Orange*. I believe the main theme of the book is this feeling of hostility from the younger to the older generation.' The lawyer asked rhetorically, 'What possible explanation can there be for this savagery other than this film?' Anyone who made the obvious retort, 'Robbery,' would have been howled down.

Initially, Kubrick robustly defended his film and the right to freedom of speech. In January 1972 some Florida newspapers announced that, on moral grounds, they would not carry advertising for *A Clockwork Orange* or any other X-rated films. Kubrick promptly withdrew the film from the area. 'It's Kubrick's picture,' shrugged a representative of the Florida State Theaters chain, 'and he can do with it as he wants' – an indication of Kubrick's influence over Warners; almost no other director enjoyed the luxury of being able to make such a gesture at the expense of profit.

His stubbornness, insistence on the smallest detail and relentless pressure on every member of the distribution chain, from cinema owner to chief executive, induced a state of awed respect for Kubrick inside the company. 'Talk about him in Hollywood,' remarked one visitor from London, 'and it's like you're talking about Jesus Christ.' Critical of Warners' 'mishandling' of foreign distribution, Kubrick compiled a database of cinemas all over the world, with which he directed the sales and distribution strategy for *Clockwork Orange*. Ted Ashley praised his ability, rare among creative artists, to combine 'aesthetics . . . and fiscal responsibility'. Following repeated revelations of shortcomings in Warners' methods, Kubrick was credited by many with being behind the decision to fire the head of its international operations, Norman Katz.

On 27 February the *New York Times* unexpectedly published under the headline 'Now Kubrick Fights Back' an attack written by Kubrick on an obscure critic, Fred M. Hechinger, who discerned 'a deeply anti-liberal totalitarian nihilism' in the film. 'An alert liberal,' he went on, 'should recognise the voice of fascism.' Kubrick unleashed quotes from Robert Ardrey's *African Genesis*, Arthur Koestler's *The Ghost in the Machine* and Jean-Jacques Rousseau's *Confessions* to annihilate this feeble assertion.

Anthony Burgess found himself co-opted into the firing line. The New York Film Critics chose *A Clockwork Orange* as Best Film, and Kubrick as 1972's Best Director, but he declined to attend the presentation at Sardi's restaurant, using the excuse of his dislike of flying. Instead, a fuming Burgess collected the plaques and delivered them to Kubrick in London, where the BBC prevailed on him to make yet another TV appearance, this time before an invited audience, to defend a film from which he increasingly felt alienated and to which he had contributed relatively little.

The packed studio was hostile, and unsympathetic to Burgess's argument that if literature or drama had a causal relationship to human action, millions would have been incited by *Hamlet* to kill their uncles. Presenter Jimmy Savile, a radio disc jockey transmogrified into a TV spokesman for the common man, particularly angered Burgess by giving the last word to a man in the audience who had served a long jail sentence for violent assault. Had reading affected his actions? asked Savile unexpectedly. Indeed it had, said the felon, and without giving Burgess the opportunity to respond, Savile ended the programme.

Later, Burgess would exaggerate his anger at this and other con-

frontations with the press and public over the film. In his autobiography, he painted himself as the victim of a manipulative Savile
and an even more Machiavellian Kubrick. 'This weighting of what
was meant to be a free discussion with a dramatic conclusion that
confirmed the prejudice of so many made me boil and wish to inflict
GBH on Savile,' he wrote. 'I was also sickened by the manner in
which a book that, all of ten years before, had made very little
impact on the reading public was now becoming a kind of invisible
primer of evil . . . Kubrick filed the nails of his other hand in Borehamwood and left me to be the target of vile accusations.'

At the time, however, Burgess was a good deal less censorious.
In a 1972 interview he told *Transatlantic Review*, 'I think it's a
good film, and it's not often an author says that about an adaptation.
Kubrick loves British authors and books . . . He is immensely well-
read and a great chess player.' Burgess's praise is all the more for-
bearing for the fact that it preceded the huge success which the film
brought to his career. He complained at the time of the interview
that he hadn't been able to find a copy of his novel for sale anywhere
in London. A laconic footnote remarked, 'Penguin published *A
Clockwork Orange* a few weeks later and sold fifty thousand copies
in the first fortnight.' Such success even blunted Burgess's resentment
that the film was now officially titled *Stanley Kubrick's A Clockwork Orange*, with Burgess's name relegated to the also-rans of the
credits.

In March the film received four Oscar nominations – Best Picture,
Best Director, Best Screenplay and Best Editing. But when the Academy of Motion Picture Arts and Sciences approached stars to present
the awards, many, including Barbra Streisand, refused to do so or
even to attend the ceremony for fear of appearing to honour so
infamous a film. In the event, it won nothing, but William Friedkin,
whose *The French Connection* took Best Director and Best Film,
told the press, 'Speaking personally, I think Stanley Kubrick is the
best American film-maker of the year. In fact, not just this year,
but the best, period.'

On 26 March, the *Detroit News*, nudged by the Florida precedent,
announced that it too would henceforth refuse advertising for
X-rated films, charging that 'a sick motion picture industry is using
pornography and an appeal to prurience to bolster theater attendance'. No particular film was singled out, but the first to suffer was

A Clockwork Orange. Kubrick's pungent letter to the editor was published on 9 April. This time it was his turn to detect fascism; he compared the Detroit decision, at length, to Hitler's justification of book burning. Warners issued the letter as a press release the next day, obviously having been supplied with the text well in advance. On 19 April *Variety* published it in full.

The fuss, which many people began to suspect was orchestrated and timed by Warners and Kubrick, kept *A Clockwork Orange* in the news until the start of summer, at which point admissions had peaked. In July 1972, Warners and Kubrick began negotiations with Aaron Stern of the MPAA rating authority on changes that would give the film an R rating, allowing it to be sold to television. Ideals about censorship, so sternly maintained in public, were privately allowed to slip as less revealing out-takes were substituted for thirty seconds of footage from the speeded-up three-way sex scene and the simulated gang rape shown to Alex during his aversion therapy. On 30 August Warners announced it would pull the X-rated version in October and release an R-rated edition in time for Christmas.

By now, *Variety* suspected that much of Kubrick's indignation about censorship was oriented towards publicity. In a pointed post-script to its report, highlighted in heavy print, it remarked, 'There remains one mystery in the saga of the *Clockwork Orange* alterations. Did Kubrick agree to the changes now to open up as many bookings as possible, thus "compromising" himself in the view of many film buffs, or did the MPAA considerably soften its request for changes this time from what it was demanding pre-release? Much trade opinion opts for the latter.' A greater mystery is, why cut only the sex scenes, which, in the context of the period, are mild? The American censor clearly didn't feel that the film any longer risked inciting violence – if it ever had. When the film's violence became an issue in the next part of its release, it would seem to some industry observers that Warners and Kubrick, deciding that eroticism had been milked dry, were switching their publicity effort to the next most promising element.

As Kubrick had hoped, *A Clockwork Orange* returned him to the limelight. No longer regarded as a middle-aged back-number, he was offered his share of prestigious properties, including William Peter Blatty's novel of diabolical possession *The Exorcist*. Blatty's contract with Warners called for mutual approval of a director. They agreed on a shortlist of Arthur Penn, Kubrick and Mike Nichols, but were turned down by all. 'Kubrick [said he] could produce for himself, thank you kindly,' said Blatty. William Friedkin finally won the project, the acclaim, the box office millions and the Oscar for Best Director.

The success of *The Exorcist*, which went well over budget but was, in its day, the fourth-biggest money-maker of all time, grossing $88 million worldwide, rankled with Kubrick for years. He became convinced that Warners paid for retakes with funds 'borrowed' from the profits of *A Clockwork Orange*. When *Barry Lyndon* was forced to shut down later in the year, Kubrick recalled Friedkin's budget blow-out and said, 'Now it's my turn.' *The Exorcist*'s success also planted in Kubrick's mind the idea of making his own horror film, later to bear fruit in *The Shining*.

Kubrick remained an elusive figure, seldom emerging from behind the high gates of Abbots Mead except to go to Borehamwood. In the wake of *Clockwork Orange*, Joseph Losey tried to set up a meeting, but Kubrick made his excuses. Aside from their natural rivalry, he resented what he saw as similarities between *King and Country*, Losey's 1964 film about a World War I court-martial for cowardice, and *Paths of Glory*. In July 1972, Kubrick, responding to a further overture from Losey, who had just released *The Assassination of Trotsky*, wrote to him, 'I have admired all your films and *Trotsky* was no exception.' He added, however, that he didn't rate it as one of his best. Losey, stung, retorted that he had seen *A Clockwork Orange* in Paris and 'would say about it much as you say about *Trotsky*. I found it technically brilliant and much more exciting as to images than any of your previous pictures, but I also found it unclear, dangerous and, I regret to say, gratuitous.'

This exchange decisively killed any possibility of a friendship between the two men, but Losey retained a grudging respect for Kubrick. Lecturing at Dartmouth College in 1975, he summed up the fate of film-makers like himself and Kubrick who elected to work outside the studio system. In his notes for the lecture, he wrote, 'I cannot think of a rich director excepting perhaps Kubrick, or Visconti, who inherited it [i.e. money]. Kubrick – six or seven films, no personal life. Bresson – obscure and poor. Buñuel – nearly twenty years wasted. [Richard] Lester – five years without work; Welles – one step ahead of the debt collectors – how many unrealised films – a ruin – a magnificent one . . . ; Resnais – five or six years without work – only five or six features – really poor. All more or less happy. Like me.'

1974 brought an ironic postscript to *Blue Movie*. For three years, Southern's script of his novel had rattled around Hollywood, until John Calley of Warners decided to produce it on a $14 million budget. Calley was living with Julie Andrews at the time, and persuaded her – 'for love, art and a lot of money,' says Southern – to play Angela Stirling, the squeaky-clean Hollywood star who agrees to go All The Way for Boris Adrian's film. On this basis, Mike Nichols, whose eyes had been opened to porn's possibilities by three visits to *Deep Throat*, agreed to direct.

All seemed set, until Warners tried to reacquire the rights to Southern's book and script from his friend Ringo Starr, who then held the option. Southern recalled:

Ringo was quite ready to step aside now that there was an actual production ready to roll. He didn't want any participation. He just wanted to see the book made into a movie. Enter the villain of the piece: Ringo's lawyer (who shall remain nameless) in absolute hysteria, ranting about how he (the lawyer) was 'going to look like a *schmuck* if the picture gets made and we [i.e. Starr and his company] don't have a piece of it'. John Calley and I were prepared to give him a piece, but it turned out that Mike Nichols wanted to retain all points so he could use them to make deals with actors. That proved to be the deal-breaking stipulation.

The film was offered to David Lean, who was briefly interested, but elected not to go ahead. In 1981 Blake Edwards, who had married Julie Andrews, fictionalised the incident in his comedy *S.O.B.*, in which a director with a flop on his hands decides to rescue it by adding sex scenes. Andrews appears demurely but defiantly bare-breasted, a pale shadow of what *Blue Movie* might have been.

*

Goodtimes, the British company run by David Puttnam and Sandy Lieberson, assembled the most intriguing project offered to Kubrick after *A Clockwork Orange*. In 1971 Puttnam had become interested in the career of Hitler's architect Albert Speer, after reading an interview with him in *Playboy*. Speer joined the National Socialist Party in 1931 and rose with it, and Hitler, whose intimate he remained until the end of the war. In 1942, Hitler put Speer in charge of war production. Though responsible for using hundreds of thousands of slave labourers to run the Reich's munitions works, Speer denied any knowledge of the extermination of the Jews. Tried at Nuremberg, he accepted his share of responsibility while continuing to claim ignorance of Nazism's worst excesses. 'Of these dreadful things, I knew nothing,' he assured his daughter Hilde in a letter written from prison in Spandau in 1952. The judges, won over by his charm, accepted his claim, and he was imprisoned for a relatively lenient twenty years.

On his release, Speer published *Inside the Third Reich: The Secret Diaries*, his revealing but blinkered view of the Nazi regime. Puttnam and Lieberson bought the screen rights, and Andrew Birkin was hired to write a screenplay. It portrayed Speer, whom both Birkin and Puttnam had come to know well, as a man who'd made a decision at twenty-three in the grip of youthful idealism, and had been forced to live with it ever since. Birkin approached the story much as Kubrick would have done, as the tale of a good-natured but weak boy who is destroyed because he cannot resist the forces of history. He showed his screenplay first to his mentor Carol Reed, who slyly pointed out the trap into which he had fallen, that of sympathising with his character to the extent of losing touch with reality.

'Andrew, it's wonderful,' he said. 'You've done a wonderful job. You've shown us what it was like to live in the Depression after the Great War, inflation rampant and the rest of it, and this young man with his head full of dreams, meeting Hitler. They plan for a new Germany together – it's just tremendous and it's all going so well for them too, it's all going *so* well – and then tragedy! They lose the war.'

Despite these moral ambiguities, Paramount were interested in the project, but proposed a journeyman Hollywood director who, Birkin, Lieberson and Puttnam realised, would emasculate the project. They discussed radical British film-makers like Nicolas Roeg, at which point Lieberson brought up Kubrick's name. Birkin mentioned having worked with him on *2001* and 'Napoleon', and since Kubrick had encouraged Birkin's early screenwriting efforts, they decided to send the script to him.

Birkin also knew that Kubrick had a keen interest in the Nazis. While shooting backgrounds for *2001* in the former German colony of South-West Africa, Birkin had found a bookshop in the town of Swakopmund still stocked with postcards of Nazi leaders and boxes of pre-war Nazi Party yearbooks and magazines, all in their original packaging, and being sold for their cover price to an obviously receptive white community. The local museum also contained a cabinet inlaid with a picture of what appeared to be Christ surrounded by children but proved, on closer inspection, to be Hitler flanked by young Nazis.

Birkin brought a quantity of this memorabilia back to London, and showed it to Kubrick, who asked to keep it. 'He was very intrigued by the Third Reich business,' recalls Birkin. 'I think you'll find there's a lot in common with Hitler and why he wanted to do "Napoleon".' Birkin sent the Speer screenplay to Kubrick, who rang back and complimented him. 'And he was obviously interested,' says Birkin. 'But he said, "I'm Jewish. I can't get involved in this."' Birkin sensed that Kubrick's decision had less to do with the attractiveness of the theme than with his fear of a potential public-relations gaffe. As he'd explained on *2001*, 'I've got to think about the publicity too.'

By 1974, 'Napoleon' had the odour of a white elephant, and a dead one at that. Ian Holm, one of Kubrick's choices to star, had made *Napoleon and Love*, a series for Thames TV which critic Clive James described as 'seeming as endless as the Gobi . . . a turkey of fabulous dimensions, able to trot for hundreds of miles before laying its enormous egg'. Burgess gave up waiting and published *Napoleon Symphony* as a novel, jointly dedicated to his wife and to Kubrick, '*maestro di color*'. Since the making of *A Clockwork Orange*, Burgess had resigned himself to being best remembered for the scandal surrounding the film. On lecture tours in the United States he carried a 16mm print, 'which he showed,' commented his friend, the novelist Paul Theroux, 'to impress or amuse his audiences'.

Kubrick began casting around for a new film to offer Warners which might exploit his mountain of Napoleonic research. After *War and Peace*, the most filmed novel set in that period was William Makepeace Thackeray's *Vanity Fair*, the story of Becky Sharp, a girl from the wrong side of the tracks who lives on her wits in early-nineteenth-century London, marries for money, neglects her child, loses her husband and is left sadder but no wiser after having done little but mar the lives of those around her. It had already been filmed in 1923 and 1932, and a third time, as *Becky Sharp*, in 1935. There was also talk of a BBC TV adaptation and perhaps a new Hollywood film, so Kubrick discarded it.

As an alternative, he came across – by chance, he said – *The Memoirs of Barry Lyndon Esquire*. Thackeray's second novel, obscure to the point of invisibility, also deals with a young person (male this time) who lives on his wits in early-nineteenth-century London, marries for money, neglects his child, loses his wife and is left sadder and wiser after having done little but mar the lives of those around him.

Redmond Barry, intended by Thackeray to be a parody of the feckless young Irishman, sentimental, romantic and gullible, doesn't have the spirit of Becky Sharp; Thackeray subtitled the book 'A Novel Without a Hero'. Barry resents the fact that, over the previous century, the English have bought, won or stolen most of Ireland, including his own ancestral estate. Forced to run away (inevitably as the result of a girl, and by a trick played on him by another suitor), he bumbles through the Seven Years' War, only to emerge empty-handed. A born gambler, he bets his life and fortune, but is cheated, seduced, misled and finally destroyed by the shrewder, more ruthless English and Prussians.

Throughout, Barry is his own worst enemy. Though he marries the wealthy and beautiful heiress of his dreams, he is bored with her almost from the moment they leave the ceremony, and throws himself into whoring and gambling. He has a child, but the boy, Brian, inherits his father's nature. Arguments between Brian and Viscount Bullingdon, Barry's stepson, turn Bullingdon into an implacable enemy who undermines Barry's authority in his own house and, after a scandalous scuffle in front of an audience of the aristocrats with whom he's anxious to curry favour, destroys his hopes of a peerage.

It's not hard to see what attracted Kubrick to *Barry Lyndon*, over and above its Napoleonic setting. It resonated with the *bildungsroman* of Albert Speer's story. It also, as Gene Phillips points out, 'echoes a theme which appears in much of the director's best work, that through human error the best laid plans often go awry, and hence man is often thwarted in his efforts to achieve his goals'.

Like Spartacus and Alex DeLarge (and Hitler and Napoleon), Barry is also, as Kubrick said of Humbert Humbert at the time of *Lolita*, 'the outsider who is passionately committed to action against the social order . . . the outsider in the Colin Wilson sense – the criminal, maniac, poet, lover, revolutionary . . . fighting to do some impossible thing'. In addition, he has an autobiographical dimension. 'There's a lot of that character in Stanley,' Gavin Lambert feels. 'Not the defeated Barry but the fuck-the-world Barry. That great moment after the marriage when they get into the coach and Marisa Berenson says something stupid, and he just blows smoke rings. Fabulous! It's very Kubrick-esque. A gesture I could very easily see him do. It's his wicked, humorous side coming out. It's a wonderful comment on her, and why he's married her, and this extraordinary cold indifference there is at the centre of him. It's a fable; not a realistic film in any sense. It's his Ophuls side.'

Kubrick may also have had a hidden agenda in making *Barry Lyndon*. In the wake of *A Clockwork Orange*, he preferred to be seen not as an alien dangerously loose in Britain but as someone who had adopted it as his home, who loved the country, and was prepared to wear his heart on his sleeve by making the best British historical film ever, from the work of a classic British author. He also recognised that, at forty-five, he was due for his masterpiece. Given the rate at which he made films, this production would set the tone for the last and, hopefully, richest part of his career. Many people in the film industry still regarded him as iconoclastic and ingenious, but perhaps not entirely of the first rank. 'I think there are probably only two really genuinely original film-makers in this country,' Paul Newman said in 1975. 'Kubrick is one and the other is Cassavetes. That doesn't necessarily mean that they're good, but they're original.'

Barry Lyndon's defects as a film subject are multitudinous. The novel has plenty of dialogue and some colourful incidents, including battles and duels, but no equivalent of the ball on the eve of

Waterloo which is the major set-piece of *Vanity Fair*. The fact that the book is told in the first person, and in a way that doesn't lend itself to being used as a voice-over as had been the case with *Lolita*, was an added disadvantage, though Kubrick would add a rueful voice-of-God commentary, spoken superbly by Michael Hordern.

Kubrick wrote a bare-boned 243-page script that removed the more outrageous coincidences. Redmond Barry's family are no longer the ancient and rightful owners of the Lyndon estates, sold generations before to an Englishman. Nor does the Chevalier de Balibari, the professional gambler on whom Barry is sent to spy, and whose associate he becomes, turn out to be his uncle in disguise. Kubrick also truncated Barry's courtship of Lady Lyndon, which occupies much more time in the book. Originally Barry won her only by out-manoeuvring the many candidates who, as old Sir Charles tells Barry apoplectically just before his death, 'have always turned up to apply for the situation'. The antipathy between Barry and Viscount Bullingdon assumes greater importance, culminating in a duel where Barry, succumbing to his Irish sentimentality and taking pity on the terrified young man, fires into the ground, only to have Bullingdon use his second shot to smash his leg, which has to be amputated. Many linking scenes were also inserted, some of them eccentric. To cover Barry's desertion from the British army, Kubrick wrote in a comic sequence where two gay officers stage a tearful parting waist-deep in a river while Barry steals the horse and despatches of one of them. He also extracted two incidents from *Vanity Fair*: the reading of Sir Charles Lyndon's obituary (Lord Steyne's in the novel), and Lord Wendover's speech about his friends (said of Becky Sharp in the novel).

Once he had finished his screenplay, Kubrick removed all hints of the setting, period and source of the story – Barry became 'Roderick' – and, heading it 'New Stanley Kubrick Film Project', sent it to Warners. David Hemmings had told Kubrick that, on *Blow-Up*, Michelangelo Antonioni hadn't written a script at all, but had simply slipped pages from Julio Cortázar's short story under the doors of his stars each evening, telling them, 'These are tomorrow's scenes.' Convinced that anything Antonioni could do, he could do better, Kubrick argued that the draft script and the book itself constituted enough material to start shooting; the rest would be written as they went along.

John Calley agreed to invest $2.5 million, with the proviso that stars take the leading roles. The decision was to cost Warners dear. One can only speculate on the reasons for Calley, Steve Ross and Ted Ashley making it. Perhaps they simply had too much on their minds. 1972 was election year, and Richard Nixon was threatening to regulate the move of media companies like WCI into cable TV. Ross, no stranger to corporate graft, made a list of key politicians up for re-election and told his executives to get busy with campaign contributions. Embarrassingly, a payment of $137,856 to Richard Nixon's campaign came to light in Ted Ashley's name. Charles Colson, Nixon's special assistant, later charged with obstruction of justice in the Watergate hearings (and who memorably displayed above his bar at home the motto, 'If you've got them by the balls, their hearts and minds will follow'), remained on WCI's payroll as a consultant on cable regulation right up to his indictment.

By the time Nixon was out of office and WCI had bought its commanding position in cable, the budget of *Barry Lyndon* was up to $9 million and it was too late to do anything about it. Calley told *Time* magazine, 'It would make no sense to tell Kubrick, "OK, fella, you've got one more week to finish the thing." What you would get then is a mediocre film that cost, say, $8 million, instead of a masterpiece that cost $11 million. When somebody is spending a lot of your money, you are wise to give him time to do the job right.'

Kubrick's first choice to play Barry was Robert Redford, who was in England shooting *The Great Gatsby* for Jack Clayton. Redford and Kubrick came to a tentative agreement, and it's intriguing to imagine what changes his offhand screen presence would have imposed on *Barry Lyndon*. The critic David Thomson has pointed out how effective a change of pace it could have been for Redford to play a scoundrel. However, in the autumn of 1972 Redford dropped out, preferring a heroic role in George Roy Hill's undistinguished version of William Goldman's script about post-World War I barnstorming pilots, *The Great Waldo Pepper*. Warners and Kubrick hurriedly trolled the available stars, and announced that Ryan O'Neal had been cast as Barry and Marisa Berenson as Lady Lyndon in 'The Luck of Barry Lyndon', to start shooting in March 1973.

O'Neal had shot to fame in 1970 as the bereaved hero of Arthur Hiller's *Love Story*, from Erich Segal's lachrymose novel, but since then his career had been in screwball comedy, mostly for Peter Bogdanovich, who directed both of his major successes, *What's Up, Doc?* and *Paper Moon.* He was the world's number-two box-office draw, below Clint Eastwood and above Burt Reynolds, and looked a good investment, justifying his fee – unpublicised – of $800,000.

O'Neal was both astounded and flattered to be offered the role. When journalist Pat McGilligan asked him at the end of production if he considered this 'the most serious film you've ever made', he responded presciently, 'Probably that I'll *ever* make.'

'You don't expect to graduate to bigger things?' McGilligan pressed.

'Than *Barry Lyndon*?' O'Neal said. 'Jeez, yeah. I'm going to do a police story, play a sniper. C'mon. It's *hard*.'

O'Neal is credible as the naive boy of the first reels, blushingly co-operating in the erotic games proposed by his provocative cousin Norah, but the moral decline Thackeray describes once he gets into the army is beyond his powers. Though the commentary observes that 'he was soon very far advanced in the science of every kind of misconduct,' in the image which accompanies this declaration, a long-lens view of the marching army with Barry in the front rank, his face remains the bland and open countenance of someone who would blush if he farted in the bath.

As in *A Clockwork Orange*, the supporting cast exist in the shadow of the main character, who is in every major scene. The film is half over before Marisa Berenson appears as the Countess of Lyndon, bored wife of ageing, gouty Sir Charles, and after that she has little to do but languish elegantly as she had done in Luchino Visconti's *Death in Venice* and Bob Fosse's *Cabaret.* A fashion model descended on her father's side from the art historian Bernard Berenson and on her mother's from *haute couture* designer Elsa Schiaparelli, Berenson epitomised to Kubrick the haughty melancholy of the formal portraits by Gainsborough and Romney which are the best evidence of how the rich of late-eighteenth-century England saw themselves. 'There is a sort of tragic sense about her,' Kubrick said. O'Neal, unimpressed, found her 'overbred, vacuous, giggly and lazy'.

For the rest of his cast, Kubrick called as much as possible on people he'd worked with before, and therefore didn't have to audition – a process he increasingly disliked. Patrick Magee was Balibari, Steven Berkoff, unrecognisable in powder and wig, one of his clients and victims, Lord Ludd. Norman Rossiter, who had appeared in *2001*, played Captain Quin, the strutting recruiting officer with whom young Barry fights the faked duel that forces him to leave home. Philip Stone from *Clockwork Orange* was Lady Lyndon's well-meaning but browbeaten clerk Graham. Minor performers were chosen by proxy via video. Ken Adam's niece Nikki was sent to Germany with a camera to record local actors. After that, Kubrick chose seasoned character performers whose familiarity gave the film a reassuring solidity. Hardy Kruger, taking over from Oskar Werner, whom Kubrick fired after three weeks on the film, was Captain Potzdorf, a canny Prussian who sees through Barry and blackmails him into becoming his spy, and Murray Melvin the pickle-faced Reverend Runt, the Lyndons' chaplain and tutor. Viscount Bullingdon as an adult was played by unknown American Leon Vitali, who was to assume an important role in the Kubrick entourage.

From the start, Kubrick decided to ravish the senses of his audience; if you had them by the eyeballs, their hearts and minds would follow. If it succeeded, the film would cut for a generation the benchmark for the recreation of the past on film, just as *2001: A Space Odyssey* had defined their future.

Ken Adam was in Villefranche working on Herbert Ross's thriller *The Last of Sheila* when he got Kubrick's call offering him the production design of this massive project. With memories of *Dr Strangelove*, Adam viewed the prospect nervously. 'I was very reluctant to work on *Barry Lyndon*,' he says. 'I loved the man, but at the same time I felt he was bad for me psychologically, with this continual questioning of one's talent and capability, and his enormous brain. As an artist, whatever you do, part of it is an instinctive process; something that you can't intellectualise. You read a story, you have a concept, you talk to the director, then try to design it within those boundaries. But with Stanley I always felt there was a questioning characteristic.'

After weeks of haggling, Adam and Kubrick couldn't agree on a fee. 'Well, I'll have to use the second-best production designer in the business,' Kubrick said provocatively. Adam, grateful to be off the hook, said, 'Stanley, be my guest.'

Kubrick hired Wilfrid Shingleton, who had shown his ability to recreate authentic period sets with his masterly decor for David Lean's *Hobson's Choice*, but a month later he rang Adam again. 'This time [he was] in his little boy persona,' says Adam. 'He told me, "Ken, I suppose we can get together on your fee. The production designer I've got now doesn't seem to understand my concept."' Between jobs and out of excuses, Adam gave in.

Immediately, the two men collided over a fundamental concept. All designers prefer to build their own sets, using time-wasting and expensive locations only as a last resort. Kubrick wanted, on the contrary, to shoot everything in real eighteenth-century houses. Furthermore, he intended, wherever possible, to film by candlelight.

He'd already made some progress towards this during the 'Napoleon' research, though he and John Alcott had calculated that however many candles one crammed into a scene, the light level would be well under that demanded by most film stocks and lenses. Still perhaps preoccupied on some fundamental level by the giant 165mm Graflex lens of his first boyhood camera, Kubrick scoured the world for lenses that admitted more light. Finding them took three months. The best was a Zeiss 50mm developed by NASA for use on the moon. Its large aperture reduced the depth of field severely, but Kubrick asked Californian engineer Ed DiGiulio to fit it to a camera. After some inspired engineering, DiGiulio succeeded, but had to rebuild the camera.

Once he had lenses large enough to admit the light, Kubrick turned his attention to candles. In the eighteenth century most had been made from animal fat, which smoked and stank. The aristocracy preferred beeswax, which burned almost without smoke, smelled of honey and, since the candles themselves were translucent, gave an even, golden light. Price's candle company in Battersea still produced beeswax candles for the Roman Catholic Church, the rubrics of which at the time required any ritual object to be predominantly of natural origin. Kubrick visited their factory, where he saw a massive dipping machine producing candles five feet long and an inch and a half thick made of 65 per cent beeswax. He ordered enough to light a hundred ballrooms.

Originally, Kubrick had hoped to film all of *Barry Lyndon* in England – ideally no more than ten miles from his home. It had worked for his other films, so why not for this one? In response, his team pointed out that authentic eighteenth-century buildings were comparatively rare in England, especially around London. Stubbornly, Kubrick insisted on a full-dress location search. 'You never know what you will find around the corner,' he said. His garage became a sort of operation room, with large maps of the home counties on all the walls. Ken Adam recalled, 'He would mark out a radius of five miles, or ten or twenty, from Borehamwood. Then he employed some very young people, including my niece, who really weren't photographers but knew how to click a camera, to look for locations within those areas. They couldn't use flash. Every picture had to be taken with a tripod.'

Adam sensed that Kubrick lacked the skill to assess a building from the point of view of shooting a film there. Except for a few small interiors on *A Clockwork Orange*, he'd never needed to do so before. He became easily distracted by what Adam thought of as trivia: 'the details of who might have lived here; what they did; what they thought'.

Conferences on the design of *Barry Lyndon* assumed the proportions and, increasingly, the absurdity of grand opera. 'Every night we had sessions of projecting transparencies of these buildings,' says Adam. 'I could tell that Stanley was more drawn to the Victorian era than to the rigidity of the eighteenth century. We would get into terrible arguments.

' "I like that wallpaper," he would say.

' "It's Victorian, Stanley."

' "*Prove* it."

'It was a continuous compromise. To get him out to look at locations was a major achievement. And once he got to these places, he discovered that these kids hadn't known where to point the camera. They didn't have anything like a script. So some of these houses had renovations, or were in places impossible to film.'

In the hope of reconciling the rival demands of a dozen bickering experts, Kubrick convened a make-or-break design meeting at which he laid out the rules of debate. Each person would have one minute in which to put his or her point of view, and at the end Kubrick would decide.

'To be sure it's fair,' Kubrick continued, 'everyone must have sixty seconds *exactly*. What we need is a bell to signal when their time is up.' Turning to one of the helpers, he ordered, 'Get me a catalogue of bells. No, better, get me every catalogue of every bell manufacturer . . .'

No decisions were made that day, or most days.

Ken Adam, line producer Bernard Williams and Kubrick's financial comptroller Jan Harlan all urged him to abandon his fantasy of shooting close to home and to shoot the film in Ireland, where, they pointed out, many large houses remained intact. Moreover Ireland was, after all, where part of the story was set. As logistical problems piled up, Kubrick moved towards a decision to shoot at Ardmore Studios near Dublin, which, providing the visiting company imported all its own technicians, was regarded for purposes of winning the British government's Eady Fund support as British.

Kubrick had picked the worst of times to make a period film with an Irish setting. 1973–74 was to be the bleakest of bleak midwinters for both Britain and Ireland. Prime Minister Edward Heath, whose Conservative administration had ousted Labour in 1970, found it impossible to curb the trades unions, which staged a series of strikes, including one by coalminers which crippled the country. Hoping to wait them out, Heath introduced a three-day working week in mid-December 1973, cutting electricity and public services in the hope that the belt-tightening which helped lick Hitler would wear down the National Union of Mineworkers. The principal result was a series of electricity blackouts, during one of which the *2001* food lockers defrosted at Kubrick's house and he had to throw an impromptu party to use up the food. In February 1974 an election would return Labour and Harold Wilson to power.

Unrest in Ireland added to the sense of national disaster. Since the so-called Bloody Sunday in January 1972, when British paratroopers killed thirteen civilians in Londonderry, the Irish Republican Army had waged a persistent terror campaign in Britain, planting bombs and assassinating politicians and public figures with apparent impunity. Over the next few years their victims would include Ross McWhirter, co-editor of *The Guinness Book of Records*, shot on his London doorstep after offering a reward for information leading to the arrest of IRA members; MP Airey Neave, blown up by the IRA splinter group the INLA as he left the House of Commons; and Lord Louis Mountbatten, his boat mined off the Irish coast. On 29 May 1974 the British imposed direct rule on Northern Ireland. On 7 August, a Protestant militiaman shot down outside his home would become the five hundredth victim of sectarian violence in three years.

It was at this point, with *Barry Lyndon* ready to start shooting and Kubrick mulling over the move to Ireland, that he had an alarming visitor. 'One day,' said an assistant, 'a stranger arrived at Kubrick's house and said something which severely unnerved him.' Whoever made the threat, and of whatever it consisted, it was a potent one. 'Overnight the entire production was switched to Ireland,' said the assistant. 'We never discovered what the stranger had said, but Kubrick had an absolute phobia about any stranger who approaches him. He worries constantly about being kidnapped, about his family's safety.'

Some reports suggest that the visitor may have been mentally deranged, but others hold that he represented the Irish Republican Army. The IRA has long been a bogeyman of non-Irish commercial interests. It was widely believed, despite a lack of hard evidence, to have extorted money from film units working in the Irish Republic. During his tenure at Columbia, David Puttnam tried to shoot a biography of the Irish Republican hero Michael Collins, only to be dissuaded by Cadbury-Schweppes, the British affiliate of the Coca-Cola company which controlled Columbia. 'One of our night-watchmen,' Dominic Cadbury said, 'might end up being shot as a warning.' Puttnam cancelled the film.

As liaison with the Irish army, which would supply some personnel, mostly bandsmen, Bernard Williams had retained retired Colonel Bill O'Kelly. He assured Williams that Kubrick, an American with no observable political sympathies, would have little to fear from the IRA, and his production even less so, particularly since it was bringing work to the chronically impoverished Irish film industry. Nor could any IRA threat have been in response to *A Clockwork Orange*, since the film had been banned in the Republic of Ireland in 1973 before it reached the cinemas.

So, in the autumn of 1973, Kubrick uprooted the production and moved it bodily to Ardmore, where shooting began on 17 September. The film was unlucky from the moment the unit arrived in Ireland. It rained constantly, and casual Irish business methods troubled the production even more; it was, remarked one senior production executive, 'a nightmare'. A cast and crew of 170 moved with the slowness and expense of a small army, and with just as much concern for its own comfort. John Alcott griped later, 'Barry Lyndon had the worst food of any film I ever worked on.' The militant Irish electrical trades unions, which had instigated a series of damaging strikes between 1962 and 1964 to win the concession that all visiting film productions had to employ a number of their members, threatened to declare the production 'black', so Kubrick hired a dozen of them, whom he told to 'go and drink tea' until the shoot was finished.

Occasionally the bad weather was useful. Bob Anderson, the coach of the British Olympic fencing team whom Kubrick had hired to handle the film's swordplay, was taken aback when Kubrick, having read that duels were traditionally fought at dawn, insisted that the fight between O'Neal and the delinquent Lord Ludd (Steven Berkoff) take place at the correct hour, with the trees dripping from the night's rain, and real, not Nujol-generated mist. Anderson worked out a flashy finale to the duel, with Barry slipping his foil around his body to plant it threateningly over Ludd's heart, and Kubrick, despite the difficult and constantly changing weather conditions, insisted on fifteen takes.

He also fussed continuously with the script. Ken Adam says, 'It was a very strange way of making that picture. Stanley believed there were very few screenwriters as good as Thackeray. Barry Lyndon was, in his mind, like a screenplay. It didn't turn out that way and Stanley was working night after night, trying to get the script right.' Once, when the copy of the novel which Kubrick had printed up as a script fell open at the passage they were about to film, he took it as an omen and did the scene exactly as Thackeray described. The tension of the whole process brought Kubrick out in a nervous rash, which didn't improve his temper. After ten weeks he had spent $2.5 million but shot only 10 per cent of the film. In the hope of saving money and time, he proposed shooting the German and Continental locations in Ireland as well. Adam insisted that houses of the right size simply didn't exist there. Nor were the styles of architecture and design anything like those of Austria and Prussia. 'Show me,' Kubrick demanded.

As one technician on Full Metal Jacket put it, 'If he thought you were right, he'd admit it. But if he believed you were wrong, he'd spend a million dollars to prove it.' Kubrick was more than ready to justify his punishing methods. 'If a picture is flawed,' he says, 'that flaw is forever. The ideal way to make a film would be to wrap up after every scene and go away for a month to think.' The alternative was to continue working until he was satisfied that every nuance had been explored.

Barry Lyndon would make Kubrick notorious as the director who demanded twenty, thirty, fifty takes of a scene. The rehearsal method he'd perfected on *A Clockwork Orange*, with up to ten days spent improvising with the actors before the scene was shot, developed on *Barry Lyndon* into a sort of rehearsal-on-camera. Charlie Chaplin had been the first to employ this technique, retaking a scene repeatedly – not because the earlier takes might be usable in the final film, but because the tension of working with lights blazing and film in the camera stimulated both his invention and that of the performers.

'Is it true he drives people to exhaustion and paranoia?' Pat McGilligan asked Ryan O'Neal.

'Exhaustion, yes.'

Was it true that he did twenty-five takes of some scenes?

'Of *everything*,' grated O'Neal.

Murray Melvin recalled, 'Stanley was pressing me to my limit and I was failing every time. He'd seen something in my performance that he wanted brought out. We did forty-eight takes. I still had not got it. He called a short break. When he started again, the clapper boy said, "One-oh-nine, take one." I dried immediately. Stanley had changed the slate number so I wouldn't be embarrassed. I did another twenty-seven takes before he finally said, "OK, Murray. I can do something with that."' From behind the camera, someone muttered, 'And I bet he uses take three.'

As the shoot of *Barry Lyndon* lengthened, so did the list of those who didn't last the distance. The legend of Kubrick the tyrant gathered even more strength. 'He either drains you dry,' remarked one crew member, 'or the picture overruns into prior commitments, or you can't stand Stanley another minute.' Working on weekends and holidays was expected. 'A key member of the production team of *Full Metal Jacket*,' noted a journalist, 'blanched at the vehemence of Kubrick's reaction when he asked for Christmas Day off.' Adrienne Corri, whom Kubrick tried unsuccessfully to recruit to dub the actors in French and Italian, rounded a corner to find an assistant repeatedly kicking the set and muttering, 'Think of the mortgage, think of the mortgage.'

As Christmas approached, Kubrick realised that he couldn't continue under these conditions. The supply of stately homes was drying up, and the deficiencies of his scriptless shooting method were increasingly apparent. After consultation with Bernard Williams, he suggested putting the cast and crew on unpaid holiday over Christmas and the New Year. Ryan O'Neal agreed to an eight-week break, and the crew were so relieved at the thought of being with their families for the holidays that they accepted the offer with relatively little complaint. Warners made it official when it announced from Hollywood that the film was 'breaking for the holidays'. The people lending their houses as locations, John Calley explained, wanted them back for Christmas.

Shooting picked up again in the New Year, and almost immediately halted when the production office at Ardmore received a threat on Kubrick's life. Bernard Williams was in Salisbury, arranging shooting at some English locations, including Wilton House, where he'd filmed part of *Lady Caroline Lamb*, when he received a call from the production office in Dublin. An officer of the Special Branch had called from Dublin Castle, he was told, with the news that, according to their intelligence, Kubrick was a potential IRA target. Williams was incredulous, but the person ringing him assured him, 'Stanley freaked.'

In fact, Kubrick and his family had already fled to Britain the previous night on the ferry from Dun Laoghaire under assumed names. Bob Anderson remembers how the news flashed around the production office that morning, and the shock it engendered in the already dispirited unit. 'I don't know what the exact threat was,' says Ken Adam, 'but we certainly were aware of the possibilities, and remember that Stanley I think was very worried by the reception of *A Clockwork Orange*. He was seriously concerned about the reaction of the media and these habitual crackpots, so I think whatever happened in Ireland must have seriously worried him.'

Whether he was right to be worried is another question. While the first threat to Kubrick in England was almost certainly unconnected with the IRA, it's possible that terrorists were involved in some form of intimidation in Dublin. Kevin Rockett, the Irish film historian, points to the scenes of the British army on the march which dominate the first half of the film. Most of them were shot in County Kilkenny, which has a history of radical Republicanism. If anything was likely to trigger a threat against the production from some IRA sympathiser, believes Rockett, it was the sight of massed British redcoats in a Kilkenny field. Having received one threat already, a nervous Kubrick would probably not have needed a second. The unit waited for three days, then returned to London. *Barry Lyndon* never shot in Ireland again.

Clearly Kubrick associated the threats against his life less with *Barry Lyndon* than with *A Clockwork Orange*. As Ken Adam says, it was *Clockwork Orange* which, he believed, had raised the heat of debate and turned him into a potential target. One can well understand his desire in early 1974 to cut himself loose from the film, especially in Great Britain. And the time was propitious to do so. As *Variety* noted on 16 January, the film, having finished eleventh on 1972's UK box office hits, after Ken Russell's *The Devils* but ahead of *Straw Dogs*, was approaching its third anniversary in London, having earned almost $3 million in the UK alone.

On sober consideration, early in 1974 Warners and Kubrick privately agreed to withdraw *A Clockwork Orange* from distribution in the UK, but to make no public announcement of the fact. With its theatrical distribution largely over, the film would be allowed quietly to fade from sight, in the hope that controversy would fade with it. The secret was kept until 1979, when Adrian Turner, then the National Film Theatre's programme manager, arranged a retrospective of Kubrick's work to coincide with the publication of Michel Ciment's book *Kubrick*. Turner planned a stage discussion with cameraman John Alcott on working with Kubrick. 'We were at Joe Allen's restaurant in London,' recalls Turner, 'and I asked John how we might get a clip from *Orange*. He said, "Don't worry. I'll just call Stanley." Later that afternoon, an embarrassed John called me and said, "I called Stanley and he said, 'John, I know what you want and I'm sorry I can't let you have it.'" So we weren't even allowed to have a clip for an evening which honoured Alcott's career.' Warners confirmed that they and Kubrick had 'absolutely withdrawn [the film] from distribution' five years earlier. The notice in the NFT programme booklet was the first public acknowledgement of their action.

The ban occasionally reached absurd extremes. When Malcolm McDowell was shooting in Russia following the Chernobyl disaster, the Russian authorities offered to run a season of his films to raise money for the victims. Kubrick, however, refused to lend a print of *A Clockwork Orange*. In 1992 a small London repertory cinema, the Scala, created a test case by advertising a screening of the film. (It had already shown it on other occasions, but covertly.) Warners took the manager to court. She was fined £1000 and forbidden from screening any other Warner Brothers films. In September 1993, Warners, on Kubrick's behalf, acted against the television station Channel 4 to prevent them from showing a documentary, *Forbidden Fruit*, which dealt with the banning of *Orange* and included some clips. An injunction was granted, but overturned by the Court of Appeal. Channel 4 screened the programme on 5 October. The press pointed out that, in his letter to the *Detroit News* about their refusal to advertise the film, Kubrick had protested against all censorship. Kubrick didn't reply.

Barry Lyndon shot for three hundred days over two years, with two major shutdowns and a resulting budget blow-out to $11 million. Ken Adam became one of many to fail before the end. '*Barry Lyndon* was not for me a happy experience,' sighs the designer. 'It ended up in me becoming very ill.' According to Adrienne Corri, a technician noticed Adam standing trembling with a chocolate biscuit in his mouth and a burning match in his hand. He was trying to ignite the biscuit like a cigar. He immediately left the production for a long rest, and hasn't worked for Kubrick again.

Shooting by candlelight had proved slow and exhausting. In some cases, notably the gambling scenes where Barry and the Chevalier play cards in the middle of a room crammed with aristocrats dressed in the height of eighteenth-century fashion, it became almost unendurable. 'The heat was very nasty,' said one actress in the scene, 'and remember, my dear, we all had on this heavy white-lead make-up they wore in the eighteenth century to cover the ravages and filth.' When they shot in stately homes, the candles became downright dangerous, and Adam had to design aluminium shields to protect the ceilings.

Even after all his preparation, Kubrick was seldom satisfied. One of the film's most elaborate sequences was a birthday party for

Barry's beloved son Brian, which featured a conjurer on a raised
stage and rides for the children in a tiny carriage pulled by sheep.
Publicity claimed that a thousand candles lit the scene, though the
real figure was more like two hundred. When they were all alight,
Kubrick mounted a ladder to study the effect, then climbed down
and walked off the set. 'Fifteen minutes later, we were stood down,'
says Marisa Berenson. 'Stanley didn't like it.' Like many other
scenes, it was shot months later, outdoors, in the grounds of Castle
Howard in Yorkshire.

The autumn of 1974 was spent scoring the film. Traditional
musician Sean O'Riada provided a series of keening, reedy fife and
drum pieces for the first half, which were played by the Irish folk
group The Chieftains on authentic original flutes and drums. For
the second half, Leonard Rosenman, a veteran with impressive
qualifications both as a serious musician – he'd studied composition
and theory with Arnold Schönberg – and as composer of the scores
for classic films like *East of Eden* and *Rebel Without a Cause*, was
given the job of adapting and re-recording Handel, Bach, Mozart,
Schubert and Vivaldi. It was no easy task. Rosenman conceded that
Kubrick was 'brilliant, but he reduces everyone to slaves. After the
105th take on one piece of music he complained that the orchestra
was one-third of a beat off. That was it. I threw down my baton,
grabbed him by the neck and tried to strangle him.'

In September 1974, executives from Warners' New York office
flew to London to see the film, which they hoped to release just
before Christmas, giving it a chance of Oscars in 1975. But Kubrick
refused to show them anything. When they protested, Kubrick
assured them that, once *Barry Lyndon* won its inevitable Academy
Awards, 'it would go through the roof'. He declined even to supply
a print to the MPAA Censorship board. Instead, the assessors were
flown to London at the expense of the production, put up at the
Dorchester, and wined and dined before seeing the film at a special
private screening.

The British press saw it a few days later. Julian Senior, alerted
by now to Kubrick's methods, had booked Warners' preview theatre
for thirty consecutive evenings, and been forced to cancel each time,
to the fury of the projectionists and other producers and executives
who needed to view films. When Kubrick was finally ready to unveil
Barry Lyndon, the projection staff were so aggrieved that they

refused to show it until Kubrick rang them with a personal appeal. The screening itself was a disaster. In an excess of hospitality, Warners had laid on a generous buffet and quantities of alcohol. After the first hour, the screening room began to reverberate with snores.

Once the film opened in the West End, Kubrick's interest in how it was received became even more intense. Five minutes into one of its first screenings at Warners' flagship Leicester Square cinema, a Kubrick assistant burst into the manager's office and demanded that the film be stopped and restarted, as the projectionist was showing it in the 1.85:1 ratio, not the 1.66:1 which Kubrick preferred. When the manager declined, the assistant responded with the familiar wail, 'But what am I going to tell Stanley?'

The public and critical reaction to *Barry Lyndon* was confusion and boredom. Films like *Lawrence of Arabia* had accustomed them to films with a knowing, cynical view of the past. They expected characters who enjoyed a sense of history, and spoke as they never would have spoken in real life: 'kings talking like kings never had sense enough to talk,' in the phrase of the American poet and humorist Don Marquis.

In David Lean's films, scriptwriter Robert Bolt ensured that no character, however minor, lacked pithy one-line dialogue that implied a gnomic perception. Even in a Hollywood epic like *Ben-Hur*, Andre Morell as a centurion was allowed, with a perspective uncommon among professional soldiers of the time, to comment of Christ's teaching that it was 'quite profound, some of it'. In *Barry Lyndon*, Morell, playing Lord Wendover, whose palm Barry greases liberally in hopes of achieving a peerage, has no such opportunities. Never once does he, or any of the characters, step outside the limits of historical time and position.

Michel Ciment spoke for many people when he remarked that *Barry Lyndon* had the stately pace of a silent film. The comparison pleased Kubrick. 'I think that silent films get a lot more things right than talkies,' he said. He didn't particularise, except to say how pleased he was with perhaps the film's most successful moment, where Barry and Lady Lyndon, after covertly eyeing one another over the gaming table, meet in the colonnade outside. As she stands silent in the moonlight, the night breeze stirring the plumes on her hat, the soundtrack takes up its most evocative piece, Schubert's

Trio in E Flat. Barry walks up behind her and takes her hand. She turns and they kiss, all in silence. In accepting praise for the reticence of this scene, Kubrick failed to mention the fact that he'd shot a long exchange of dialogue between the couple, then discarded it because the scene fell at exactly the point where the three hours seven minutes running time dictated an intermission. Barry's wordy wooing now takes place while the audience is buying ice cream and popcorn.

In scenes like this – too few in the film – *Barry Lyndon* does achieve the tense suppression of emotion typical of the best silent screen acting. In others, however, where groups of people pose in formal precision on baize lawns amid a scatter of daffodils before yet another stately home, the film is more like a *tableau vivant*. Most critics attacked this static, graphic stillness. Charles Champlin in the *Los Angeles Times* rated it 'the motion picture equivalent of one of those very large, very expensive, very elegant and very dull books that exist solely to be seen on coffee tables'. Stanley Kaufman in the *New Republic* dismissed it as 'three hours and four minutes of pictures'. British critic Michael Billington called it 'all art and no matter; a series of still pictures which will please the retina while denying our hunger for drama. And far from recreating another century, it more accurately embalms it.'

Yet *Barry Lyndon*'s hieratic stiffness and stillness were to become its most memorable qualities, and to elevate it to near-mythic status among the directors of New Hollywood like Martin Scorsese, who revered both Kubrick and the film. In a cinema increasingly preoccupied with action, and indiscipline in language and performance, *Barry Lyndon* moved to the more stately rhythm of another age – one in which animal appetites and urges flexed their muscles against the constrictions of an ordered society. The formal settings of the film, the measured movements of armies, the rituals of cards, courtship and duels are like the squares on a chessboard, on which the characters move awkwardly, seldom of their own volition. If any film reflects Kubrick's vision of a world under rational control, it is *Barry Lyndon*.

Chapter Fifteen

Kubrick in Hell

> 'And the Lord said unto Satan, "Whence comest thou?"
> Then Satan answered the Lord, and said, "From going
> to and fro in the earth, and walking up and down in
> it." '
>
> Job 1: 7

Because Kubrick had invested so much time and effort in *Barry Lyndon*, its commercial failure, the worst of his career, depressed him acutely. The film grossed only $9.5 million in the American domestic market, much less than the $30 million needed for Warners to see a profit.

As he'd assured Warners, however, it did garner Oscar nominations – seven of them: Best Picture, Director, Adapted Screenplay, Cinematography, Art Direction, Music and Costume Design. From the start, however, the cards were stacked against it winning. The smart money that year was on the phenomenon of *Jaws*, but though Steven Spielberg's thriller was nominated for Best Picture, Academy members denied him a Best Director nomination. Despite this leaving the field open for Kubrick, the major awards went to Milos Forman's *One Flew Over the Cuckoo's Nest*, including Best Actor for Jack Nicholson. *Barry Lyndon* won for Music (principally an acknowledgement of The Chieftains' accompaniment to the early scenes), Cinematography, Art Direction and Costume Design, but Kubrick was again cheated of personal recognition.

This snub, taken with the film's commercial failure and the threats on his life, reinforced Kubrick's sense of isolation, and he responded as he always did to criticism or hostility, by ostentatiously turning his back. Systematically, he cut himself off from all but a few people. Julian Senior compared him to 'a medieval silversmith' at work in his tower. Enemies drew parallels with Howard Hughes. From 1975 to 1978, Kubrick became a little of both, with the image, as Peter Evans wrote in *New York* magazine, of someone with 'a passion for secrecy [who] does not care to have anyone know the details of his life'.

Within this cocoon, Kubrick's life was anything but sensational. 'Stanley did all the cooking and the laundry,' says Adrienne Corri. 'Christiane drifted off to the bottom of the garden and painted.' With Corri, Kubrick felt relaxed enough to discuss his real concerns. 'How do you make sure all the socks come back from the laundry?' he asked her plaintively, as irritated as any housewife by the perennial offences against order and logic offered by the washing machine, dishwasher and vacuum cleaner. Thereafter, socks became a motif of Corri's relationship with Kubrick. For the Christmas after *A Clockwork Orange* she sent him a pair of red ones, a reminder of the fact that this was all he permitted her to wear in her rape scene.

Preoccupied with the trivial in his private life, Kubrick was occasionally moved to make a rare public pronouncement about matters that were just as inconsequential. In November 1976, he wrote to Adrian Turner to endorse a piece Turner had written about the London Film Festival's method of allocating tickets. Neither he nor Vivian, Kubrick complained, had been able to buy seats, while a family across the road got four places for a number of films. Most directors of his reputation would have rung the Festival and received complimentary seats as a courtesy, but Kubrick preferred to hover between anonymity and notoriety – Ulysses and No Man at the same time.

Old acquaintances like Alex Singer came to resent Kubrick's failure to keep in touch, or even to respond to notes or calls. Ken Adam invited Kubrick to a dinner party in his Belgravia home. He accepted, but as the guests sat down, a courier arrived with a parcel containing an expensive architectural photo lens and a note from Kubrick. Reminding Adam that he had introduced him to photography on *Barry Lyndon* by encouraging him to buy his first still camera, Kubrick asked for the lens to be placed on the chair he would have occupied; Adam's guests would find it far more communicative than him. The calculatedly dramatic gesture attracted far more attention and comment than Kubrick would have if he had turned up in person or ignored the invitation altogether – as he no doubt intended.

In 1978, Kubrick unexpectedly added his name to those of sixty-two others, including Robert Altman and François Truffaut, on an advertisement in the trade press deploring the boardroom conflict which had led Arthur Krim, Robert Benjamin and three other executives to resign from United Artists after its takeover by the Transamerica Corporation. The advertisement questioned 'the wisdom of the Transamerica Corporation losing the talents of these men'. The industry found Kubrick's endorsement puzzling. Krim and Benjamin had run United Artists at the time when he and Harris had experienced their greatest problems with the company. The poor release of *The Killing* and UA's subsequent purchase of the TV rights at a discount were directly attributable to the Krim/Benjamin management. Nevertheless, Kubrick signed, probably at the urging of Warner Brothers, who had guaranteed the $100 million line of credit with which Krim, Benjamin and the others set up their own independent production company, Orion.

With time on his hands, Kubrick became adept at managing his reputation, and jealous of attempts to tarnish it. Interviews, always rare, became rarer still. 'I'm not going to be asked any conceptualising questions, right?' he demanded of one journalist. 'It's the thing I hate most. I've always felt trapped and pinned down and harried by those questions. Truth is too multi-faceted to be contained in a five-line summary.'

Attempts by writers to examine his life or career in detail were scrutinised and, more often than not, thwarted, usually by the same method. Kubrick would initially agree to co-operate, on condition that he had the right to authorise the text. He would then withhold approval until the deadline passed or the writer lost patience. In 1968 the magazine *Books* recorded eight hours of conversation under this restriction, but was permitted to use only four sentences. It filled the allocated pages with this handful of words, eked out with the repeated sentence, 'We interviewed Stanley Kubrick for eight hours and he only let us use four sentences.'

In 1970, British critic David Austen had begun a book for publisher Peter Cowie about Kubrick's work, with the promise of an interview from him. Before they could meet, Austen became ill and

Neil Hornick replaced him, but Kubrick continued to be helpful, supplying prints of *Killer's Kiss* and *Paths of Glory*. At the same time, using Ray Lovejoy as a go-between, he extracted an agreement from Cowie that nothing would be printed before he'd vetted it for factual errors.

A formal letter from Kubrick's lawyer followed, with a memo requiring Cowie's signature. Cowie queried the terms, which gave Kubrick wide powers of veto, and tried to incorporate some guarantee that the author's independence would be respected. Kubrick's lawyer replied that he wasn't satisfied with Cowie's attempts to provide an objective standard in relation to 'valid criticism'. The publisher would have to rely on Kubrick to be fair.

Hornick submitted his manuscript, only to have it rejected by Kubrick, 'not so much because of any factual errors,' Cowie explained, putting the Kubrick view, '. . . but because your chapter on each film gives him (and Lovejoy) the impression of a "mixed review", a summary of the bad points, which, in his view, almost always outweigh the good.' As he had done with Arthur Clarke on the novel of *2001: A Space Odyssey*, Kubrick never listed his grievances or supplied the promised amended manuscript, and Cowie cancelled the book.

Offers of films continued to arrive on Kubrick's desk, many from Warners, who remained enthusiastic about his work. To Gene Phillips, to whom he gave a few brief interviews for *Stanley Kubrick: A Film Odyssey*, published in 1975, Kubrick confided that he still hoped to make 'Napoleon', but admitted that the chances were increasingly slim, since he estimated that it would cost between $50 and $60 million and would run three hours. Nobody had forgotten Sergei Bondarchuk's 1971 multinational *Waterloo*, with Rod Steiger, which cost Columbia $25 million and earned only $1.4 million.

Even in isolation, Kubrick never lost touch with events in America. The *New York Times* was delivered by air mail every day, as were video cassettes of US television documentaries and sitcoms, and football and baseball games. At night he monitored short-wave broadcasts that kept him up to date on the deteriorating situation in Vietnam.

He had taken to driving again, though circumspectly. He even bought a white 928S Porsche to replace his Mercedes. 'Sometimes I drive it at eighty or ninety miles an hour on the motorway,' he insisted to a journalist in 1987, though Alexander Walker remarked, 'I don't think it's often driven faster than the family saloon,' and nobody ever saw it out of the yard. Like Kubrick's radios, stereos, TVs, cameras and projectors, it was a trophy, a collectible: the best of its kind, state of the art, just as valuable to him and an equal source of pleasure if it stayed in the garage.

If Kubrick did venture out, it was usually in one of the family's four-wheel-drive vehicles. When he did so, he remained in constant touch with home via the latest electronic gadget: walkie-talkie, CB radio, car phone. Friends got used to calls at odd hours, sometimes from the car, though Kubrick always rang off when approaching any driving hazard, even one as unthreatening as an intersection. He took intense satisfaction in being able to reach out across Britain, and even beyond, via his electronic network. Alexander Walker was taken aback to receive a late-night call criticising him for attending Imelda Marcos's Manila Film Festival, thereby giving support, as Kubrick saw it, to a corrupt regime. Walker hardly heard from him again for years until, in a hotel in Switzerland, Kubrick tracked him down at 1.15 a.m. to discuss the Lockerbie aircraft bombing.

When Warners' East Coast publicity department omitted a late-night screening of *Barry Lyndon* from its display ad in the *New York Times*, Kubrick noticed and rang them. Worried that his films might not be showing in the best venues, he had Warners summarise the programmes presented over the last few years at all the cinemas in European capitals, the length of runs, and their box office receipts. He insisted on the right of approval on all new prints and all advertising. Few infractions of the rules under which his films were screened escaped his attention. Many French cinemas lacked the 1.66:1 mask needed to frame *Barry Lyndon* correctly, so Kubrick supplied one to every theatre. Jan Harlan was sent around Europe to monitor cinemas' compliance, and accidentally locked himself out of his Mercedes in France *profonde*. Kubrick told him to wait where he was. Next morning, a new set of keys, helicoptered from Paris, were waiting at his hotel. Kubrick had looked up the chassis number of the car in his filing system and ordered duplicates.

The alarming variability among cinema projectors and sound systems continued to irritate him. Exhibitors in midwestern cities would be startled by a low, toneless Bronx murmur announcing, 'This is Stanley Kubrick. Your number two projector is out of alignment. An engineer will be there this afternoon. Meanwhile don't use it.' Fretting over such details, a classic symptom of the passive/ aggressive personality ('Oh, I suppose I'll have to do it myself'), gave Kubrick a sense of control and at the same time confirmed his belief in human fallibility. When Julian Senior tried to tell him about the successful Paris run of *Barry Lyndon*, Kubrick cut him off. 'Why are you telling me that?' he said. 'I can't do anything if it's *good* news. It's only when there are *problems* that I can intervene.'

Kubrick's ability to participate in the screening of his films, even in the furthest corners of the world, was viewed jealously by other directors who had no such control. Federico Fellini told American journalist Charlotte Chandler, 'I understand that Kubrick is able to watch carefully over each film. Someone told me he even has plans of the major theatres around the world, and if he sees that the first rows of seats are too close to the screen in a theatre in Tokyo, he wants them to take out those rows.' Fellini, however, didn't pursue this practice himself, a fact which would have disappointed Kubrick, who so admired the *maestro* for his refusal to produce commercial films. But, as Fellini explained, 'If you take the time and energy for what you have already done, it is not without price. It has to be at some sacrifice to your next project, which is delayed. I am disappointed, but it's absolutely impossible to try to be there in two thousand situations.'

Barry Lyndon might be shown in the right ratio in Belgrade, but while Kubrick was ensuring this was the case, Fellini was raising money for his next film. The statistics speak for themselves. Between 1974, when *Barry Lyndon* was released, and the completion of his next film, *The Shining*, in 1980, Fellini made *Casanova*, *Prova d'orchestra* and *La Città delle donne*.

All this time, Kubrick actively sought a home even more remote and secure than Abbots Mead, with enough space to make him totally self-sufficient. He was also alarmed by the increase in traffic on the road outside his property: two of his cats had been run over. He found a replacement in 1977, when Childwick (pronounced 'Chillick') Bury, the estate of the horse trainer Harry Joel, came on the market. Situated two miles outside St Albans in rural Hertfordshire, Childwick Bury was technically a manor, comprising not only a huge house, parts of which dated back to Elizabeth I, but also forest, pasture and a tiny village, Childwick Green.

Joel had built a large stable block next to the house, which Kubrick saw would adapt well into offices and cutting rooms. The house itself, a rambling Elizabethan pile encrusted with additions, had little architectural interest, but hedges, walls and trees made it nearly invisible as well as unapproachable. And it was remote – a quarter of a mile from the nearest road, the A1081. It had its own cricket pitch, and plenty of space for Kubrick to practise with his guns, though, once he moved in, he confined his target shooting to the nearby shooting club. He completed the purchase of the house, grounds and stable block in 1977, just as he was getting ready to make *The Shining*, and was in the process of renovating and moving into it throughout shooting.

In 1974, Ed DiGiulio, who had built the lenses for *Barry Lyndon*, sent Kubrick a 35mm demonstration reel for Garrett Brown's newly invented Steadicam, a gyro-stabilised camera harness which allowed an operator to walk, run or even climb stairs while retaining a rock-steady film image. Kubrick telexed DiGiulio:

Demo Reel On Hand-Held Mystery Stabilizer Was Spectacular And You Can Count On Me As A Customer. It Should Revolutionise The Way Films Are Shot. If You are Really Concerned About Protecting Its Design Before You Fully Patent It, Suggest You Delete Then Two Occasions On The Reel Where The Shadow On The Ground Gives the Skilled Counter-Intelligence Photo Interpreter A Fairly Clear Representation Of A Man Holding a Pole With One Hand With Something Or Other at the Bottom Of The Pole Which Appears To Be Slowly Moving. But My Lips Are Sealed. I Have a Question. Is There a Minimum Height At Which It Can Be Used?

Kubrick's eye wasn't as sharp as he thought – the Steadicam has no visible moving parts – but Brown's invention, for which he shared an Oscar in 1978, had planted the vision of a style which was to dominate Kubrick's next two films, *The Shining* and *Full Metal Jacket*.

Though Kubrick had turned down *The Exorcist*, Warners offered him *Exorcist II: The Heretic*. He refused. What could one do to top the first one, with its projectile vomiting, he asked: vomit in other colours, perhaps? It was a wise move, since John Boorman's attempt at the sequel was a disaster.

The proposal stuck in Kubrick's memory, however. As early as 1966, he'd told a friend he would 'like to make the world's scariest movie, involving a series of episodes that would play upon the nightmare fears of the audience'. The horror genre, like pornography, science fiction and the war film, intrigued Kubrick precisely because of its accumulated mass of inherited plot ideas and visual clichés. By scraping off the barnacles and showing the material in a new light, he hoped, as he'd done with *2001*, to demonstrate his abilities in the most striking way. The challenge of Cocteau's Orphée remained as powerful as ever: 'Astonish me.'

Horror fiction, having all but disappeared with the collapse of pulp magazines like *Weird Tales* during World War II, underwent an intense revival and period of revision in the 1970s. The atmospheric style pioneered by American writer Shirley Jackson with *The Haunting of Hill House* and by Ray Bradbury in his short stories inspired a new crop of writers, and a revival of interest in such classics as Bram Stoker's *Dracula* and Mary Shelley's *Frankenstein*.

In 1973, British author Brian Aldiss published *Frankenstein Unbound*, a post-modernist novel which sent a time traveller in an armoured battle-wagon back to the world of Mary Shelley and involved him in a sexual liaison with the author. Aldiss aimed to strip away the trappings of a score of movie versions and restore Shelley's original to its place at the heart of the Age of Enlightenment's visionary literature. The same year, he also published *Billion Year Spree*, a history of science fiction co-written with David Wingrove. Aldiss says:

In that book I mentioned *Strangelove*, *A Clockwork Orange* and *2001*, and in a footnote I remarked, not entirely seriously, that this made Stanley Kubrick the 'great sf writer of the age'. Kubrick picked up the paperback of *Billion Year Spree* on a railway bookstall and was impressed by this, because he could see it was just slipped in, and wasn't meant to be sucking up to him. He rang me and said, 'Let's meet and have a meal.'

We had a wonderful meeting. In those days Stanley used to dress like Che Guevara: green battledress, a tam o'shanter, a floppy beard. We repeated the lunch a bit later. He said to me, 'Why don't you send me a book or two of yours? Maybe there's something I could film.' Extremely generous.

Aldiss sent Kubrick a collection of his short stories which contained 'Super Toys Last all Summer Long', written in 1969 for a special issue of *Harpers and Queen* magazine. Only two thousand words long, 'Super Toys' is set in a future where birth control is rigorously imposed. While waiting for permission to bear a real child, an executive in a company that produces androids – flesh and blood artificial humans – brings home an android boy, David, together with his android teddy bear, as companions for his wife. Neither the reader nor David, who frets to his teddy that his mother doesn't love him, knows until the end that he's artificial. Aldiss couldn't imagine what Kubrick saw in the story or why he wanted to adapt it, though he surmises it was the theme of the failure of mother and child to communicate. He recalls:

Stanley was intrigued by the story, but then *Star Wars* came out. We had another lunch, and it was clear that he was very jealous of *Star Wars*. He didn't think it was as good as *2001*. He said, 'Couldn't we cook up between us a really good science fiction movie?'

He said that what we really wanted was a whole lot of archetypal situations: a poor young boy who somehow had to make good, and had to fight some terrible evil in order to win the hand of the princess. Then we realised we were actually describing *Star Wars*.

But then he reverted to 'Super Toys'. He made me an offer for it. He would buy the story outright, and I would work on the script. He made me sign a contract which was actually very disadvantageous to me. Among other things, if I called in an agent to negotiate for me, the deal was immediately off. If, on the completed film, the credit read just 'Script by Brian Aldiss and Stanley Kubrick,' I would be paid $2 million. But if he called in another writer, I got zilch.

I could see this might create problems. He could just call in someone at the very end, get them to contribute a few lines of dialogue, and I would have nothing. But Stanley is very fascinating. And I wanted to have a go. The $2 million didn't really interest me all that much. I was more concerned about how we might adapt the story.

I said, 'This is a vignette. I don't see how you can make it into a movie,' but he reminded me that he had done almost the same thing with Arthur Clarke's 'The Sentinel'. And he said something that I think is axiomatic: that it's easier to expand a small thing into a large one than vice versa. Maybe he was thinking of *Barry Lyndon*.

More likely, Kubrick had in mind a new novel by Stephen King, *The Shining*, of which John Calley had just sent him advance proofs. The book had been brought to Warners by an independent production group, the Producers' Circle, led by Robert Fryer, which had already successfully filmed other best-sellers, including *Voyage of the Damned* and *The Boys from Brazil*.

In 1977, King was still at the start of his enormously successful career. He had published only *Carrie*, *Salem's Lot* and, as 'Richard Bachman', *Rage*. Within a few years, however, he would become the *wunderkind* of modern horror fiction, a literary Steven Spielberg with the same ability to search out the sinister in even the most prosaic suburban setting. 'I have a very common nature,' says King, 'which is why my books sell. I am not capable of being fancy.' Brian De Palma had turned *Carrie* into a successful film, but while many scriptwriters flirted with transferring his combination of folksy setting and bloody horror to the screen, most failed. King wasn't surprised. 'It's tough to break the gap between the warmth in the novel that makes the characters seem worth loving and caring about, set off against the horrors. When they make the movie they concentrate on the moment when the monster comes out and starts waving his claws. I don't think that's what people are interested in.'

The Shining was King's longest and most ambitious novel to that date. Set in a snowbound Colorado resort hotel, the Overlook, it detailed the mental and moral deterioration of the winter caretaker, Jack Torrance, under the building's evil influence. A sullen ex-teacher with literary ambitions but a history as well of heavy drinking and domestic violence, Torrance has taken the job in the hope that it will help him to overcome a writing block and finish a novel. Once he and his wife Wendy and young son Danny are alone, however, the spirits which haunt the hotel begin to affect him as they did a previous caretaker, who killed his family with an axe.

King's most inventive creation is a topiary garden, the creatures of which, sculpted from living shrubs, come to life as the hotel becomes snowbound. Wendy and Danny are saved by the hotel's chef, Hallorann, who battles through the snow to rescue them, having recognised in Danny the same precognitive and telepathic ability which he possesses, and which his grandmother called 'Shining'. The hotel and its garden burn, and Torrance with them, while Hallorann takes Wendy and Danny under his wing, intending to nurture the boy's psychic abilities.

Kubrick agreed to make *The Shining* for Warners. This left his project with Brian Aldiss up in the air, but he found a characteristically cavalier method to escape from this. Among the more unusual clauses in their contract was one which specified that Aldiss could not leave Britain except with Kubrick's agreement. Aldiss thought little of it when he signed, and when Kubrick suspended work on 'Super Toys' to prepare *The Shining*, he accepted an invitation to attend a conference in Florida. He sent Kubrick a postcard from there, and on his return was astonished to receive a terse call informing him that, in view of this breach of contract, he was fired.

'But you weren't working either!' Aldiss protested. 'We were taking a break.'

Kubrick expressed indifference. A contract was a contract, and he regarded himself, he told Aldiss, as free of all obligations. The two men didn't speak again for five years.

King's contract with Warners stipulated that he write the first draft screenplay of *The Shining*, but there was little hope that he and Kubrick would agree on an approach to the story. To King, the hotel was simply haunted, and the thrust of the story was the innocent characters' rescue from its ghosts. His script, the first he'd written, stressed the essential decency of Torrance, and placed the blame for his acts on the hotel itself and its topiary beasts. As in the book, six-year-old Danny was the main character.

Kubrick saw the book in an entirely different light. This was Jack Torrance's story, and everything else, in particular the supernatural element, was peripheral. Some critics have assumed that Kubrick saw himself in Torrance, and that the story of a man who immures himself with his family in a remote country retreat was autobiographical, but his true inspiration was Stephen Crane's story 'The Blue Hotel', which he remembered from James Agee's 1948 adaptation during the time both were involved with the TV series *Omnibus*. Crane's story – more like a fable – tells of three men, stranded in a Nebraska town by a blizzard, whose game of cards in an eerily painted hotel degenerates first into a fist fight, then a murder as a stupid and apparently paranoid player, 'The Swede', goads one of the others into killing him by claiming he's being cheated. The Swede *is* being cheated, as it turns out, but Crane suggests that, by making an issue of it, the victim connives at his own killing.

'That feller was lookin' for trouble,' observes one of the characters in the aftermath.

'Like all troubled men,' says another, smoothly carrying on the thought. 'And we helped him find it, and we trapped him into it.'

'The Blue Hotel', says Kubrick, suggested the 'psychological misdirection' of *The Shining*. He saw Torrance as a man like the Swede, in search of his own destruction, who surrenders to the imagined horrors of the hotel in order to rid himself of his troublesome family, and, finally, to destroy himself. Jack's decline into paranoia and homicidal mania was a textbook illustration of Kubrick's Manichaean belief in Evil as a force that can be embodied, the entity Michael Herr called 'the Shadow'. If there was to be evil at the Overlook, it was within Torrance, not in a telepathic six-year-old, nor in ambulant shrubbery – which would, moreover, be ruinously expensive to create.

Among the novels Kubrick had encountered in his random reading was *The Shadow Knows*, a novel by American writer Diane Johnson whose main character, a recently divorced woman prey to feelings of despair and helplessness, is menaced by – perhaps imaginary – burglars, and anonymous phone calls threatening her life.

Johnson's novel was published in 1974, but it was June 1977

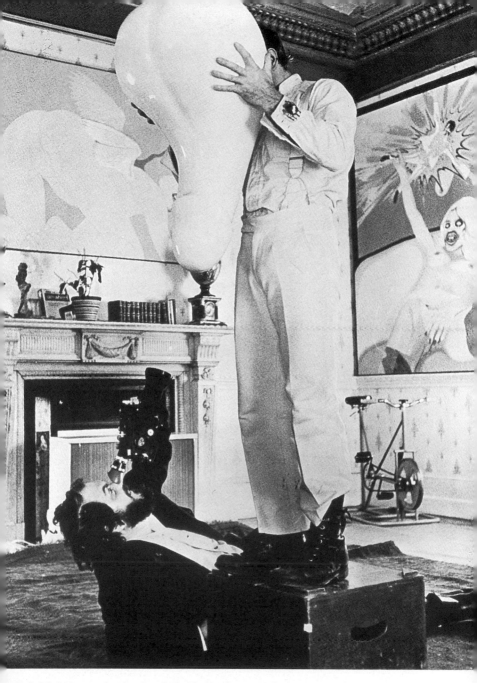

Kubrick lining up the shot in which Alex DeLarge (Malcolm McDowell) attacks the Cat Lady with one of her collection of erotic art objects in *A Clockwork Orange* (1971).

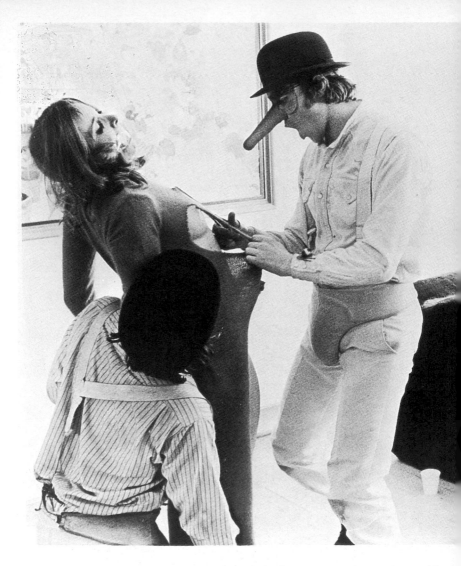

Mrs Alexander (Adrienne Corri) about to be raped by Alex and his *droogs* in *A Clockwork Orange* while Kubrick operates the camera. *Right:* Kubrick on the prison set with Michael Bryant and Malcolm McDowell.

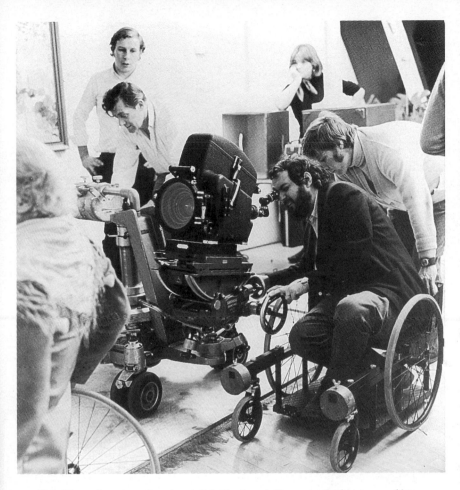

Kubrick on the prison chapel set of *A Clockwork Orange* and, *above,* one of his cost-cutting technical innovations, a wheelchair adapted into a camera platform.

The troubled *Barry Lyndon* (1975). *Top:* Kubrick directs. *Left:* Marisa Berenson as Lady Lyndon: 'overbred, vacuous, giggly and lazy', according to co-star Ryan O'Neal. *Below:* Lady Lyndon and her chaplain, the Reverend Runt (Murray Melvin), in one of the gaming-room scenes which Kubrick insisted be shot by candlelight.

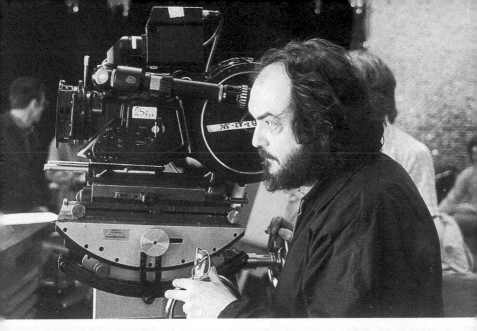

Kubrick on the set of *The Shining* (1980)
and, *below,* with director of photography
John Alcott.

Lee Ermey as Sergeant Hartman rages at the recruits in *Full Metal Jacket* (1987).

The death of Cowboy (Arliss Howard), the only scene in *Full Metal Jacket* written by the author of the original novel, Gustav Hasford.

before the author, who was married to a cardiologist and divided her time between Europe and the United States, had a call from Warner Brothers' London office, asking her conspiratorially, 'Where will you be at 11 p.m. tomorrow?'

Kubrick rang her the following night at the London Hilton, and on a number of subsequent nights, always late. At first, he hinted that he was interested in the film rights to *The Shadow Knows*, but he and Johnson soon agreed that its first-person structure made adaptation difficult. 'All the horror is subjective,' says Johnson, 'which makes it hard to film.'

Johnson was teaching a course on the gothic novel at Berkeley. Once Kubrick discovered this, their talk ranged further. What did she think about Mary Shelley's *Frankenstein*? About Dickens? 'They were literary conversations,' says Johnson. 'He talked like a writer. I enjoyed them.' After a number of such discussions, Kubrick and Christiane ventured as far as the West End to have dinner with Johnson and her husband at the Hilton. Only then did he admit that he was planning *The Shining*.

Kubrick didn't show her King's screenplay, but Johnson was left in no doubt that he didn't want to use it or to work with King, and while he'd started a treatment of his own, he didn't show her that either. After their preliminary discussions, Johnson left for California to teach the rest of her course, but it was understood that she would return to London in a few months and start work on the script of what now, with the casting of Jack Nicholson as Torrance, had become a $13 million production.

The Jack Nicholson of 1978 was a different man to the relative unknown to whom Kubrick had offered 'Napoleon'. Dark in temperament, bitter and disillusioned, the actor felt himself to be facing both a personal and vocational abyss. He'd seized the professional high ground with his Best Actor Oscar for *One Flew Over the Cuckoo's Nest*, but was still better known for his parties and his championship of recreational drugs, of which he was a self-confessed enthusiastic user, having smoked marijuana, he claimed, every day for fifteen years without ill effects. Close friends included Roman Polanski, the director of *Chinatown*, who often stayed at the Mulholland Drive house Nicholson shared with Anjelica Huston. In 1977 Huston moved out, but the couple remained close, and she continued to spend time in the house.

The same year, Nicholson launched his career as a director with the comedy Western *Goin' South*, in which he also starred as Henry Moon, an inept bankrobber about to be hanged who's rescued by a local woman prepared to marry him as a means of acquiring cheap labour to work her goldmine. Nicholson played Moon as a filthy, unshaven drifter, employing a feral grin and a degree of eye-rolling which alarmed the film's producers, as did rumours of lavish cocaine consumption during location shooting in Durango, Mexico, much, though not all of it, by Nicholson's co-star, John Belushi.

In March 1977, while Nicholson was skiing in Colorado, Polanski borrowed the Mulholland Drive house to shoot part of a photo-essay for the French magazine *Vogue Hommes* on the young girls of California – 'the younger the better,' said the editors, according to Polanski. Shortly after, Polanski would be accused of raping one thirteen-year-old model. Anjelica Huston too was arrested when police, raiding the house while she was there in Nicholson's absence, found small quantities of cocaine and hashish. Neither Nicholson nor Huston was ever charged, but Polanski, rather than face a jail sentence, fled to France in January 1978.

When Nicholson arrived in London soon afterwards to start work on *The Shining*, there were few actors better equipped mentally to play Jack Torrance. The Polanski scandal, the failure of *Goin' South*, which was received with little enthusiasm, his break-up with Huston and recent revelations about his disordered childhood – he'd been brought up to believe that his grandmother was his mother and his true mother his elder sister – combined with his drug use to induce a mental state in which manic humour alternated with depression and paranoia. 'Nicholson was very much crazier from the outset in his performance than in the book,' says Diane Johnson, 'and very much crazier than Kubrick envisioned, I think. It's what Nicholson brought to it. Nicholson was very hyped-up at the time.'

Warners installed Nicholson in the $2000-a-week Thames-side house on Cheyne Walk in Chelsea where Alex North had written his unused score for *2001*. The actor was seldom there, however, partying vigorously until well into the small hours, returning for only a few hours' sleep before the long drive to the studio. Soon even these visits ceased when he injured his back, supposedly while leaping over a low wall in the garden, and doctors laid him off for weeks.

While Diane Johnson was in California, Kubrick's scouts had found the Overlook in Oregon's Timberline Lodge on the slopes of snow-capped Mount Hood. It provided the exteriors, while the art deco interiors were copied from Yosemite Valley's Ahwanee Lodge. (Kubrick's stepdaughter Katherina receives a credit for Location Research.) Doug Milsome, Alcott's assistant, who was to become Kubrick's regular cameraman, just as Alcott himself had taken over from Geoffrey Unsworth, directed a second unit that filmed extensive coverage of the hotel, as well as the long shots of landscape which open the film. He also shot scenes of Hallorann's car and Snowcat battling blizzards to reach the hotel.

Kubrick himself never left Britain. Instead he persuaded Elstree to bulldoze its standing Street Scene set, a ten-year veteran of countless productions. In its place rose the façade of the Overlook and the entrance to the maze opposite. Production designer Roy Walker built the interiors, an intricate succession of wide corridors and vast public rooms through which Kubrick enjoyed tracking as much as he had in the trenches of *Paths of Glory* and the centrifuge set of *2001*.

The primary set was the lofty Colorado Lounge, thirty metres long, with a large staircase at one end and five floor-to-ceiling windows, each three metres wide, looking out, notionally, onto the snowbound grounds. Any interior filmed during a snowstorm demanded an army of grips outside the windows strewing expanded polystyrene snow, large quantities of which, carried on the breeze, ended up in Borehamwood High Street. *The Shining* finally took up every square centimetre of space at the studio, and its hunger for equipment strained the capacity of London's rental companies. Above all, it excited the intense interest not only of the world's press but of every member of Stephen King's growing worldwide mass of enthusiasts.

When Diane Johnson returned to London at the end of 1977, she prudently refused to work, as Kubrick wanted, at Abbots Mead and to live nearby, an arrangement which rendered writers vulnerable to summons at all hours. Instead she stayed in London and was driven to the house each day. Otherwise, the collaboration was close. 'We really did write it together,' says Johnson. 'We would sit down and talk about a scene, then I would go away and write the dialogue. Right from scratch we would discuss theories of horror and stuff like that. I really had the sense that he was working through all that for himself for the first time. We got books out of the library; people like Freud. Books about what is scary, and why do we feel scared of this book, etcetera. Bruno Bettelheim's *The Uses of Enchantment*, about the importance of fairy tales, was a useful source. So were *Wuthering Heights* and *Jane Eyre*, and the stories of Edgar Allan Poe.

'Family hate seemed quite important. We decided that in the case of *The Shining* this was a central element. I had the very strong impression that Kubrick was attracted to *The Shining* because of the father/son thing. He never said it in so many words, but that was my diagnosis of the attraction of that theme.' Jack Nicholson, himself disoriented by the publication of the details of his own fractured childhood, embraced this idea with vigour. 'If you take a sociological view of the last ten years,' he said in an interview when the film was released, 'you'd find that the most volatile element in our culture is the pressure inside the family unit.'

Kubrick later called *The Shining* 'just the story of one man's family quietly going insane together'. He originally meant the tension between Jack and Danny to be the film's most powerful element, and Jack's disturbance to be triggered by the frustrations of dealing with his ditzy wife and telepathic son. His first cut contained a long early scene in which Wendy explained the troubled relationship to a paediatrician (Anne Jackson). Some months before arriving at the Overlook, Jack, coming home drunk, had attacked Danny and dislocated his shoulder – by accident, Wendy insists. She blames this incident for Danny's retreat into a fantasy relationship with his imaginary playmate Tony, who 'lives in his mouth' and speaks through his right index finger.

Johnson and Kubrick systematically worked out a scheme for the film, starting with a treatment in which each scene had a brief one-sentence summary: 'Jack and his family arrive at the hotel.' Each of these was then expanded to include motivation: 'Filled with expectation, Jack and his family arrive at his new job at the hotel.'

After this, Johnson had an unprecedentedly free hand. She exploited it to create some of the film's most disturbing moments. Fascinated as ever by new technology, Kubrick owned one of the first electric typewriters to include computer memory. Johnson incorporated its rhythmic clatter as a motif that culminates in Wendy's discovery, surreptitiously reading the manuscript of Jack's novel, that it consists of nothing but the same phrase repeated page after page, as both exposition and dialogue. Kubrick used the computerised typewriter to produce the five hundred pages of manuscript which fill the box on Jack's table. No matter how deep Wendy scrabbled, she'd always find a neatly typed page consisting of the words 'All work and no play makes Jack a dull boy.'

When Johnson had to return to America again in January 1978 – Kubrick would start filming in May, on what was meant to be a seventeen-week shoot – the film's ending remained unwritten. Neither liked King's topiary animals: they could easily look comic. The creatures gave way to a vast maze with four-metre-high hedge walls – one more step towards a psychiatric subtext to the film, which is reinforced by a new ending.

'We agreed that blowing up the hotel was banal,' Johnson said. 'Things always blow up in horror films. It was Stanley who thought of Jack chasing Danny through the maze in the ice. I remember him ringing me in California, very excited, and asking, "What do you think of this?"' Jack, who is seen brooding over a small-scale model of the maze in one scene, ends up frozen to death in the labyrinthine passages which echo his own psychosis, a climax that again underlines Kubrick's debt to Freud.

Johnson attributes to Kubrick the film's sexual imagery: the nude girl who rises from her bath and embraces Jack, only to turn into the rotting corpse of an old woman; the scenes of apparent homosexuality, including two men in animal suits surprised in a hotel room during an intimate moment. 'There were certain images in the script which I think were always in his mind,' she says. 'There was that very strange dark bit where at the very end Wendy sees kind of strange images of what looks like oral sex between two men, and skeletons; that had nothing to do with me.' In particular Kubrick interpolated the nightmarish vision, one of the most startling in contemporary cinema, of an elevator door sliding open in slow motion to disgorge a flood of blood.

For Wendy Torrance, Kubrick chose Shelley Duvall, a gangling, toothy Texan whose film experience, aside from a cameo in Woody

Allen's *Annie Hall*, was exclusively in Robert Altman's casually constructed and often improvised films. Unaccustomed to the discipline of traditional Hollywood sets, let alone the rigour of a Kubrick production, Duvall was to have a great deal of difficulty in adjusting, and would turn in a largely unconvincing performance.

After playing Bullingdon in *Barry Lyndon*, Leon Vitali had been called back on *The Shining* as one of Kubrick's inner team of four or five full-time personal assistants. They were almost always young men, the exception being Kubrick's long-suffering secretary Margaret Adams, whose efficiency and ability to cope with Kubrick's whims seemed unimpaired by the fact that she was confined to a wheelchair. Most of the team lived in ill-concealed terror of disappointing their master. People dealing with Kubrick became accustomed to any refusal being greeted with a pleading, 'But what shall I tell Stanley?'

Kubrick sent Vitali through the American midwest looking for someone to play Danny. The boy had to be a complete amateur, and no more than six years old. Vitali interviewed five thousand boys in Denver, Chicago and Cincinnati, and videotaped several hundred of them doing improvisations, from which Kubrick chose Danny Lloyd, a five-year-old from a railroad family. During shooting, Vitali stayed on as his coach.

Both Nicholson and Duvall trailed a sense of the Hollywood Kubrick had abandoned, a community high on cocaine which still reverberated to the designer slaughter of Charles Manson, the cult leader whose group had murdered Roman Polanski's wife Sharon Tate and her friends in the most notorious and bloody mass murder in recent Californian history. The wild-eyed Manson was one of Jack Nicholson's inspirations for his playing of Torrance.

There was no possibility of either star starting low-key and working up to an intensity of feeling. Duvall, with her tombstone teeth, long Easter Island face and giant pop eyes rolling like those of a spooked horse, evoked panic the moment one saw her. 'Shelley seemed quite crazy,' says Johnson. 'She told me later that she was *driven* crazy by the process of shooting this film. She felt that Kubrick didn't like her and drove her unmercifully.'

As for Nicholson, his performance, grinning evilly even when he is being interviewed by the hotel manager Barry Nelson for the job of caretaker, imposed a level of hysteria which swept the story to new heights of manic energy. 'Jack Torrance descended into lunacy,' remarks Patrick McGilligan in his biography of Nicholson. 'His hair became mangier than Henry Moon's, his eyes zoned out, his tongue lolled around inside his mouth. Jack seemed to enjoy the murderous mood. He couldn't resist a hint of comedy, playing madness like an ape, grunting and muttering, swinging his arms hugely from side to side as he lunged down empty corridors running from ghosts and chasing his victims.' Later Nicholson was to describe his performance as 'sort of balletic'.

Stephen King, who had no sympathy with the behavioural/R.D. Laingian approach to his book contained in Kubrick and Johnson's first script, loathed the new, intensely physical, one even more. 'Kubrick just couldn't grasp the sheer inhuman evil of the Overlook,' he complained. 'So he looked, instead, for evil in the characters and made the film into a domestic tragedy with only vaguely supernatural overtones. That was the basic flaw: because he couldn't believe, he couldn't make the film believable to others. The real problem is that Kubrick set out to make a horror film with no apparent understanding of the genre. Everything about it screams that from beginning to end.'

For a while, Kubrick and Johnson tried to respect King's wishes, making Jack a victim of the hotel's diabolical tenants. Showing the Torrances around, manager Barry Nelson confides that the place is built on an old Indian burial ground and is thus cursed – a favourite theme of King's. Jack's first hallucination occurs in the empty bar as he covers his face with his hands and mutters that he'd sell his soul for a beer. When he looks up, Joe Turkel, playing Clyde, the hotel's bartender, is waiting to serve him all the booze he craves. It's a scene that might have come from a dozen other horror films.

Jack then encounters Grady, played by another survivor of *Barry Lyndon*, Philip Stone, and recognises him as the caretaker who, some years before, murdered his family and then killed himself. When Jack questions how Grady could still be in the hotel, albeit serving drinks in a patently imaginary party scene, Stone intones sepulchrally, 'I have *always* been here,' a line worthy of Boris Karloff.

Johnson also wrote an additional scene in which Barry Nelson visits Danny after his ordeal and tosses him a ball which has appeared earlier in the film as a motif of evil possession. Nelson is thus established as a creature of the Overlook, doomed to repeat a cycle of madness and murder within the hotel. This sets up the last shot of the film, in which the camera, tracking in on one of the many framed photographs that decorate the walls, reveals Nicholson as a grinning figure in a 1921 party scene. This image goes to the heart of Kubrick's Manichaean vision of the world. Evil exists. It has always existed. It always will.

But Kubrick couldn't live with the full implications of this approach. Each day, Nicholson's performance drove the story relentlessly back to the daily paranoia and social dysfunction of the actor's own life and milieu, and to Kubrick's own problems of communication with his parents and, later, his own family. To Kubrick, *The Shining* was about Evil in its widest incarnation, Michael Herr's (and Jung's) Shadow, lurking just beyond the firelight, waiting to devour us. Gradually, he removed those elements which introduced any sense of Good: the paediatrician with her calm reassurance, Hallorann's last-minute rescue (in the film he reaches the hotel, only to be promptly axed by Jack), and in particular Jack's affection for his family. Kubrick's Torrance, like the mother to the android boy in 'Super Toys Last all Summer Long', displays a motiveless hostility to Wendy and Danny from the start. The only scene of intimacy between father and son is an ominously low-key encounter in which Jack, sleepless with nightmares, takes Danny on his knee and murmurs, 'Wouldn't you like to stay here in the hotel . . . forever?'

Kubrick and Johnson watched a number of Nicholson movies to study his technique, and noted, as Johnson said, that

in some, he played a 'down' person, measured, slow. We decided he was more interesting 'up' – as an active, voluble person, like the role he played in *One Flew Over the Cuckoo's Nest*, rather than as a contemplative, brooding person. Luckily, our character was driven and energetic. We would have changed the character to fit Nicholson, but we didn't have to . . .

We had trouble getting a voice for Torrance. Jack Nicholson speaks in short blocks. It's no good having him do long speeches. Luckily, there were no long speeches required. But the character had to be a specially demanding verbal combination – intelligent, unpleasant, mordant, and sarcastic. What struck me was how

well Stanley wrote Jack. Much better than I could. Considering
the ease with which Stanley wrote Jack, you wouldn't imagine
Stanley to be the pleasant, kindly husband and father he is.

Slim Pickens was Kubrick's first choice for Hallorann, despite
the fact that the character is black, but after the experience of *Dr
Strangelove*, he had no desire to work with Kubrick again. His
agent showed the script to a fellow agent, Don Schwartz, who
decided the role was perfect for a client of his, black actor Sherman
'Scatman' Crothers. An ex-singer and bandleader, Crothers had
gone into movies in the fifties, and at sixty-seven was a fixture in
supporting roles requiring a genial, toothy African-American with
an air of beaming confidence. Though he'd never heard of Kubrick
or seen any of his films, Crothers wanted the role of Hallorann
sufficiently badly to ring up Nicholson, with whom he'd appeared
in *The King of Marvin Gardens*, *The Fortune* and *One Flew Over
the Cuckoo's Nest*, and ask him to intercede. Nicholson put in a
word for him, and Kubrick acquiesced, though with reservations
that grew as shooting continued.

The production excited enormous interest in Hollywood, as did
all Kubrick's films. In a community rendered increasingly transparent by a desperation to hype every new production, a film-maker
who gave almost no interviews and refused to discuss his work was
as rare and awe-inspiring as an alien. When Steven Spielberg arrived
in Britain in March 1978 for the launching of *Close Encounters of
the Third Kind*, chosen for the Royal Command Film Performance,
he confided to Adrian Turner, who had scheduled an on-stage interview at the National Film Theatre, that his main reason for coming
was not to meet the Queen but Kubrick, with whom he'd spent
that day. Clint Eastwood too tried to make a pilgrimage to Childwick Bury, only to be driven back at the gate by his allergy to cats.

Kubrick and Spielberg, despite the latter's reverence for *2001*,
proved to have little in common. Spielberg typified the post-war
generation of film-makers, the so-called New Hollywood. Raised
on comic books, television and fast food, they looked for facile
answers and short cuts. Their emblem was the storyboard, which
visualised each film as a moving comic book. Kubrick, raised in a
different school, never used storyboards, and spent months in the
cutting room, feeling towards his vision, less like a comic book

artist than a Renaissance painter, building up a film with a multitude of *pentimenti*. With so little basis for agreement, the relationship between Kubrick and Spielberg, which began in cordiality and mutual respect, would collapse during post-production of *The Shining*, when Spielberg moved into the studio in the wake of Kubrick's film to start shooting *Raiders of the Lost Ark*.

For the time being, however, Kubrick remained to Spielberg and most of New Hollywood a charismatic, even almost magical figure. A not-very-funny joke circulated. Spielberg died and went to heaven, but at the Pearly Gates he's denied admittance; God doesn't like film directors. Just then, a shabby balding figure in stained cords and battered sneakers cycles by.

'Isn't that Stanley Kubrick?' asks Spielberg.

St Peter spares the rider a troubled glance. 'No, it's God. He just *thinks* he's Stanley Kubrick.'

Cast and crew on *The Shining* quickly tired of the relentless regime. Scatman Crothers had no experience of direction like Kubrick's, and found the multiple takes gruelling. For the scene in which Hallorann shows Wendy and Danny through the storage rooms of the kitchen, Kubrick demanded eighty-five takes, in the middle of which Crothers broke down and cried in frustration. 'What do you want, Mr Kubrick?' he screamed. 'What do you *want*?!' For a scene without dialogue in the snow, Kubrick put the actor through forty takes, and almost as many on the scene where Torrance hits him with the axe.

Crothers' complaints and Nicholson's febrile state of mind led to an incident which has overtones of Groucho Marx. 'Somebody said something about me being too old to fall down that many times,' Crothers recalled of his death scene, 'and Nicholson jumps up and says, "Who says my man's too old to fall down? Why, he can fall down fifty or sixty times if he has to." I wound up having to go to a chiropractor I was hurting so bad. My arms and elbows and neck and head got kind of beat up.'

Nobody was ever sure if this exhausting system bore fruit, or whether it didn't simply prop up the mystique of a director who would go to any lengths to achieve his ends, and expected his cast and crew to do the same. (Kubrick's own explanation, that 'the only time I do a lot of takes is when an actor hasn't learned his lines,' is not only absurd but a slur on the professionalism of his actors.) Critics regularly used this penchant for multiple takes as a club to beat him with. 'If Nicholson's performance is what the director wants after fifty takes,' *Variety* said of *The Shining*, 'it's no wonder [Kubrick] demands the final cut. It's impossible to imagine what the forty-nine takes he threw away could look like.' Fortunately, Gordon Stainforth, one of *The Shining*'s editors, can tell us.

> That long tracking shot where Jack Nicholson pursued Shelley Duvall up the staircase while she's waving a baseball bat at him was taken fifty or sixty times. Typically, Nicholson's first take would be absolutely brilliant. Then the thing would start to get stale after about ten takes. Then you can see he's almost marking time, so that he doesn't get exhausted. Then he's going right over the top. The impression I got is that Stanley tended to go for the most eccentric and rather over-the-top ones. There were plenty of times when Stanley and I were viewing the stuff where my private choice of the best performance – or sometimes he would ask me – wasn't in, while the more eccentric was.

This bears out George C. Scott's complaint on *Strangelove*, that Kubrick used only the moments where he was at his most manic. Though Kubrick paints his backgrounds in shades, he prefers his foregrounds in the gaudiest of primaries.

When it came to the scene on the stairs where he's struck with the bat, Nicholson had no intention of taking the kind of physical punishment endured by Crothers. He requested a stunt double. Characteristically, Kubrick held a cattle-call audition of every available stunt man in the London area. Long, short and tall turned up. Once they were assembled, each in turn was given a duplicate of Nicholson's jacket and asked to stand beside the star with his back to the camera for purposes of comparison. Kubrick finally chose a young stunt man new to the business. The secretary of the stunt men's section of the actors' union Equity insisted that he couldn't work alone, but would need to have an experienced man with him. Bridling at the idea of having someone looking over his shoulder, Kubrick quixotically said that the secretary, a veteran with nothing like Nicholson's build, could do the job himself.

Kubrick gave little direction to Nicholson, to the disappointment of a young sound recordist who'd signed on in the hope of learning Kubrick's methods. After a particularly tiring series of takes, Kubrick called for a tea break and, while a member of the catering staff served it, called Nicholson over for a conference. The recordist turned up the volume of Nicholson's radio mike, and heard Kubrick mutter to his star, 'Did you see the tits on that tea girl?'

The Shining was the second Kubrick film, after *2001*, to be the subject of a behind-the-scenes documentary about its making. The director and camerawoman was Kubrick's daughter Vivian, then eighteen, who had ambitions to go into movies. She had no formal training, but Kubrick, true to his belief that the best way to learn film-making was to make a film, gave her an Aaton 16mm camera and told her to shoot as much film as she liked, with the proviso that he would have approval of the final cut. The fact that she was Kubrick's daughter, and both pretty and intelligent, gave Vivian unprecedented access to what was going on behind the scenes, up to and including Jack Nicholson removing his trousers and other members of the cast taking a revivifying toot of cocaine. In homage to the family taste for birds of prey, *Making The Shining* was an Eagle Film. It was shown on British television, after careful editing by Kubrick, who removed some of the less flattering images of himself, and had a few screenings as a promotional tool for the film's overseas distribution. Vivian, however, did not persist with her film-making ambitions. Her next, and more successful, appearance in connection with one of her father's films was as composer.

With memories of the Steadicam demonstration reel, Kubrick had Roy Walker design the sets for long smooth tracking shots, and hired the Steadicam's inventor Garrett Brown to shoot them, though John Alcott remained in charge of the lighting. 'I realised by the afternoon of the first day's work,' said Brown phlegmatically, 'that here was a whole new ball game, and that the word "reasonable" was not in Kubrick's lexicon.'

The maze set existed in three versions: one, on Radlett Aerodrome, used for the summer scenes; a second on the Elstree backlot for sequences demanding snow; and a third, partial version on a sound stage for the scenes where Danny and Wendy flee the hotel, and Jack pursues Danny into its alleys. The maze itself was made from pine boughs stapled to plywood sheets which formed empty corridors through which, in theory, technicians could move around the huge set. In practice, they became easily lost. The map attached to every call sheet didn't help, especially when the fog machines began belching oil and water vapour. 'It wasn't much use to call out, "Stanley!"' said Garrett Brown, 'as his laughter seemed to come from everywhere.'

The maze was the greatest test yet of the Steadicam, which Brown operated personally in almost every scene where it was used. Despite its remarkable qualities, the mechanism depended on smooth movement, and while one could easily carry it up and down even a spiral staircase, it resisted sudden changes of direction. Negotiating the right-angle turns of the maze at speed, following Jack as he pursued Danny, placed machine and operator under enormous strain.

Used to operating the camera himself, Kubrick had a habit, when working with Brown, of grabbing the harness and tugging at it, saying, 'Just come a little right.' In such situations the system malfunctioned, ruining the shot. Brown warned Kubrick, but he took no notice, so on the advice of Doug Milsome, who knew the political intricacies of a Kubrick unit, Brown set up a fake conversation within the hearing of Vivian, who could be relied upon, like other members of the family, to carry tales to Kubrick.

'Is it true,' Milsome asked Brown innocently, after making sure Vivian was in earshot, 'that you knocked out Sylvester Stallone?'

'Oh, yeah,' said the muscular Brown, who was well over six feet tall. 'Well, he used to grab the Steadicam pole and pull me this way and that way. And I said to him one day, "You do that again, Sly, and I'll knock you down." He did it the following day and I hit him, and he went down.'

The next day, Brown and Milsome watched in amusement as Kubrick's hand moved out to grab the harness – then snapped back. 'Er, could you just move a little to the left?' he asked tentatively.

Since Kubrick had seen his demo reel, Brown had developed a refined model, the Universal II, in which the camera is suspended under the stabilising platform rather than mounted above it, allowing much lower shooting. It was used in a shot from behind Danny as he swept along the hotel's corridors on his tricycle. 'I tried it on foot,' Brown recalled, 'and found that I was too winded after an entire three-minute take to even describe what sort of last rites I would prefer. Also, at those speeds I couldn't get the lens much lower than about eighteen inches from the floor.'

Kubrick suggested using the wheelchair camera seat he'd helped develop for *A Clockwork Orange*. With Brown seated, his lens was only a few inches above the carpet. It functioned superbly, so Kubrick set about refining it by adding a platform behind Brown for the sound recordist and Doug Milsome, co-opted as focus puller. The chair quickly metamorphosed into a fragile camera platform. Kubrick fitted a super-accurate speedometer so that shots could be precisely repeated no matter how often they were retaken. This worked so well that he wanted the same instruments fitted to his big Moviola and Ellemak dollies. By this time, the chair, careering along the halls with three or four men on board, flanked by runners to steady it at corners, was alarmingly top-heavy, especially when Kubrick, who insisted on operating the 'Pan' handle while Brown or his operator worked the 'Tilt' control, added his weight. Unsurprisingly, a tyre blew and there was almost a serious crash. Kubrick ordered that solid tyres be fitted and no more than two men at a time be carried, and shooting went on.

Brown was in awe of Kubrick's single-mindedness. 'During the year of production,' he said, 'the science of air conditioning was reinvented, and you can be certain that about every other branch of human learning was at least re-examined insofar as it touched upon the doings at Borehamwood. Laboratory science, lighting, lenses and the logistics of lunch – all were scrutinised daily.' Brown tried to moderate Kubrick's obsessiveness by engaging him in philosophical debate. 'We talked a lot about the elusive pursuit of perfection,' says Brown, 'and how you can never achieve it. By the time we'd done twenty takes, entropy had taken over. Something taped to the wall would fall off. We were all getting older.' But Kubrick was unconvinced.

The seventeen-week schedule of *The Shining* doubled, then tripled. When he got to the scenes of Shelley and Danny bolting out of the hotel into the snow, Kubrick was able to shoot them in genuine cold, since it was by then almost Christmas. According to legend, Kubrick suggested that the camera crew sleep in the camera room and not go home at all for holidays. The proposal was indignantly rejected.

Elstree's managers, who had bookings for two years ahead, start-

ing with Steven Spielberg's *Raiders of the Lost Ark*, followed by
Warren Beatty's *Reds*, watched uneasily as the shoot stretched on
into the spring of 1979. Not for the first time on a Kubrick film,
intense lighting resulted in enormous heat. Even with the air conditioning at full blast, the seven hundred thousand watts pouring
through the windows of the Colorado Lounge pushed the temperature up to 110 degrees Fahrenheit.

The set finally burst into flames and was completely destroyed,
along with part of the studio roof. Only a few close-ups remained
to be shot, and the Elstree management expected Kubrick to shoot
them elsewhere. Vain hope. Kubrick was adamant that the building
be repaired and the set rebuilt.

Principal photography didn't end until April. Anjelica Huston
joined Nicholson, and managed to wean him from the round of
parties. In interviews, she described an almost unrecognisable
Nicholson who staggered in exhausted from shooting at 10 o'clock
each night and collapsed into bed alone. Ray Lovejoy was already
assembling the film at Elstree, though since Kubrick personally cuts
all his films and the editor is, in effect, his assistant, not a foot was
cut until all shooting was finished.

Meanwhile, in another part of the complex, Vivian confronted the
problem of distilling an hour-long documentary from 120,000 feet
of footage. *The Shining*'s first assistant director, Gill Smith, rang
an old friend, Gordon Stainforth, then working as an editor for
Thames TV, and asked if he would cut the film and also act as
nursemaid to Vivian. 'She warned me,' said Stainforth, 'that Vivian
was a bit difficult, like her father, and would want everything her
way.'

Stainforth faced the accumulated footage with horror. None of
the film was identified, and since the sound had been transferred
onto magnetic tape, there was an equal amount of soundtrack, all
of which needed to be synchronised with the image. Vivian finally
decided that she would transfer everything to black and white video,
so scores of tape boxes joined the cans of film and sound stock that
cluttered the cutting rooms. 'Vivian had been scratching her head for
weeks about how to structure it,' says Stainforth. 'But she insisted on
doing it her way. She's very like her father in that. The saving grace
was, she has a photographer's eye – like Stanley.'

While Vivian pondered, Stainforth hung around the main cutting room of *The Shining*, and was pressed into service on the larger film when, in August 1979, Kubrick decided to edit at Childwick Bury, where the stable block had been converted into cutting rooms. Ray Lovejoy and his staff were dismayed at having to work so far out of London. Childwick Bury also lacked the controlled temperature storage to accommodate the mountain of film Kubrick had shot, a mountain made more overwhelming by the fact that, since he constantly rethought cuts, every centimetre had to be numbered, logged and stored in case he wanted to make a change. Since dubbing would still take place at Elstree, all footage had to be transported to Hertfordshire for cutting, then returned to the studio afterwards.

Stainforth was enrolled in the team shuffling film between Childwick Bury and Elstree. When cutting was in full swing, six assistant editors were involved, mostly in loading and unloading film cans from the large yellow Swiss van called the Unimog in which the Kubrick chauffeur Emilio ferried it back and forth. Staff accustomed to working at Elstree found the trip to the house long and exhausting – though not as exhausting as Kubrick's work schedule, which began at about noon with a series of phone calls to the United States: he didn't get down to serious editing until late afternoon.

Ray Lovejoy, with a home and family in London, was accustomed to working 9 a.m. to 6 p.m., and found Kubrick's regime increasingly wearing. By Christmas, there were recurrent clashes. An exhausted Lovejoy cut his hand at a party and was so run down he caught septicaemia and was rushed to hospital. Gill Smith took over, but had to attend a wedding one weekend. Stainforth, who was single and who had moved in with his parents in nearby Knebworth for the duration of the film, was mounting his motorbike outside the editing block one Friday evening when the Tannoy PA system barked, 'Will Gordon please come to the cutting room. Stanley wants him to do some cutting.' Stainforth recalled:

It was a fantastic moment for me. I was so nervous. And Stanley treated me just the way he probably treated Ray. Just gave me some instructions and walked out of the room. And that weekend worked really well. On Saturday evening I had dinner with Stanley and Christiane, and we kept cutting through Sunday.

On Monday morning, Ray came in, looking white, with his arm in a sling, and had a long meeting with Stanley. When Ray came out, he said, 'I want to see you and Gill in my cutting room.' And that's when he said, 'Gordon will be cutting the rest of the film.' It was one of the great moments in my life. But it caused a great deal of resentment in the lower echelons of the production. Because here was this man who had been until recently just a numbering boy, who had never worked on a feature film in his life and not even been an assistant, who becomes not even a first assistant but is, in effect, the editor.

This went on into the spring [of 1980]. There was one period where I worked fifty-seven days without a break, and ludicrous hours, like 110 hours a week. I even went onto Golden Triple Time, which is what one is paid if one doesn't have one's ten-hour break. I was being paid about £100 a week but because of overtime getting £700 in my pay packet.

Stanley was nothing like Hitchcock or Spielberg, who worked out everything in advance. The usual method is to film the scene from one angle, then put in a cutaway from a different angle, but with Stanley the cutaway would be a complete reshooting of the scene from that new angle. He just shoots one hell of a lot.

After the image was cut, Kubrick began to lay the music. He'd again decided to dispense with a composed score, and to use instead an anthology of contemporary classical music, mostly from Eastern Europe. György Ligeti, aggrieved at what he saw as the misuse of his music in *2001*, had sued MGM, but he was placated by now, and allowed Kubrick to use some of his *Lontano* in the film. Kubrick also employed part of Bela Bartok's *Music for Strings, Percussion and Celesta*, but the bulk of the score is derived from Polish composer Krzysztof Penderecki, whose music had always harmonised well with film, and who had influenced Hollywood composers like the prolific Jerry Goldsmith. Penderecki's ominous scoring for choir, and in particular his writing for strings, alternately twittering in panic or leaning queasily towards hysteria, became the perfect aural counterpoint to scenes of a manic Torrance pursuing Wendy and Danny through the hotel with an axe. He also contributed the music for the opening sequence of sweeping helicopter shots over still lakes and lonely mountain highways. Blaring electronic chords are interwoven with what sound like wordless cries, perhaps of animals, perhaps of the local Native Americans dispossessed by the Overlook's builders.

Warners had demanded the film for summer release, and Julian Senior, as diplomatically as possible, was urging Kubrick to finish. It was dubbed in eleven days, with sound and editing crews working round the clock. Right to the end, Kubrick made changes, deleting as little as one or two frames. For each change, however, a new black and white print had to be struck, and the music relaid.

With *The Shining* delivered, Gordon Stainforth returned to help Vivian with her documentary. The footage had been boiled down to less than an hour, and the pair fashioned an interim cut which they screened for Kubrick. On the whole he approved, though he did demand the deletion of some scenes, including a couple that showed cocaine being used, and others in which he got aggressive, especially with Duvall.

As a daughter's view of her father at work, *Making The Shining* is less than affectionate. Except for a few moments of murmured domestic conversation with his mother when she visits the set, Kubrick is seen as either irascible or brooding. No member of the crew is permitted to comment either on the film or on working for Kubrick, and the cast are clearly so much in his thrall that they either complain about ill-treatment, like Duvall, or, like Scatman Crothers, break down and weep – not out of frustration, insists Crothers, but from admiration. 'I love that man,' he chokes. On the time-honoured principle of the star having the major share of the lime-light, the film concentrates on Nicholson, who, under the larky exterior, is clearly living on his nerves.

During the final cut of *The Shining*, *Raiders of the Lost Ark* moved into Elstree. The fire in the Colorado Lounge had become a plus for Lucas and Spielberg, who took advantage of the damaged roof to raise the studio's ceiling height, giving them extra space to create the Well of Souls with its two giant statues of jackal-headed Anubis. The dressing rooms were filled with large baths in which thousands of snakes seethed. A false floor had been built seven feet above the actual floor of the sound stage, and strewn with sand and snakes, some of them rubber but many of them real, though not poisonous. As Harrison Ford and Karen Allen pretended to fend off cobras and pythons (kept on the other side of a glass shield), their feet knocked snakes through the cracks in the planks.

Vivian, an animal lover, became convinced that the snakes were being mistreated. Stainforth wasn't so sure, but agrees, 'There were some dead snakes around; no doubt about that.' Unconcerned that Spielberg was shooting, Vivian climbed to the camera platform and demanded that he give some thought to the reptiles' welfare. Spielberg assured her there was no problem, and that even if there were, he was too busy to deal with it. But no Kubrick would be so easily fobbed off, and a tearful Vivian called the RSPCA. Production on *Raiders* was shut down, and when it restarted a day later, the stage was lined with plastic garbage bins, in each of which three or four snakes nestled comfortably on beds of lettuce. Kubrick came in from Childwick Bury to watch. 'When there's a scandal like this,' recalls Stainforth, 'Stanley revels in it. He was positively buoyant. Of course he took Vivian's side and then there was a definite clash between Spielberg and Kubrick. And I remember Stanley puffing on his cigar, and saying with a grin, "Steve's a jerk."'

Chapter Sixteen

Kubrick in a World of Shit

> 'All I've ever asked of my Marines is to obey my orders
> as they would the word of God.'
>
> Colonel in *Full Metal Jacket*. Script by Kubrick, Michael
> Herr and Gustav Hasford

While he waited for the release of *The Shining*, Kubrick screened
the film at Childwick Bury for a few friends outside the movie
business, including David Cornwell, aka spy writer John le Carré.
Cornwell brought an American friend, Michael Herr, author of
the classic of Vietnam war reportage *Dispatches*, who had also
contributed to the screenplay of *Apocalypse Now*. Herr was happy
to meet Kubrick, since at least one film of his had affected him
profoundly. He saw *2001* the day he arrived back from the war,
and was so moved by the optimistic ending that he wept.

'Stanley invited me to an extremely private screening of *The Shining*,' says Herr, 'and then to dinner at his house. He was a big fan
of *Dispatches*. He was actively looking for a book to adapt for a
war film, probably a Vietnam war film. He was very up-front about
telling me that *Dispatches* was not that book because it didn't have
a story, and that if I knew of any books he'd be interested in
looking at them. Since I was not remotely interested in reading
about Vietnam then, I didn't know what to suggest to him. But
he'd call every couple weeks, and we'd have *long* conversations
about this and that; war and peace, life and death, books and
movies, and so forth.'

*

Two weeks before *The Shining*'s 23 May 1980 US opening, Kubrick was still making changes. The Warners brass didn't see the film until 16 May, and as late as 20 May it still lacked an American censorship certificate. Exceptionally, the MPAA allocated it an R rating, even though its board had only seen an unfinished version. Kubrick continued to tinker right up to the last day. He rejected the sound mix on the first six prints, which had to be redone. He also changed the lettering in the opening rolling titles from deep blue to white.

Warners had already decided a year before on a staggered release, launching the film on the Memorial Day weekend in New York and Los Angeles, in only ten cinemas and one drive-in. When those results had been assessed and some (hopefully) enthusiastic press comment garnered, it would go out to 750 cinemas around the country on Friday 13 June. After the first week, the strategy seemed to have worked. *The Shining* broke house records at six of its venues, although reviewers greeted it with now-predictable ambivalence. *Newsweek* called it 'the first epic horror film, a movie that is to other horror movies what *2001: A Space Odyssey* was to other space movies'. Others were less sure. *Variety* savaged the film, and especially Nicholson's performance. Stephen King disowned it, and continued to bad-mouth it at every opportunity. The deal under which Kubrick relinquished the rights in 1996 for a new three-part TV version directed by Mick Garris with King's imprimatur barred King from making any public comparisons between the two.

That Kubrick's *The Shining* succeeded as it did at the box office was a tribute to its intrinsic value rather than to any acumen on the part of Warners. The distribution pattern developed for *Jaws* and *Close Encounters of the Third Kind* had discredited the 'stepped' release. Studios like Universal and Columbia now blanketed the country with their biggest films from the first day, relying on TV and word of mouth to get a film off to a sprint start. *The Shining* felt the effect of its more sluggish release in the second week, when business dropped off 29 per cent. Warners had predicted a $1 million gross for the week. It actually made $823,649.

Length was a major problem and, not for the first time, Kubrick adjusted a film when it was already in the cinemas. He'd already dropped Anne Jackson's part as the paediatrician. Now he cut a final scene in which Barry Nelson visits Shelley Duvall in hospital.

Variety recorded that 'a Kubrick-anointed film editor was bicycled around theaters on both coasts to do the on-the-spot cutting'. After a first cut of 146 minutes, *The Shining* would eventually run almost everywhere at exactly two hours. It made *Variety*'s list of top ten moneymakers at year's end, grossing $30.9 million in US domestic rentals, but with a more imaginative release the profits would have been much greater.

The shortfall provoked Kubrick into giving an angry interview to John Hofsess of the *Washington Post*, in which he complained bitterly about the failure of Hollywood studios to give film-makers a fair share of the income from their films. Despite the continued success of *2001: A Space Odyssey*, including a 1978 sale to television, MGM still claimed the film was technically in the red. According to *Variety*, *2001* had made $20,347,000 in domestic rentals by 1973, and a further $7.5 million overseas, but MGM insisted that the cost of prints, distribution and interest on its initial investment remained unpaid. It was this unequal distribution of income, and the practice of delaying profit participation with 'creative accounting' and the so-called 'rolling break-even' system, that drove George Lucas and Steven Spielberg to make their historic deal with Paramount for *Raiders of the Lost Ark*. In return for accepting much of the risk for delivering the film on time and under budget, the film-makers took a share of every dollar paid at the box office.

The gap between the release of *The Shining* in May 1980 and the start of filming on *Full Metal Jacket* in August 1985 would be one of the longest in Kubrick's career. A lot of time went into converting Childwick Bury. Most people attributed the purchase of the estate to Kubrick's passion for privacy, and drew parallels with Jack Torrance in *The Shining*. But Christiane was as much the motivating spirit behind the move as Kubrick. She and their daughters had minds and lives of their own. Christiane exhibited her paintings from time to time, and occasionally taught art in St Albans after the local art school closed. Her work included a portrait of Kubrick, expressionless and staring, and while she specialised increasingly in flower pieces and landscapes, she often included a tiny picture of Kubrick in the corner, a fixture of their hermetic existence.

Vivian flirted with a career in the arts. *Making The Shining*, though cut to thirty minutes and bowdlerised by Kubrick, had considerable TV play, and she would compose the music for *Full Metal Jacket*. Katharina married the film catering manager Philip Hobbs, who, on the principle of 'the son-in-law also rises', was elevated to co-producer of *Full Metal Jacket*.

While Christiane transformed the house into a comfortable country retreat, Kubrick pottered around in a blue boiler suit, an outfit which, on one occasion, caused him to be mistaken for the gardener. He dictated some of the improvements, including a small viewing theatre and a huge kitchen/conservatory furnished with potted plants, armchairs and a twelve-foot table, but there was no swimming pool, no helicopter pad, no lavish provision for entertainment. If Kubrick hadn't succumbed to the lifestyle of the big-time producer/director when he lived in Hollywood, he wasn't about to do so in deepest Hertfordshire. He remained, as he had always been, happiest with one suit of clothes, his books, a chess set, a TV, a typewriter and his filing system. His sanctum was the stable block, which contained his office, cutting rooms, storage area and a kitchen where, during a production, he and the staff ate most of their meals.

Secure in his new retreat, Kubrick spent his spare time supervising the distribution of his films and fighting to protect and rescue earlier ones from the studios that produced them. He oversaw the production of all new prints and ensured their quality. When new Spanish and Portuguese prints of *The Killing* were made, he satisfied himself that the subtitles coincided with the appropriate images. Multiple takeovers and collapses within the Hollywood studio system had been less than kind to his films. Columbia lost the fine-grain picture and sound negatives of *Dr Strangelove* in a fire. All that remained were the worn and damaged negatives used to make release prints. Though it concerned him less, the printing material of *Spartacus* at Universal was also battered and incomplete.

The American company Criterion, which specialised in high-quality video-disc reissues of classic films, and had already done *2001* with Kubrick's collaboration, asked for his help in putting *Dr Strangelove* on tape and video-disc. Kubrick lent them his own 35mm fine-grain, struck from the original negative. They combined it with the better of the surviving negatives, and were well on the way to producing a superior tape when Kubrick requested his print back to make another copy. When he returned it to America, a US Customs Agent, alerted by the odd title, seized it as a possible porno film.

Transferring the film to video-disc allowed Kubrick to adjust the framing. Columbia had imposed the standard 1.85:1 ratio for early screenings, but he asked that Criterion alternate between 1.66:1 and 1.33:1, depending on the scene. Unsatisfied with the quality of the lens in the optical printer, he substituted one from his Nikon still camera, and had every frame of the film individually reshot. The result was a *Dr Strangelove* which conformed closest to his early vision.

One afternoon during the shooting of *Full Metal Jacket*, Kubrick would halt production in order to screen a new copy of *Paths of Glory* to the crew. Partway through, he leaned over to camera operator John Ward and said, 'Isn't that great, John?' Ward agreed that it was a wonderful film. 'Yes,' Kubrick sighed. 'Not a scratch anywhere.' Ward, like most of his collaborators, didn't grasp the fact that, when one's work was threatened with extinction, a new print might signify more than an agreeable viewing experience.

Universal, with the help of Jimmy Harris, would also reissue *Spartacus*, restoring some of the scenes deleted in the run-up to release, most of which Kubrick had been glad to see go. Universal couldn't locate footage of the sequence in which Laughton's Gracchus conducts John Gavin's Caesar through the streets of Rome to buy votes, nor the soundtrack of the 'oysters-and-snails' exchange between Olivier and Tony Curtis. By the time the project was ready, Olivier had died, so Anthony Hopkins dubbed his dialogue. Universal also issued a video-disc version on which Harris and the surviving principals discussed the film and its restoration, but Kubrick refused to take part or endorse this misnamed 'Director's Cut'. Nevertheless, most people agreed that *Spartacus*, for all its faults, stood up better than many epics of the period.

The problem of poor storage of original negatives by Hollywood producing companies continued to preoccupy Kubrick, and in May 1990 he would, exceptionally, add his name to those of Martin Scorsese, Steven Spielberg, Woody Allen, George Lucas and Sydney Pollack, Francis Ford Coppola and Robert Redford as a sponsor of the Film Foundation, 'dedicated to ensuring the survival of the American film heritage'.

The question 'What's Kubrick up to?' was a Hollywood perennial during the 1980s, and crafty operators used the mystery to serve their own ends. In 1983, director Matthew Chapman offered a backhanded compliment to Kubrick in the form of *Stranger's Kiss*, a film about an autocratic director (Peter Coyote) who encourages the stars of his low-budget film to have an affair, even though the girl (Victoria Tennant) is the mistress of his backer. To judge from Irene Kane's testimony, the script had few parallels with the circumstances of *Killer's Kiss*, though it was widely publicised as being based on the making of Kubrick's film.

In 1981, rumours circulated that Kubrick was about to film a sequel to *2001*, called *2010: Odyssey II*, and based on a novel by Arthur C. Clarke which described a joint US–Soviet expedition, with Heywood Floyd on board returning to the Discovery in orbit around Jupiter. Clarke's agent told Julia Phillips, producer of *Close Encounters*, that Kubrick had a copy of the manuscript of *2010* and was reading it with a view to making it his next film. Certain publishers formed an impression that Kubrick was in fact ready to start shooting, fuelling competition for the novel. The book was published worldwide in 1982, to great profit for Clarke, though publishers were surprised and disappointed when no film appeared.

Two years later, in 1984, Peter Hyams released the film of *2010*, subtitled *The Year We Made Contact*, with a script by Clarke and Hyams. *2010* is really *2001: A Space Odyssey* as Clarke would have preferred it. It turns Floyd and Bowman into fully-realised characters, giving Floyd a young wife, a son, a beach house with a dolphin pool in the living room. Bowman, whose parents were seen only as genial TV images in the first film, returns from his incorporeal state to revisit his widow and brush the hair of his dying mother. Even HAL has a family. Through the computer expert Chandra and HAL's sister intelligence SAL, we learn why he broke down.

Clarke, who makes a brief appearance in the film as an oldster on a bench outside the White House, underlined its adversarial nature by introducing a fake *Time* magazine cover on which the rival American and Soviet political leaders face one another. Clarke is the American, Kubrick his opponent. Was Kubrick ever interested in making *2010*? It seems unlikely. Who circulated the rumour that he was? We will probably never know, though some people may have recalled the old Italian proverb 'Revenge is a dish that the connoisseur prefers to eat cold.' (Ironically, in 1996, when Arthur

Clarke announced the publication of *3001*, newest episode in the saga of *2001*, the same rumours of Kubrick's interest began again.)

Kubrick continued to take an interest in new films, albeit at a distance. Director Albert Brooks, smarting over the failure of his *Modern Romance* – the story of a man unwilling to commit emotionally to his girlfriend but too frightened of loneliness to let her go – which producers Columbia were threatening to bury, was astonished to receive a call from Kubrick, whom he'd never met. 'I've been trying to do a movie like *Modern Romance* forever,' he told Brooks. 'How did you do it?' They continued to correspond until Brooks, visiting London, suggested they meet in person. 'Um, that is not a good thing to do,' Kubrick responded. His letters ceased abruptly, though many years later he rang, once again out of the blue, and said, 'Albert, I'm thinking of making a movie. What do you think of Steve Martin?'

Reading occupied much of Kubrick's day at Childwick Bury. 'It's intimidating, especially at a time like this,' he told Michel Ciment, 'to think of how many books you should read and never will. Because of this, I try to avoid any systematic approach to reading, pursuing instead a random method, one which depends as much on luck and accident as on design. I find this is also the only way to deal with the newspapers and magazines which proliferate in great piles around the house – some of the most interesting articles turn up on the reverse side of pages I've torn out for something else.' The randomness didn't end at home. In a bookshop he'd grab books off the shelves without looking at their titles, just as, buying clothes with Ruth Sobotka, he had backed into Klein's and snatched the first thing he saw.

Among the books he read was Thomas Keneally's documentary novel *Schindler's Ark*, published in 1983, and *Perfume*, by German writer Patrick Süskind, about a homicidal perfume maker in eighteenth-century France who creates scents so potent that those who smell them lose their will. Both revived his interest in his Middle European roots, as Keneally's book in particular was also to do with Steven Spielberg. The news that both had already been optioned, Keneally's on Spielberg's behalf by Universal, turned him away from period settings and the Jewish diaspora in particular, but both books continued to preoccupy him.

He also studied gun and military hardware magazines, and books like *Dispatches* which put the Vietnam war into historical and social perspective. He'd followed the war on television and short-wave radio, and through video cassettes sent from the US. The TV images of weary 'grunts' and rice paddy fire-fights became indelibly imprinted on his mind, as they did on those of all his generation back in the United States.

He told a journalist in 1968, 'It's great that anything that goes on long enough that's terrible and comes into the living room every night in vivid, sync-sound-dialogue newsreel form makes a big impression on people. It will produce a more active body politic.' This last sentence falls flatly from the lips of someone as politically neutral as Kubrick. Never a dove, he became progressively more right wing throughout the seventies and eighties, though his political point of view on Vietnam – or, for that matter, anything else – remained unformed. Diane Johnson feels 'he certainly wasn't a hawk on Vietnam.' As for politics in general, she saw him as 'like a lot of liberals who find themselves out of sympathy with public policy. He was now the father of teenage girls, and he had what I would call straitlaced ideas. He liked having guns in the house.'

The editing of *The Shining* coincided with the Iran hostages affair, and the unsuccessful attempt by a US military team to rescue the Americans being held in the US Embassy in Tehran. The mission ended in confusion and humiliation in the desert, when bad communications and mechanical failure disastrously aborted the mission. Gordon Stainforth often had dinner with Kubrick and Christiane at this time. They discussed the crisis, but Stainforth never discovered Kubrick's view of the events. 'He was slightly mysterious. I never could work out where he lay on the political spectrum. Bit of a mystery.' One might infer from his penchant for ironic views of conflict and voice-of-God commentaries in his films that Kubrick saw himself more as a historian, committed to the detached perspective and the long view. An exchange with a journalist from *Eye* magazine in 1968 says a great deal by saying nothing.

'And you're glad that we're getting out of Vietnam, if we are?' prompted the reporter.

Kubrick responded simply, 'Sure.'

*

At a London publisher's party in 1984, Texas science fiction writer Lisa Tuttle was startled to catch the eye, over the heads of the crowd, of a tall young man whose rueful down-turned mouth and receding hairline looked familiar.

'I was getting very uneasy,' says Tuttle, 'thinking, "Who is this guy staring at me?" And he walked over and he said, "*Lay*-suh?" And I realised it was Gus Hasford.'

Tuttle had first met Gustav Hasford at the Clarion science fiction writers' conference in New Orleans in the mid-seventies. At that time he hadn't published anything, though as a correspondent for the Marine Corps magazine *Leatherneck* between 1966 and 1968, attached to the First Marine Division in Vietnam, he'd started work on a novel, *The Short Timers*.

Tuttle had been struck by the mixture of artlessness and erudition in the lanky Alabaman. 'Gus was very strange,' she remembers. 'He always led a kind of chaotic life. He was very much a kind of innocent, a sophisticated redneck. Because he'd read a lot and knew a lot, he'd speak about things in a kind of sophisticated way, then suddenly shift into this shitkicker attitude of "I don't know nuthin'. I'm just a redneck. I like to drink beer. I don't understand why people are scared of me, just because I know how to kill a man with my bare hands." ' Whether Hasford *could* kill anyone is doubtful. 'Actually my body count was a standing joke,' he'd admit later. 'I killed as many of them as they did of me.' His worst injury resulted from a rations drum landing on his head during a helicopter supply drop.

Most people who met Gus, however, needed little convincing of his deep emotional disturbance. Michael Herr, from whose *Dispatches* Hasford took the epigraph of *The Short Timers* ('I think that Vietnam was what we had instead of happy childhoods') remembers him as 'sort of a scary guy. Very smart, very big, a born writer, possibly sociopathic, deeply paranoid, seriously awkward around most people . . . I was very fond of Gus, but he wasn't one of those people you can take just anywhere. And if Gus thought that you liked him, sooner or later he began to wonder what your problem was.'

After New Orleans, Tuttle lost touch with Hasford, who accompanied some of his new friends back to Los Angeles. For a while he stayed with author Harlan Ellison, then lived on the street in a

Volkswagen for eight months on a budget of $2 a day until he found work as a security guard.

The Short Timers took seven years to write and three to find a publisher. Morrow brought it out in 1979, after films like *Apocalypse Now* and Michael Cimino's *The Deerhunter* had drawn Vietnam back onto the American national agenda. The *Los Angeles Times* hailed it as 'a savage, unforgiving look at a savage, unforgivable time'.

When Tuttle met Hasford again in London, she asked, 'What are you doing here?' Hasford told her, 'I'm working with Kubrick.'

Kubrick was alerted to *The Short Timers* by a report in *Kirkus Reviews* just after its publication in 1979, but didn't read it until 1982. He was impressed by the book's starkness and simplicity, the 'economy of structural statement', as he later put it. With its terse sentences, thumbnail characterisation and reliance on the ritualised dialogue of boot camp and the front line, it was already halfway to being a screenplay. However, a Munich businessman with no links to the movie business had already optioned the book, and Kubrick couldn't acquire the rights until 1983, by which time the fuss had died down and Hasford was almost forgotten.

'*Shorty*', as Hasford always abbreviated the title of his book, follows a group of young recruits on a 385-day 'short time' enlistment as they pass through boot camp at Parris Island, South Carolina, and then as Marines 'in country'. The Corps systematically desensitises them to violence and eradicates all individuality, leaving them, in the word of British critic Penelope Gilliatt, 'nulled'.

The instrument of this change is Sergeant Gerheim, a bug-eyed drill instructor, ranting, monomaniac, inventively and comically obscene, who drives the boys so relentlessly that the lumbering Pratt, rechristened 'Gomer Pyle' after Jim Nabors' gormless TV Marine, cracks and kills Gerheim, then himself. The main character, nicknamed 'Joker' by Gerheim, observes this and everything else with sardonic detachment. Posted to Vietnam in 1968, Joker and his friends are embroiled, and many killed, in that year's Tet offensive and the destruction of the ancient city of Hué. Forced to kill his best friend 'Cowboy', who is lying wounded and being used as bait by a sniper, Joker finds himself in command, and, as the book ends, moves the remains of the platoon on to the next skirmish. 'I am in a world of shit,' he muses, 'but I am alive and I am not afraid.'

Hasford's equilibrium hadn't been improved by the brief acclaim for *The Short Timers*, which sold well but not spectacularly. He'd started a second novel, *The Phantom Blooper*, in which Joker, living out a battlefield myth of Vietnam, switches sides and becomes commander of a Viet Cong commando group, but found no publisher in a market now saturated with Vietnam books. As Hasford drifted around California, his physical and mental health deteriorated. A tireless reader and book collector, he'd taken to stealing books from libraries and squirreling them away in remote apartments and rented storage. He was also already suffering from the diabetes that would kill him.

The news that Kubrick had bought his book exhilarated Hasford. He viewed it as the long-awaited payback for a wasted life. 'Most of my friends are middle-aged accountants and solicitors, not writers or actors,' he told a friend. 'They make about $50,000 a year. I've been writing for twenty years. I've really just made the same as they have, but in one lump sum.' He anticipated becoming rich from the movie tie-in reprint of the book: 'Even a dud film will sell about two million copies in the US. Even *Benji* sold two million! If Stanley was to make the worst movie he'd ever made, it'd still be a Stanley Kubrick movie.'

Late in 1982, Michael Herr had a call from Kubrick. 'Stanley rang to say he'd found a book that really impressed him,' says Herr. He already knew *The Short Timers*. Morrow had sent him a set of galleys in 1978 with a request for a cover blurb. He'd refused. 'I was so tapped out at that point on Vietnam as a subject and Vietnam as a piece of my own experience and the Vietnam that I'd just spent so many years getting into my own book and then into *Apocalypse Now*, that I couldn't deal with Gus's great book. But I read it again with Stanley, and we agreed to work on the film together.'

The clincher for Herr was the sense of historical detachment he felt in Kubrick's approach, 'a certain tact and distance' which contrasted with the relish of Francis Ford Coppola and Michael Cimino, directors of *Apocalypse Now* and *The Deerhunter*. Kubrick believed the film, as *The Shining* had done, should convey some of the sense of naked evil represented by Jung's image of the Shadow. Coppola had done this overtly in *Apocalypse Now*, personifying it in the tiger lurking in the jungle and in Marlon Brando's Kurtz, muttering 'The horror, the horror,' as he expires in his temple hideout. But while Coppola's vision of Vietnam was operatic, replete with well-tagged metaphors, each with its visual *leitmotif*, Kubrick looked for the poetic; truth subsumed within language, rhetoric indissoluble from form.

In writing the script, he followed the method he'd used with *2001*, *Barry Lyndon* and *The Shining*. Instead of going straight to screenplay, he would turn the book into an extended treatment in prose form. He and Herr met every day for a month, breaking down the narrative, as he had with Diane Johnson on *The Shining*, into brief scenes, each one of which was given a title and recorded on a file card. 'Then, working at home in London, I wrote a draft, in prose,' Herr says, 'sending pages out to Stanley most days via his driver. We'd talk that night about what I'd done that day ... In this way, I finished a draft in something like eight or nine weeks. Then Stanley rewrote my draft, and then I rewrote his draft.' Kubrick rang Herr almost daily. 'I think of it now as one phone call lasting three years,' Herr says.

Seeking his 'non-submersible' elements, Kubrick focused on ritual moments, often concerned with death. The first third of the film, lasting forty-four minutes, would show the recruits torn down and rebuilt emotionally and intellectually by the ruthless, raving Gerheim, renamed 'Hartman' for the film. The sequence is a sustained rite of passage, illuminated from within by other rituals, like the boys ganging up on Pratt to punish him for the incompetence that has led to all of them being penalised. They tie him to his bunk and beat him with cakes of soap wrapped in towels – even Joker, who has done his best to befriend and help the hapless boy. True to this vision, Pratt/Pyle, when he cracks, does so in ritual form, parroting the rote elegy to his weapon drummed into all the recruits before using it on Hartman, then himself.

In 'Nam itself, which occupies the remaining seventy-two minutes of the film, life is increasingly bound by rituals and rules. As a war correspondent, Joker is expected to use the approved circumlocutions. Kubrick told Penelope Gilliatt, 'Vietnam was probably the first war that was run ... as an advertising agency might run it.' Joker's commanding officer/editor explains, 'If we move Vietnamese, they're *evacuees*. If they come to us to be evacuated, they're *refugees.*' A memo from GHQ instructs that the term 'Search and Destroy' is to be replaced by 'Sweep and Clear'. 'There are only two stories in the paper,' says the editor. 'Soldiers giving half their pay to buy gooks toothbrushes and deodorant – Winning Hearts and Minds. And ones about combat action resulting in a kill – Winning the War.'

Joker and his photographer friend Rafter Man fall into the same habit in conversation, mouthing the catchphrases that Kubrick obviously relishes: 'Outstanding!' 'It's a negative.' Combat is 'trigger time', the front line 'in the grass' or 'in the shit'. Base camp is 'in the rear with the gear'. Vietnamese are 'zipperheads', 'gooks', 'Charlie' or 'Mister Charles'. 'We have Condition Red and we are expecting rain,' says Cowboy's lieutenant, Mr Touchdown. 'Are we taking care of business, sir?' Joker asks, and the lieutenant confirms that 'We're getting some pretty good kills.'

Rock lyrics, movie lines and slogans substitute for conversation. Joker has 'Born to Kill' lettered on his helmet. 'Animal Mother', the most brutally pragmatic of the recruits, has 'I am Become Death', part of the phrase from the *Upanishads* which Robert Oppenheimer, head of the Manhattan Project which developed America's atomic bomb, claims to have recalled as he watched the first nuclear device explode in the American desert. Joker habitually slips into an imitation of John Wayne at his most offhandedly heroic, until Animal Mother challenges him, 'You talk the talk. Do you walk the walk?' Whether Joker can 'walk the walk' becomes the point of the film's last sequences. The original ending showed that he still retained too much humanity to do so. Having shot Cowboy, Joker finds that the Viet Cong sniper is a girl. As she lies dying in the rubble, surrounded by a ring of soldiers looking down at her – a recurring visual motif of this and other Kubrick films – the men debate what to do with her. When nobody else, Joker included, can bring themselves to act, Animal Mother cuts off the girl's head, which the platoon uses as a football. The scene was shot but, to the chagrin of Adam Baldwin, who played Animal Mother, Kubrick substituted a more compassionate conclusion in which the girl begs the men to kill her, and Joker does so.

As work on the script progressed, Hasford received, in his words, 'a series of marathon transatlantic phone calls and letters' from

Kubrick soliciting his opinion of what he and Herr had written. One conversation lasted seven hours. 'We chewed over every line of that movie,' said Hasford. 'There isn't a word or phrase that hadn't at some time been debated.'

Most of his book is in the film. Some of the changes Hasford applauded. Others troubled him, including the last shots, in which the platoon, led by Joker, harmonise on the Mickey Mouse Club theme as they march on to their next objective. He had used the song in the book, but not at the end, and not with such heavy irony. However, he wasn't about to argue. Kubrick would make him famous. Kubrick would make him rich.

By the middle of 1983, Herr and Kubrick had finished a script. The first draft, which told the story in flashback, starting with Joker's funeral and ending with the decapitation, included a laconic voice-over spoken by Joker – a type of writing at which Herr was expert, since he'd supplied a similar commentary for *Apocalypse Now*. Kubrick, rightly, didn't think *The Short Timers* would work as a title. He found a phrase in a gun magazine which conveyed some of the things the film would deal with: the armouring of boys so that they would become killing machines; the celebration of American military technology; the revelation that, while bullets were hard, certain qualities of the spirit were harder: 'It's a hard heart that kills,' Hartman says. 'A rifle is only a tool.' *The Short Timers* became *Full Metal Jacket* – a title, like two others Kubrick invented, *One-Eyed Jacks* and *Killer's Kiss*, with the shuffling beat of wire brushes on a snare drum. Hasford approved of the change.

At this point, Herr recalls, 'Stanley felt, for various complicated reasons ... that it might be a good idea to have Gus come to England.' Chief among these was Hasford's growing emotional investment in the film. Herr thought it was a bad idea, but he met Hasford at the airport and, with some trepidation, brought him to Childwick Bury. 'My instincts turned out to be correct,' he says. 'As I expected, Stanley, in spite of having worked with Jim Thompson, had never met anything like Gus before ... Although he and Stanley had logged in over a hundred telephone hours, face to face Gus was totally uncommunicative. After that evening, I don't think they ever saw each other again. They continued their phone relationship, but it became increasingly strained.' While Hasford and Herr were going through this punishing process, Kubrick's first screenwriter, Howard Sackler, who wrote *Fear and Desire*, was dying in Ibiza, Spain, burned out at fifty-two.

Kubrick refused to let the screenplay out of his sight, so Warners CEO Terry Semel and agent Mike Ovitz, head of CAA, which represented many of the people involved in the film, flew to London to read it. Semel immediately approved the project. Under Steve Ross, Warner Communication Industries had become the fastest-growing and most innovative of all showbiz conglomerates. A Kubrick film, reasoned Semel and Ross, would add lustre to a production slate which otherwise favoured mass-market entertainment. In January 1984, *Variety* announced that Warners would back *Full Metal Jacket*, which Kubrick would write, produce and direct in the autumn. Herr wasn't mentioned, and Hasford only as author of the novel.

Variety also noted that Kubrick would 'launch a nationwide search for new faces to play the young Marines. "Kubrick plans to stick very closely to that age in casting the film," says WB [Warner Brothers].' Kubrick played on his mystique, letting wannabe actors do much of the work of casting for him. In March 1984 he told the world's press that he wanted audition tapes from anyone who felt able to play an eighteen-year-old Marine. They should stand against a plain background in jeans and a white T-shirt with a card showing their name and a contact number, then perform a dramatic scene of no more than three minutes. After that he wanted a minute on themselves and their interests. Then they should hold up a sheet with their name, address, phone number, age and date of birth. A series of close-ups, full-length shots and left and right profiles would finish the tape, which should then be sent to Warners in London.

A reporter for a Boston paper monitored one video company which offered to tape audition pieces for the film. At the height of the search they did thirty pitches a day. The same thing was happening in a dozen other cities around the world. Julian Senior was inundated with tapes. A few who applied in this way got jobs as extras, but all the major roles would go to Hollywood professionals. The fallout in publicity, on the other hand, was phenomenal. Everyone soon knew about *Full Metal Jacket*.

After the first wave of tapes, Kubrick, via Leon Vitali, who had been appointed casting director, more discreetly invited proposals from professionals. In Los Angeles, New York and London, agencies were nominated as the contact point, and actors could go there for a taped audition – an eerie experience for most, since they were ushered into an empty room with a tiny video camera on a tripod, and directed by a ghostly voice to make their pitch. In particular American, Canadian and Vietnamese performers resident in Britain made audition tapes at Kubrick's expense.

From the start, Kubrick was looking for men who could 'walk the walk and talk the talk'. Matthew Modine was an obvious choice, since he'd already played Vietnam vets twice, in Alan Parker's film of William Wharton's novel *Birdy* and Robert Altman's adaptation of David Rabe's play *Streamers*. To play drill instructor Hartman, Kubrick hired Tim Colceri, a thirty-six-year-old ex-Marine NCO invalided out of Vietnam. Adam Baldwin, who became the six-foot-four Animal Mother, had kicked off his career as the kid hired by a smart newcomer to a tough school to protect him in Tony Bill's *My Bodyguard*. Kevyn Major Howard, who played the fresh-faced but bloodthirsty Rafter Man, and Arliss Howard, as Cowboy, were young lower-echelon performers with lots of TV and a few film roles to their credit.

Once Modine was cast, he told his friend Vincent D'Onofrio, a burly off-Broadway actor who had never made a film, to send Kubrick an audition tape. After four more taped auditions, D'Onofrio was cast as the lumbering 'Gomer Pyle'. On Kubrick's orders he gained sixty pounds, changing him from the scrawny redneck of the book into a bumbling baby. His sheepish face, amiable and confused, is one of the first things seen in the film. Seated in a barber's chair, he and a dozen other recruits are shaved to the scalp, their individuality ending up on the floor with their hair.

To attempt to recreate Vietnam in the suburbs of London seemed the height of absurdity, but to Kubrick that was probably its greatest recommendation. Hué was reconstructed at Beckton, on a square mile of the Thames marshes owned by British Gas. The area was dominated by a gasworks, scheduled for demolition, which had already been used for films, including Michael Radford's version of George Orwell's *1984*. Teams with explosives and earth-moving machinery spent a week toppling some buildings, caving in and half-destroying others. After this, gangs with sledgehammers and a

wrecking ball selectively battered the remnants under the direction
of production designer Anton Furst. Palm trees from Spain and
thousands of plastic plants from Hong Kong completed the effect,
while tons of old tyres provided the silent black thunderheads of
smoke above the burning ruins. Before each shot, a team with ham-
mers and a modified flame-thrower further 'distressed' any walls
which might appear in the action, and seared the ground, sometimes
accidentally setting the actors' boots or trousers on fire.

Fortunately, Beckton's reinforced concrete construction, square
windows and ground-level openings for garages and storage echoed
almost exactly the colonial architecture of South-East Asia. Kubrick
went through the ritual consultation of archives and original magazines from which posters, cinema marquees and street signs of the
period were copied. There are cribs from Tim Page's photographs
of murdered Vietnamese civilians powdered white with lime and
Larry Burrows' scenes of Marines crouched at the open doors of
Cobra gunships.

Like the Gotham City which Furst would create for Tim Burton's
Batman a few years later, this Hué was a confection, a decor, evok-
ing rather than recreating wartime Indochina. So effective was the
improvisation that, though it was announced by *Variety* that Kubrick would be importing ten Vietnam-era tanks from Fred Ropkey,
an Indianapolis collector who supplied vehicles to war films, it's
only after repeated viewing that one notices the entire *matériel*
consists of two tanks, two helicopters and a few trucks. Kubrick
had learned the lesson of *Apocalypse Now*: hardware wasn't the
point.

The Parris Island assault course and the base at Da Nang were
recreated at Bassingbourne Air Base, and an old asbestos factory
on an industrial estate in Enfield was chosen for the barracks,
though these scenes were left until last, since Kubrick wanted the
actors to be as thoroughly indoctrinated as the 'maggots' they
played. To put them in the right frame of mind, he hired a short,
crop-haired, snake-eyed and strident ex-Marine sergeant, Lee
Ermey, who'd been technical adviser on *Apocalypse Now* and
Sidney J. Furie's *The Boys in Company 'C'*, in which he actually
played a drill sergeant. Ermey was the film's real discovery, as potent
a creation as Strangelove: foam-flecked, foul-mouthed, Cagney-
esque, raving on the dizzy lip of mania. In his audition, he reeled

off fifteen minutes of obscenity, never using the same word twice. Kubrick had him do his routines while Leon Vitali pelted him with tennis balls and oranges. He never flinched or stopped talking, and his blink-rate remained reptilianly low.

Kubrick decided to use Ermey to play Hartman instead of Colaceri, a decision which Colaceri, who had been cooling his heels in his London hotel for weeks, took ill. 'Maybe he should have got a real killer to play the other roles,' he growled when he heard the news. 'Then he could have dispensed with actors altogether.' As a consolation prize, Kubrick cast him as the nameless Cobra gunner who sprays helpless peasants from the open doorway as Joker and Rafter Man are flown up country. Yelling 'Get some! Get some!' at each burst, he offers the callow reporters their first real taste of combat. 'How can you shoot women and children?' asks Joker queasily. 'Easy,' Colaceri grins. 'You just don't lead 'em so much. Ain't war hell?'

Ermey proved no less convincing under the pressure of production than he had in rehearsal. A 250-page transcript of his tirades provided the material for most of the opening Parris Island sequence, in which he threatens to rip out the recruits' eyes and brain-fuck them, tear off their heads and shit down their necks. When Joker dares to mutter one of his John Wayne impressions, Ermey rages, 'Who's the slimy little shit twinkle-toes cocksucker down there who just signed his own death warrant?' Ermey also had by heart the cadence counts used to keep recruits trotting at a steady speed ('I don't know but I've been told/Eskimo pussy is mighty cold...')

'Lee, I want it *real*,' Kubrick told him just before they started shooting.

Ermey replied, 'Stanley, I wouldn't give it to you any other way.'

In the middle of an outburst directed at Arliss Howard, Ermey's memory failed him, so he extemporised. 'I bet you're the kind of person who'd fuck a person in the ass,' he roared, 'and not even have the common courtesy to give him a reach-around.' Kubrick was delighted. 'We'll keep that in,' he said. 'But Lee – what's a reach-around?' Ermey said, 'Stanley, use your imagination.'

Shooting on *Full Metal Jacket*, intended to last eighteen weeks, started at the end of August 1985. In the long gap since *The Shining*, many of Kubrick's old crew had gone on to other things. John

Alcott turned down the offer to direct the photography. He couldn't, he explained to an exasperated Kubrick, take the strain any more. Doug Milsome, who'd been his assistant, was promoted to replace him. Alcott was to die during the production of *Full Metal Jacket*.

Garrett Brown also declined to operate the Steadicam, so Kubrick hired a young British operator, John Ward. Ward arrived at Beckton to find Kubrick and his son-in-law and line producer Philip Hobbs installed in one of a series of demountable Portakabins. A Winnebago recreation vehicle served as Kubrick's on-set residence. 'We went into one of the Portakabins,' said Ward. 'It was empty, except for two chairs. Phil and Stanley sat down. I wondered what I was supposed to do – keep standing, or crouch down so as not to be higher than their heads?'

Ward got the job as operator of both the Steadicam and the film's ten other cameras (he can be seen as the combat cameraman filming Cowboy's platoon after the battle), but was warned by everyone that he would probably end up burned out by Kubrick's abrasive methods. He survived, but, for him, the Kubrick legend didn't. 'He has a vision. The problem is he doesn't always know what the vision is. People tell you before you work for him that he's one of these great *auteur* directors who knows how to do everyone's job and is perfect at it. And he doesn't.

'As an example, the film speed we used was 400 ASA. We didn't use the standard 85 filter because Stanley wanted the washed-out look of Vietnam combat photography. The sun is always shining but there's often thin cloud, so you get the soft look of a wet climate.'

When Ward asked Kubrick, 'What are we shooting?' – meaning the speed at which he wanted to rate the film – Kubrick replied, '640 ASA.'

'So you're *over*-rating it slightly,' Ward said.

'No. That's normal,' Kubrick replied. 'We're not using the 85 filter so it's two-thirds of a stop faster.'

'I said, "Hang on, it's two-thirds of a stop *slower* with the 85 . . ."' recalls Ward. 'And I looked over his shoulder, and Doug Milsome was shaking his head at me, as if to say, "I've had this conversation, and it's no use."'

*

Full Metal Jacket was almost as great a logistical challenge as *Barry Lyndon*. The number of performers in front of the camera seldom exceeded a dozen, but their environment demanded no less complex management than did the eighteenth century. As many as ten cameras would be operating on most days, some of them belonging to Kubrick, who had providently rented them to Warners. First Assistant Director Terry Needham acted like a general, rolling in tanks and trucks, calling down helicopter strikes, marshalling teams to ignite mountains of tyres soaked in oil. On such days, smoke hung not only over Beckton, but suburbs miles away. There were complaints from people ten miles downriver whose washing was ruined.

Kubrick supervised by remote control, via walkie-talkie. 'We had two channels,' recalls John Ward, 'so people like Terry Needham had to walk around with two walkie-talkies. One was Stanley's private channel, which was also used by Doug Milsome, Anton Furst, Terry Needham, and the other one was for the rest of the crew.' Kubrick worked on the assumption that anything he said on his private channel couldn't be overheard, but in practice someone was always within earshot, so the production leaked information like a sieve.

It soon became clear that Kubrick had underestimated both the complexity of the shoot and his own stamina. Almost sixty, and leading a sedentary life, he lacked the energy to stay up all night, then work through a gruelling twelve-hour day. John Ward recalls:

He'd come in in the morning knackered. In the scene where Cowboy and Eightball and the Doctor are pinned down and Joker doesn't know how to help them, Stanley was in the same position. He didn't know how to get them across this open space. It was in the script that Animal Mother took off with the M60 and they all had to chase after him, but how he started that process off, got it into their heads, wasn't clear. We shot the bit where they all blaze away at the side of the building five times.

He used to phone up from the car twenty minutes before he arrived. On this day, Terry Needham said, 'Fine, Stanley, we're all set up and waiting. The actors are dressed and ready.' Then Emilio drove up, and Stanley got out, and said, 'Why are you set up here, Terry?'

'But you said . . .'
'I want to be up at the square.'
'But the square's not dressed, Stanley.'
'How can I work if it's not ready?'
Then he was in his caravan with the Marks and Spencers sandwiches having a bit of shut-eye because he'd been up all night watching umpteen channels of television.

Both Kubrick's parents, who had been in retirement in California, died during the production, Gert on 23 April 1985, and Jack on 18 October. Toba Metz Kubrick Adler, Kubrick's first wife and Gert's lifelong friend, was left $20,000 and two rings. Stanley received only the plaques and awards he'd sent to his parents to keep, and the money he'd lent them in their old age. Kubrick's detractors claim he didn't close down the production for the deaths. Stories like this circulate constantly about Kubrick. They may even be factually accurate, though one can never know their psychological truth. Kubrick is monomaniac but not heartless. Reviewing *Barry Lyndon*, Adrian Turner had suggested that, in the scene of Barry's young son Brian dying, Kubrick showed a callous detachment. Kubrick sent him a rare mild rebuke, saying he meant the scene to be moving. It was as close as he'd come to confessing emotion since Curtis Harrington saw him crying over the rejection of *Fear and Desire*. Observing the world as he did, like a voyeur, placed a protective barrier between his mind and the realities of existence.

As on all Kubrick films, the cost and schedule of *Full Metal Jacket* began to expand at an alarming rate. The Enfield warehouse location for the Parris Island barracks was discarded, and Furst built a new interior at Pinewood which echoed the whiteness and symmetry of *2001*.

As he concentrated on Cowboy's platoon for the last sequences, Kubrick wanted the camera, as in *Paths of Glory*, to be perceived as a member of the group, giving the audience a sense of participation and shared danger. Gilbert Adair rightly praises the 'amazing fluidity [of] a long, suave virtuoso sequence-shot of the advancing squad, filmed from behind by a slowly forward-tracking Steadicam'.

John Ward had been handling the Steadicam alone, but during the scene, shot in rural Kent, where Joker and Rafter Man, arriving from Da Nang, meet Mr Touchdown on the road, propeller wash and dust from a helicopter nearly knocked him over. Kubrick decided he needed a sturdier man, and tried once again to get Garrett Brown. Brown pleaded prior commitments, but suggested a French operator, Jean-Marc Bringuier. Kubrick imported Bringuier from Paris and tried him out in the scene where Animal Mother sprints over rough ground in an attempt to rescue Cowboy. Even with Adam Baldwin weighed down by his M60 machine gun, Bringuier couldn't keep up, and suggested they fit the camera to the sidecar of a motor cycle. With great difficulty this was done, and a bulldozer was brought in to smooth the ground. The entire crew watched the result at rushes. Since the Steadicam can't handle abrupt movements, the technique that worked when it was fitted to a wheelchair on carpeted corridors in *The Shining* failed when it was attached to a sidecar.

'That motorcycle goes,' said Kubrick abruptly after he'd seen the results. Bringuier protested, but Kubrick cut him off. 'And you can go with it,' he concluded.

Warners would have liked *Full Metal Jacket* for the summer of 1986 but, knowing Kubrick's laborious methods, were resigned to having it for Christmas. Had they known it would shoot for thirty-nine weeks, use a million feet of film, cost $17 million and not open until summer 1987, they might have thought twice about funding it. As costs and delays mounted, an emissary was sent to the set. John Ward remembers:

> Paul Hitchcock, then head of the Warners Suite at Pinewood, came down to Beckton to see how things were going. He arrived, and Margaret Adams, Stanley's production secretary, called Stanley. He was in the Winnebago. He came out, took Terry's walkie-talkie and said to Margaret, 'Tell Paul Hitchcock I'm too busy to see him, and never to come to my set again.' Hitchcock got in the car and went back to Pinewood.
>
> A few weeks later, we had lunch, Dougie [Milsome] and Paul and a few other people, and I said, 'How does he get away with it?' Paul said, 'Look, Warner Brothers told me to visit Stanley on the set. I visited Stanley on the set. Stanley told me to go away. I went away. Everybody's happy.'

Gus Hasford was another less than welcome visitor. Kubrick had extended him an invitation to drop in sometime, but left the details carefully vague; so vague, in fact, that Hasford didn't know the exact location. Undeterred, he asked Lisa Tuttle if she'd drive him there for a surprise visit. 'I said, "OK. Do you know where it is?"' recalls Tuttle. 'He had the name of the place, Beckton, and he said something that surprised me, that we could drop in at Hay-on-Wye at the same time.' (Hay-on-Wye, famous for its second-hand book-shops, is on the opposite side of England from Beckton.) 'Finally we got to this little village over near the Welsh border and went into the local pub and asked where the filming was going on. Of course they just stared at us.'

Hasford did finally find the real Beckton and get onto the set, taking with him a group of friends dressed in military fatigues in the hope of being mistaken for extras, but he wasn't happy with what he saw, nor with the changes wrought by Kubrick and Herr. This began a protracted wrangle that was to obsess the increasingly unstable Hasford. 'Gus was so mad, he was just crazy,' says Tuttle. 'He was just going to screw everything up for no reason. It became a matter of principle. He wanted it acknowledged that it was his work and that he'd done some work on the script. There was talk about giving him more money, but Gus just got angry about that. "I don't want the money. It's a matter of principle." The film was going to have to be pulled. He wasn't going to allow it to be shown. He got really grandiose.'

Kubrick placated him with a co-screenwriting credit. According to Hasford, he was first offered 'Additional Dialogue' but refused, demanding parity with Kubrick and Herr. 'Gus wrote a number of scenes at Stanley's invitation,' says Herr, 'and one of them, "The Death of Cowboy", was used in the film; maybe four lines of dia-logue. But Stanley felt, for several reasons (one of the chief ones being that it would be bad PR to have a pissed-off Vietnam vet around), to give Gus a screenplay credit.' As a quid pro quo, Herr received an additional credit as Associate Producer.

Warners rescheduled the film for Christmas 1986, which would have put it up against its only major competitor, Oliver Stone's Vietnam film *Platoon*. Unfortunately this date had to be postponed when Lee Ermey's untrained voice, unequipped for Kubrick's multiple takes, broke down. Soon after starting up again, Ermey crashed his car in Epping Forest, caving in all his ribs on one side and injuring his face. He couldn't film for more than four months. Matthew Modine also strained his shoulder on the assault course. Summer 1987 became the new release date, and *Platoon*, having got in first, took Oscars for Best Film, Best Director, Best Sound and Best Editing. Still, it was *Full Metal Jacket* that everyone was waiting for. When Julia Phillips tried to pitch a war story to production executive Dawn Steel, she volleyed it back with a casual, 'I think Mr Kubrick is going to say everything left to be said about Vietnam.'

It was against a sense of missed opportunities and inflated expectations that Kubrick embarked on the post-production of *Full Metal Jacket*. His manner, tested by delays and fatigue, didn't improve. 'Stanley tried not to lose his temper because he felt it demeaned him in the eyes of the crew,' said a friend, 'but of course he did lose it, and it eroded his control. It always does in these situations.' Kubrick became increasingly nervous that someone would sneak a preliminary look at the film. Not even technicians at the Rank film laboratory knew what it looked like. Two burly 'assistants' accompanied each delivery of film, and stood over the lab staff as it was fed through the baths. After a few weeks of this, Rank told Kubrick to take his business elsewhere.

Relationships with some of the young actors on the film, never warm, deteriorated. Kevyn Major Howard, who was dating one of the production secretaries and eventually married her, became Kubrick's particular *bête noir*. He was more friendly with Arliss Howard, with whom he played chess. The greatest clash, however, took place with someone who wasn't even in the film, although, like thousands of others, he had sent in an audition tape.

Kerry Shale had relocated in Britain from Canada and was among London's most sought-after voice-over actors when he was asked by his agent to test for the trailers for *Full Metal Jacket*. He jumped at the chance – not only because it meant working with one of his heroes, but because such work paid well. The going rate was £120 a session for a test, and an additional £140 if one was chosen, with repeat fees that could push the sum into five figures. Bob Sherman, who had done the trailers for *The Shining*, told Shale he'd cleared £10,000 for the full campaign.

Shale was surprised to find that the test recording would take place not in a Soho dubbing theatre, as was usual, but at Childwick Bury. Kubrick's driver Emilio picked him up at seven p.m. in a Land Rover and drove him to the house. Shale was also taken aback that Kubrick would direct the recordings – the first time in Shale's more than a hundred trailer commentaries that a director had been present. Shale never forgot those visits.

We waited for Stanley to get up; his working day began at about seven p.m. When he came in, he was avuncular, slightly distant but polite. All the lights were turned off except for an Anglepoise lamp on the script. Stanley is over in the corner, in the dark. It's all very quiet. There's a guy with a Nagra tape recorder. He pokes his microphone in my face and says 'Take One.' It's not what I'm used to, but this is Kubrick. I know from friends who've been in his films that he likes lots of takes, but that's OK. I would do anything for this man.

Shale did forty takes of the test. Afterwards, Kubrick asked him to do some background voices for the scene of the editorial conference at the *Leatherneck* office which would be used in the trailer. With Kubrick and Vitali, he recorded background muttering. 'Normally one gets paid extra for that sort of thing,' says Shale, 'but I told myself I would dine off this for years. It was all I could do not to ask him for his autograph.'

Shale's agent tried repeatedly to finalise a fee with Vitali, but never managed to contact him. Vitali continued to call Shale at his home, always on Friday nights or weekends, when his agent wasn't available. Shale returned half a dozen times to Childwick Bury, each time on a Saturday or Sunday. Each time he pressed Vitali about his fees, and each time Vitali apologised profusely, pleading pressure of work, and promised he would negotiate a deal.

The next call came on a Sunday morning; Vitali wanted Shale that night. Shale had been invited to a party that he couldn't avoid, and would be dubbing a film all that day.

The film was called *Slugs*, and I knew what it was going to be like. 'God! There are slugs in the water supply! AARGH!!!' I told Vitali, 'Leon, my voice is going to be shot. On top of it, there's this party. Cigarette smoke, and everyone talking. I won't sound the same.'

Vitali said, 'But what will I tell Stanley? I've said you'll be there. Anyway, it's just a test. It won't be used. It's just for continuity, because you've done all the others.'

Shale acquiesced. Emilio picked him up at the party in south London and drove him and his girlfriend all the way to Childwick Bury, on the opposite side of the city.

Stanley came into the room, and I hadn't said much more than 'Hello, Stanley,' when he said, 'What's the matter with your voice?'

I looked at Leon, and he just gave me a panicky stare. Obviously he hadn't told him anything. I felt sorry for him, because I'd seen how frightened he was of Stanley's disapproval. I decided not to drop him in the shit, so I told him I'd been working all day.

'It's no good to me if your voice is different,' Stanley said.

'But it's just a test.'

'What do you mean, "*Just* a test?" It's part of the film. Everything is important. Well, you'll have to come back tomorrow.' And he walked out.

My girlfriend and I were put into the car with a very junior cutter. She was gibbering. She'd been working for weeks on the film, always at night, and she'd been sent home with the equivalent of shellshock.

Some weeks later, Shale embarked on a marathon recording for BBC radio. On the evening of the second day, a Saturday, Vitali rang and said they needed him the following day. Shale, remembering the previous occasion, refused. Vitali pleaded that this was the Big One, for the North American release, but Shale was adamant. He had gone to bed when Kubrick himself rang just before midnight.

'He said, "What's this about you not being available? We need you. Warners are expecting the trailers . . ." Here was one of the greatest directors in the American cinema, and he was begging me. I told him, "Stanley, my voice will be tired. You remember what happened last time." He said it didn't matter. I just had to be there.'

Again Shale was driven to Childwick Bury. Again he sat down at the Nagra, in the dark. Individual sheets were handed to him, all with variations on the same text: 'Stanley Kubrick's *Full Metal Jacket*. Coming soon to a theatre near you.'

As I left, Stanley and Leon said, 'We're very pleased. We'll see you in a few months for the British trailers and TV campaign.' I said, 'Thanks. And call my agent.' And Leon did this thing. 'What? You mean nobody has? I can't believe it! Heads will roll!' and so on.

Three or four months later, Leon rang and left a message on my answerphone: 'Stanley wants you to do the British trailers. It's urgent. Please call back.' I didn't call. The next morning he rang again, but I was in the bath. My girlfriend answered, and Leon asked her to get me out of the bath. I refused, and said, 'Tell him to call my agent.' That was the last I ever heard.

Shale claims that, long after the film's release, Kubrick's office did contact his agent, claiming he'd agreed to do all the recordings for his test fee alone, and offering £120 a session. Shale took the case to Equity, which refused to fight an expensive court battle over it, so a bitter Shale accepted £1000 in settlement.

Gus Hasford was no happier with Kubrick. By the time the film was released, he had ended up, improbably, in Perth, Western Australia, where he finished his second novel, *The Phantom Blooper*. He continued to press Kubrick for what he regarded as just payment, but to no effect, until he asked for advice from his famously litigious friend Harlan Ellison, who had won suits against Hollywood's most powerful TV and film companies. 'Harlan called me recently,' he wrote to Lisa Tuttle on 23 October 1986, 'and gave me the name of his lawyer, the dropping of which rang Stanley like a tuning fork.' The following April, he announced gleefully, 'Stanley and I have reached a compromise. The compromise is that he gave me everything I wanted.' The letter was written on a xerox of a telegram from Kubrick, assuring him that a signed contract, a cheque and a video copy of the final cut were on their way by courier.

Money and fame brought Hasford no peace. James Caan showed some interest in a crime novel he'd written, and he acquired

Kubrick's lawyer Louis Blau as a representative, but soon he was wandering again, compulsively stealing books. At Kubrick's request, Jimmy Harris tracked him down to negotiate with him. He found him increasingly disoriented and manic, living in squalor in San Luis Obispo, north of Los Angeles, surrounded by thousands of stolen books, including some from the private subscription London Library, which had admitted him only on recommendations from Kubrick and Herr. Shortly after, he was arrested for the thefts. Unexpectedly, Joe Hyams had a call from Kubrick, asking if Hyams' friend Clint Eastwood, a major force in local government in that area, could intercede. Eastwood rang the judge, who reassured him that Hasford, obviously mentally unstable, would probably be given a suspended sentence and psychiatric help. Eastwood passed on this news, and was disgruntled to receive neither acknowledgement nor thanks from Kubrick.

'The whole aftermath of *Full Metal Jacket* involving Gus was crazed and very sad for my wife and me,' says Herr. 'I received a few long, mad letters from him – brilliantly written, since he was incapable of writing a bad sentence, but quite nuts. Then he died, as much of loneliness as from diabetes. Someone, a friend of his, wrote in one of the alternative LA papers that Stanley and I had as good as killed him.'

Chapter Seventeen

In Castle Kubrick

*'All before. Nothing else ever. Ever tried. Ever failed.
No matter. Try again. Fail again. Fail better.'*

Samuel Beckett, *Worstword Ho*

Full Metal Jacket justified Warners' faith in it, and in Kubrick, by grossing $38 million in the first fifty days of release. Reviews were mixed, but predominantly enthusiastic. Those which compared the film to *Platoon* tended to describe *Full Metal Jacket* as the other, darker side of Oliver Stone's humanistic memoir.

Nothing underlined the contrast more than the films' music scores. The best-remembered music from *Platoon* is Samuel Barber's elegiac *Adagio for Strings*, but in *Full Metal Jacket* the tone is set by Johnny Wright's nasal and jingoistic 'Goodbye my Sweetheart, Hello Vietnam'. Vivian Kubrick assembled and composed *Jacket*'s score. Vintage pop like Nancy Sinatra's 'These Boots are Made for Walking' and The Trashmen's gibbering 'Surfin' Bird' made up seventeen minutes. She added a further twenty-two minutes of synthesiser sounds, resembling, suggested the *New York Times*, 'detonated bombs, doors swinging on rusty hinges and asthmatic exhaling, with drum harmonics and French horn-like blasts'.

To avoid accusations of nepotism, the music credit read 'Abigail Mead'. Kubrick didn't like Vivian's initial suggestion, 'Moses Lumpkin', so she adapted the name of the family's first London house, Abbots Mead – which, she was pleased to find, meant 'a father rejoices' in old English. Kubrick submitted the score for a possible Oscar, but the twenty-eight-member Academy music committee turned it down unanimously: there were too many pop tunes, it said, and besides, noises and drums didn't count as music. Vivian had a consolation prize when 'I Want to be a Drill Instructor', her recording, discreetly cleaned up, of Lee Ermey's cadence chants set to beat-box drum patterns, reached number two on the British pop charts in October 1987 and earned a silver record.

In 1989, Julia Phillips tried to interest Kubrick in filming Anne Rice's fantasy novel *Interview with the Vampire*, with funding from record executive David Geffen. Phillips had pitched Rice's story to Geffen as 'the *2001* of vampire movies'. She explained, 'If *2001* was really three separate movies, a little past, a little present, a little future, with the monoliths there as the linkage – the glue – then the vampire epic would be three separate movies – only instead of going forward, go back; the monoliths are the blood-sucking vampires themselves . . .' Geffen sent a copy of the novel to Kubrick for his consideration, though he wasn't convinced it was Kubrick's kind of project. Nor was Kubrick, but this approach and others like it revived his interest in fantasy, and in 1990 he rang Brian Aldiss again.

'I believe we had a difference of opinion,' he told Aldiss casually, 'but that was many years ago.' Over those years Kubrick's repu-tation for eccentricity had not decreased, and Aldiss decided that he had to accept his oddities as part of the territory. He and his wife drove over from Oxford to Childwick Bury for lunch in the big kitchen/conservatory – 'Steak and string beans, as I recall,' says Aldiss, 'which was his usual meal at the time.'

They talked about 'Super Toys' again. The reasons for Kubrick's renewal of interest soon became clear. Seeing and admiring *E.T.: The Extraterrestrial* had given him a new concept. He now saw 'Super Toys', to which he had given the working title, not a million miles from *E.T.*, of 'A.I.' (for 'artificial intelligence'), as sentimental, dream-like – a fable.

Aldiss didn't share Kubrick's enthusiasm for Spielberg's film. He thought it a kiddie picture: 'It was smartly made, but it was not for me.' But the two men started work again. Each day, Emilio would pick up Aldiss at his home in Oxford and drive him to Childwick Bury, then return him each night, often very late. From the start, it wasn't a happy collaboration for Aldiss:

I couldn't see how we could turn this vignette into a film. We stuck at it for a while, but it wasn't working. Then, gradually, I realised; this time it wasn't *Star Wars*, it wasn't *E.T.* It was fucking *Pinocchio*! The Blue Fairy! I worked with him for about six weeks, and I couldn't get rid of that Blue Fairy. [In Collodi's story, a blue fairy intervenes at crucial times in the life of the puppet Pinocchio, helping him in his attempt to transcend his wooden nature and become human.]

At various times, he decided that the story might go in different directions. He thought about some sort of Utopian future, so I wrote about half a dozen of these. The other side of it, and a more worthwhile one, I thought, was the Jewish side. Kubrick wanted the little boy, David, to be rejected and to be kicked out into what was referred to as Tin City; it was a sort of Skid Row for old robots and androids. They were going to be used until they were dead, in a kind of concentration camp.

It was an odd way for the plot to move, but at least we were getting somewhere. But then I came in one day, and he said, 'Brian, this concentration camp stuff is all shit.' And in flew the Blue Fairy again.

Kubrick lectured Aldiss on his theory of screenwriting. 'All you need,' he told him, 'is six non-submersible units. Forget about the connections for the moment. You just get six really good non-submersible units.' Aldiss recalled, 'We got two, and he was really excited. "Now be a genius, Brian," he said, "and do the next one."' They never found the other four, though Kubrick knew roughly that they would involve elemental forces: ice, water, fire.

Aldiss was impressed by Kubrick's willingness to use his prestige and his worldwide connections.

In the middle of a discussion, he'd call in one of his assistants and say, 'Get Hans Moravec on the line.' He's the world's leading expert on artificial intelligence. The guy would come back in half an hour and say, 'Stanley, Moravec isn't in the States right now. He's in Japan on a lecture tour.'

Kubrick would say, 'OK, get him in Japan.'

'Uh, Stanley, how would I do that?'

'Well, ring Warners in Tokyo. Tell them to get off their backsides and find Moravec.'

'But Stanley, it's midnight in Tokyo . . .'

An hour later, Moravec would be on the line. Stanley would ask, 'Can we do so-and-so? No? Then what about so-and-so? No? OK. Thanks, Hans.' He was relentless in his pursuit of what he actually wanted.

At this point, Kubrick decided to try other writers. He faxed some notes to Arthur Clarke for his comments, and asked, 'How much do you want to work with me again?' Clarke responded with a brief summary of how he thought the story might progress. However, as for working with Kubrick again, he told Aldiss later, 'He hasn't got that much money.' As an alternative, Clarke nominated Bob Shaw, an amiable Ulsterman with a reputation for low-key science fiction. Kubrick read some of Shaw's work, then rang and invited him to the house. 'I was very impressed,' Shaw says. 'His car picked me up at the nearest railway station and took me to the house. There were these electrically controlled gates. We ate in the kitchen, which was about the size of the average ballroom. He asked me, "Do you like Chinese food?" I said, "Yes." He must have given some kind of invisible signal, because a door opened and a waiter came out and served us a Chinese banquet. I often wondered what would have happened if I'd said, "No, I prefer Indian." Maybe another door would have opened and an Indian would have come out.'

Kubrick said he'd been rethinking 'Super Toys', in particular another of its characters. Henry Swinton, David's 'father', is an android engineer who has just launched a new product, a synthetic 'serving man' with a computer brain 'capable of dealing with any situation he may encounter in the home'. Kubrick told Shaw he now believed that the serving man was the key to the story. He offered him a six-week contract to work on the script. Before Shaw left, Kubrick gave him copies of Aldiss's story, *Pinocchio*, and a book called *Mind Children*, about artificial intelligence, and said he wanted all these combined in the script.

Shaw started work on a treatment in which the serving man played a large part. A week later, he was back at Childwick Bury.

It was the same thing: the station, the car, the meal. Then he said, 'Well, what have you got for me?' I read him out my treatment, but I could see his face getting gloomier and gloomier. Finally he stopped me and said, 'What's all this stuff about the butler?' I said, 'But we agreed that he was to be the main character.' Stanley said, 'No, no, he's peripheral. What else have you got?' Of course I didn't have anything.

Shaw rang Aldiss in desperation. 'Brian, he wants more ideas. I don't have any. Do *you* have any ideas?' Aldiss sent him three short drafts of possible new directions. Shaw continued:

After that, our relationship deteriorated. I kept coming up with story lines but he didn't like any of them. In the middle of the six weeks, I went to a science fiction convention in Vancouver. I was the guest of honour, and it had been publicised everywhere. When I arrived back I got a letter from Warner Brothers' solicitors telling me I'd done an unforgivable thing by leaving the country while under contract.

I fixed that up with Stanley, and offered to work a week or two longer to make it up. He kept asking me to write sample pages of script. But I couldn't write a script without having a story, and I think he formed the opinion that I was a pretty useless sort of a bugger.

After Shaw, Kubrick approached another British science fiction writer, Ian Watson. Aldiss and Watson are not friendly, and Aldiss wrote to Kubrick explaining that he would find it difficult to work with him. Kubrick immediately responded with a letter saying that, in view of his refusal to work with Watson, their deal was off again. Aldiss denied vehemently that he was refusing to work with Watson; he was merely pointing out that there might be diplomatic problems. But it was clear that Kubrick was once more looking for a way out, as he had five years before. He found it when Aldiss wanted to go on holiday to Europe with his family. Remembering their falling-out over his trip to Florida, Aldiss told Kubrick in advance this time. Kubrick's reaction was the same: Aldiss couldn't be spared.

'I'm going anyway,' he said.

'I'll get an injunction,' Kubrick threatened. He didn't, but Aldiss never worked on the project again.

Writing continued with Watson. He lived too far away to work at Childwick Bury, so Kubrick installed a fax machine in Watson's house so they could correspond quickly. Watson completed a first draft script, for which, he boasted, he was paid 'an eighth of a million pounds'.

In the writing, 'A.I.' expanded far beyond its original parameters as a surrogate *E.T.* The story is set in a future where New York city and large areas of the east coast of the United States are underwater, and where an artificial boy searches for a means of becoming human. Early in 1996, the rumour page on one Kubrick site on the Internet recorded: 'Kubrick has been filming two months of "A.I." every five years. He's using a young actor and filming his progress as he grows older. So far Kubrick has filmed four months/ten years.'

In the nineties, Kubrick's urge for anonymity and privacy became increasingly the stuff of legend. He was so well known as a recluse and only occasional film-maker that when he entered into a dispute with neighbours in 1991 over some trees near Childwick Bury which he claimed were felled without proper authorisation, and managed to videotape them doing it, the event was reported around the world.

In July 1993, *New York Times* drama critic Frank Rich was having dinner with friends in Joe Allen's restaurant in London when a man at a nearby table interrupted their conversation and introduced himself as Stanley Kubrick. He was clean-shaven, with short grey hair, and seemed to be homosexual. This didn't strike Rich as incongruous. 'Everyone always thought HAL the computer acted like a jealous gay lover in *2001*,' he explained. 'And *Full Metal Jacket* was full of homoeroticism.' A friend of Rich's recognised another man at the table as a Conservative Member of Parliament. The two men's companions looked like rent boys.

'Kubrick' told Rich he took issue with some things written about him in the *New York Times*. He wasn't a recluse, he insisted, and he no longer wore a beard. As he left, Rich asked for an interview. The man said he was going to Dublin on the pre-production of his new film, but gave a number where he could be called the following week.

Next morning, Rich took the precaution of checking with Julian

Senior at Warner Brothers, who laughingly told him he'd been con-
ned by this man, and that he wasn't the first. In Bournemouth,
entertainer Joe Longthorne had been so convinced that he gave
'Kubrick' free seats, invited him backstage and, after he had
promised to fix Longthorne up with some Las Vegas club dates,
put him up in luxury at a local hotel. Other people who'd run into
the man over the years claimed he made homosexual overtures to
them, inviting them back to his decidedly unmysterious house in
the north London suburb of Harrow.

In 1996, journalist Martin Short tracked down 'Kubrick'. He
proved to be Alan Conway, a small-time con man with a record
for theft and obtaining money under false pretences in Australia,
France, Switzerland and Ireland. He didn't look anything like Kubrick, but such was the need of some people to believe they'd met
the legend that he was able to carry off the imposture for years.

In 1991, after briefly reconsidering *Perfume* and a biography of
Colette as possible subjects, Kubrick read and bought the rights to
a slim novel called *Wartime Lies* by Louis Begley, a Pole who had
relocated in New York after World War II. Begley's book, told
entirely without dialogue in the style of the nineteenth-century
writers he admires, like Benjamin Constant, is the story of Maciek,
the young son of a wealthy Jewish family forced to flee when the
Germans invade Poland. He becomes the responsibility of his beautiful aunt Tania, who resourcefully finds ways of hiding in occupied
Warsaw. She takes a collaborationist lover, and, when his protection
fails, flees with Maciek into the countryside, where she supports
them by dealing in black-market vodka. The relationship between
them becomes so intimate that it will colour the rest of Maciek's
life.

There were obvious resonances between *Wartime Lies* and 'Burning Secret'. It also recalled the concentration camp theme of 'A.I.'
and the forthcoming *Schindler's Ark*, renamed *Schindler's List* by
Thomas Keneally's American publishers, which was going through
a laborious process of adaptation with various screenwriters. Brian
Aldiss feels Kubrick hoped to get in ahead of Spielberg.

Terry Semel visited Kubrick in London and gave the go-ahead
after he'd been handed a copy of Begley's novel and ordered to read
it. Warners announced the project in April 1993, with the working

title 'Aryan Papers' – the term for the documents needed in occupied Europe to avoid deportation. In what may have been a smoke-screen comparable to that which preceded *Barry Lyndon*, Kubrick said the story was set in the aftermath of the fall of the Berlin Wall. Joseph Mazzello, one of the children trapped among the dinosaurs in Spielberg's *Jurassic Park*, would play Maciek. For his aunt, Uma Thurman and Julia Roberts were mentioned.

All this was news to Louis Begley, a soft-spoken and reserved lawyer in a large Manhattan practice who had turned down other approaches to film *Wartime Lies*, but who accepted Kubrick because of his admiration for *Paths of Glory*. He'd seen *Dr Strangelove* and *Full Metal Jacket* too, but fled from *A Clockwork Orange* because he was 'so scared'. (Michael Herr made a similar admission.) For a few months after the sale, Begley received calls from London, demanding background information. Kubrick asked, for instance, if he had the music for a song mentioned in the story. When Begley said he didn't, Kubrick asked if he could sing it. Begley sang it down the line and Kubrick recorded it.

Steven Spielberg began shooting *Schindler's List* in Krakow on 1 March 1993. A month later, the trade press announced that Phil Hobbs was in Denmark on Kubrick's behalf, scouting forests for 'Aryan Papers'. Two thousand photographs were sent back to Childwick Bury for assessment and filing. The Danish Film Institute supplied, according to a *Variety* report, 'crates of videos of Danish feature films', from which they assumed Kubrick would choose Danish performers. Kubrick wrote to the mayor of Aarhus describing his 'gratitude and relief' at having found in that town the location and facilities he needed. But as Spielberg's production gained pace, and it became clear that it would open by Christmas 1993, Kubrick's interest in 'Aryan Papers' waned. Instead, some European film magazines announced that he would revive 'A.I.' Then, utterly unexpectedly, in December 1995, Warners issued a press release that Kubrick would make *Eyes Wide Shut*, from a screenplay by British novelist Frederic Raphael, starring none other than Tom Cruise and his redheaded Australian wife Nicole Kidman.

For Warners, it was the dream team incarnate. Executives from Los Angeles were eager to attach themselves to this obvious money machine, but Kubrick remained as aloof as ever. Rumours sped around London of his cavalier treatment of a Warners executive sent to approve the project. Arriving in London, the man was booked into the Dorchester, which was used by most visiting Warners executives. Julian Senior supplied him with a copy of the screenplay. Some hours later, a contact at the Dorchester alerted Senior that the executive had sent down the screenplay with directions to make half a dozen xerox copies. At this news, Kubrick reportedly told Senior, 'Get the script back from him. Tell him if he wants to know any more about it, he can wait until I've finished shooting.'

Initially, *Eyes Wide Shut* was rumoured to be an adaptation by Raphael of his obscure 1971 novel *Who Were You With Last Night?* Kubrick had read the script, liked it and collaborated, mostly by phone, on rewrites with Raphael, who lived in the Périgord region of France.

Tom Cruise and Nicole Kidman negotiated deals with Kubrick and Warners while Cruise was in Britain making *Mission: Impossible*. Both, according to *Variety*, 'flipped over the script and were anxious to work with Kubrick'. Though Kidman seemed ideal casting for one of the women, Cruise's interest in such a project was puzzling. Most people assumed that, for New Hollywood, the mystique of Kubrick remained sufficiently powerful to transcend even the worst gossip about his abrasive methods and difficult personality.

The unwillingness of anyone to discuss the project fed the rumour mill. By the summer of 1996, some papers were suggesting that Kubrick, hearing of director Brian De Palma's problems with his producer/star Cruise on *Mission: Impossible*, had shelved the film in favour of reactivating *Wartime Lies*. Kubrick took the time to make a public statement that he hadn't talked to De Palma for more than ten years, and was continuing with *Eyes Wide Shut*. Harvey Keitel and John Malkovich were rumoured to be joining the cast. Malkovich dropped out, but Keitel remained, joined by Jennifer Jason Leigh.

The Kubrick websites on the Internet gleefully announced that in one scene Cruise would wear a dress. Another rumour suggested that Kubrick, in a reminder of his attempt to employ Henri Cartier-Bresson on *One-Eyed Jacks* and his use of Weegee on *Dr Strangelove*, had asked Helmut Newton, the fashion photographer famous for his erotic and sado-masochistic imagery, to shoot a special series of stills, in the hope that he would 'loosen up' the stars. For a film with only three principals, the resources were lavish. Kubrick took over the Rothschilds' giant country house Mentmore for some scenes, and hired an entire floor of London's Lanesborough Hotel for a week, including its $6000-a-night Royal Suite. Retracing his *2001* steps, Kubrick began shooting at the mansion of Luton Hoo, which had been the site for an unused portion of the earlier film.

By mid-1997, however, the Dream Team had begun to crumble. Keitel quit, to be replaced by director and occasional actor Sydney Pollack. All Keitel's scenes were reshot. Cruise and Kidman complained about the many other projects kept on hold, hostages to Kubrick's lapidary methods. And Kubrick himself, of course, said nothing at all. By mid-summer, rumours circulated that Pollack had been imposed on Kubrick by Warners, since he'd directed Cruise before, and might act as a calming influence. Some even speculated that Pollack might be the studio's watchdog, poised to take over the direction of *Eyes Wide Shut* in an emergency.

Principal photography of *Eyes Wide Shut*, which began officially on 7 November 1996 and ended late in February 1998, earned the dubious honour of being the longest continuous shoot in motion picture history. Frederic Raphael found the work fulfilling, even educative, but remains in the dark as to why Kubrick chose him. 'I frankly have no idea. He reads a lot, though he never talked about anything I'd written.'

Kubrick *had* seen *The Man in the Brooks Brothers Shirt*, a short film Raphael directed from the Home Box Office anthology *Men and Women*.

'That was a pretty good movie,' he told him. 'You're a pretty good director.'

Raphael demurred. 'I had Ernie Day as cameraman, but with only a week to shoot . . .'

Kubrick brushed aside his objections. 'No, cummon, you're a pretty good director. And that's why you're never gonna come on the set.'

Raphael delivered the first portion of his script just before Christmas 1994 and worked for many more months on the adaptation, during which he transposed Schnitzler's story to modern New York. 'Although we parted with, as they say, expressions of mutual esteem,' he says, 'I have no idea whether I will ever speak to Stanley again. I could imagine, God help me, being lured back into it again. He sort of spoiled me for other people. Not because it was such fun writing for him, or so quick, but just because of that extraordinary obsessive hermetic concern with this particular story and ... not how we are going to do it together, but how it's going to be done with us.'

Now rising seventy, Kubrick is entering the last and, for the majority of great film-makers, normally the most agreeable part of his career. After three score years and ten, the tributes begin: the life achievement awards, the honorary Oscars, doctorates, master classes, medals. In March 1997 he received the first of these traditional accolades when the Directors' Guild of America gave him its D.W. Griffith Award for lifetime achievement. Kubrick sent a perfunctory video acknowledgement, and asked Jack Nicholson to collect the award for him in Hollywood. In his message, Kubrick paid tribute to Griffith as an innovator, but pointed out accusingly that the great director had spent the last seventeen years of his life in poverty and obscurity, rejected by the industry he did so much to found. In a summation that puzzled many, he compared Griffith to Icarus, and suggested that the moral of his fate was to 'forget about the wax and feathers, and do a better job on the wings'. In August, he was awarded the Venice Festival's honorary Palme d'Or.

On past form, Kubrick will shrug off all subsequent testimonials as he did these two. The honours of New Hollywood matter to him as little as did those of the Old. He has set his face so resolutely against the acceptance of his peers that he's unlikely to change now. Nor should we wish him to. One feels no pleasure at the thought of a grey, untidy Kubrick blinking in the blaze of Oscar night, accorded a standing ovation by people who have never seen his films or, if they have, understand them or their value hardly at all.

As for university courses and master classes, what has he to teach that is not already in his films? Only this – 'You may one day be as great a film-maker as myself, if only you oppose utterly and to the limits of your energy every attempt to impose on your work any will but your own.' Easy to articulate, but difficult – almost impossible – to follow.

Early in his life, Kubrick made a decision that to live and work on his own terms was worth the price of ostracism. Half a century later, personalities like his, thrown up by the post-war technological revolution, are legion: Microsoft's Bill Gates, Apple Computers' Steven Jobs, Steven Spielberg and George Lucas made the precocious but dysfunctional teenage *savant* a widely understood, if not always socially accepted figure. But Kubrick did it the hard way, when there were no role models, no well-blazed paths. That he guards his reclusiveness is no surprise, if one considers the blood and pain invested in it. Stanley Kubrick will be Stanley Kubrick to the end.

Max Ophuls loved to slide into the past with his films, his camera gliding down empty streets and corridors to find another world where choices were clearer, emotions sharper. If he were to do that with Kubrick, the image on which he would settle might well be that of a young man in a rumpled shirt, hunched over a concrete chessboard in Washington Square under a streetlamp.

Moths bump and circle, distant sirens keen, *kibitzers* jostle and mutter, but the young man is indifferent. His mind is ranging that cold, clean level of reality where every problem may be solved by the application of intelligence. He scowls and shakes his head as the *potzer* across the board tentatively shoves forward a pawn and puts his rook at risk. *You'd dare play a move like that against me?* Kubrick thinks. *You dare play such a move against . . . The Master?*

Notes

PROLOGUE: THE SKULL KING

All quotes from William Read Woodfield and Adrienne Corri in this chapter are from interviews with the author in Beverly Hills and London, 1994 and 1995.

Kirk Douglas's 'talented shit' and the story of Kubrick suggesting he be credited with the script of *Spartacus* are from *The Ragman's Son*. Tony Curtis's quotes appear in *Tony Curtis: The Autobiography*. Sam Fuller delivers his famous encapsulation of cinema in Jean-Luc Godard's 1965 *Pierrot le Fou*. Malcolm McDowell spoke to the London *Evening Standard* on 31 December 1971. Calder Willingham's quote is from Robert Polito's *Savage Art: The Biography of Jim Thompson*. Barbara Greene is from *Land Benighted* (Geoffrey Bles, London, 1938). Christiane Kubrick quoted by Jeremy Bernstein in 'How About a Little Game?' in the *New Yorker* magazine, 11 December 1966. Jack Nicholson quotes from *Newsweek*, 26 May 1980.

CHAPTER ONE: KUBRICK UNDER THE LENS

All quotes from David Vaughan in this chapter are from an interview with the author, New York, 1995.

'I am a camera' is from John van Druten's play of the same name adapted from the story 'Sally Bowles' in Christopher Isherwood's *Berlin Stories*. David Thomson on Kubrick is from *A Biographical Dictionary of Film* (André Deutsch, London, 1994). Kubrick spoke about Max Ophuls to *Eye* magazine, August 1968. Gilbert Adair on Kubrick's use of language is from *Hollywood Vietnam: From The Green berets to Full Metal Jacket*. Michael Herr made his remarks about 'The Shadow' in his introduction to the published screenplay of *Full Metal Jacket*. 'There is something inherently wrong with the human personality' from *Newsweek*, 26 May 1980. Gustav Hasford quote from a letter to Lisa Tuttle, 23 October 1986. Michel Ciment's comment about Kubrick's cultural roots is from his book *Kubrick*. Adrian Turner quote from 'Shine on

Stanley K' in the *Guardian*, 23 December 1988. Malcolm McDowell's quote from the London *Evening Standard*, 31 December 1971.

CHAPTER TWO: KUBRICK IN CLASS

All quotes from Alexander Singer, David Vaughan and Ken Adam are from interviews with the author in Beverly Hills, New York and London 1995 and 1996.

'Developers' is from *NYC Access* by Richard Saul Wurman (Access, NY, 1983). 'The tension' appears in *Time* magazine, 16 December 1929. H.G. Wells wrote 'What seems to me inevitable' in his introduction to the published screenplay of *Things to Come* (Cresset, London, 1936). 'Kubric the *nudnik*' quoted by Vincent LoBrutto in *Stanley Kubrick: A Biography*. 'I think the big mistake in schools' quoted from Gene Phillips's *Stanley Kubrick: A Film Odyssey*. 'A great story is a kind of miracle' is from 'Kubrick Country' by Penelope Houston in *Saturday Review*, 25 December 1971. 'I want to take my own kind of pictures' recounted in 'Tell Me, Who is Kubrick?' by Hollis Alpert, *Esquire*, July 1958. Enrico Ghezzi was writing in his introduction to *Stanley Kubrick, Ladro di Sguardi: Fotografie di fotografie 1945–1949*. Walter Trueman and Fred Stettner were interviewed in New York, 1996/97. 'Class creep' is from 'Tell Me, Who is Kubrick?' 'He was constantly at war' from 'In Search of Stanley K' by Mark Carducci in *Millimetre*, December 1975.

CHAPTER THREE: KUBRICK IN THE CITY

All quotes from Alan Kaufman, Alexander Singer, Gavin Lambert, William Read Woodfield and Brian Aldiss are from interviews with the author in New York, Beverly Hills, Hollywood and Oxford, 1995 and 1996.

'Chess ability is quite specific' from a report by William Hartston, the *Independent*, London, 30 May 1996. Kubrick on chess is from Alexander Walker's *Stanley Kubrick Directs*. Pete Hamill on boxing is from 'Blood on Their Hands', *Esquire*, June 1996. The comments on editing and acting are from *Film Acting* by Veseveolod Pudovkin, translated by Ivor Montagu (Faber, London, 1935). Kubrick on editing is from interview with Tim Cahill in *Rolling Stone*, 27 August 1987. Jeremy Bernstein's comment from 'How About a Little Game?' 'A mind-game guy' is from John Joyce's documentary on Kubrick for Channel 4, 1996. Lyn Tornabene on Kubrick and chess from 'Contradicting the Hollywood Image', *Saturday Review*, 28 December 1963. Kevyn Major Howard on Kubrick from John Joyce documentary. Shelley Duvall's comment recounted by Adrian Turner.

CHAPTER FOUR: KUBRICK ON THE THRESHOLD

All quotes from Alex Singer, Curtis Harrington and Gavin Lambert are from interviews with the author, Hollywood, 1995. 'Some oddball thing' from 'Tell Me, Who is Kubrick?' Gene Phillips's quote from *Stanley Kubrick: A Film Odyssey*. David Thomson on Kubrick is from *A Biographical Dictionary of Film*. 'Odyssey' appears in a letter to Joseph Burstyn held in the archives of George Eastman House, Rochester, NY. Kubrick on affinity between criminals and soldiers from *New York Times* magazine, 12 October 1958. 'Young Man with Ideas and a Camera', by Thomas M. Pryor, *New York Times*, 14 January 1951. Paul Mazursky quote from lecture at National Film Theatre, London, 1989. Kubrick's letter to Theodore Huff is held in the archives of George Eastman House. Mark Carducci quote from 'In Search of Stanley K'. Details of James Agee's movements drawn from *James Agee: A Life* by Laurence Bergreen (E.P. Dutton, NY, 1984). Mark van Doren's recommendation for *Fear and Desire* held in archives of George Eastman House. Kubrick's comments on James Agee's physical condition and on *Fear and Desire* from Film Forum 2 publicity notes. Kubrick's summary of *Fear and Desire* from Burstyn papers, George Eastman House. Paolo Cherchi Usai from 'Checkmating the General: Stanley Kubrick's *Fear and Desire*' in *Image*, Spring/Summer 1995. John McCarten in the *New Yorker*, 11 April 1953. Kubrick's comments on *Fear and Desire* quoted by Janet Maslin, *New York Times*, 14 January 1994. 'Pain is a good teacher' is from *New York Times* magazine, 12 October 1958.

CHAPTER FIVE: KUBRICK AND CRIME

Comments by Alexander Singer, James B. Harris, David Vaughan and Adrienne Corri are from interviews with the author, Beverly Hills, Santa Monica, New York and London, 1995. *I, The Jury* (E.P. Dutton, NY, 1947). Kubrick on Spillane to Irene Kane quoted by Mark Carducci, 'In Search of Stanley K'. Remarks to Hollis Alpert appear in 'Tell Me, Who is Kubrick?' Kubrick on Sackler's script in *Stanley Kubrick Directs*. Irene Kane's quotes *passim* are from *How to be a Movie Star, Or A Terrible Beauty is Born*, written as 'Chris Chase'. Foster Hirsch quotes *passim* from *Film Noir: The Dark Side of the Screen* (Da Capo, NY, 1981). Alpert quote from 'Tell Me, Who is Kubrick?' Kubrick on post-synching dialogue from *Stanley Kubrick Directs*. 'He came into my office dressed like a bum' quoted by Carducci in 'In Search of Stanley K'. Kubrick on failure of *Killer's Kiss* from *Stanley Kubrick Directs*.

CHAPTER SIX: KUBRICK AT THE TRACK

Quotes from James B. Harris, Alexander Singer, Gavin Lambert and David Vaughan are from interviews with the author, Beverly Hills, Santa Monica, Hollywood and New York, 1995.

Many details of Jim Thompson's life and most quotes are from Robert Polito's *Savage Art: A Biography of Jim Thompson*, including Robert Goldfarb on the format of the script of *Clean Break*. 'Did you say "Coop"?', Sterling Hayden on the rushes of *The Killing* and the comment on the unnamed electrician from 'Tell Me, Who is Kubrick?' *Time* reviewed the film on 4 June 1956. Richard Dillard on Calder Willingham is from *Contemporary Novelists* (St Martin's, NY, 1972).

CHAPTER SEVEN: KUBRICK IN THE TRENCHES

All quotes from Richard Anderson, David Vaughan, William Read Woodfield and James B. Harris are from interviews with the author in Bel Air, Beverly Hills, New York and Santa Monica, 1995.

A report of the incident on which *Paths of Glory* is based appeared in the *New York Times*, 2 July 1934, under the headline 'French Acquit 5 Shot for Mutiny in 1915: Widows of Two Win Awards of 7 Cents Each.' Brooks Atkinson's review of the play *Paths of Glory* appeared in the *New York Times*, 27 September 1935. Details of Jim Thompson's work on *Paths of Glory* from Robert Polito's *Savage Art*. Kirk Douglas quote from *The Ragman's Son*. Richard Fleischer quote about Kirk Douglas from *Just Tell Me When to Cry* (Carroll and Graff, NY, 1993). Calder Willingham's version of the writing of *Paths of Glory* and Stan Margulies' memo quoted from *Savage Art*. Peter Ustinov wrote about Max Ophuls in *Dear Me*. Kubrick on Timothy Carey from *Rolling Stone* interview, 1987. 'Kirk doesn't like it' from 'Rebels with a Cause' in *Filmfax*. Account of Kirk Douglas's reaction to the cutting of *Paths of Glory* from author's conversation with David Slavitt, Paris, 1995. Adrian Turner's quote from 'Shine on, Stanley K'.

CHAPTER EIGHT: KUBRICK AND THE TEN-FOOT KANGAROO

All quotes from James B. Harris are from conversation with the author, Santa Monica, 1996.

Marlon Brando's 'I beat the army' from *Playboy* interview, January 1979. Richard Fleischer quote from *Just Tell Me When to Cry*. Brando on *The Killing* from Manso's *Brando*. 'I'll get Cary Grant' is from conversation with James B. Harris. Brando's 'the rivers and woods' is quoted in Manso. *The Authentic Death of Hendry Jones* by Charles Neider (Frederick Muller, London, 1957). Sam Peckinpah's involvement in *One-Eyed Jacks* detailed in David Weddle's *If They Move, Kill 'em* (Faber, London, 1996), from which most of Peckinpah's quotes are taken, and Paul Seydor's *Peckinpah: The Western Films* (University of Illinois Press, 1980). Some details of the writing of *One-Eyed Jacks* are from Manso's *Brando*, others from Fiore's *The Brando I Knew* and Anna Kashfi's *Breakfast with Brando*. Maurice Girodias's purchase of *Lolita* detailed in Brian Boyd's *Vladimir Nabokov: The American Years*. Other facts from *The Good Ship Venus: The Erotic Voyage of the Olympia Press* by John de St. Yorre (Hutchinson, London, 1994). Quotes from *Lolita* (Olympia Press, Paris, 1955). Graham Greene's review of *Wee Willie Winkie* appeared in *Night and Day*, October 1936. Geoffrey Shurlock's response to *Lolita* and Kubrick's thoughts on the censorship negotiations on *Lolita* are from *The Cutting Room Floor* by Laurent Bouzereau (Citadel, NY, 1994). 'You're bigger and stronger' and the Cartier-Bresson story from *The Brando I Knew*. Kubrick's press statement quoted in the Paramount Pictures pressbook for the film. 'It was an ass-breaker' is from 'The Method in His Madness' by Chris Hodenfield, *Rolling Stone*, 20 May 1976.

CHAPTER NINE: KUBRICK IN CHAINS

All quotations from James B. Harris and William Read Woodfield are from interviews with the author, Santa Monica and Beverly Hills, 1996.

The facts behind Trumbo's work on *Spartacus* are laid out best in the article 'A Good Business Proposition: Dalton Trumbo, *Spartacus* and the End of the Blacklist' by Jeffrey B. Smith in *Velvet Light Trap*, April 1989, from which all Trumbo's quotes on the subject are taken. Kirk Douglas on Fast's script for *Spartacus* and all other aspects of the film from *The Ragman's Son*. Ustinov on *Spartacus* is from *Dear Me*. Simon Callow's *Charles Laughton: A Difficult Actor* (Methuen, London, 1987). Some details of Mann's firing from *Scratch an Actor* by Sheilah Graham (Granada, London, 1970). 'It had everything but a good story' is from Kubrick's interview with Joseph Gelmis in *The Film Director as Super-Star*. Kubrick on his method of working with actors from *Stanley Kubrick, Movie-Maker* in the London *Observer*, 4 December 1960.

CHAPTER TEN: KUBRICK IN LOVE

All quotes from James B. Harris, Diane Johnson and Brian Aldiss are from interviews with the author, Santa Monica, Paris and Oxford, 1996.

'A girl with a beautiful body and a sick mind' quoted by Peter Sellers, BBC interview, included in *Arena*'s three-part study of Peter Sellers, 1995. Kubrick's wire to Nabokov and anecdotes *passim* about his involvement in the film from Brian Boyd's *Vladimir Nabokov: The American Years*. 'It concerns the outsider' from *New York Times*, 17 October 1959. 'More erotic weight' is from interview in *Eye* magazine, August 1968. Richard Corliss from his British Film Institute study of *Lolita*. Some details about this period in James Mason's career from conversation with the author, London, 1984. Kenneth Tynan on the meeting between Peter Sellers and Mike Nichols is quoted in *The Life of Kenneth Tynan* by Kathleen Tynan (Weidenfeld and Nicolson, London, 1987). Quotes on the censorship of *Lolita passim* from Jack Vizzard's *See No Evil*. Lindsay Anderson's comment about Kubrick recalled by Gavin Lambert, conversation with the author, Hollywood, 1996. Anthony Harvey on Kubrick from interview with John Andrew Gallagher in *Film Directors on Directing* (Praeger, NY, 1989). Oswald Morris on Kubrick from interview with Morris by Adrian Turner, 1997. 'He seemed to be acting on another planet' from *Shelley II: The Middle of My Century*. 'She knew the script' from *The Making of Feature Films: A Guide*, Ivan Butler (Penguin, London, 1971). Richard Corliss on Sue Lyon from his BFI Guide to the film. Exchange between Harris and Shurlock from *The Cutting Room Floor*.

CHAPTER ELEVEN; KUBRICK DESTROYS THE WORLD

All material in this chapter from Ken Adam, Adrienne Corri, Diane Johnson, Gavin Lambert and James B. Harris is from interviews with the author, London, Paris, Hollywood and Santa Monica, 1996. All comments by Gil Taylor are from an unpublished interview with Richard Walker, 12 February 1993. Much background material on Terry Southern's involvement was provided by Lee Hill's unpublished *A Grand Guy: The Art and Life of Terry Southern*, and from conversations with the author.

'You read books' is from *Rolling Stone* interview, 1987. Kubrick on childbirth is from *Playboy* interview, September 1968. Christiane Kubrick's comments on living in New York are from *The Times*, 5 February 1973. Kubrick on his chess computer from '*Strangelove* Outtake: Notes from the War Room' in *Grand Street* 49 (1993). Jeremy Bernstein's description of Kubrick's notebooks from 'How About a Little Game?' 'I'm distrustful of delegating authority', *Time* magazine, 3 January 1972, as is Malcolm McDowell's description of Kubrick's filing system. 'I found myself tossing away' is from *Stanley Kubrick Directs*. Terry Southern in his 'rather heavy rap' with Kubrick from *A Grand Guy*. 'Film by fiat, film by frenzy' and Southern's account of his hiring appear in '*Strangelove* Outtake'. The reference to Scott playing 'an American college professor' is from a *New York Times* report by A.H. Weiler, 31 December 1962. Sterling Hayden on *Strangelove* from *Newsweek* magazine, 3 January 1972. Conversation between Mo Rothman and Terry Southern reported by Southern in '*Strangelove* Outtake'. Peter Sellers's 'Kubrick is a god' and 'a state of comic ecstasy' quoted in *The Life and Death of Peter Sellers* by Roger Lewis. Sterling Hayden recalled by Janette Scott in BBC *Arena* documentary on Sellers, 1995. Sellers's telegram is from '*Strangelove* Outtake'. 'I was going to do them all' is from *The Life and Death of Peter Sellers*. Comment from Bert Mortimer about Sellers's fear of balancing on the bomb from *Arena*. Peter Bull on his role from *I Say Look Here*. Jeremy Bernstein from 'How About a Little Game?' Victor Lindon and Kubrick on Sellers's injury from '*Strangelove* Outtake'. Dan Blocker's rejection on *Strangelove*, Southern on Slim Pickens and description of the pie fight from '*Strangelove* Outtake'. Peter Bull tells the *Candid Camera* anecdote in *I Say Look Here*. Anthony Harvey on the first cut of *Strangelove* from *Film Directors on Directing*. *New York Times* review by Bosley Crowther, 24 June 1962. Kubrick's letter about the writing credits of *Strangelove* in 'Kubrick Threatens Suit on *Strangelove* writer' in *New York Morning Telegraph*, 12 August 1964. George C. Scott quote from interview in *Playboy*, December 1980. Southern on Kubrick's 'generosity' is in Hollis Alpert's 'Offbeat Director In Outer Space', *New York Times* magazine, 16 January 1966, as is Kubrick's comment about Southern 'getting more work'. Kubrick on *nouvelle vague* technique in *Cinema '65* (Paris), January 1965.

CHAPTER TWELVE: KUBRICK BEYOND THE INFINITE

All quotes from Andrew Birkin and Ken Adam are from interviews conducted with the author, London, 1996 and 1997.

Alexander Walker's reminiscence of Kubrick in New York from *It's Only a Movie, Ingrid*. Roger Caras's meeting with Kubrick and Caras's resulting correspondence with Clarke, along with many other details of the production of *2001: A Space Odyssey* appear in *Odyssey: The*

Authorised Biography of Arthur C. Clarke by Neil McAleer (Gollancz, London, 1992). Others are quoted from Piers Bizony's *2001: Filming the Future*. Brian Aldiss on Arthur Clarke from *The Billion Year Spree: The True History of Science Fiction* (Weidenfeld and Nicolson, London, 1973). Kubrick on *Things to Come* from Arthur Clarke's 'Destination 2001 – Kubrick at the Controls' in *New York* magazine, 18 April 1968. 'Stanley was in some danger', from *Odyssey*. 'Is there never to be any age of happiness?' from H.G. Wells's introduction to the published screenplay of *Things to Come*. Clancy Sigal quoted from '2001: An Informal Diary of an Infernal Machine', in *Town* magazine, July 1966. Robert O'Brien on *2001* as no 'Buck Rogers kind of space epic' quoted by Hollis Alpert in 'Offbeat Director in Outer Space'. Anthony Burgess on Kubrick and codes from interview with Carol Dix in *Transatlantic Review* 42/3, May 1972. Gil Taylor's remarks on the heat of the lighting on the centrifuge from unpublished interview with Richard Walker, 12 February 1993. Wally Veevers spoke to John Brosnan for *Future Tense*. Clancy Sigal from '2001: An Informal Diary of an Infernal Machine'. The story of Alex North's score for *2001* and its replacement by recorded music is told by Robert Townson in *The Odyssey of Alex North's 2001* in the liner notes to Jerry Goldsmith's recording of the North score, Varese Sarabande, 1993. Clarke on Kubrick delaying the publication of the novel of *2001* from *Odyssey*. 'We have lost two presidents' from *Let Me Entertain You* by David Brown (Morrow, NY, 1990). Some details of Kubrick's special effects innovations for *2001* were taken from a 12pp 'Notes on Special Effects for *2001: A Space Odyssey*', dated 9 January 1969, written by Kubrick for circulation to voters in the photographic section of the Academy of Motion Picture Arts and Sciences. The resemblance of some visual effects to the experiments of Jordan Belson was remarked by Pauline Kael in her article 'Trash, Art and the Movies' in *Harper's*, February 1969, and reported in *Variety*, 29 January 1969 under the headline 'Sez Paulene [sic] Kael: Kubrick "Followed" Belson Experiment'.

CHAPTER THIRTEEN: KUBRICK AMONG THE THUGS

Quotes from Adrienne Corri, Andrew Birkin, Gavin Lambert and Bertrand Tavernier are from conversations with the author, London, Hollywood and Paris, 1995 and 1996.

'Deliberate obscurantism' is from the *New York Times* review, reprinted, like all others of any significance, in *The Making of Kubrick's 2001*. Renata Adler quoted in *A Year in the Dark* (Berkley, NY, 1969).

'Mostly Negroes' is quoted by Kubrick in his *Rolling Stone* interview, 1972. 'A Clockwork Utopia' in *Rolling Stone*, 20 January 1972. Kubrick on drugs is from *Eye* magazine, August 1968. Clancy Sigal's quote from '*2001*: An Informal Diary of an Infernal Machine'. Story of *Earth II* from interview with William Read Woodfield by the author, Beverly Hills, 1995. Gordon Stainforth on the props for *2001* from interview with the author, London, 1995. Kubrick to Anthony Harvey quoted in interview with John Andrew Gallagher in *Film Directors on Directing*. Malcolm McDowell on Kubrick eating from London *Evening Standard*, 31 December 1971. Kubrick on battle plans for 'Napoleon' from Joseph Gelmis in *The Film Director as SuperStar*. Comments to Gene Phillips in *Stanley Kubrick: A Film Odyssey*. Kubrick's letter to Jack Nicholson quoted by Mark Carducci in 'In Search of Stanley K'. Quotes by Kubrick *passim* on 'Napoleon' from Gelmis interview. Anthony Burgess described the origins of *nadsat* and the phrase 'clockwork orange' in 'Juice from a Clockwork Orange' in *Rolling Stone*, 8 January 1972. Details of Terry Southern's involvement in *Clockwork Orange passim* from Lee Hill's unpublished *A Grand Guy* and interview for *Backstory 3*. Adrian Turner described the Burgess screenplay to the author, London, 1996. *New York Times* report on *Clockwork Orange* deal, 3 February 1970. Julian Senior's 'We are emotionally committed' is from the *Guardian*, 3 May 1996. 'Who is the real Malcolm McDowell?' from 'Malcolm McDowell: A Clockwork Top Banana' in *Burke's Steerage* (Putnam, NY, 1976). 'If Malcolm hadn't been available' from *Playboy* interview. Allen Jones's account of meeting with Kubrick from conversation with the author, 1995. Wendy/Walter Carlos's account of composing the music for *Clockwork Orange* in *Empire*, December 1993. Account of BBC screening of *2001* and Kubrick's reaction recalled in letter to the author from David Thompson, London, 1996. Robert Hughes wrote on 'The Decor of Tomorrow's Hell' in *Time* magazine, 17 December 1971. Kubrick on modern art from Ciment's *Kubrick*. Malcolm McDowell to Kirk Douglas about Kubrick in *The Ragman's Son*. Anthony Burgess on *Clockwork Orange* as 'a theological dissertation' and the use of his book as a script from *You've Had Your Time*. Eric Swenson on the alternative ending to the novel quoted by Jeremy Campbell in 'More Sex, Please, We're American' in London *Evening Standard*, 31 January 1979. Malcolm McDowell on Kubrick taking screen credit from 'Malcolm McDowell: A Clockwork Top Banana' in *Burke's Steerage*. *Rhapsody: A Dream Novel* by Arthur Schnitzler (Doubleday, Doran, NY, 1927). *Napoleon Symphony* by Anthony Burgess (Knopf, NY, 1974). Conversation with Julian Senior from Ciment's *Kubrick*. *Variety* on the previews of *Clockwork Orange* reported in 'London Junkets for Kubrick Fans' on 22 December 1971 and 'NY-to-London Critics Paid Their Own Way' on 29 December 1971. Burgess on being barred from *Clockwork Orange* screening as 'old' from *You've Had Your Time*. John Trevelyan on *Clockwork Orange* in *What the Censor Saw* (Michael Joseph, London, 1973). Burgess on Kubrick 'paring nails' from *You've Had Your Time*.

CHAPTER FOURTEEN: KUBRICK IN THE AGE OF ENLIGHTENMENT

All quotes in this chapter from Andrew Birkin, Gavin Lambert, Ken Adam, Adrienne Corri and Adrian Turner are from interviews with the author in London and Hollywood, 1995 and 1996.

Tony Parsons quotes from 'Forbidden Fruit', *The Times Saturday Review*, 30 January 1993. 'Now Kubrick Fights Back' appeared in the *New York Times*, 27 February 1972. Burgess on Jimmy Savile from *You've Had Your Time*. Interview with Burgess on Carol Dix in *Transatlantic Review*. The *Hollywood Reporter* noted Kubrick's comments on the *Detroit News*'s banning of advertisements for *Clockwork Orange* on 12 April 1972. The theatre's motives were analysed in '*Detroit News* Submits a Log of Conscience' in *Journal of the Producers' Guild of America*, September 1972. Questions about Warners' and Kubrick's motives for agreeing to the cuts in *Clockwork Orange* appear in 'Facesaver: Dr Stern or Dr Kubrick?' *Variety*, 30 August 1972. William Peter Blatty on Kubrick from *The Exorcist: From Novel to Film* (Bantam, NY, 1974). Joseph Losey on Kubrick quoted in *Joseph Losey: A Revenge on Life* by David Caute (Faber, London, 1994). Terry Southern on *Blue Movie* from Lee Hill's unpublished *A Grand Guy*. Details of the attempted filming of Albert Speer's life supplied by Andrew Birkin and Sir David Puttnam. Clive James on 'Napoleon and Love' in the *Observer*, 17 March 1974. Paul Theroux on Burgess in the *New Yorker*, 7 August 1995. Gene Phillips quoted from *Stanley Kubrick: A Film Odyssey*. Paul Newman on Kubrick from interview with Leonard Probst, *Off Camera* (Stein and Day, NY, 1975). John Calley on *Barry Lyndon* from *Time* magazine, 15 December 1975. Patrick McGilligan's interview with Ryan O'Neal from the *Boston Globe*, 17 December 1975. 'There is a sort of tragic sense about her' and 'Overbred, vacuous, giggly and lazy' from *Time* magazine, 15 December 1975. Death threat against Kubrick detailed in 'The Heat from 1,000 Candles' in *New York* magazine. Details of Kubrick's search for lenses, together with other technical details, from special *Barry Lyndon* issue of *American Cinematographer*, March 1976. Problems with Michael Collins film described by Sir David Puttnam.

John Alcott's complaint about the food on *Barry Lyndon* from Bernard Cohn. Fights on *Barry Lyndon* described by Bob Anderson, telephone interview with the author, London, 1995. 'If a film is flawed' quoted from *Inside Oscar* by Mason Wiley and Damien Bona (Ballantine, NY, 1993). Ryan O'Neal quote from McGilligan, *Boston Globe*. Murray Melvin quote from 'The Heat from 1,000 Candles'. *Variety* reported John Calley's announcement of the Christmas suspension of *Barry Lyndon* shooting on 28 November 1973, under the headline 'Kubrick "Extruded". Delays his *Lyndon* not to Intrude on Irish Mirth'. Reports on the takings of *Clockwork Orange* in the UK appeared in *Variety*, 16 January 1974 ('Think *Orange* Took $2,500,000 in Great Britain'). 'The heat was very nasty' is from 'The Heat from 1,000 Candles'. Leonard Rosenman quote from documentary on Kubrick by John Joyce, Channel 4, 1995. 'Go through the roof' from 'The Heat from 1,000 Candles'. Exchange between Kubrick and Michel Ciment in *Kubrick*.

CHAPTER FIFTEEN: KUBRICK IN HELL

All quotes from Adrienne Corri, Brian Aldiss, Diane Johnson and Gordon Stainforth are from interviews with the author in London, Oxford and Paris, 1996.

Steven Spielberg on *Barry Lyndon* in *Sight and Sound*, Spring 1977. Letter of 23 November 1976 about tickets at London Film Festival supplied by Adrian Turner. Complains about 'conceptualising questions' from *Rolling Stone* interview, 1987. The manuscript of Neil Hornick's unpublished book is on deposit in the library of the British Film Institute, London, together with the text of the letter from Kubrick's lawyers and publisher Peter Cowie. Kubrick on his Porsche from *Rolling Stone* interview, 1987. 'I don't think it's often driven faster' from Alexander Walker in 'Vietnam on Thames', London *Evening Standard*, 25 June 1979. Many of the Kubrick anecdotes in this chapter were recalled by Adrian Turner in conversation with the author. The story of Jan Harlan's Mercedes appears in Turner's 'Shine on Stanley K' in the *Guardian*, 23 December 1988. Julian Senior's remarks from his interview with Michel Ciment in *Kubrick*. Fellini spoke to Charlotte Chandler for *I, Fellini* (Random House, NY, 1995). Details of the history of Childwick Bury from *The Hertfordshire Village Book* (Hertfordshire Federation of Women's Institutes, 1986). Kubrick's exchanges with Ed de Giulio and Garrett Brown on the Steadicam are from 'The Steadicam and *The Shining*' in *American Cinematographer*, August 1980. 'The world's scariest movie' is quoted by Hollis Alpert in 'Offbeat Director in Outer Space'.

Stephen King's comments from interview with Eric Norden in *US Play-boy*, June 1983. Nicholson's 'If you take a sociological view' is from *Making 'The Shining'*. *Jack's Life* by Patrick McGilligan (Norton, NY, 1994). Stephen King on the film of *The Shining* quoted in *The Films of Stephen King* by Ann Lloyd (Brown Books, London, 1993). Scatman Crothers quote from *Scatman* by Jim Haskins with Helen Crothers (Morrow, NY, 1991). 'It happens when actors are unprepared' from *Rolling Stone* interview. Stunt casting for *The Shining* recalled for the author by Derek Ware, London, 1995. Garrett Brown on operating the Steadicam and quotes about working with Kubrick *passim* from 'The Steadicam and *The Shining*'. Anecdote about Kubrick pulling Brown's arm recalled by John Ward in conversation with the author, London, 1996.

CHAPTER SIXTEEN: KUBRICK IN A WORLD OF SHIT

Quotes from Lisa Tuttle, Diane Johnson, Gordon Stainforth, John Ward and Kerry Shale are from interviews with the author in London and Paris, 1996.

Michael Herr quotes *passim* from a letter to the author, 29 February 1996. Details of the delayed censorship of *The Shining* appeared in *Variety* as follows: 'Down to Wire "R" Allows Sun. Ads on Kubrick's *Shining*', 21 May 1980 (censor's certificate); '*Shining* B.O. Drops After Strong Preems', 4 June 1980 (release pattern): 'Kubrick Snips *Shining*', 28 May 1980 (post-release cuts). *Newsweek* review 26 May 1980. Reports on the money made by *2001* quoted by John Hofsess in '*The Shining*: Stanley Kubrick is Hoping His Film of Stephen King's Horror Story Will be a Monster Hit', *Washington Post*, 1 June 1980. Albert Brooks's experience with Kubrick described in *Premiere*, January 1997. Kubrick on reading from Ciment's *Kubrick*. Comments on the TV coverage of Vietnam and 'You're glad we're getting out of Vietnam' from interview in *Eye* magazine, August 1968. 'Most of my friends' from 'The Write Stuff' by Tracy Hayward, *Cinema Papers*, September 1987. 'Vietnam was probably' from 'Mankind on the Late, Late Show' in London *Observer*, 6 September 1987. Hasford on working with Kubrick from 'The Write Stuff'. 'We chewed over every line' from interview with Lee Hill in the Calgary *Herald*, 11 July 1987. *Variety* report on launching of *Full Metal Jacket*, 'Kubrick Planning *Full Metal Jacket* for Warners in '84', appeared 18 January 1984. Invitations to audition were published in many papers, e.g. 'Stanley Kubrick: On the Cheap' in *Boston Globe*, 7 February 1984. Details of buying tanks and guns appeared in *Variety*, 19 September 1984 ('Tanks a Lot'). Colaceri's 'Maybe he should have

got a real killer' and Ermey's 'a reach-around' from John Joyce's documentary on Kubrick, Channel 4, 1996. Gilbert Adair's comment from
Hollywood Vietnam: From 'The Green Berets' to 'Full Metal Jacket'.
Details of Hasford's visit to Beckton from Lisa Tuttle in letter to author,
24 January 1996. 'Harlan called me recently' quoted by Lisa Tuttle from
letter to her from Hasford, 4 April 1987.

CHAPTER SEVENTEEN: IN CASTLE KUBRICK

All quotes from Brian Aldiss, Bob Shaw and Louis Begley are from
conversations with the author, New York and Oxford, 1996.

Controversy over Vivian Kubrick's music for *Full Metal Jacket*
reported in *Los Angeles Times*, 28 January 1988. Kubrick's lawsuit with
neighbours over the cutting of trees reported in the *Daily Mail*, 23 April
1991 ('Court to See Kubrick's Drama of the Lost Trees') and the *Independent*, 3 May 1991. Reports on Kubrick's plans for 'Wartime Lies' include
Variety, 4 April 1993 ('Kubrick's Got His Next Pic'), Leonard Klady's
'Cinefile' column in *Variety London*, 11 May 1993, and in 'Kubrick's
Next Film: Sssssssshhhhhhh!' in the summer 1993 issue of *Entertainment
Weekly*. Accounts of his choice of Aarhus as a location appeared in
Hollywood Reporter, 5 October 1993. *Premiere* magazine's French edi-
tion published reports on the plot of 'A.I.' in December 1993. The story
that Kubrick has been periodically shooting a young actor for 'A.I.' was
first aired on the Kubrick Rumour Page on the Internet in May 1996
and reported by Peter Lennon in the *Guardian*, 3 May 1996. Frank
Rich's encounter with the Kubrick imposter reported in the *Guardian*,
20 August 1993. Martin Short's 'Being Kubrick' appeared in *Vanity Fair*,
April 1996. The casting of *Eyes Wide Shut* was reported in *Variety*, 31
December 1995 ('Kubrick, Kidman, Cruise Open *Shut* Deal'). Kubrick
hiring the Lanesborough Hotel reported in *The Times* City Diary, 2
January 1997.

Filmography

1951

Day of the Fight
  Documentary. Producer/Director/Lighting Cameraman: Stanley Kubrick. Assistant Director: Alexander Singer. Commentary: Robert Rein,
  spoken by Douglas Edwards. Music: Gerald Fried. Editor: Julian
  Bergman.

Flying Padre
  Documentary. Producer: Burton Benjamin. Director/Lighting Cameraman: Stanley Kubrick. Narration script: Bob Hite. Editor: Isaac Klein-
  erman. Music: Nathaniel Shilkret.

1952

  Documentary for the US State Department about the World Assembly
  of Youth.

The Seafarers
  Documentary. Producer: Lester Cooper. Director/Lighting Camera-
  man/editor: Stanley Kubrick. Script: Will Chasan. Narrator: Don Hol-
  lenbeck. Commissioned by the Atlantic and Gulf Coast District of the
  Seafarers' International Union.

Mr Lincoln
  Five-part dramatised biography of Abraham Lincoln for television
  series *Omnibus*. Producer: Richard de Rochemont. Script: James Agee.
  Second Unit Director: Stanley Kubrick.
  With: Royal Dano (Lincoln).

1953

Fear and Desire
  Associate Producer: Maurice Perveler. Director/Producer/Editor/Light-
  ing Cameraman: Stanley Kubrick. Script: Howard O. Sackler. Music:
  Gerald Fried. Production Manager: Robert Dierkes. Make-up: Chet

Fabian. Set Design and Construction: Herbert Leibowitz. Assistant Director: Steve Hahn. Dialogue Director: Toba Kubrick.
With: Kenneth Harp (Corby/The General), Steve Coit (Fletcher/The adjutant), Paul Mazursky (Sidney), Frank Silvera (Mac), Virginia Leith (Girl), David Allen (Narrator).

1955

Killer's Kiss

Producers: Morris Bousel, Stanley Kubrick. Director/Editor/Lighting Cameraman/Original Story: Stanley Kubrick. Script (uncredited): Howard O. Sackler. Music: Gerald Fried. Choreographer: David Vaughan. Dancer: Ruth Sobotka.
With: Frank Silvera (Vincent Rapallo), Jamie Smith (Davy Gordon), Irene Kane (Gloria Price), Jerry Jarret (Albert), Ruth Sobotka (Iris), Mike Dana, Felice Orlandi, Ralph Roberts, Phil Stevenson (Hoodlums), Julius Adelman (Mannequin Factory Owner), David Vaughan, Alec Rubin (Shriners).

1956

The Killing

Producer: James B. Harris. Director/Writer, from Lionel White's novel *Clean Break*: Stanley Kubrick. Additional Dialogue: Jim Thompson. Lighting Cameraman: Lucien Ballard. Second-Unit Photography: Alexander Singer. Art Director: Ruth Sobotka Kubrick. Editor: Betty Steinberg. Music: Gerald Fried.
With: Sterling Hayden (Johnny Clay), Jay C. Flippen (Marvin Unger), Marie Windsor (Sherry Peatty), Elisha Cook Jr (George Peatty), Colleen Gray (Fay), Vince Edwards (Val Cannon), Ted de Corsia (Randy Kennan), Joe Sawyer (Mike O'Reilly), Timothy Carey (Nikki Arano), Kola Kawarian (Maurice Oboukhoff), James Edwards (Parking attendant), Jay Adler (Leo), Joseph Turkel (Tiny).

1957

Paths of Glory

Producer: James B. Harris. Director: Stanley Kubrick. Script: Stanley Kubrick, Calder Willingham, Jim Thompson, from *Paths of Glory* by Humphrey Cobb. Lighting Cameraman: George Krause. Editor: Eva Kroll. Art Director: Ludwig Reiber. Music: Gerald Fried.
With: Kirk Douglas (Colonel Dax), Ralph Meeker (Corporal Paris),

Adolphe Menjou (General Broulard), George Macready (General Mireau), Wayne Morris (Lieutenant Roget), Richard Anderson (Major Saint Auban), Joseph Turkel (Private Arnaud), Timothy Carey (Private Ferol), Peter Capell (Colonel Judge), Suzanne Christian (German Girl), Bert Freed (Sergeant Boulanger), Emile Meyer (Priest), John Stein (Captain Rousseau), Jerry Hausner (Tavern Owner), Harold Benedict (Captain Nichols).

1960

Spartacus

Executive Producer: Kirk Douglas. Line Producer: Edward L. Lewis. Director: Stanley Kubrick. Script: Dalton Trumbo, from novel by Howard Fast. Lighting Cameraman: Russell Metty. Second Unit Lighting Cameraman: Clifford Stine. Editors: Robert Lawrence, Robert Schultz, Fred Chulack. Production Designer: Alexander Golitzen. Art Director: Eric Orbom. Set Decorators: Russell A. Gausman, Julia Heron. Titles: Saul Bass. Technical Advisor: Vittorio Nino Novarese. Costume Designers: Peruzzi, Valles, Bill Thomas. Composer: Alex North.

With: Kirk Douglas (Spartacus), Laurence Olivier (Crassus), Jean Simmons (Varinia), Charles Laughton (Gracchus), Peter Ustinov (Batiatus), John Gavin (Julius Caesar), Tony Curtis (Antoninus), Nina Foch (Helena), Herbert Lom (Tigranes), John Ireland (Crixus), John Dall (Glabrus), Charles McGraw (Marcellus), Joanna Barnes (Claudia), Harold J. Stone (David), Woody Strode (Draba), Peter Brocco (Ramon), Paul Lambert (Gannicus), Robert J. Wilke (Captain of Guard), Nicholas Dennis (Dionysius), John Hoyt (Roman officer), Fred Worlock (Laelius), Dayton Lummis (Symmachus).

1962

Lolita

Producer: James B. Harris. Director: Stanley Kubrick. Script: Vladimir Nabokov, from his novel. Lighting Cameraman: Oswald Morris. Art Director: William Andrews. Set Designer: Andrew Low. Editor: Anthony Harvey. Music: Nelson Riddle. Love Theme by Bob Harris. With: Sue Lyon (Dolores Haze, called 'Lolita'), James Mason (Humbert Humbert), Peter Sellers (Clare Quilty/Dr Zempf), Shelley Winters (Charlotte Haze), Diane Decker (Jane Farlow), Jerry Stovin (John Farlow), Suzanne Gibbs (Mona Farlow), Gary Cockrell (Dick

Schiller), Marianne Stone (Vivian Darkbloom), Cec Linder (Physician), Lois Maxwell (Nurse Mary Lord), William Green (George Swine), C. Denier Warren (Mr Potts), Isobel Lucas (Louise), Maxine Holden (Hospital Receptionist), James Dyrenforth (Mr Beale).

1964

Dr Strangelove or How I Learned to Stop Worrying and Love the Bomb
Producer/Director: Stanley Kubrick. Line Producer: Victor Lyndon. Script: Peter George, Stanley Kubrick, Terry Southern, from George's *Two Hours to Doom/Red Alert*. Lighting Cameraman: Gilbert Taylor. Editor: Anthony Harvey. Production Designer: Ken Adam. Art Director: Peter Murton. Special Effects: Wally Veevers. Music: Laurie Johnson.
With: Peter Sellers (Group Captain Lionel Mandrake/President Merkin Muffley/Dr Strangelove), George C. Scott (General 'Buck' Turgidson), Sterling Hayden (General Jack D. Ripper), Keenan Wynn (Colonel 'Bat' Guano), Slim Pickens (Major T.J. 'King' Kong), Peter Bull (Ambassador DeSadesky), Tracy Reed (Miss Scott), James Earl Jones (Lieutenant Lothar Zogg), Jack Creley (Mr Staines), Frank Berry (Lieutenant H.R. Dietrich), Glenn Beck (Lieutenant W.D. Kivel), Shane Rimmer (Captain G.A. 'Ace' Owens), Paul Tamarin (Lieutenant Goldberg), Gordon Tonner (General Faceman), Robert O'Neil (Admiral Randolph), Roy Stephens (Frank).

1968

2001: A Space Odyssey
Producer/Director: Stanley Kubrick. Line Producer: Victor Lyndon. Script: Stanley Kubrick and Arthur C. Clarke, from Clarke's short story 'The Sentinel'. Lighting Cameraman: Geoffrey Unsworth. Additional Photography: John Alcott, Gilbert Taylor (uncredited), Editor: Ray Lovejoy. Production Designers: Tony Masters, Harry Lange, Ernie Archer. Costumes: Hardy Amies. Special Effects Designer: Stanley Kubrick. Special Effects Supervisors: Wally Veevers, Douglas Trumbull, Colin Cantwell, Frederick Martin, John Jack Malick, Tom Howard, Con Pederson, Bryan Loftus, Bruce Logan, David Osborne. Music: Aram Katchaturian, Gyorgy Ligeti, Johann Strauss, Richard Strauss.
With: Keir Dullea (David Bowman), Gary Lockwood (Frank Poole), William Sylvester (Dr Heywood Floyd), Dan Richter (Moonwatcher), Douglas Rain (Voice of HAL 9000), Leonard Rossiter (Dr Smyslov),

Margaret Tyzack (Elena), Robert Beatty (Halvorsen), Sean Sullivan (Michaels), Frank Miller (Misson Controller), Penny Brahms (Stewardess), Vivian Kubrick (Floyd's daughter).

1971

A Clockwork Orange

Producer/Director: Stanley Kubrick. Line Producer: Bernard Williams. Script: Stanley Kubrick, based on the novel by Anthony Burgess. Lighting Cameraman: John Alcott. Editor: Bill Butler. Production Designer: John Barry. Art Directors: Russell Hagg, Peter Shields. Electronic Music: Walter Carlos. Costume Designer: Milena Canonero.

With: Malcolm McDowell (Alex Burgess, alias Alex DeLarge), Patrick Magee (Mr Alexander), Michael Bates (Chief Guard), Warren Clarke (Dim), John Clive (Stage Actor 'Lardface'), Adrienne Corri (Mrs Alexander), Carl Duering (Dr Brodsky), Paul Farrell (Tramp), Clive Francis (Joe the Lodger), Michael Gover (Prison Governor), Miriam Karlin (Miss Weber, the Cat Lady), James Marcus (Georgie), Aubrey Morris (Mr Deltoid), Godfrey Quigley (Prison Chaplain), Sheila Raynor (Mum), Madge Ryan (Dr Branom), John Savident (Conspirator), Anthony Sharp (Minister of the Interior), Philip Stone (Dad), Margaret Tyzack (Conspirator).

1975

Barry Lyndon

Producer/Director: Stanley Kubrick. Script: Stanley Kubrick, from the novel by William Makepeace Thackeray. Lighting Cameraman: John Alcott. Editor: Tony Lawson. Production Designer: Ken Adam. Art Director: Roy Walker. Musical Adaptation: Leonard Rosenman. Costume Designers: Ulla-Britt Soderlund, Milena Canonero.

With: Ryan O'Neal (Redmond Barry), Marisa Berenson (Lady Lyndon), Patrick Magee (Chevalier Balibari), Hardy Kruger (Captain Potzdorf), Marie Kean (Mrs Barry), Gay Hamilton (Nora Brady), Murray Melvin (Rev Runt), Godfrey Quigley (Captain Grogan), Leonard Rossiter (Captain Quin), Leon Vitali (Lord Bullingdon), Frank Middlemass (Sir Charles Lyndon), Diana Koerner (Lischen), Andre Morell (Lord Wendover), Arthur O'Sullivan (Captain Freny), Philip Stone (Graham), Steven Berkoff (Lord Ludd), Anthony Sharp (Lord Hallum), Michael Hordern (Narrator).

1980

The Shining

Producer/Director: Stanley Kubrick. Script: Stanley Kubrick and Diane Johnson, based on the novel by Stephen King. Lighting Cameraman: John Alcott. Editor: Ray Lovejoy. Production Designer: Roy Walker. Art Director: Les Tomkins. Costume Designer: Melina Canonero. Second Unit Lighting Cameraman: Doug Milsome. Electronic Music: Wendy Carlos.

With: Jack Nicholson (Jack Torrance), Shelly Duvall (Wendy Torrance), Danny Lloyd (Danny Torrance), Scatman Crothers (Hallorann), Barry Nelson (Stuart Ullman), Philip Stone (Delbert Grady), Joe Turkel (Lloyd), Anne Jackson (Doctor), Tony Burton (Larry Durkin), Lia Beldam (Young woman in bath), Billie Gibson (Old woman in bath), Lisa Burns, Louise Burns (Grady Girls).

1987

Full Metal Jacket

Producer/director: Stanley Kubrick. Line producer: Philip Hobbs. Script: Stanley Kubrick, Michael Herr and Gustav Hasford, from Hasford's novel *The Short Timers*. Lighting Cameraman: Douglas Milsome. Editor: Martin Hunter. Music: Vivian Kubrick as 'Abigail Mead'. Production Designer: Anton Furst. Art Direction: Rod Stratford, Les Tomkins, Keith Pain. Costume Designer: Keith Denny.

With: Matthew Modine (Joker), Adam Baldwin (Animal Mother), Lee Ermey (Sergeant Hartman), Vincent D'Onofrio (Gomer Pyle), Dorian Harewood (Eightball), Arliss Howard (Cowboy), Kevyn Major Howard (Rafter Man), Ed O'Ross (Mr Touchdown), Tim Colceri (Helicopter machine-gunner), Papillon Soo Soo (prostitute).

Bibliography

Adair, Gilbert, *Hollywood's Vietnam: From The Green Berets to Full Metal Jacket*, William Heinemann, London, 1989

Adam, Ken, *Production Design: Ken Adam*. Catalogue for travelling exhibition assembled by Verband der Szenenbildner, Filmarchitekten und Kostumbildner in der Bundesrepublik Deutschland E.V. (S/F/K) Kulturreferat der Landeshauptstadt, Munchen, 1994

Agel, Jerome (editor), *The Making of Kubrick's 2001*, New American Library, New York, 1970

Bizony, Piers, *2001: Filming the Future*, Aurum, London, 1994

Blatty, William Peter, *The Exorcist: From Novel to Film*, Bantam, New York, 1974

Bloom, Harold (editor), *Vladimir Nabokov's Lolita*, Chelsea House, New York, 1987

Boyd, Brian, *Vladimir Nabokov: The American Years*, Chatto & Windus, London, 1991

Brosnan, John, *Movie Magic*, Macdonald, London, 1974

Brosnan, John, *Future Tense*, Macdonald & Jane's, London, 1978

Brosnan, John, *The Primal Screen*, Orbit, London, 1991

Brown, David, *Let Me Entertain You*, William Morrow, New York, 1990

Brunetta, Gian Piero (editor), *Stanley Kubrick: Tempo, Spazio, Storia e Mondi Possibili*, Pratiche Editrice, Parma, 1985

Burgess, Anthony, *A Clockwork Orange*, William Heinemann, London, 1962

Burgess, Anthony, *Stanley Kubrick's A Clockwork Orange*, Based on the Novel by Anthony Burgess. Illustrated screenplay, with an introductory note by Stanley Kubrick, Lorrimer, London, 1972

Burgess, Anthony, *You've Had Your Time*, Heinemann, London, 1990

Chase, Chris, *How to be a Movie Star, Or a Terrible Beauty is Born*, Harper & Row, New York, 1974

Ciment, Michel, *Kubrick*, Calmann-Levy, Paris, 1980

Clarke, Arthur C., *The Lost Worlds Of 2001*, New American Library, New York, 1972

Clarke, Arthur C., with Peter Hyams, *The Odyssey File*, Ballantine, New York, 1984

Cobb, Humphrey, *Paths of Glory*, Viking, New York, 1935

(Cobb, Humphrey) Howard, Sidney, *Paths of Glory*, Adapted for the stage, and with an introduction by Howard, Samuel French, New York, 1936

Corliss, Richard, *Talking Pictures*, Overlook Press, New York, 1974

Corliss, Richard, *Lolita*, British Film Institute, London, 1994

Coyle, Wallace, *Stanley Kubrick: A Guide to References and Resources*, G.K. Hall, Boston, 1980

Curtis, Tony (with Barry Paris), *Tony Curtis: The Autobiography*, William Heinemann, London, 1994

Douglas, Kirk (with Linda Civitello), *The Ragman's Son: An Autobiography*, Simon & Schuster, London, 1988

Elley, Derek, *The Epic Film*, Routledge & Kegan Paul, London, 1984

Fellig, Arthur, *Weegee by Weegee*, Da Capo, New York, 1975

Fiori, Carlo, *The Brando I Knew*, Hart-Davis, MacGibbon, London, 1974

Gallagher, John Andrew, *Film Directors on Directing*, Praeger, New York, 1989

Geduld, Carolyn, *Film Guide To 2001: A Space Odyssey*, Indiana University Press, Bloomington, 1973

Gelmis, Joseph, *The Film Director as Superstar*, Doubleday, New York, 1970

George, Peter (as Bryant, Peter), *Two Hours to Doom*, T.V. Boardman, London, 1958

George, Peter, with Stanley Kubrick and Terry Southern, *Dr Strangelove or How I Learned to Stop Worrying and Love the Bomb*, Bantam, New York, 1964

Ghezzi, Enrico (editor), *Stanley Kubrick, Ladro di Sguardi, Fotografie di fotografie 1945–1949*, Bomplani, Rome, 1994

Haskins, Jim, with Crothers, Helen, *Scatman: An Authorized Biography of Scatman Crothers*, William Morrow, New York, 1991

Hasford, Gustav, *The Short Timers*, Harper & Row, New York, 1979

Herr, Michael, with Stanley Kubrick and Gustav Hasford, *Full Metal Jacket*. Illustrated screenplay, with an introduction by Herr, Knopf, New York, 1987

Kagan, Norman, *The Cinema of Stanley Kubrick*, Continuum, New York, 1994

King, Stephen, *The Shining*, Doubleday, New York, 1977

Koestler, Arthur, *The Gladiators*, Macmillan, New York, 1939

Lewis, Roger, *The Life and Death of Peter Sellers*, Century, London, 1994

Lloyd, Ann, *The Films of Stephen King*, Brown Books, London, 1993

LoBrutto, Vincent, *Stanley Kubrick: A Biography*, Donald I. Fine, New York, 1996

Manso, Peter, *Brando*, Weidenfeld & Nicolson, London, 1994

Mason, James, *Before I Forget*, Hamish Hamilton, London, 1981

Monaco, James, *The Films of Stanley Kubrick*, The New School Department of Film, New York, 1974

Morley, Sheridan, *James Mason: Odd Man Out*, Weidenfeld & Nicolson, London, 1989

Nabokov, Vladimir, *Lolita: A Screenplay*, McGraw-Hill, New York, 1974

Nabokov, Vladimir, *The Annotated Lolita*, Edited and with a Preface and Notes by Alfred Appel Jr., Penguin, London, 1991

Nelson, Thomas Alan, *Kubrick: Inside a Film Artist's Maze*, Indiana University Press, Bloomington, 1982

Phillips, Gene D., *S.J.: Stanley Kubrick, A Film Odyssey*, Popular Library, New York, 1975

Polito, Robert, *Savage Art: A Biography of Jim Thompson*, Knopf, New York, 1995

Shepherd, Donald, *Jack Nicholson: An Unauthorised Biography*, Warner Books, London, 1992

Thackeray, William Makepeace, *The Memoirs of Barry Lyndon Esq.*, with an Introduction by J.P. Donleavy, Penguin Books, London, 1975

Vizzard, Jack, *See No Evil: Life Inside a Hollywood Censor*, Pocket Books, New York, 1971

Walker, Alexander, *Stanley Kubrick Directs*, Harcourt, Brace Jovanovich, New York, 1972

Walker, Alexander, *It's Only a Movie, Ingrid: Encounters on and off Screen*, Headline, London, 1988

Winters, Shelley, *Shelley II: The Middle of My Century*, Simon & Schuster, New York, 1989

Yule, Andrew, *Fast Fade: David Puttnam, Columbia Pictures, and the Battle for Hollywood*, Delacorte, New York, 1989

Index